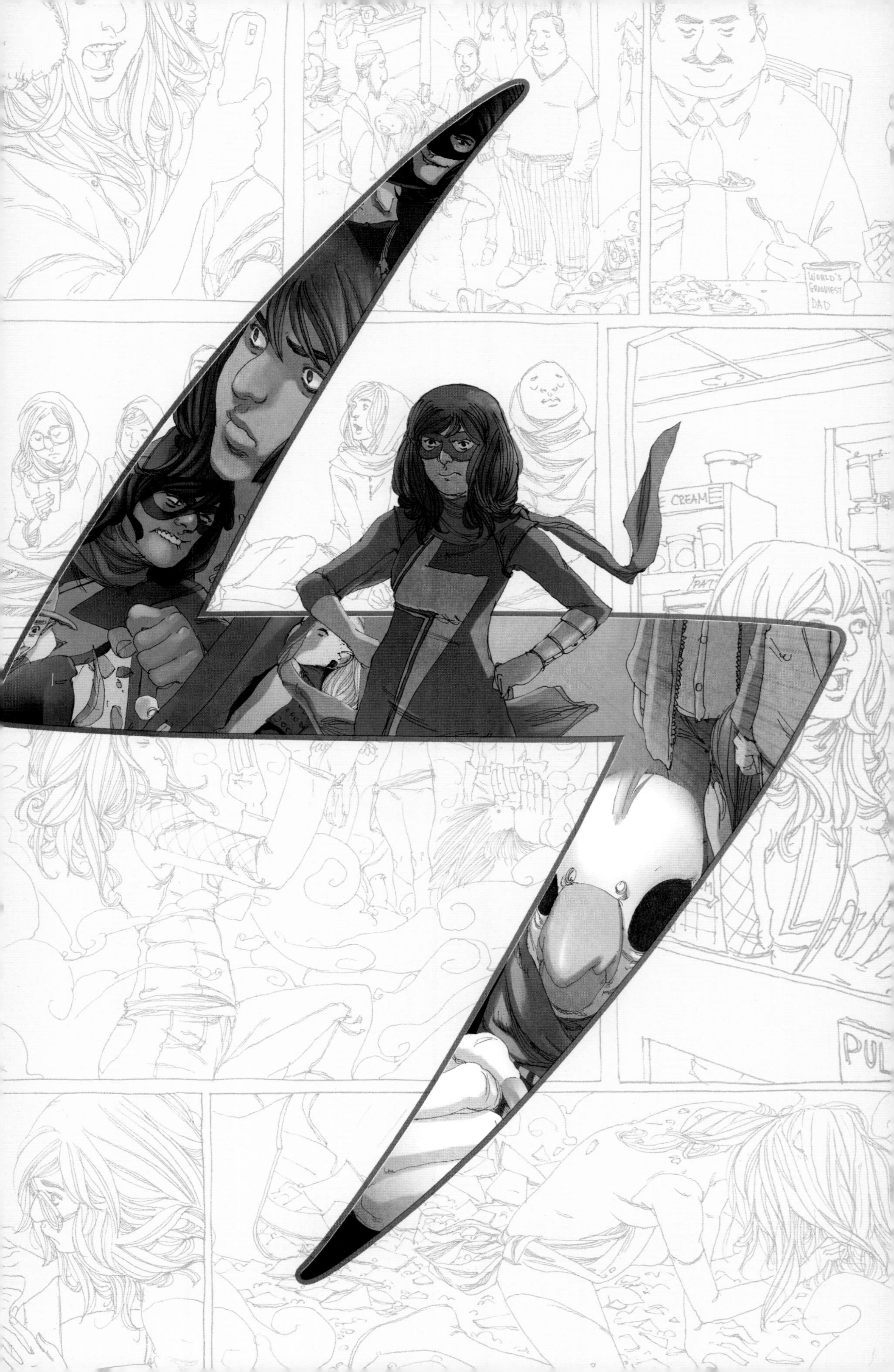
WORLD'S GROOVIEST DAD
CREAM

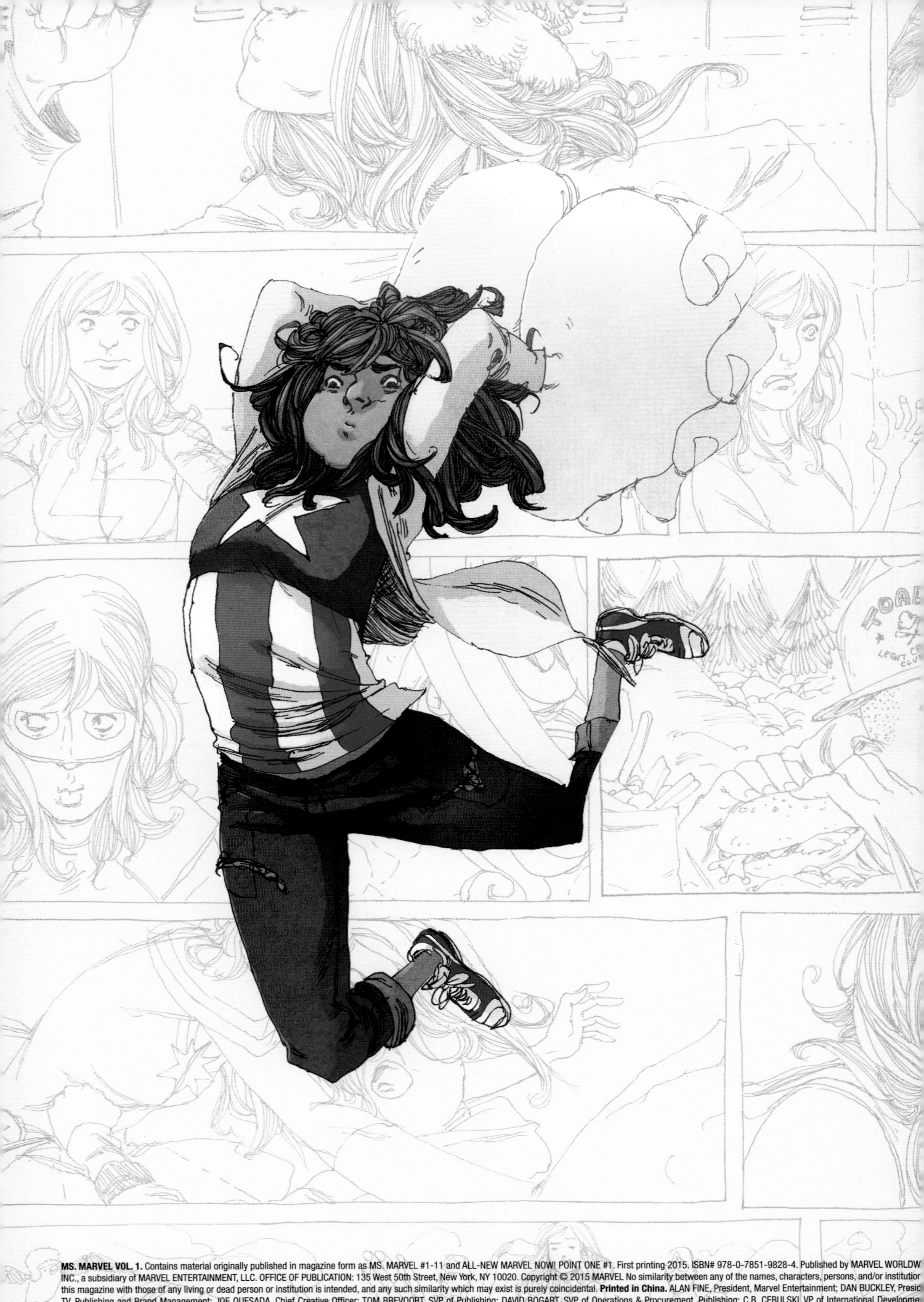

MS. MARVEL VOL. 1. Contains material originally published in magazine form as MS. MARVEL #1-11 and ALL-NEW MARVEL NOW! POINT ONE #1. First printing 2015. ISBN# 978-0-7851-9828-4. Published by MARVEL WORLDW INC., a subsidiary of MARVEL ENTERTAINMENT, LLC. OFFICE OF PUBLICATION: 135 West 50th Street, New York, NY 10020. **Printed in China.** ALAN FINE, President, Marvel Entertainment; DAN BUCKLEY, Presid TV, Publishing and Brand Management; JOE QUESADA, Chief Creative Officer; TOM BREVOORT, SVP of Publishing; DAVID BOGART, SVP of Operations & Procurement, Publishing; C.B. CEBULSKI, VP of International Developme Brand Management; DAVID GABRIEL, SVP Print, Sales & Marketing; JIM O'KEEFE, VP of Operations & Logistics; DAN CARR, Executive Director of Publishing Technology; SUSAN CRESPI, Editorial Operations Manager; ALEX MORAL Publishing Operations Manager; STAN LEE, Chairman Emeritus. For information regarding advertising in Marvel Comics or on Marvel.com, please contact Jonathan Rheingold, VP of Custom Solutions & Ad Sales, at jrheingold@ma com. For Marvel subscription inquiries, please call 800-217-9158. **Manufactured between 4/17/2015 and 6/15/2015 by R.R. DONNELLEY ASIA PRINTING SOLUTIONS, CHINA.**

10 9 8 7 6 5 4 3 2 1

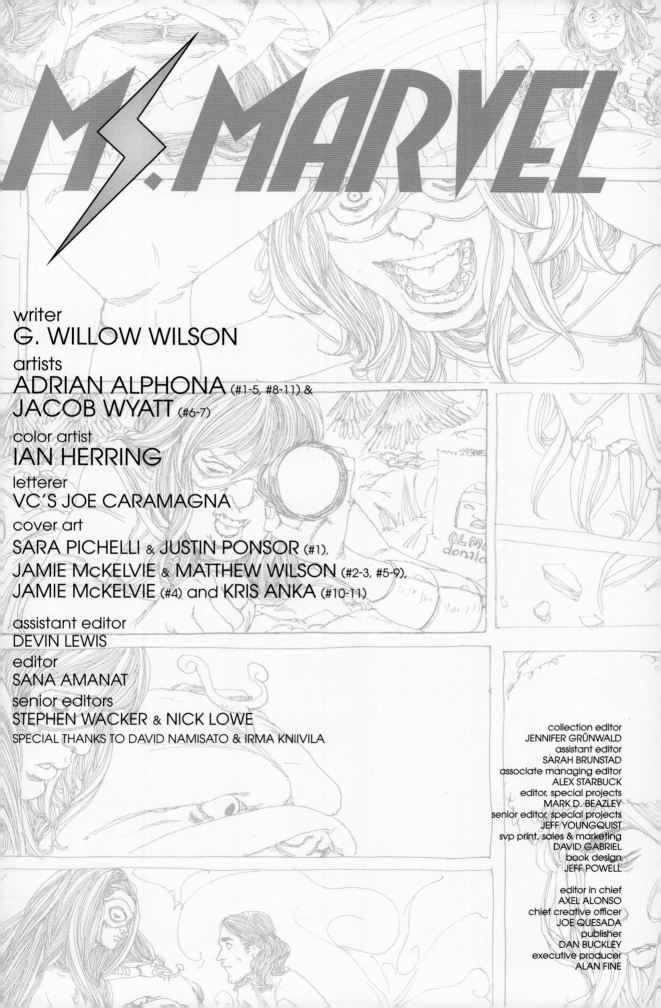

MS.MARVEL

writer
G. WILLOW WILSON

artists
ADRIAN ALPHONA (#1-5, #8-11) &
JACOB WYATT (#6-7)

color artist
IAN HERRING

letterer
VC'S JOE CARAMAGNA

cover art
SARA PICHELLI & JUSTIN PONSOR (#1),
JAMIE McKELVIE & MATTHEW WILSON (#2-3, #5-9),
JAMIE McKELVIE (#4) and **KRIS ANKA** (#10-11)

assistant editor
DEVIN LEWIS

editor
SANA AMANAT

senior editors
STEPHEN WACKER & NICK LOWE

SPECIAL THANKS TO DAVID NAMISATO & IRMA KNIIVILA

collection editor
JENNIFER GRÜNWALD
assistant editor
SARAH BRUNSTAD
associate managing editor
ALEX STARBUCK
editor, special projects
MARK D. BEAZLEY
senior editor, special projects
JEFF YOUNGQUIST
svp print, sales & marketing
DAVID GABRIEL
book design
JEFF POWELL

editor in chief
AXEL ALONSO
chief creative officer
JOE QUESADA
publisher
DAN BUCKLEY
executive producer
ALAN FINE

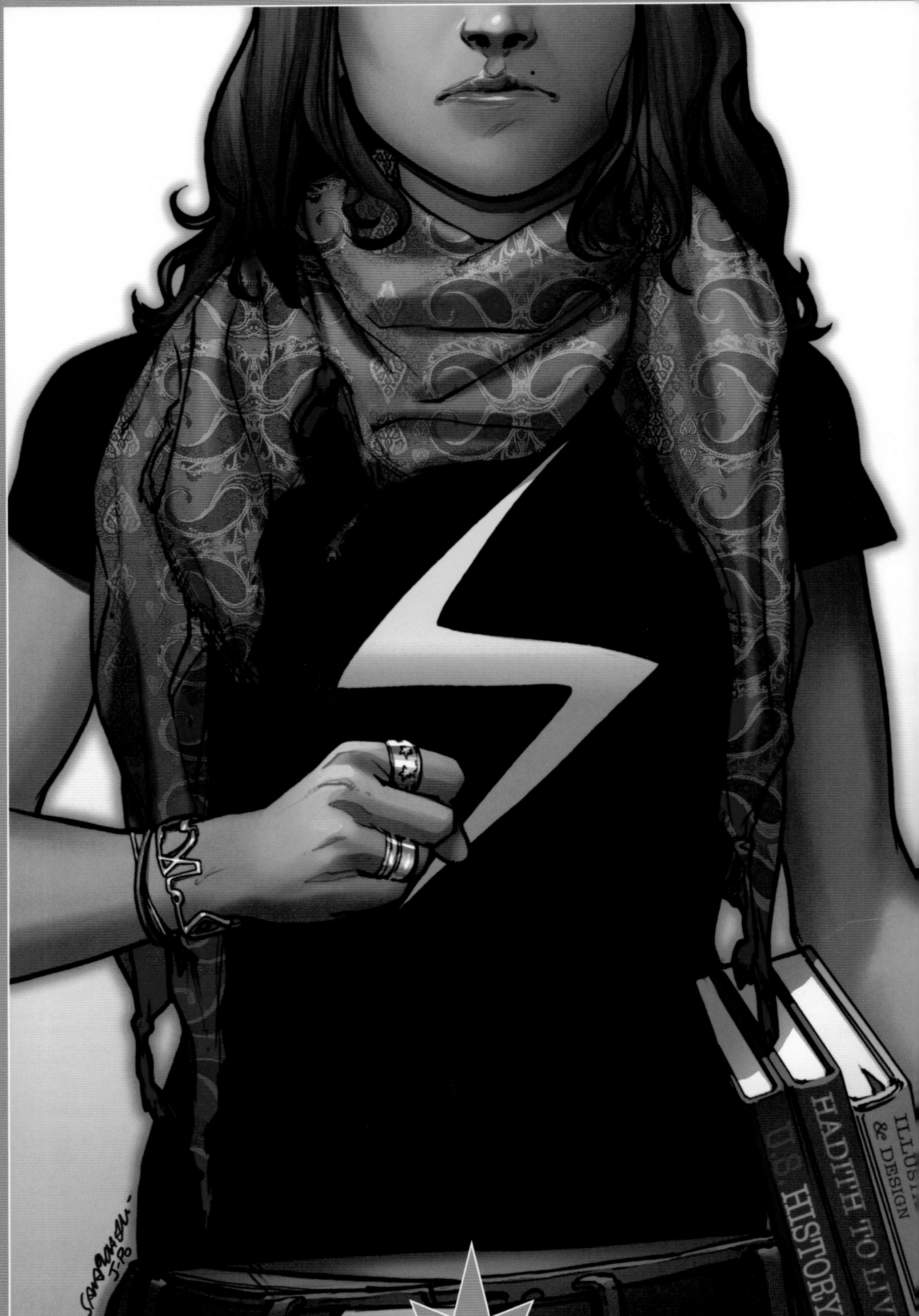
U.S. HISTORY
HADITH TO LIVE
& DESIGN
1

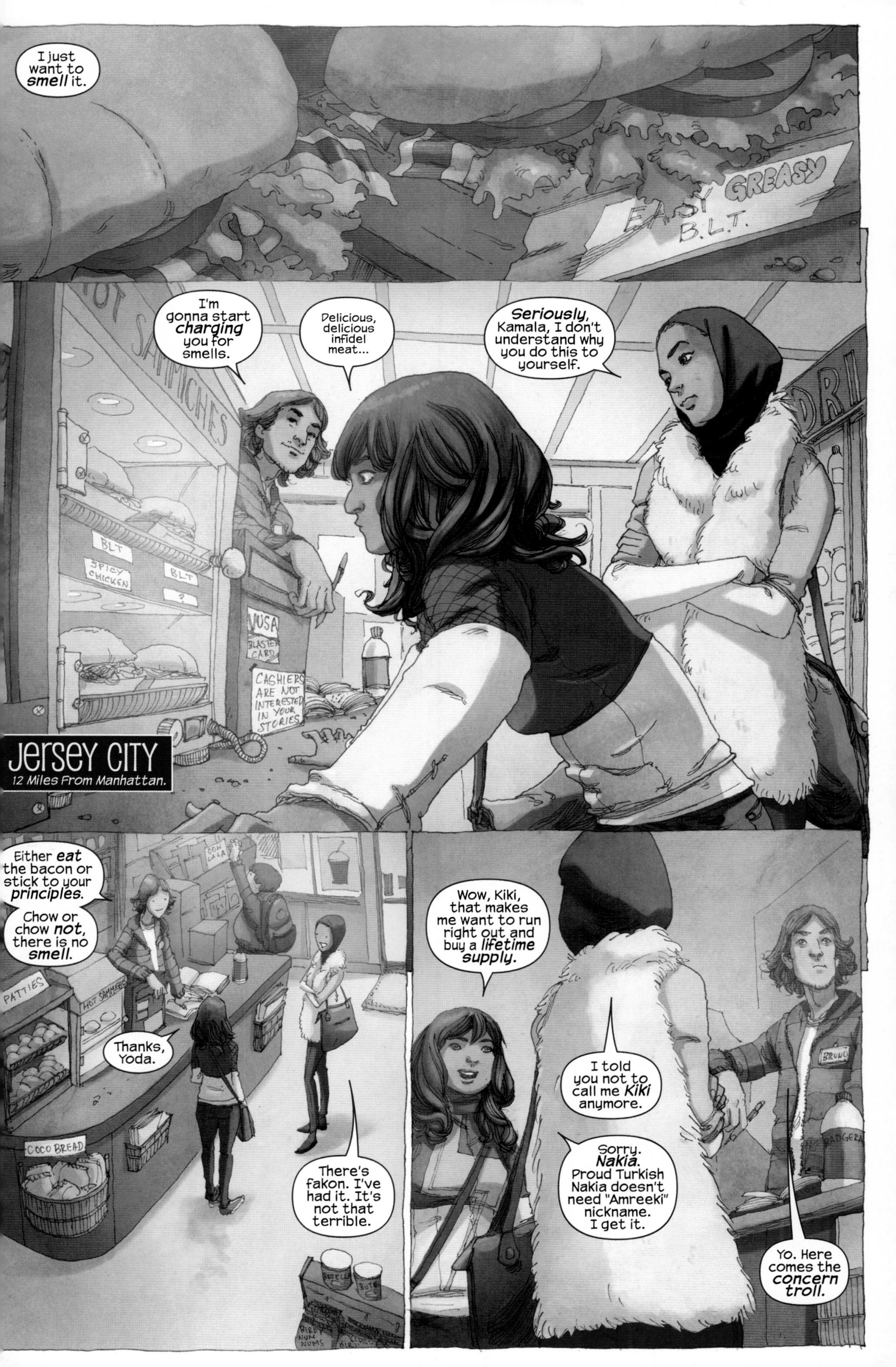
I just want to *smell* it.
EASY GREASY B.L.T.
HOT SAMMICHES
I'm gonna start *charging* you for smells.
Delicious, delicious infidel meat...
Seriously, Kamala, I don't understand why you do this to yourself.
BLT
SPICY CHICKEN
BLT
VISA
BLASTER CARD
CASHIERS ARE NOT INTERESTED IN YOUR STORIES
JERSEY CITY
12 Miles From Manhattan.
Either *eat* the bacon or stick to your *principles*.
Chow or chow *not*, there is no *smell*.
PATTIES
HOT SAMMICHES
Thanks, Yoda.
COCO BREAD
There's fakon. I've had it. It's not that terrible.
Wow, Kiki, that makes me want to run right out and buy a *lifetime supply*.
I told you not to call me *Kiki* anymore.
Sorry. *Nakia*. Proud Turkish Nakia doesn't need "Amreeki" nickname. I get it.
BRUNO
Yo. Here comes the *concern troll.*

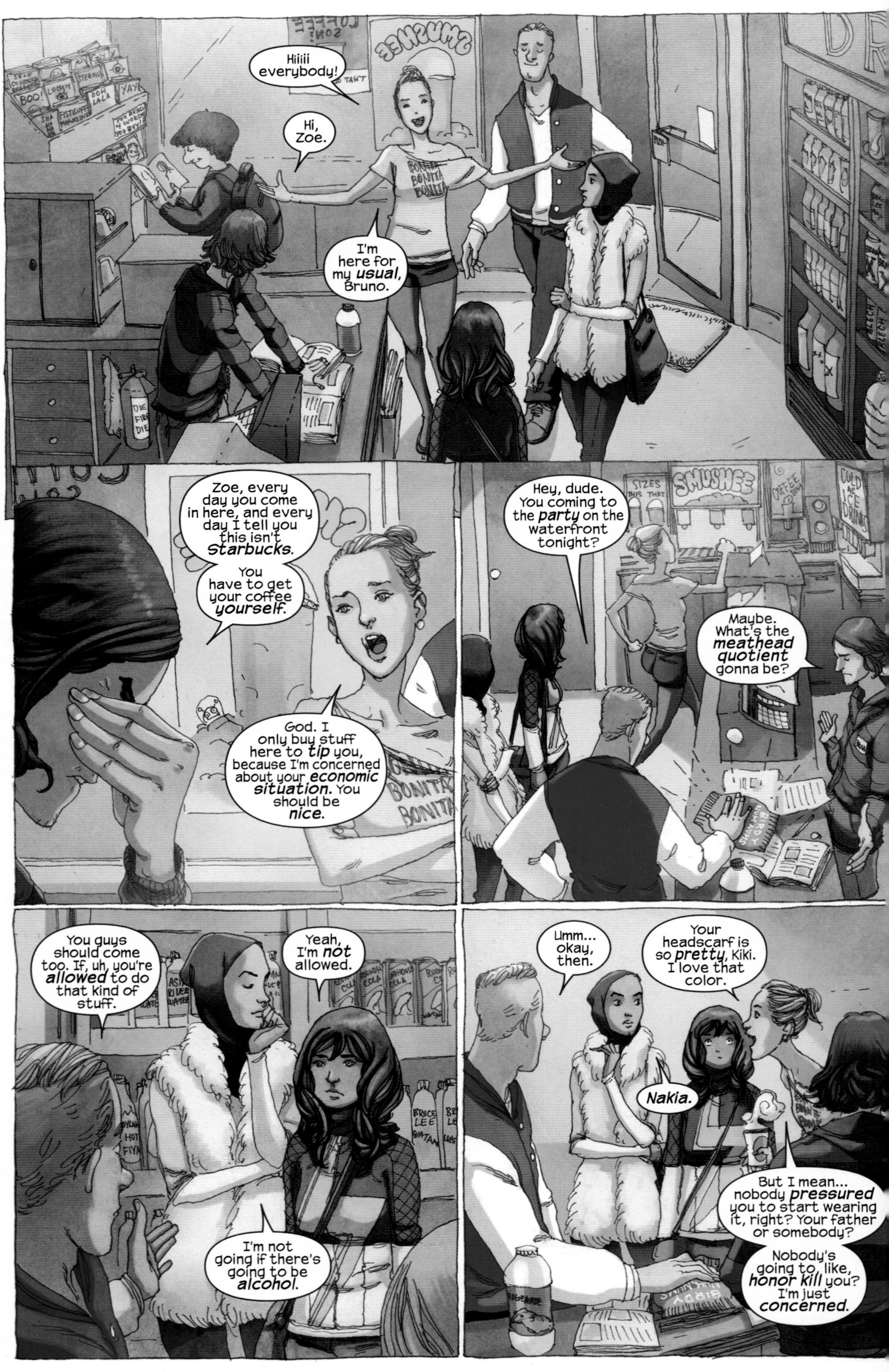
Hiiiii everybody!
Hi, Zoe.
I'm here for my *usual*, Bruno.
Zoe, every day you come in here, and every day I tell you this isn't **Starbucks**.
You have to get your coffee *yourself*.
God. I only buy stuff here to *tip* you, because I'm concerned about your *economic situation*. You should be *nice*.
Hey, dude. You coming to the *party* on the waterfront tonight?
Maybe. What's the *meathead quotient* gonna be?
You guys should come too. If, uh, you're *allowed* to do that kind of stuff.
Yeah, I'm *not* allowed.
I'm not going if there's going to be *alcohol*.
Umm... okay, then.
Your headscarf is so *pretty*, Kiki. I love that color.
Nakia.
But I mean... nobody *pressured* you to start wearing it, right? Your father or somebody?
Nobody's going to, like, *honor kill* you? I'm just *concerned*.

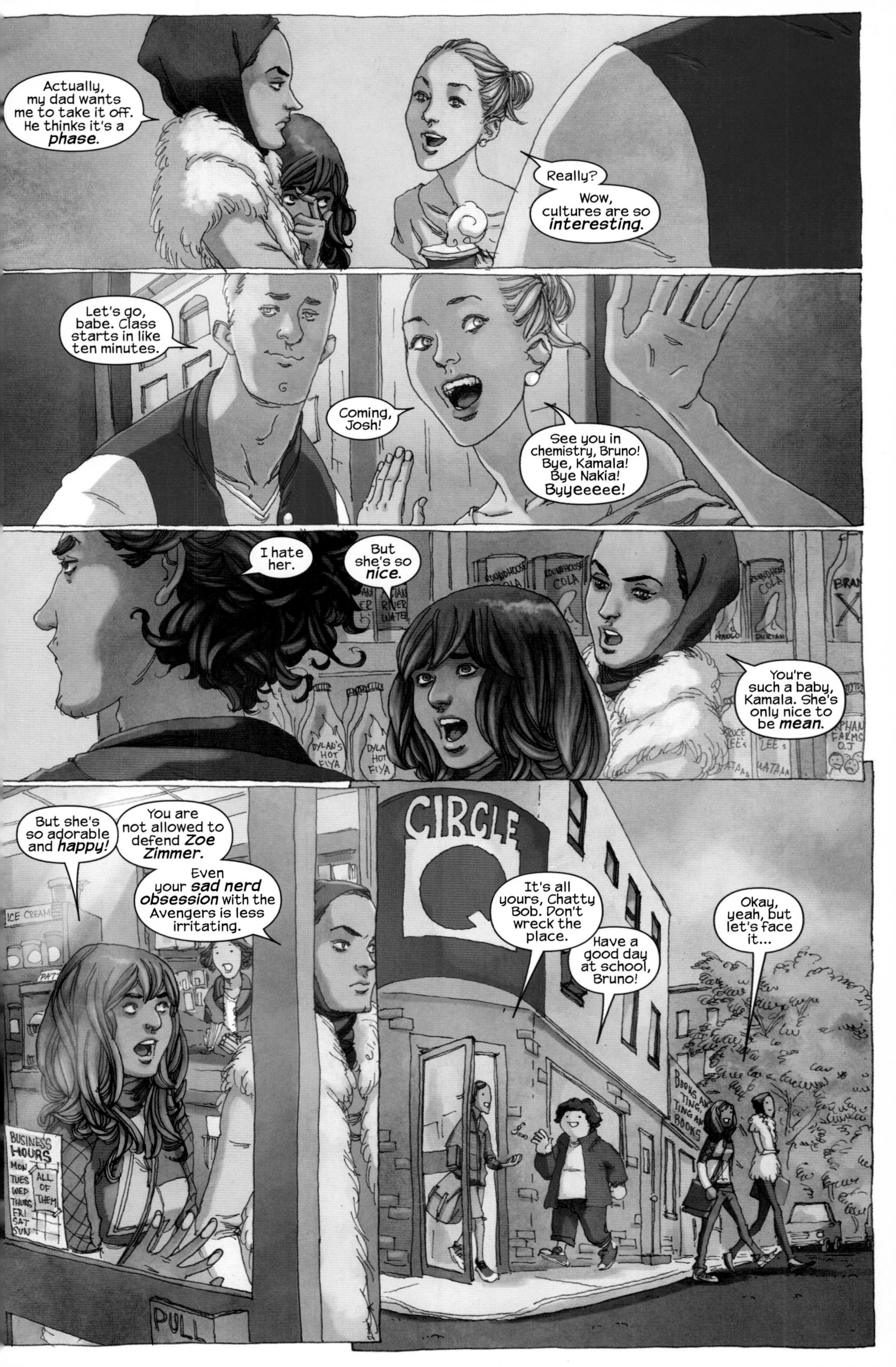

Actually, my dad wants me to take it off. He thinks it's a *phase*.
Really?
Wow, cultures are so *interesting*.
Let's go, babe. Class starts in like ten minutes.
Coming, Josh!
See you in chemistry, Bruno! Bye, Kamala! Bye Nakia! Byyeeeee!
I hate her.
But she's so *nice*.
You're such a baby, Kamala. She's only nice to be *mean*.
But she's so adorable and *happy*!
You are not allowed to defend *Zoe Zimmer*.
Even your *sad nerd obsession* with the Avengers is less irritating.
CIRCLE Q
It's all yours, Chatty Bob. Don't wreck the place.
Have a good day at school, Bruno!
Okay, yeah, but let's face it...
ICE CREAM
BUSINESS HOURS
MON TUES WED THURS FRI SAT SUN
ALL OF THEM
PULL

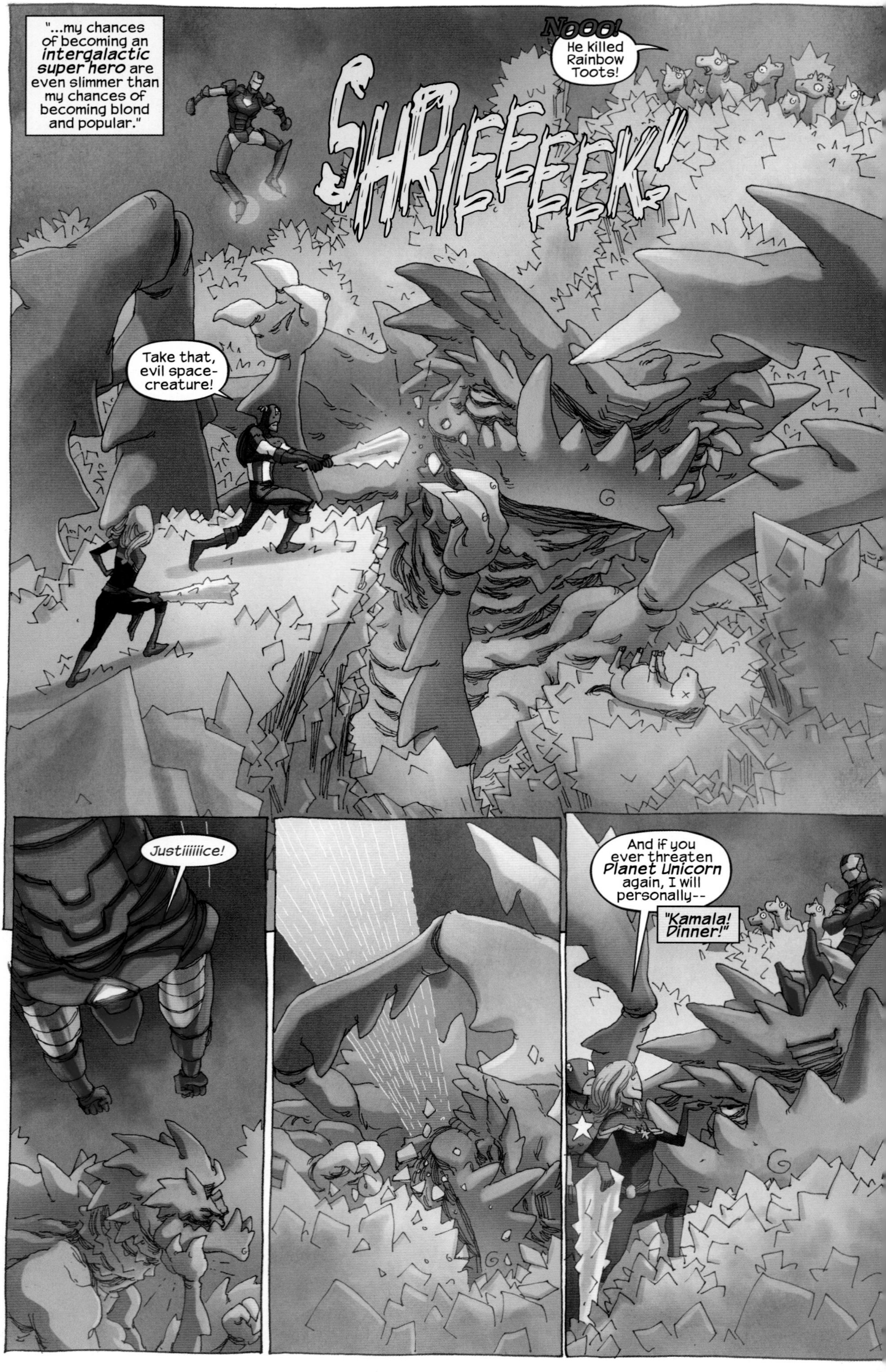

"...my chances of becoming an *intergalactic super hero* are even slimmer than my chances of becoming blond and popular."
NOOO! He killed Rainbow Toots!
SHRIEEEEK!
Take that, evil space-creature!
Justiiiiiice!
And if you ever threaten *Planet Unicorn* again, I will personally--
"Kamala! Dinner!"

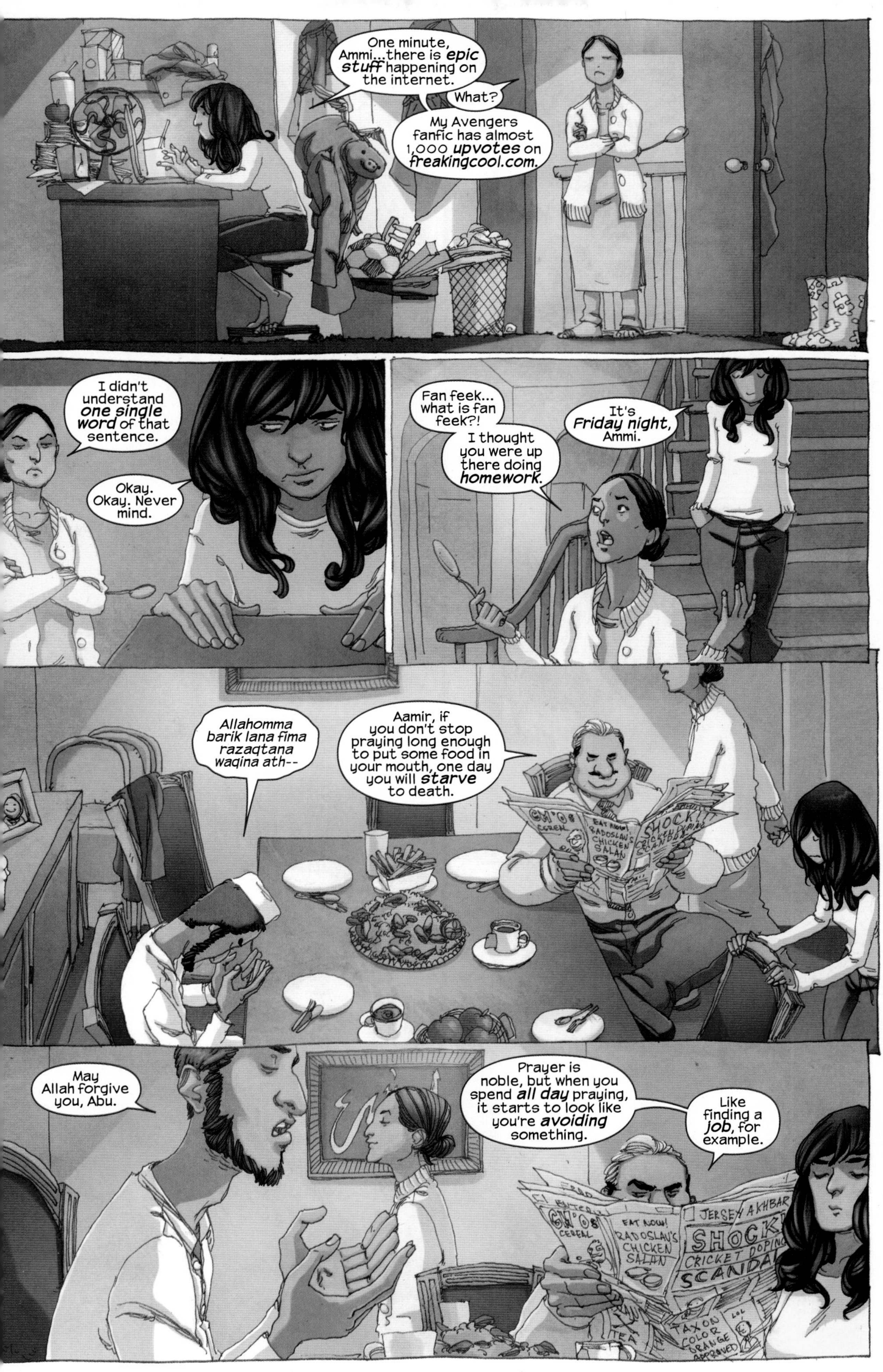

One minute, Ammi...there is epic stuff happening on the internet.
What?
My Avengers fanfic has almost 1,000 upvotes on freakingcool.com.
I didn't understand one single word of that sentence.
Okay. Okay. Never mind.
Fan feek... what is fan feek?!
I thought you were up there doing homework.
It's Friday night, Ammi.
Allahomma barik lana fima razaqtana waqina ath--
Aamir, if you don't stop praying long enough to put some food in your mouth, one day you will starve to death.
SHOCK!!
EAT NOW! RADOSLAW'S CHICKEN SALAN
May Allah forgive you, Abu.
Prayer is noble, but when you spend all day praying, it starts to look like you're avoiding something.
Like finding a job, for example.
JERSEY AKHBAR
SHOCK!
CRICKET DOPING SCANDAL
EAT NOW! RADOSLAW'S CHICKEN SALAN
CEREAL
TAXON COLOR ORANGE APPROVED

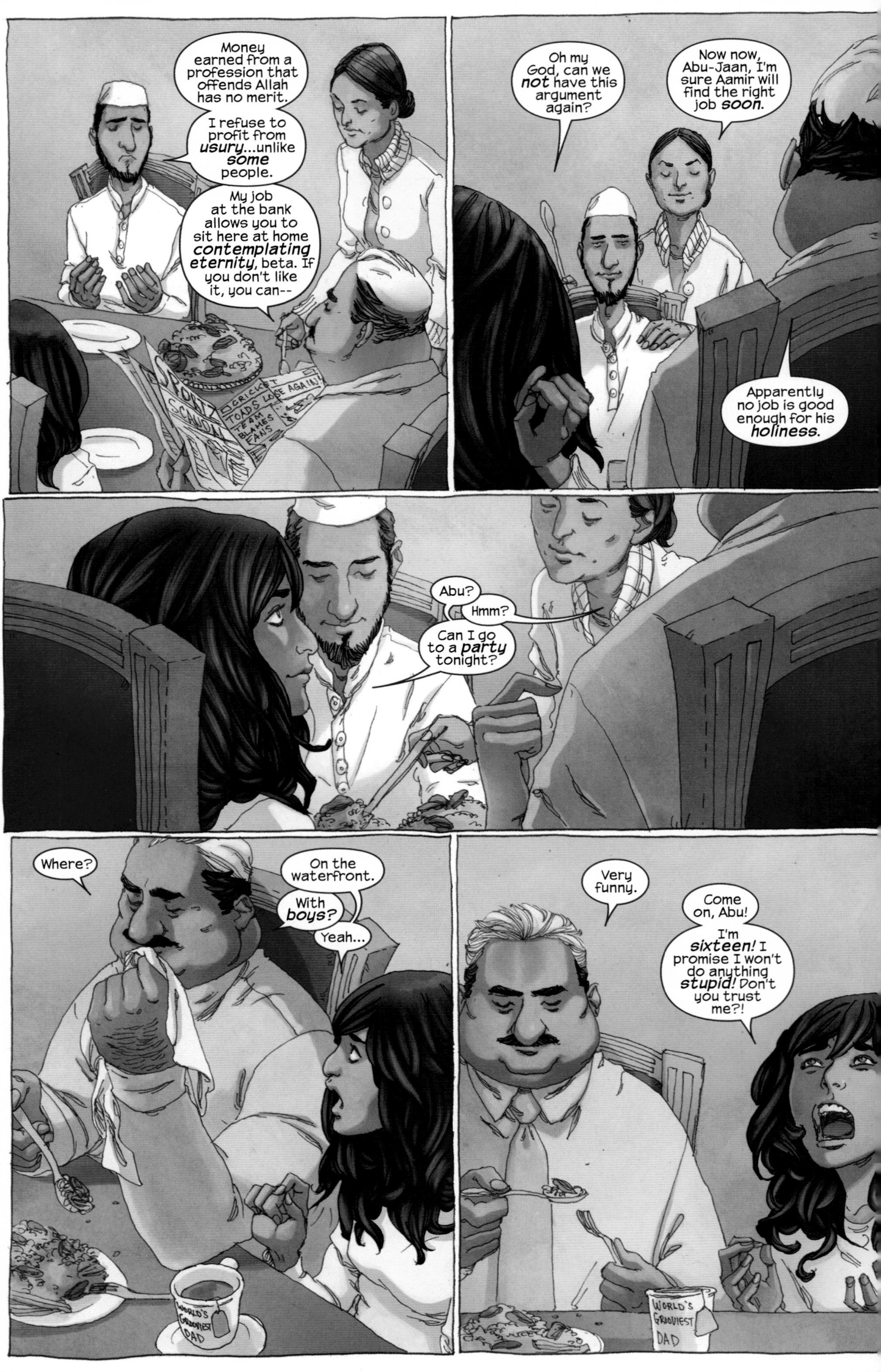

Money earned from a profession that offends Allah has no merit.
I refuse to profit from *usury*...unlike *some* people.
My job at the bank allows you to sit here at home *contemplating eternity*, beta. If you don't like it, you can--
TEAM BLAMES FANS
Oh my God, can we *not* have this argument again?
Now now, Abu-Jaan, I'm sure Aamir will find the right job *soon*.
Apparently no job is good enough for his *holiness*.
Abu?
Hmm?
Can I go to a *party* tonight?
Where?
On the waterfront.
With *boys?*
Yeah...
WORLD'S GROOVIEST DAD
Very funny.
Come on, Abu!
I'm *sixteen!* I promise I won't do anything *stupid!* Don't you trust me?!
WORLD'S GROOVIEST DAD

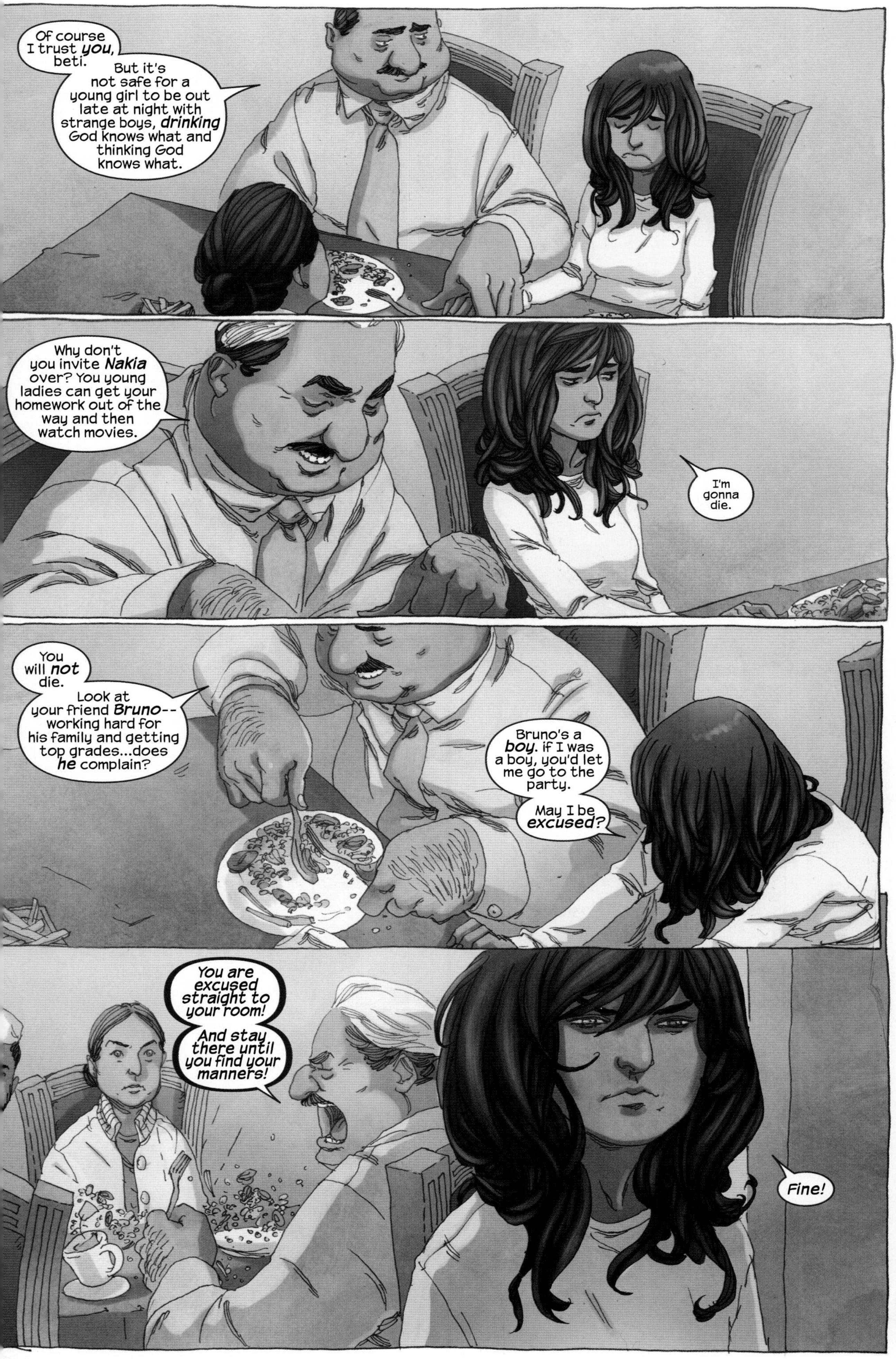
Of course I trust *you*, beti.
But it's not safe for a young girl to be out late at night with strange boys, *drinking* God knows what and thinking God knows what.
Why don't you invite *Nakia* over? You young ladies can get your homework out of the way and then watch movies.
I'm gonna die.
You will *not* die.
Look at your friend *Bruno*--working hard for his family and getting top grades...does *he* complain?
Bruno's a *boy*. if I was a boy, you'd let me go to the party.
May I be *excused?*
You are excused straight to your room!
And stay there until you find your manners!
Fine!

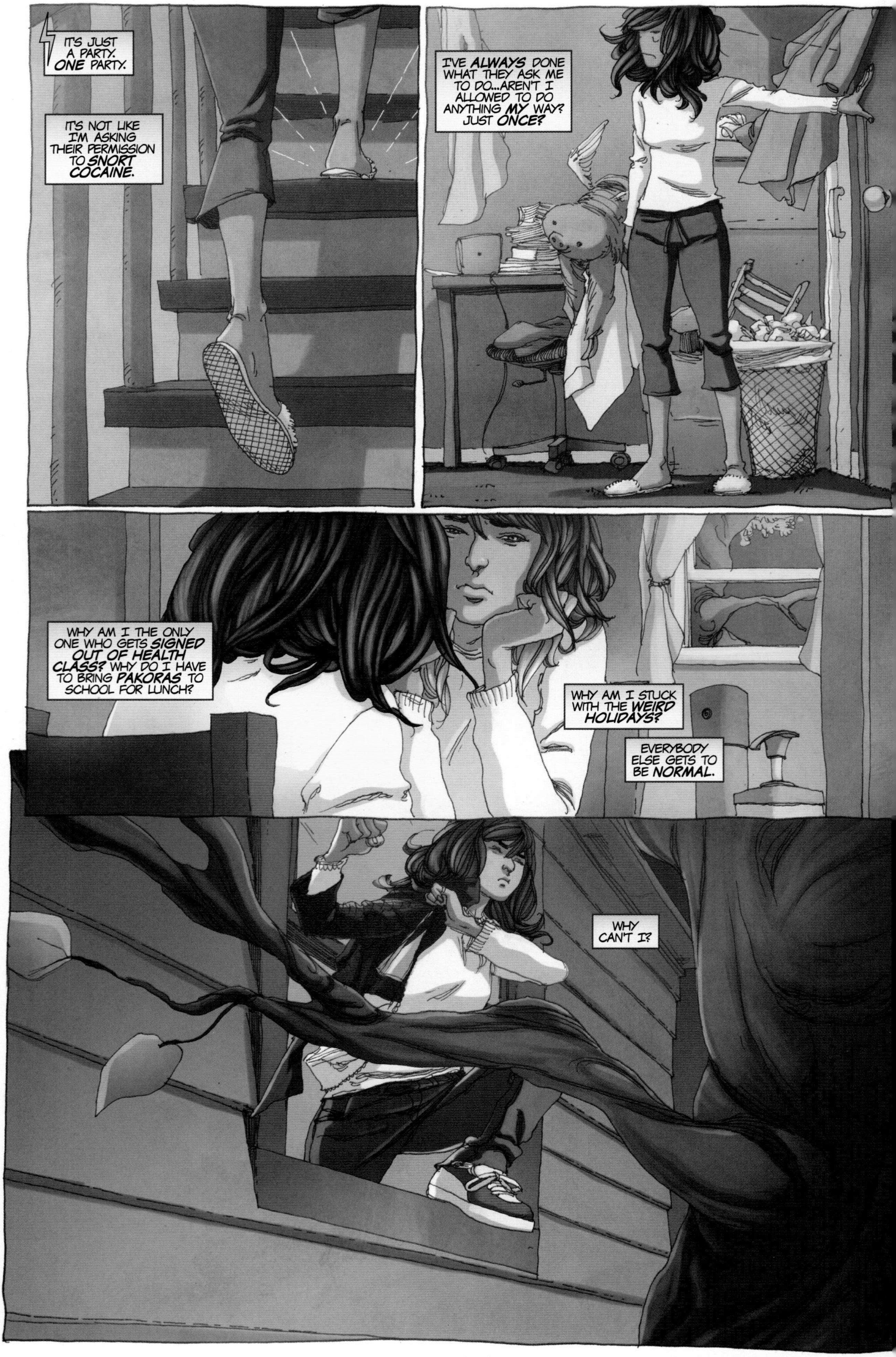
IT'S JUST A PARTY. ONE PARTY.
IT'S NOT LIKE I'M ASKING THEIR PERMISSION TO SNORT COCAINE.
I'VE ALWAYS DONE WHAT THEY ASK ME TO DO...AREN'T I ALLOWED TO DO ANYTHING MY WAY? JUST ONCE?
WHY AM I THE ONLY ONE WHO GETS SIGNED OUT OF HEALTH CLASS? WHY DO I HAVE TO BRING PAKORAS TO SCHOOL FOR LUNCH?
WHY AM I STUCK WITH THE WEIRD HOLIDAYS?
EVERYBODY ELSE GETS TO BE NORMAL.
WHY CAN'T I?

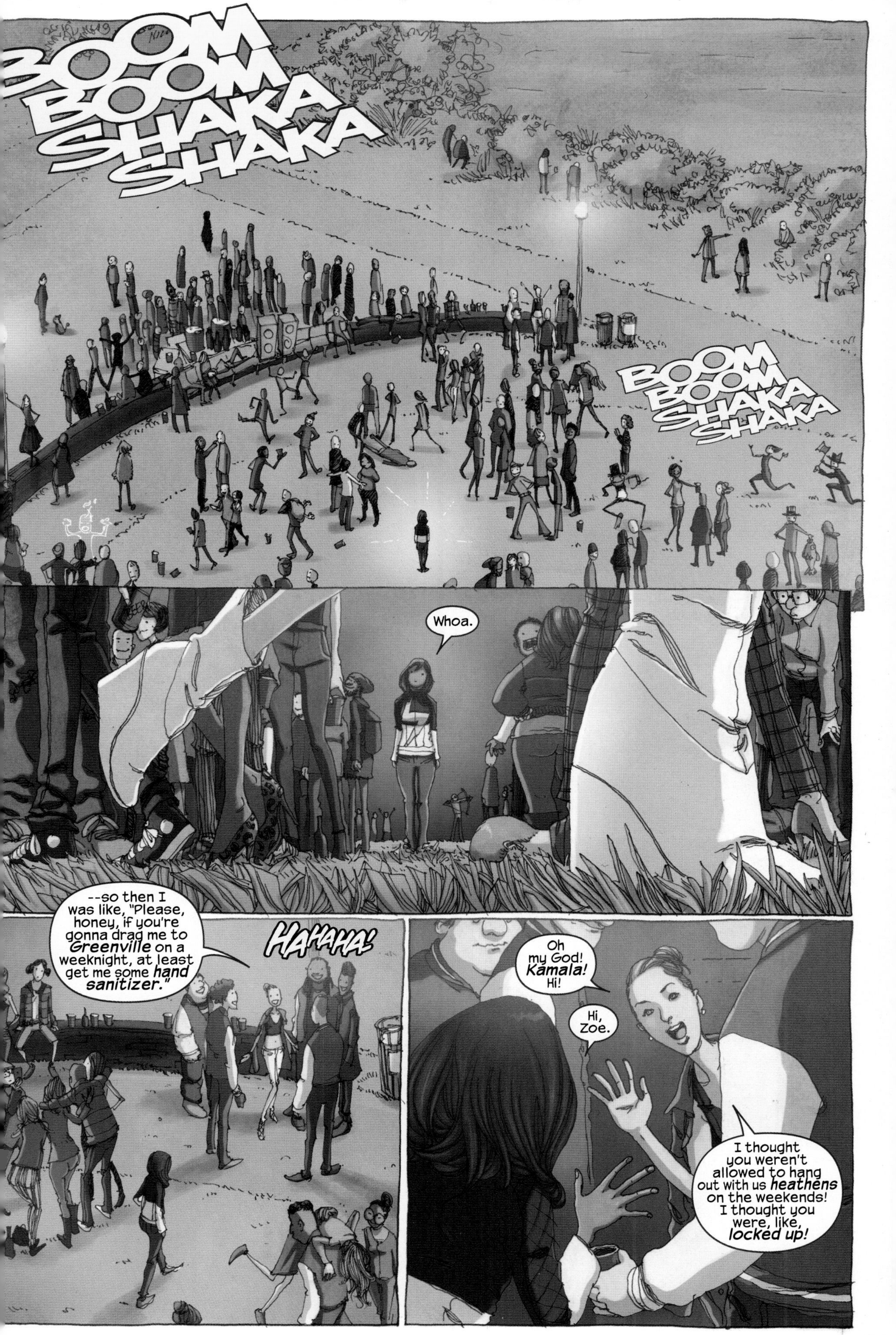
BOOM BOOM SHAKA SHAKA
BOOM BOOM SHAKA SHAKA
Whoa.
--so then I was like, "Please, honey, if you're gonna drag me to Greenville on a weeknight, at least get me some hand sanitizer."
HAHAHA!
Oh my God! Kamala! Hi!
Hi, Zoe.
I thought you weren't allowed to hang out with us heathens on the weekends! I thought you were, like, locked up!

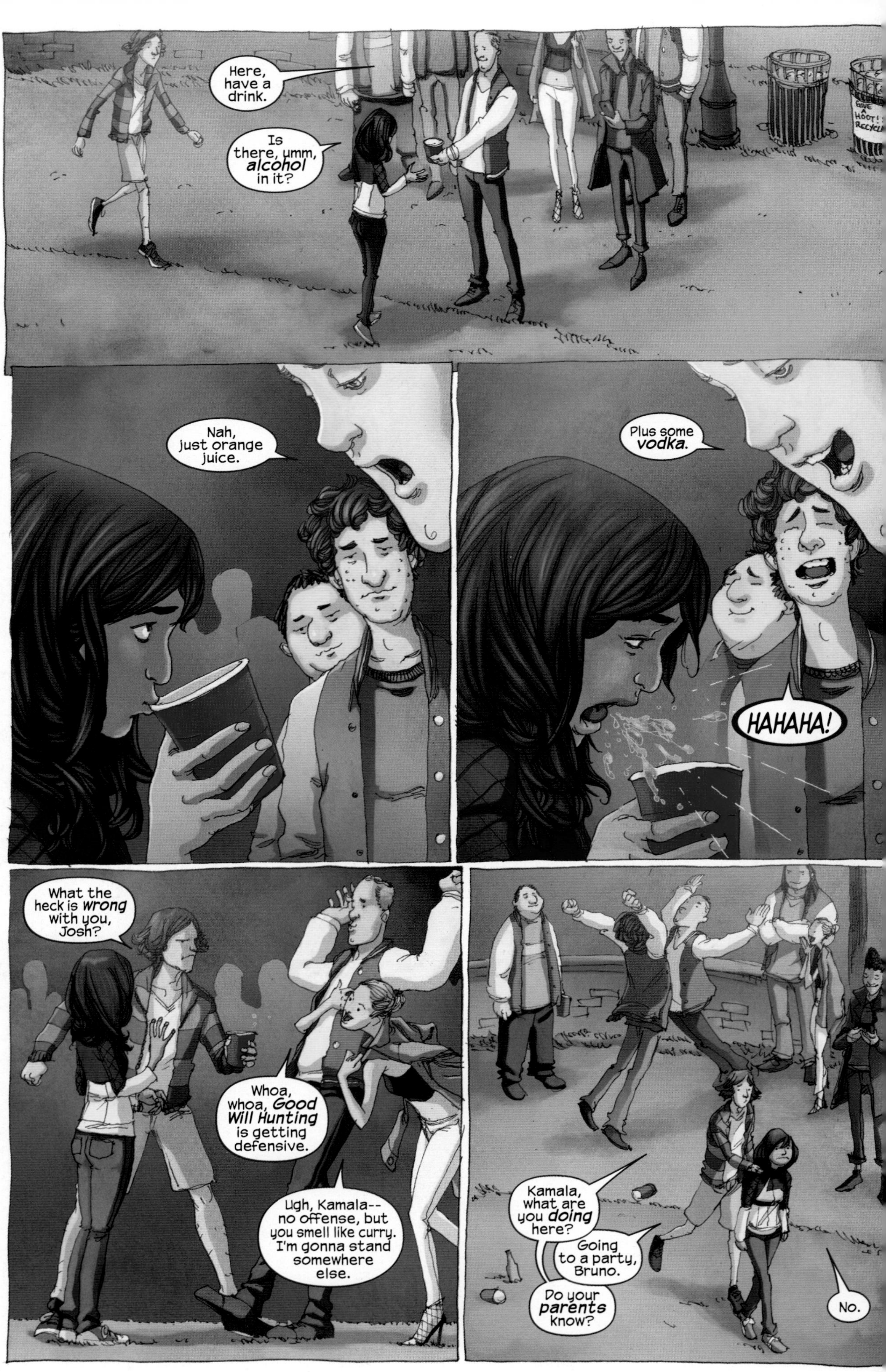

Here, have a drink.
Is there, umm, alcohol in it?
Nah, just orange juice.
Plus some vodka.
HAHAHA!
What the heck is wrong with you, Josh?
Whoa, whoa, Good Will Hunting is getting defensive.
Ugh, Kamala-- no offense, but you smell like curry. I'm gonna stand somewhere else.
GIVE A HOOT! RECYCLE
Kamala, what are you doing here?
Going to a party, Bruno.
Do your parents know?
No.

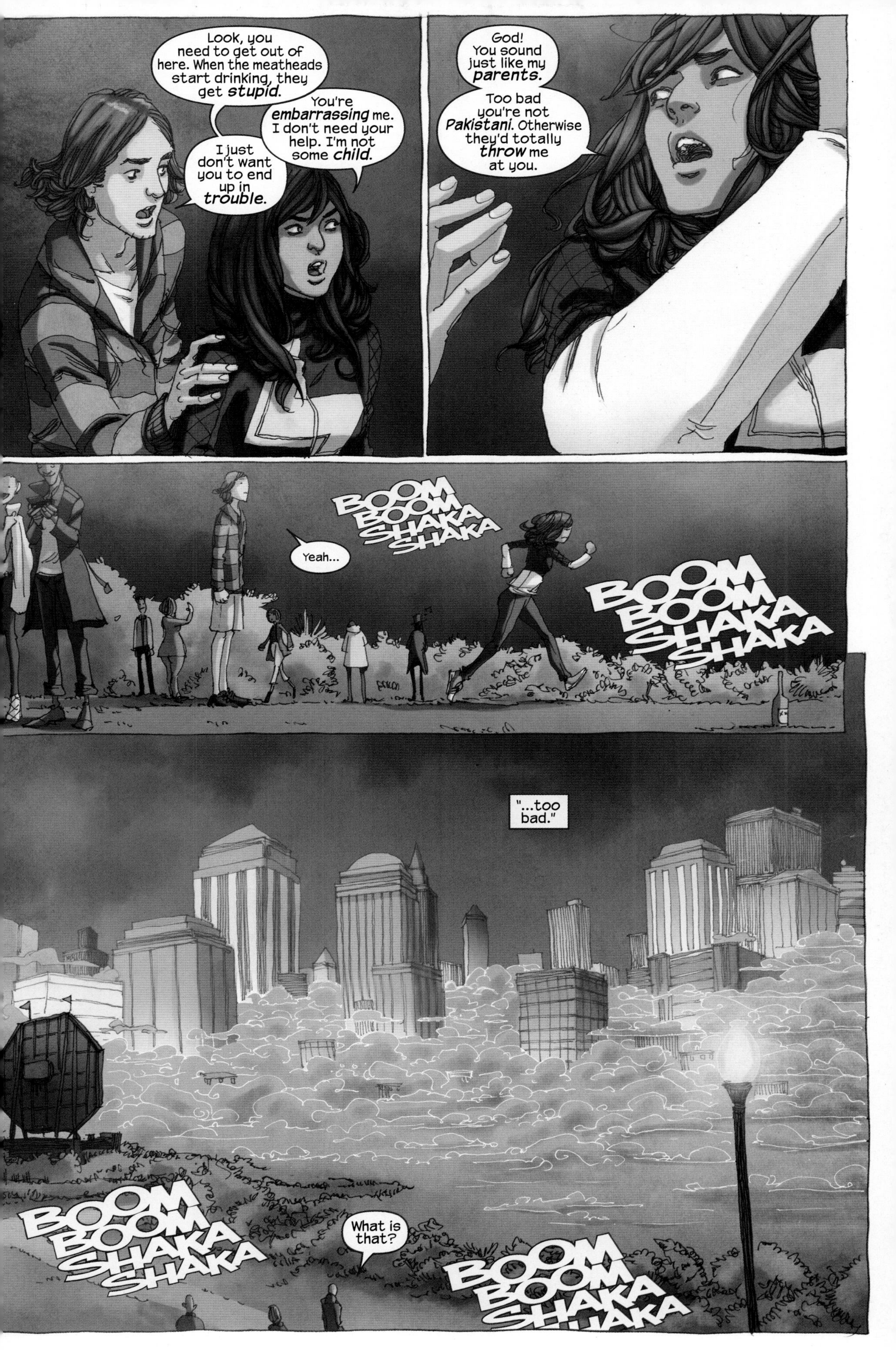

Look, you need to get out of here. When the meatheads start drinking, they get stupid.
You're embarrassing me. I don't need your help. I'm not some child.
I just don't want you to end up in trouble.
God! You sound just like my parents.
Too bad you're not Pakistani. Otherwise they'd totally throw me at you.
BOOM BOOM SHAKA SHAKA
Yeah...
BOOM BOOM SHAKA SHAKA
"...too bad."
BOOM BOOM SHAKA SHAKA
What is that?
BOOM BOOM SHAKA SHAKA

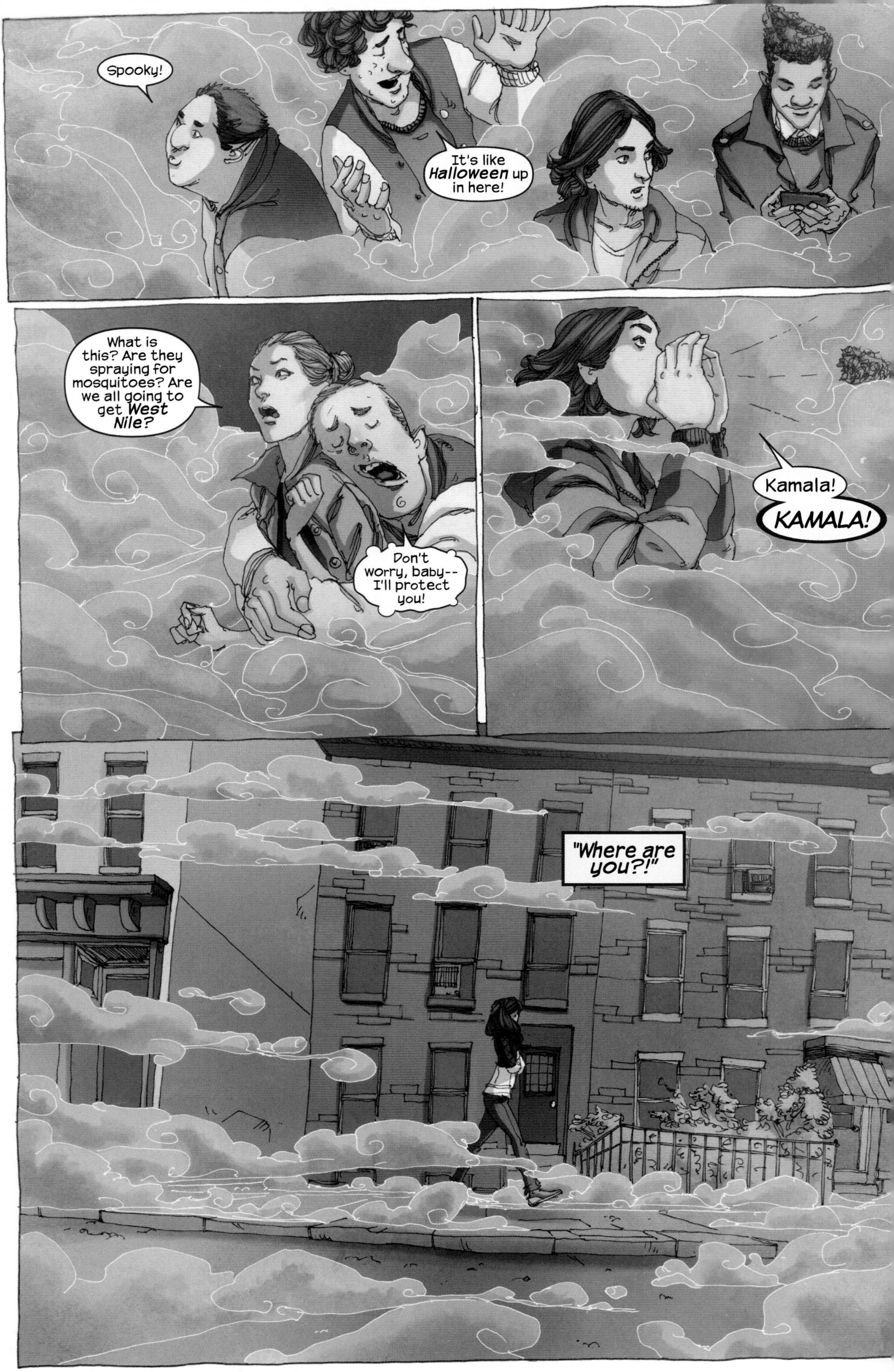
Spooky!
It's like Halloween up in here!
What is this? Are they spraying for mosquitoes? Are we all going to get West Nile?
Don't worry, baby-- I'll protect you!
Kamala!
KAMALA!
"Where are you?!"

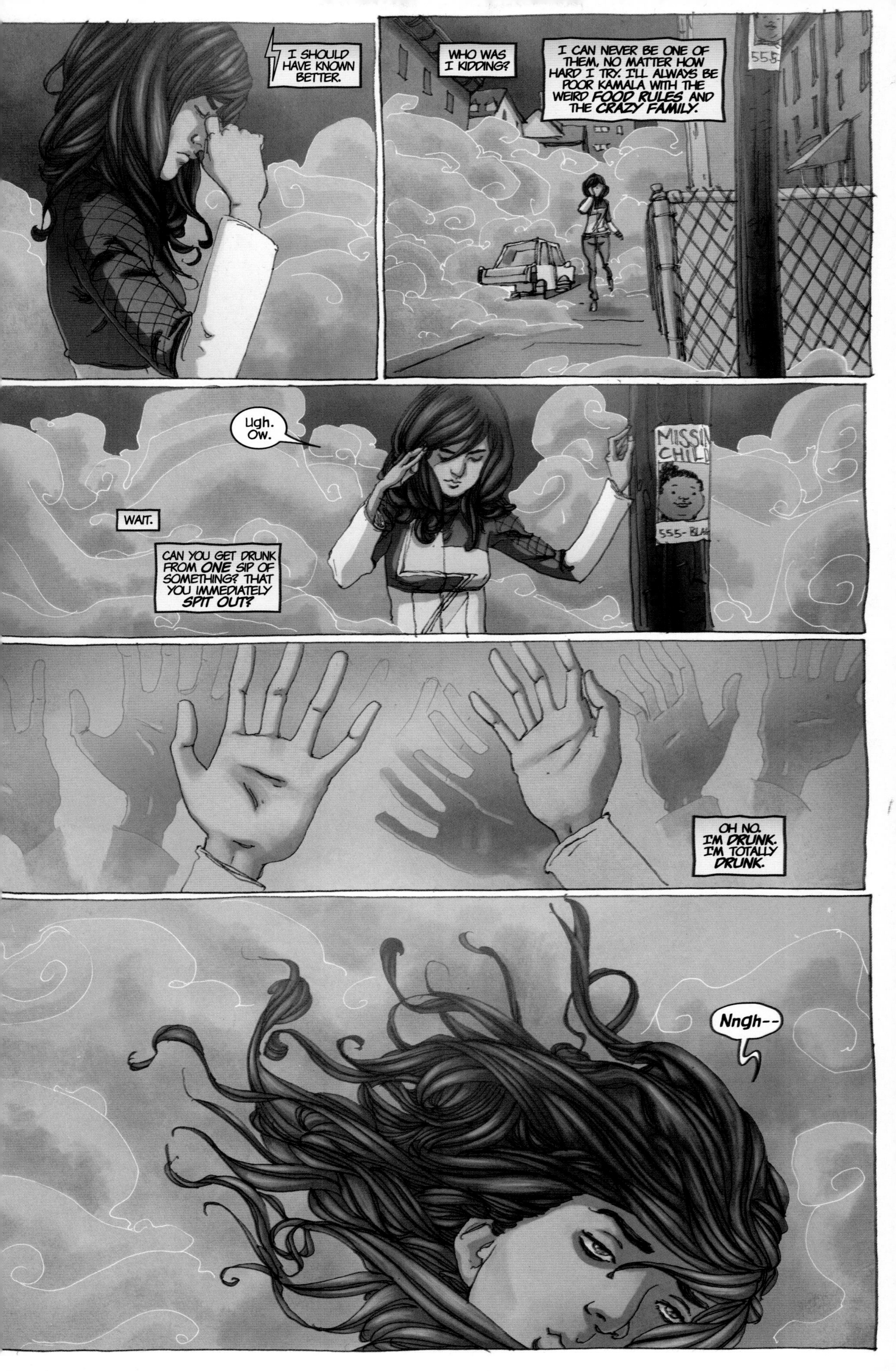
I SHOULD HAVE KNOWN BETTER.
WHO WAS I KIDDING?
I CAN NEVER BE ONE OF THEM, NO MATTER HOW HARD I TRY. I'LL ALWAYS BE POOR KAMALA WITH THE WEIRD FOOD RULES AND THE CRAZY FAMILY.
Ugh. Ow.
WAIT.
CAN YOU GET DRUNK FROM ONE SIP OF SOMETHING? THAT YOU IMMEDIATELY SPIT OUT?
MISSIN CHILD
555-BLA
OH NO. I'M DRUNK. I'M TOTALLY DRUNK.
Nngh--

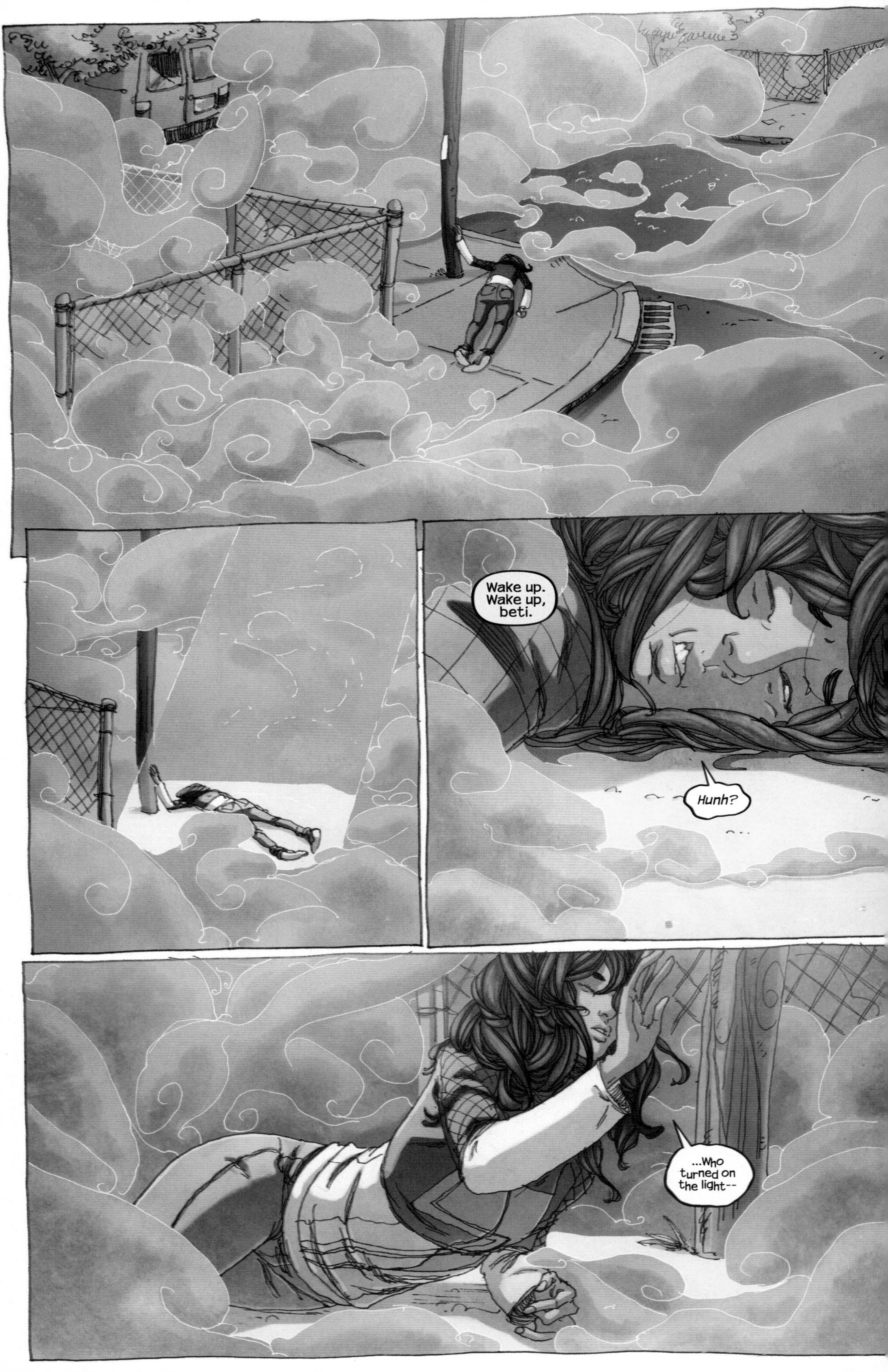
Wake up. Wake up, beti.
Hunh?
...Who turned on the light--

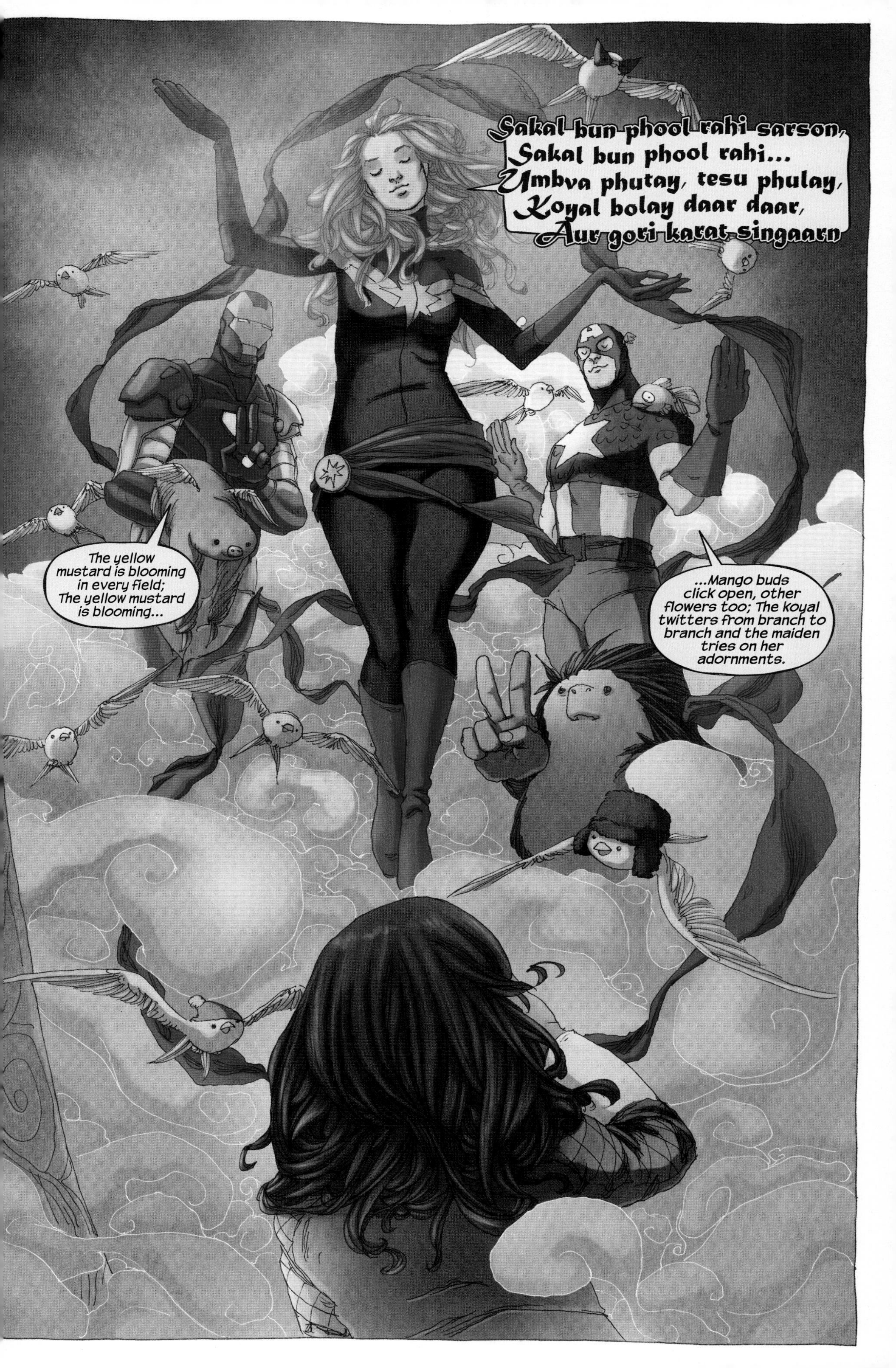
Sakal bun phool rahi sarson, Sakal bun phool rahi... Umbva phutay, tesu phulay, Koyal bolay daar daar, Aur gori karat singaarn
The yellow mustard is blooming in every field; The yellow mustard is blooming...
...Mango buds click open, other flowers too; The koyal twitters from branch to branch and the maiden tries on her adornments.

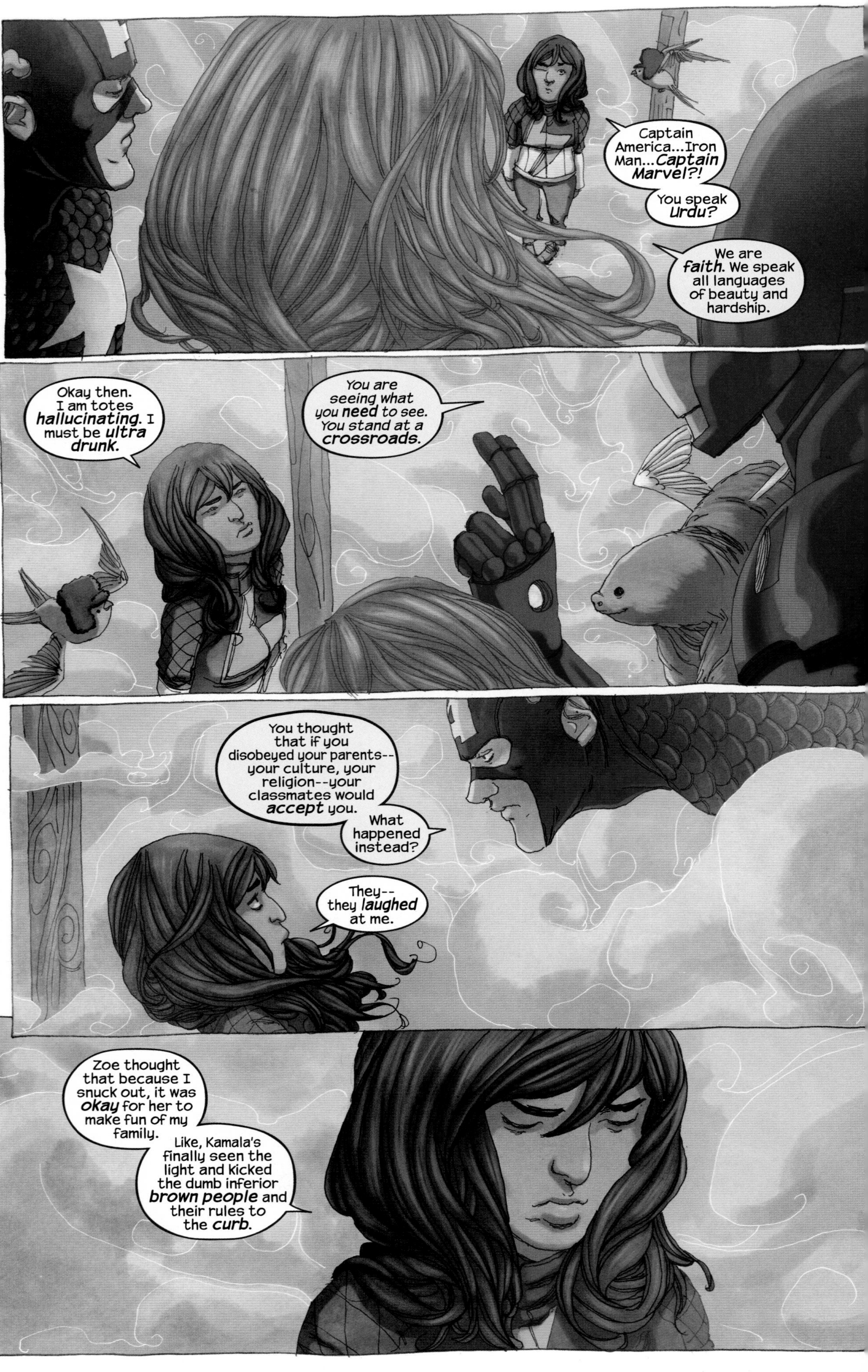
Captain America...Iron Man...Captain Marvel?!
You speak Urdu?
We are faith. We speak all languages of beauty and hardship.
Okay then. I am totes hallucinating. I must be ultra drunk.
You are seeing what you need to see. You stand at a crossroads.
You thought that if you disobeyed your parents--your culture, your religion--your classmates would accept you.
What happened instead?
They--they laughed at me.
Zoe thought that because I snuck out, it was okay for her to make fun of my family.
Like, Kamala's finally seen the light and kicked the dumb inferior brown people and their rules to the curb.

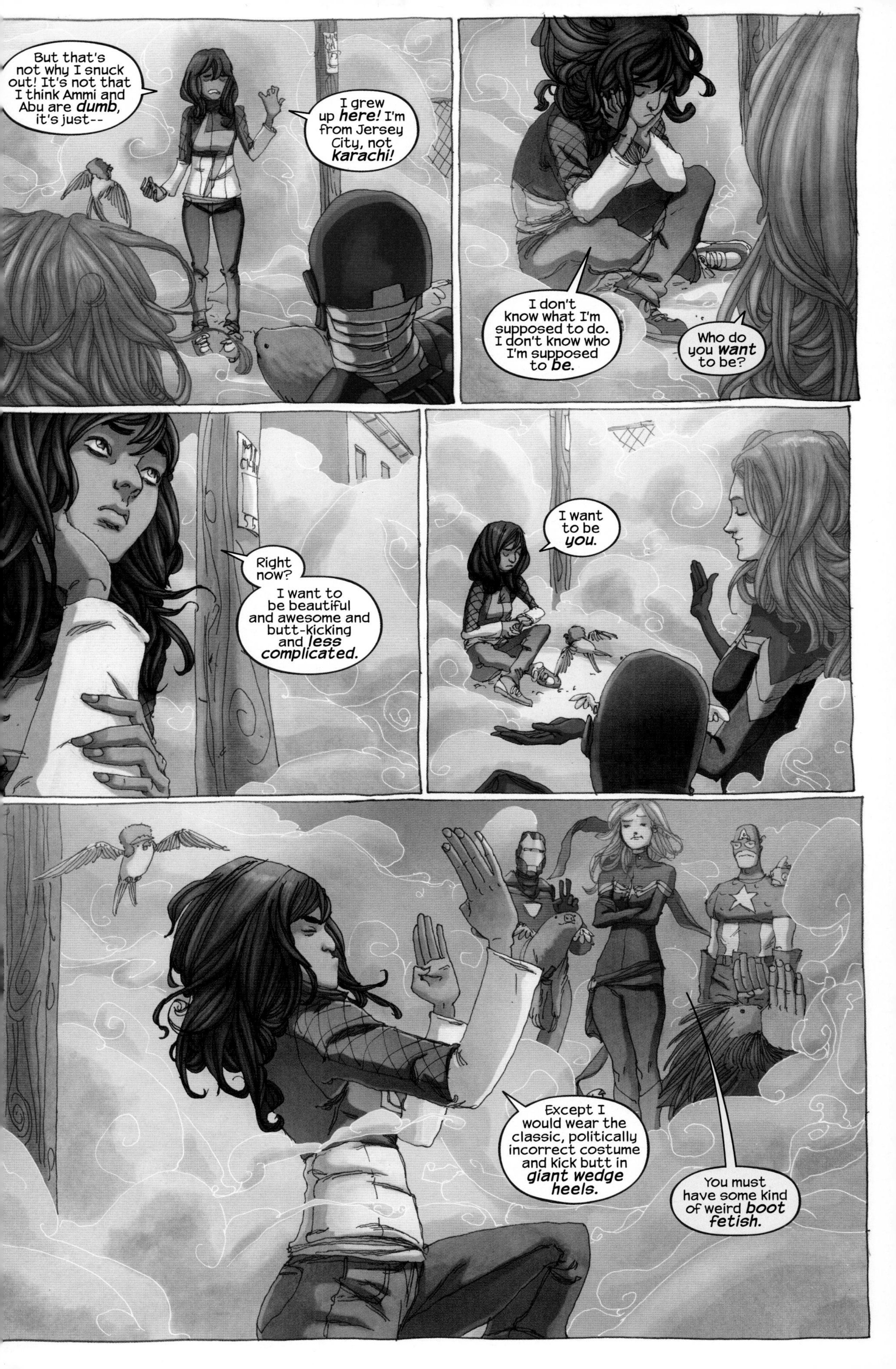
But that's not why I snuck out! It's not that I think Ammi and Abu are *dumb*, it's just--
I grew up ***here!*** I'm from Jersey City, not ***karachi!***
I don't know what I'm supposed to do. I don't know who I'm supposed to ***be***.
Who do you ***want*** to be?
Right now?
I want to be beautiful and awesome and butt-kicking and ***less complicated***.
I want to be ***you***.
Except I would wear the classic, politically incorrect costume and kick butt in ***giant wedge heels***.
You must have some kind of weird ***boot fetish***.

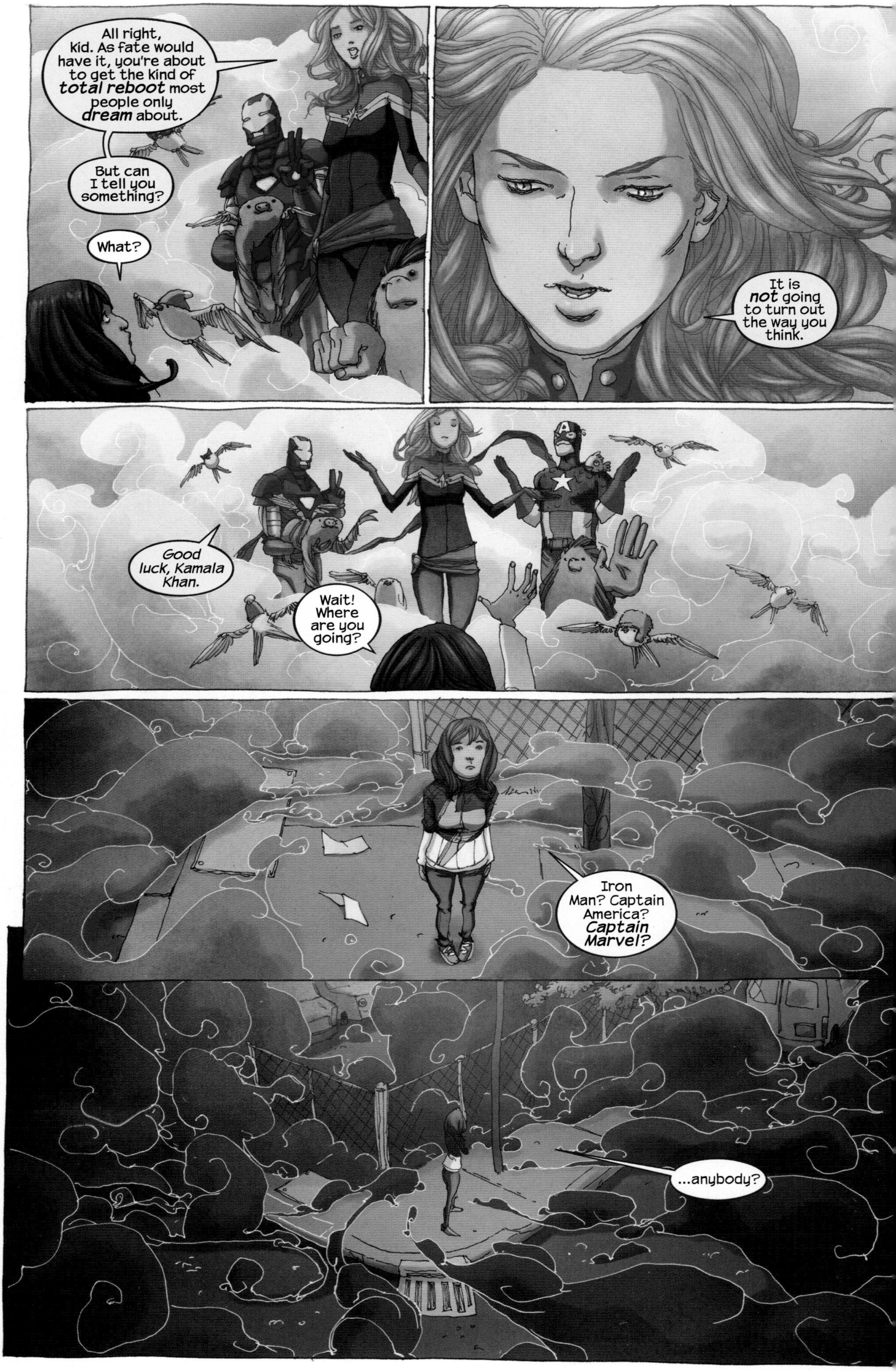
All right, kid. As fate would have it, you're about to get the kind of **total reboot** most people only **dream** about.
But can I tell you something?
What?
It is **not** going to turn out the way you think.
Good luck, Kamala Khan.
Wait! Where are you going?
Iron Man? Captain America? ***Captain Marvel?***
...anybody?

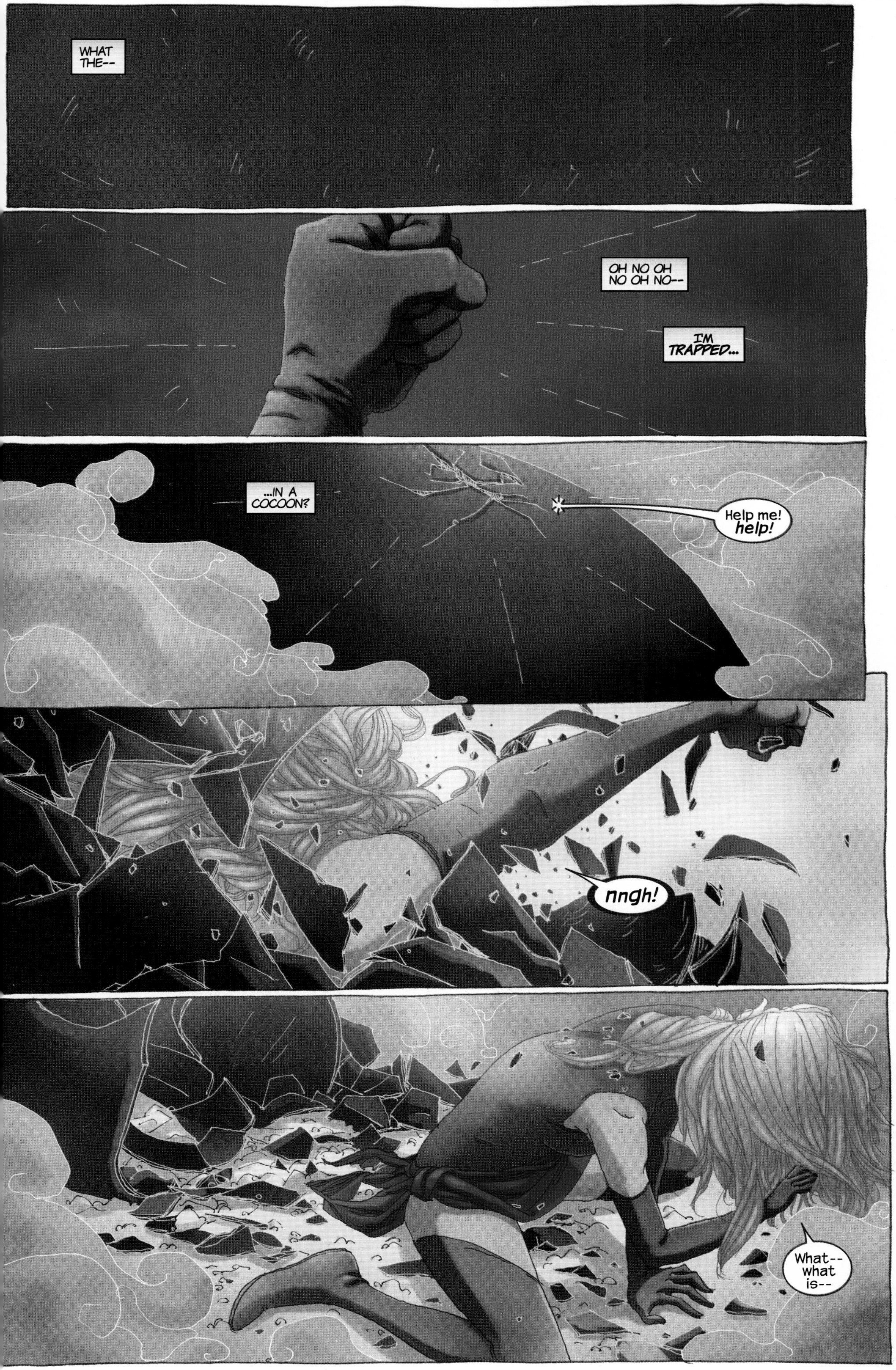
WHAT THE--
OH NO OH NO OH NO--
I'M TRAPPED...
...IN A COCOON?
Help me! help!
nngh!
What-- what is--

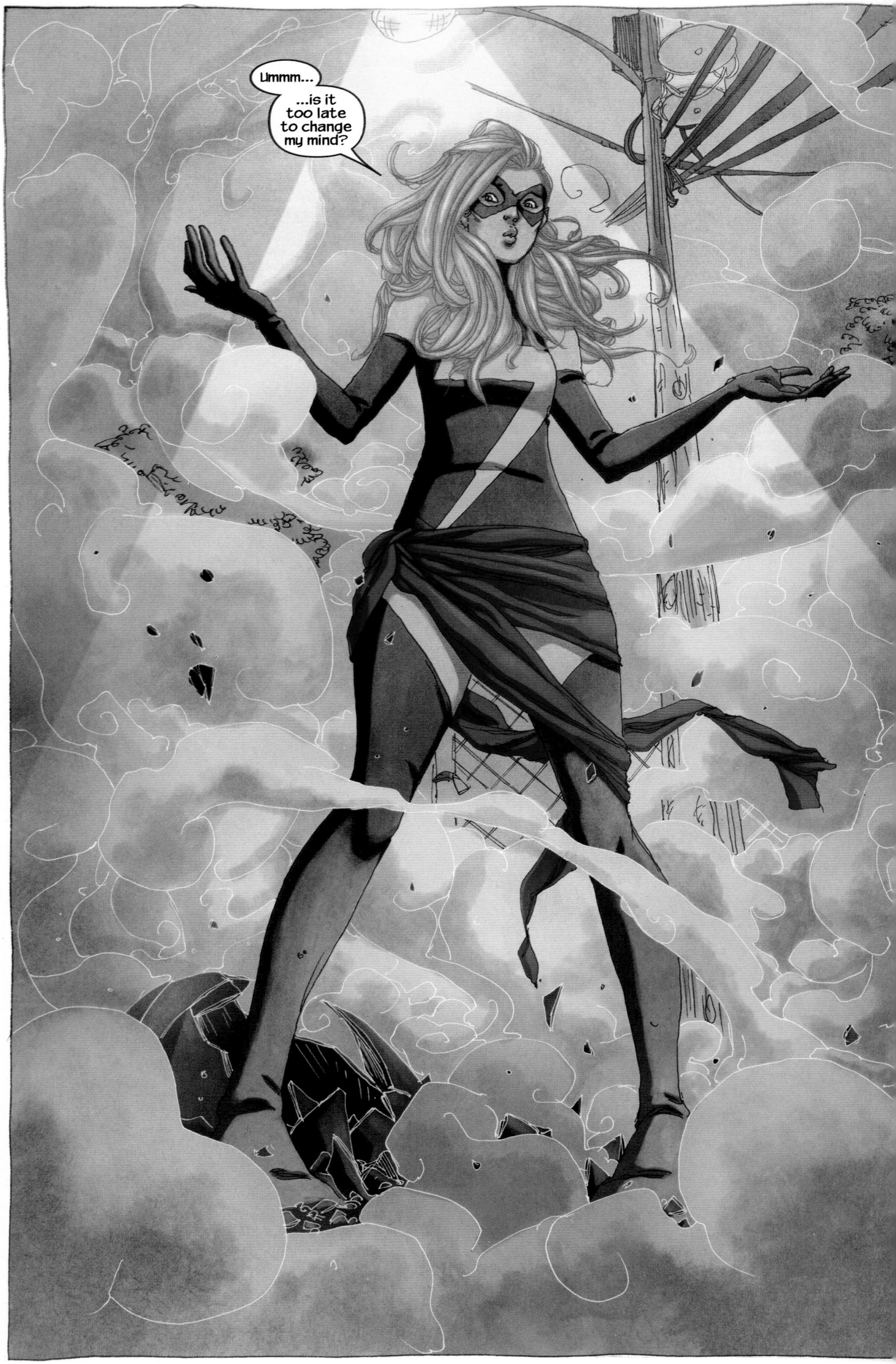
Ummm...
...is it too late to change my mind?

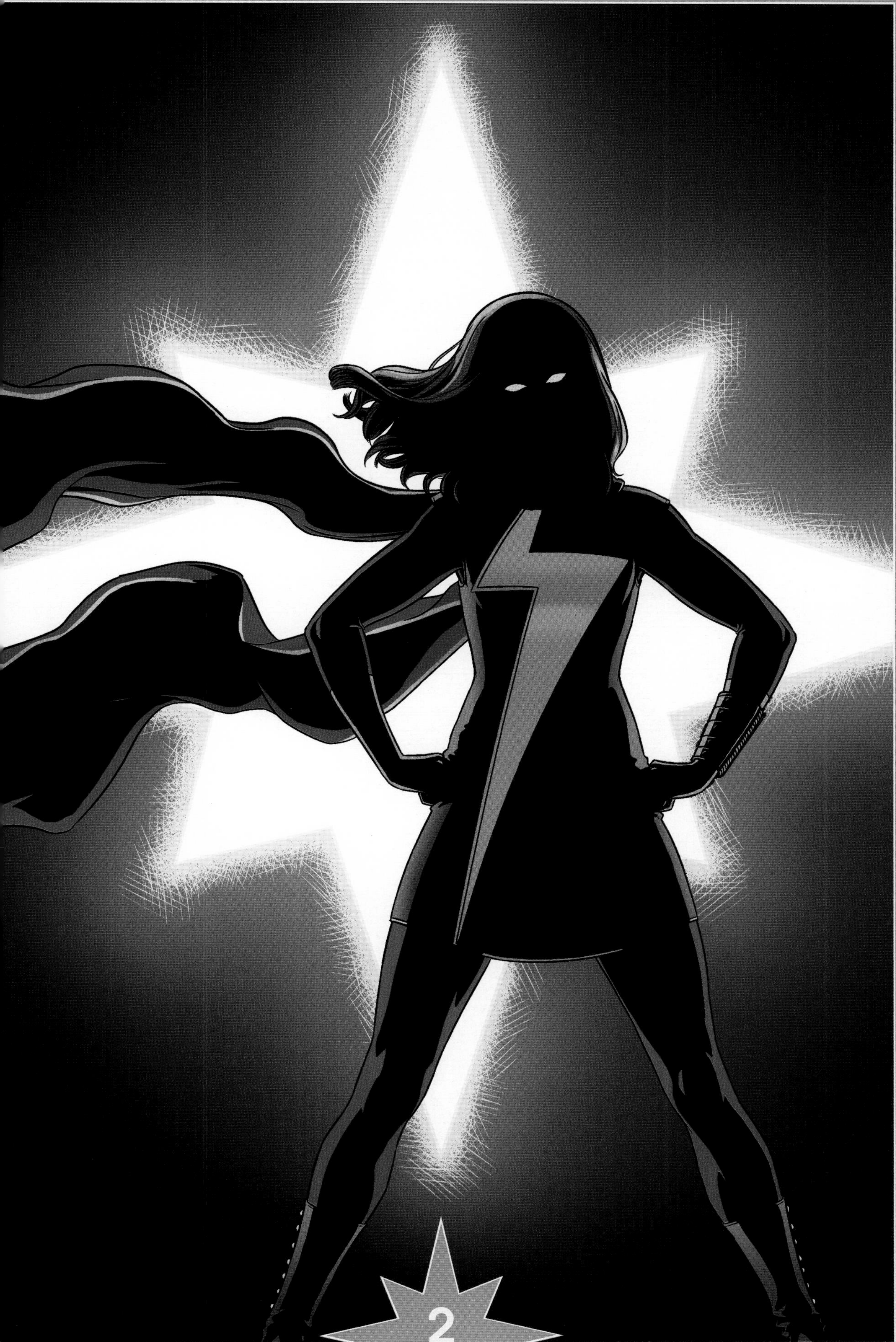
2

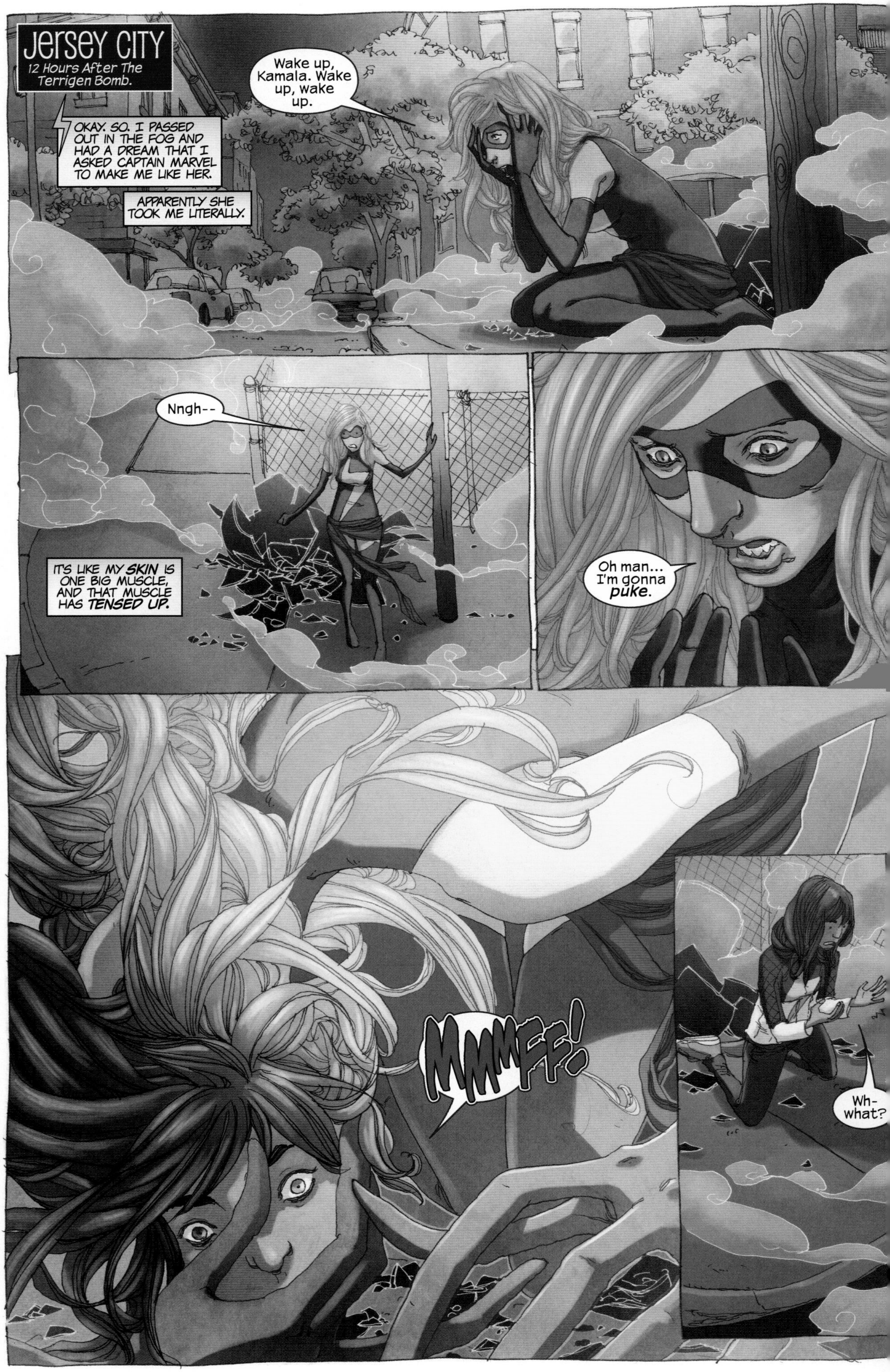
JERSEY CITY
12 Hours After The Terrigen Bomb.
Wake up, Kamala. Wake up, wake up.
OKAY. SO. I PASSED OUT IN THE FOG AND HAD A DREAM THAT I ASKED CAPTAIN MARVEL TO MAKE ME LIKE HER.
APPARENTLY SHE TOOK ME LITERALLY.
Nngh--
IT'S LIKE MY SKIN IS ONE BIG MUSCLE, AND THAT MUSCLE HAS TENSED UP.
Oh man... I'm gonna puke.
MMMFF!
Wh- what?

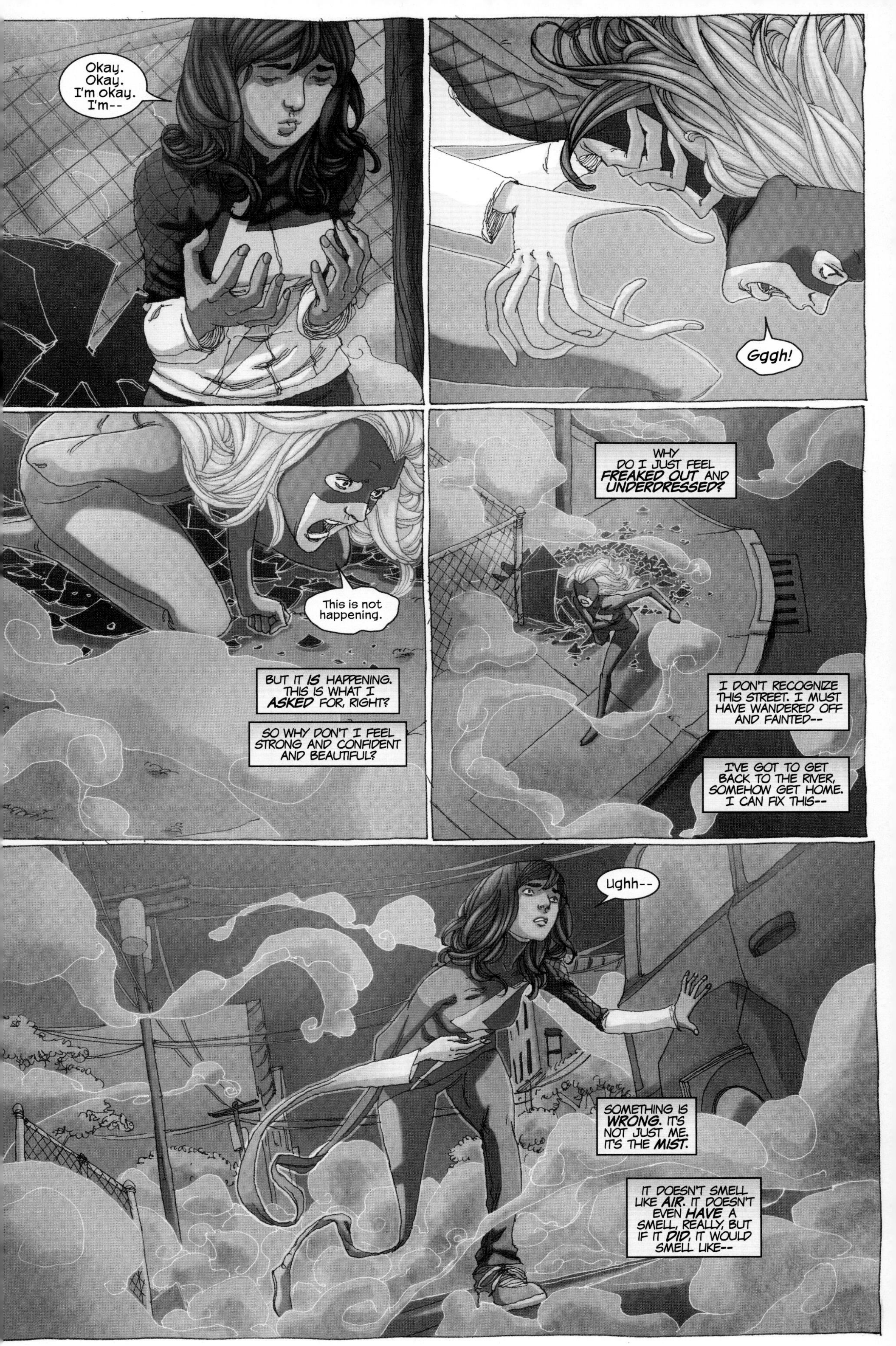
Okay. Okay. I'm okay. I'm--
Gggh!
This is not happening.
BUT IT IS HAPPENING. THIS IS WHAT I ASKED FOR, RIGHT?
SO WHY DON'T I FEEL STRONG AND CONFIDENT AND BEAUTIFUL?
WHY DO I JUST FEEL FREAKED OUT AND UNDERDRESSED?
I DON'T RECOGNIZE THIS STREET. I MUST HAVE WANDERED OFF AND FAINTED--
I'VE GOT TO GET BACK TO THE RIVER, SOMEHOW GET HOME. I CAN FIX THIS--
Ughh--
SOMETHING IS WRONG. IT'S NOT JUST ME. IT'S THE MIST.
IT DOESN'T SMELL LIKE AIR. IT DOESN'T EVEN HAVE A SMELL, REALLY, BUT IF IT DID, IT WOULD SMELL LIKE--

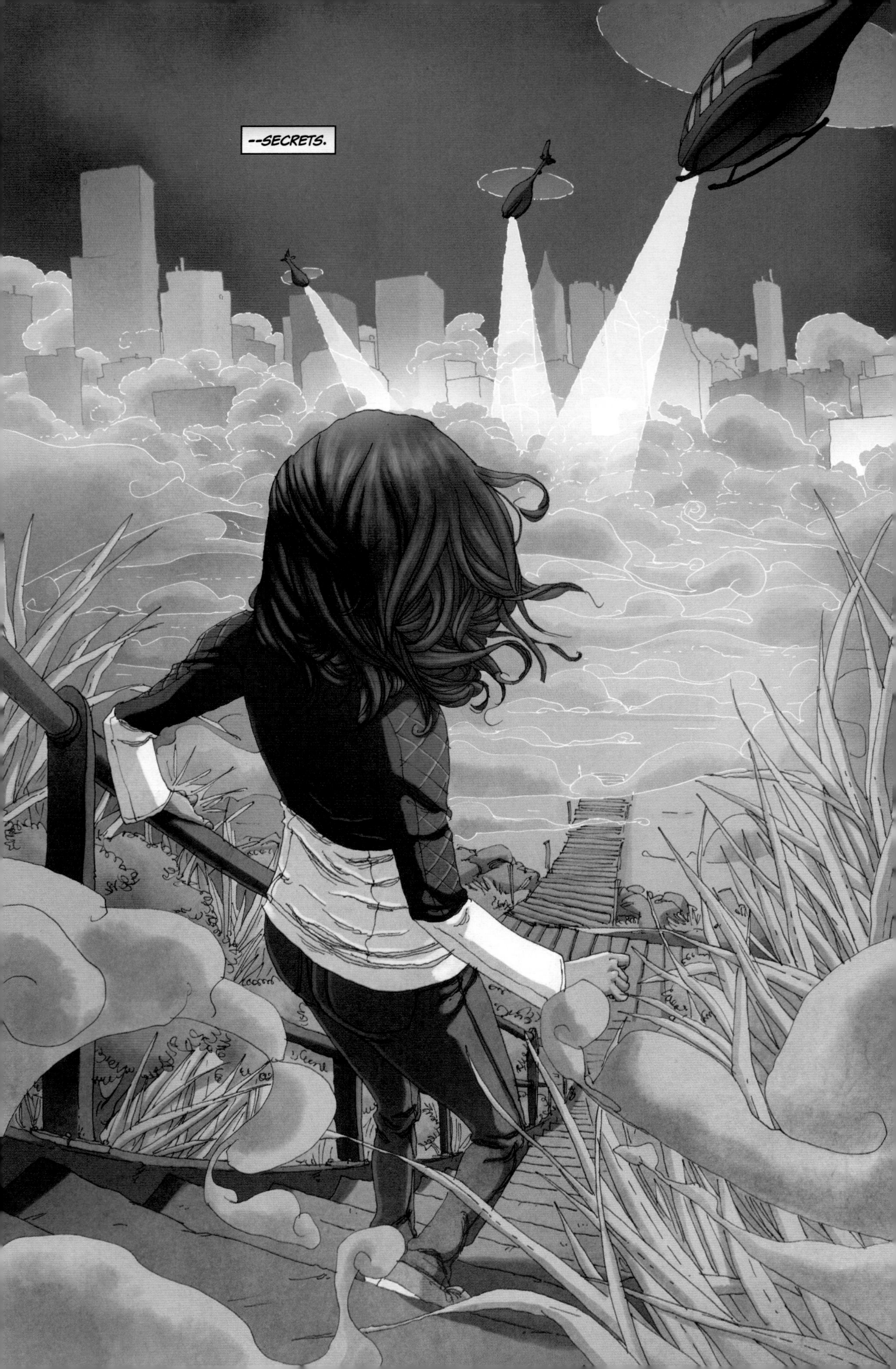
--SECRETS.

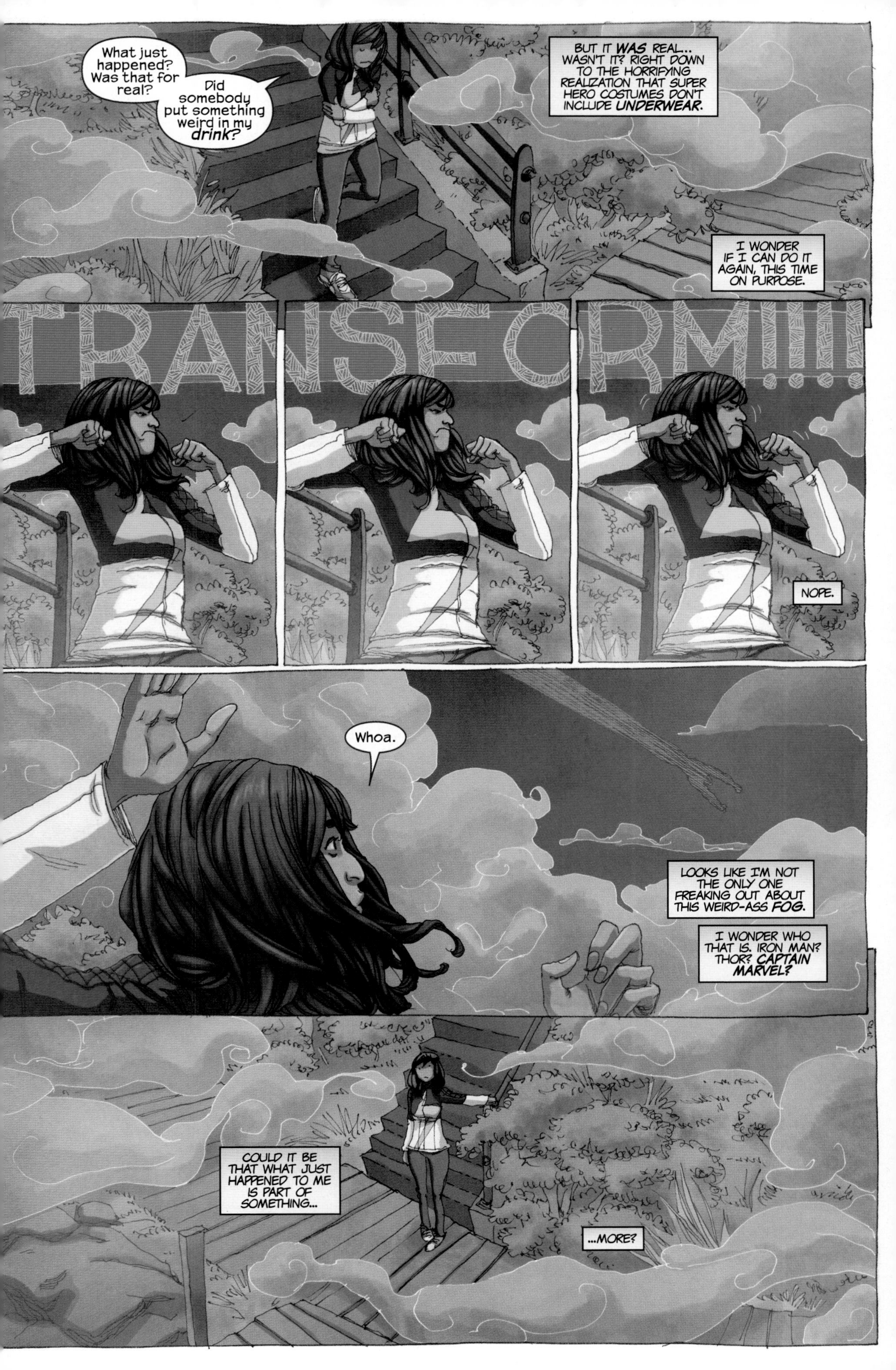

What just happened? Was that for real?
Did somebody put something weird in my drink?
BUT IT WAS REAL... WASN'T IT? RIGHT DOWN TO THE HORRIFYING REALIZATION THAT SUPER HERO COSTUMES DON'T INCLUDE UNDERWEAR.
I WONDER IF I CAN DO IT AGAIN, THIS TIME ON PURPOSE.
TRANSFORM!!!!!
NOPE.
Whoa.
LOOKS LIKE I'M NOT THE ONLY ONE FREAKING OUT ABOUT THIS WEIRD-ASS FOG.
I WONDER WHO THAT IS. IRON MAN? THOR? CAPTAIN MARVEL?
COULD IT BE THAT WHAT JUST HAPPENED TO ME IS PART OF SOMETHING...
...MORE?

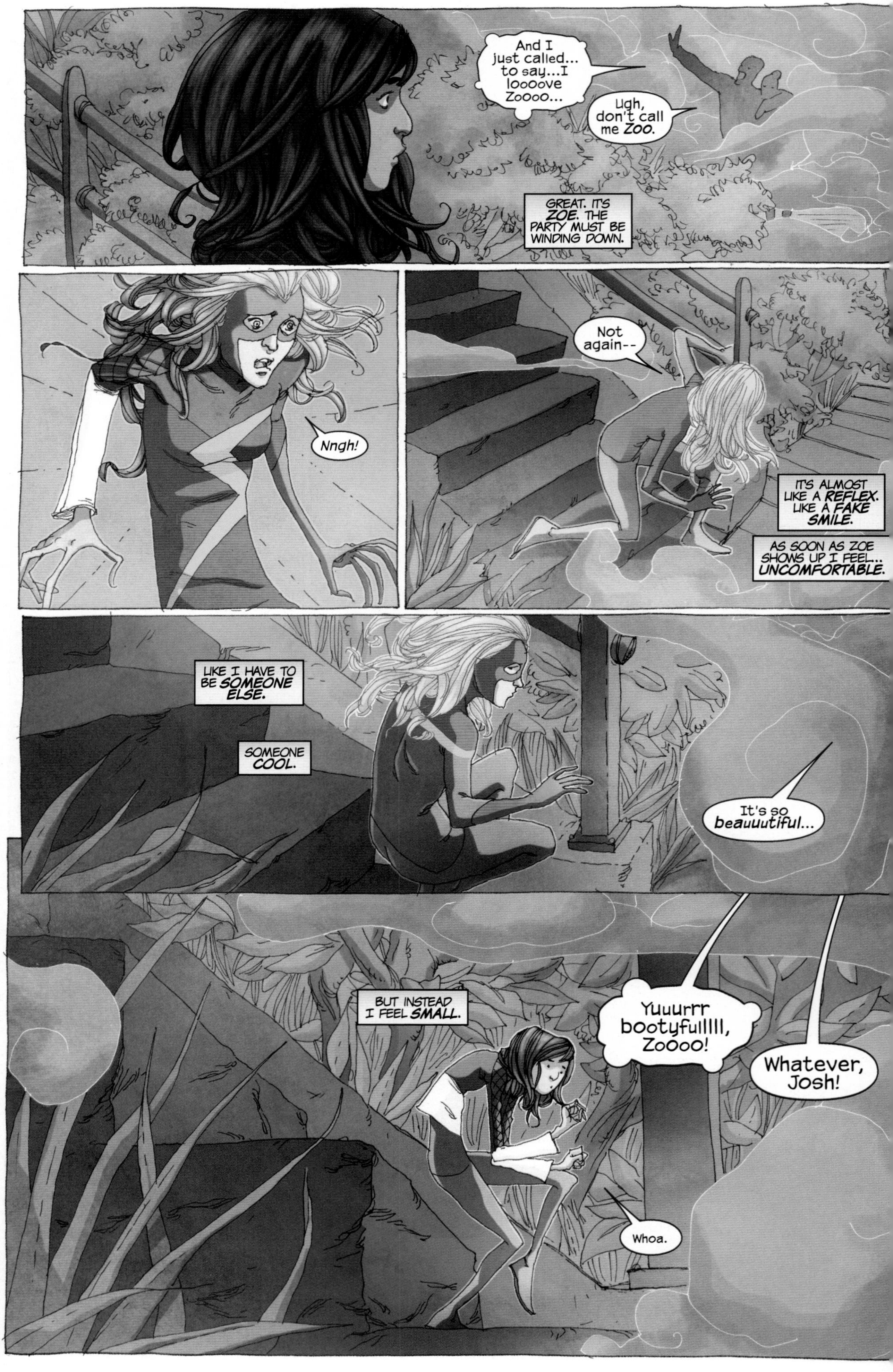
And I just called... to say...I loooove Zoooo...
Ugh, don't call me ZOO.
GREAT. IT'S ZOE. THE PARTY MUST BE WINDING DOWN.
Nngh!
Not again--
IT'S ALMOST LIKE A REFLEX. LIKE A FAKE SMILE.
AS SOON AS ZOE SHOWS UP I FEEL... UNCOMFORTABLE.
LIKE I HAVE TO BE SOMEONE ELSE.
SOMEONE COOL.
It's so beauuutiful...
BUT INSTEAD I FEEL SMALL.
Yuuurrr bootyfullllll, Zoooo!
Whatever, Josh!
Whoa.

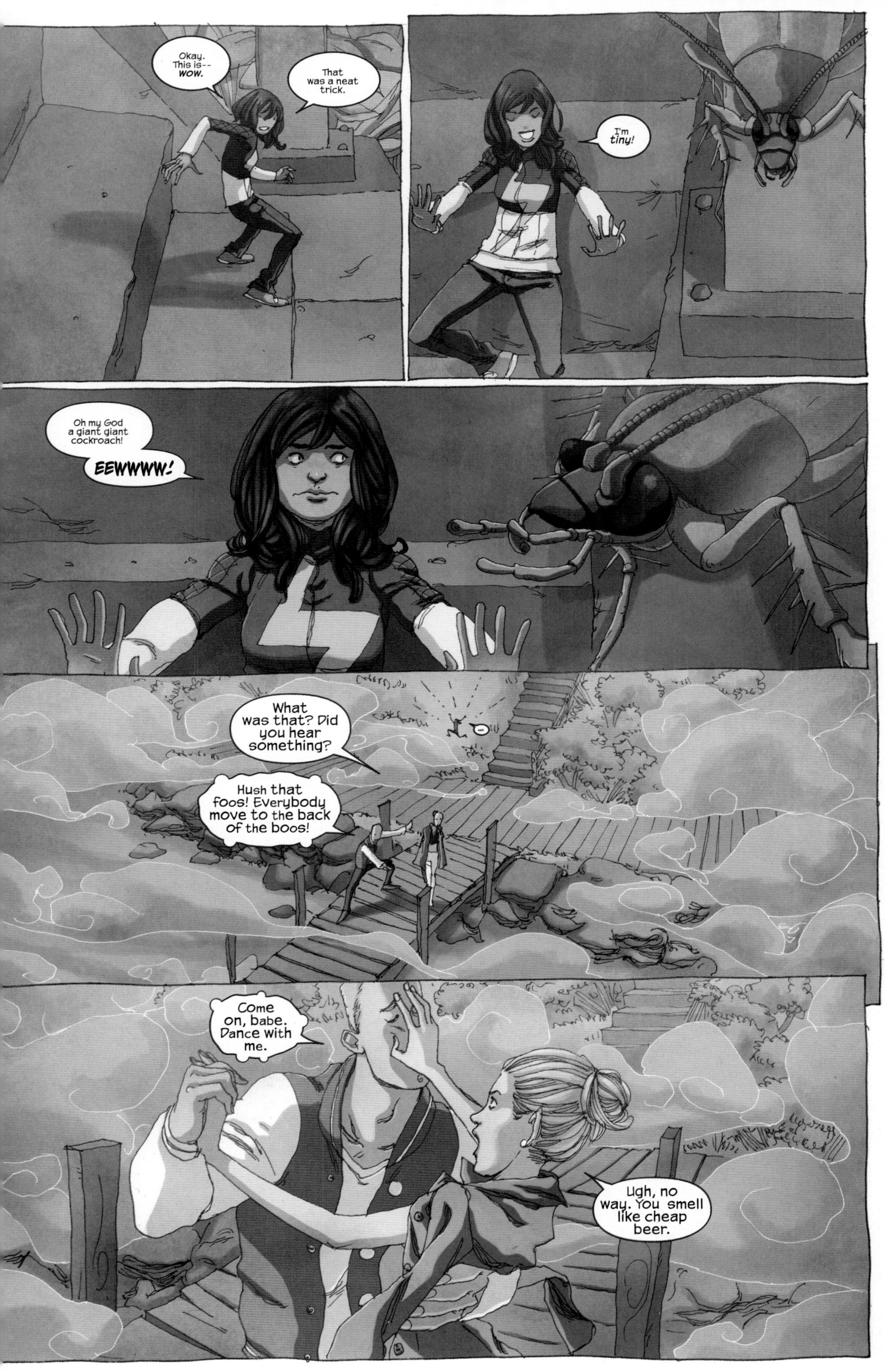

Okay. This is-- WOW.
That was a neat trick.
I'm tiny!
Oh my God a giant giant cockroach!
EEWWWW!
What was that? Did you hear something?
Hush that foos! Everybody move to the back of the boos!
Come on, babe. Dance with me.
Ugh, no way. You smell like cheap beer.

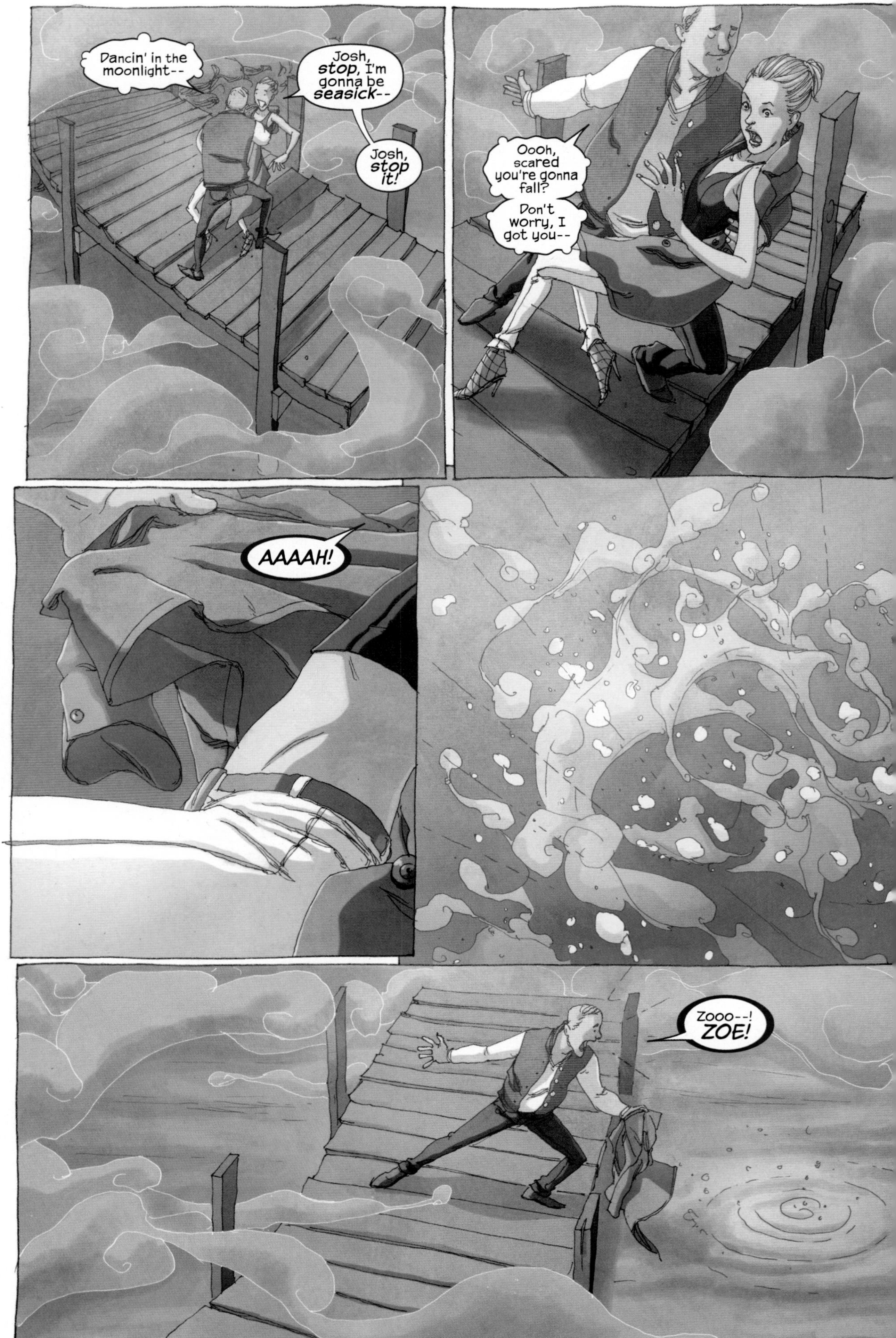
Dancin' in the moonlight--
Josh, stop, I'm gonna be seasick--
Josh, stop it!
Oooh, scared you're gonna fall?
Don't worry, I got you--
AAAAH!
Zooo--! ZOE!

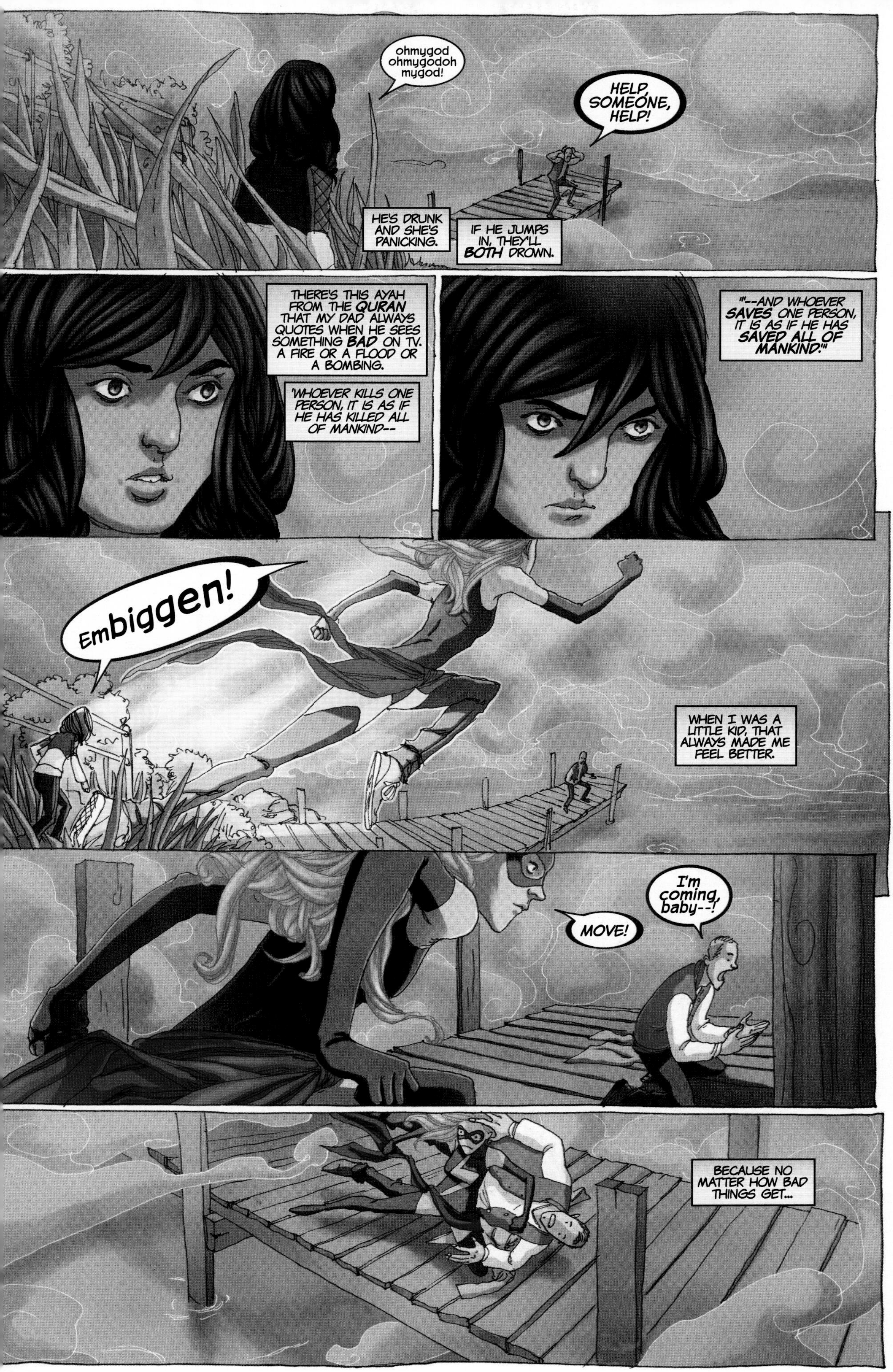

ohmygod ohmygodoh mygod!
HELP, SOMEONE, HELP!
HE'S DRUNK AND SHE'S PANICKING.
IF HE JUMPS IN, THEY'LL BOTH DROWN.
THERE'S THIS AYAH FROM THE QURAN THAT MY DAD ALWAYS QUOTES WHEN HE SEES SOMETHING BAD ON TV. A FIRE OR A FLOOD OR A BOMBING.
'WHOEVER KILLS ONE PERSON, IT IS AS IF HE HAS KILLED ALL OF MANKIND--
"--AND WHOEVER SAVES ONE PERSON, IT IS AS IF HE HAS SAVED ALL OF MANKIND.'"
Embiggen!
WHEN I WAS A LITTLE KID, THAT ALWAYS MADE ME FEEL BETTER.
MOVE!
I'm coming, baby--!'
BECAUSE NO MATTER HOW BAD THINGS GET...

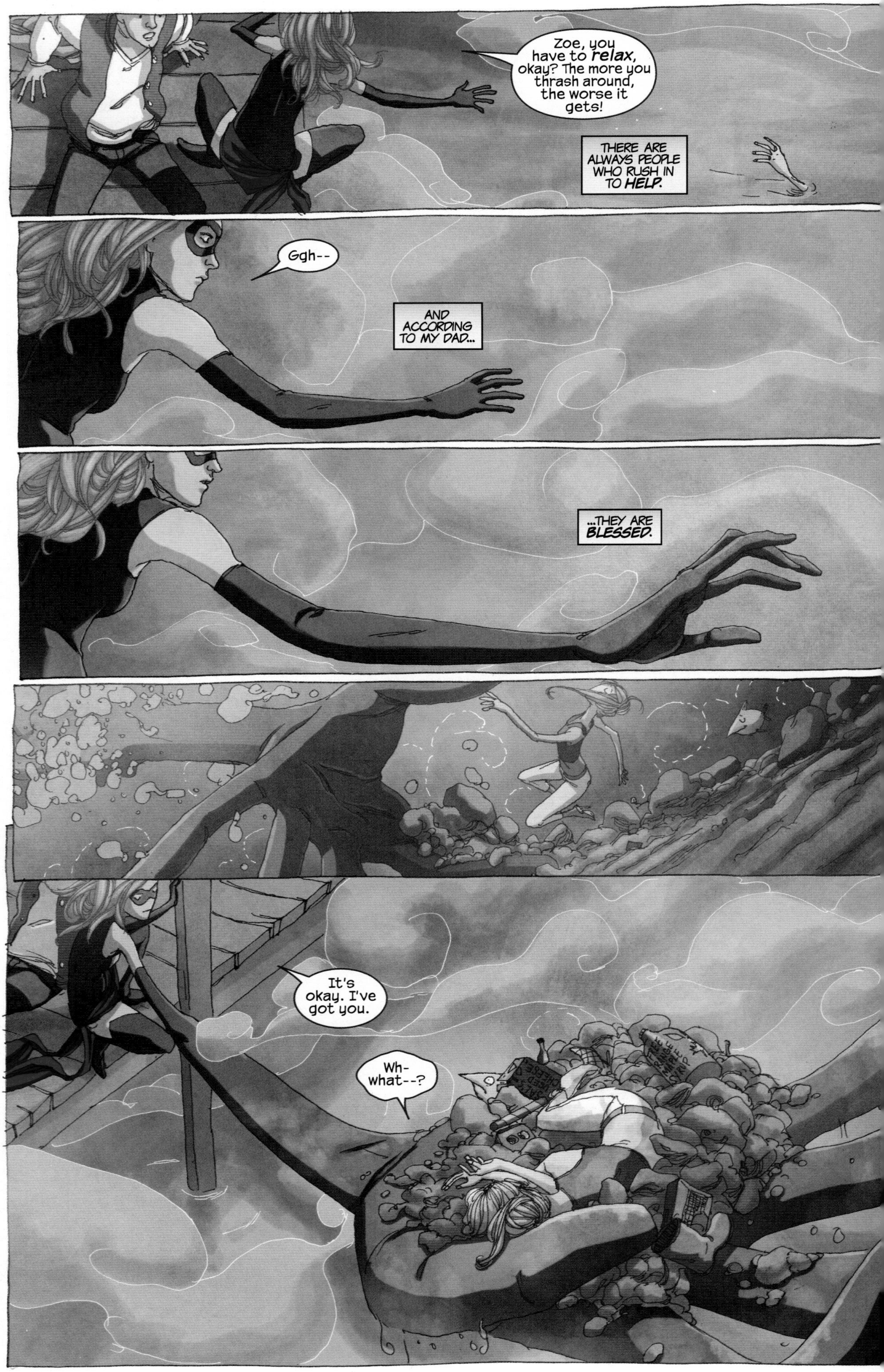
Zoe, you have to **relax**, okay? The more you thrash around, the worse it gets!
THERE ARE ALWAYS PEOPLE WHO RUSH IN TO **HELP**.
Ggh--
AND ACCORDING TO MY DAD...
...THEY ARE **BLESSED**.
It's okay. I've got you.
Wh- what--?

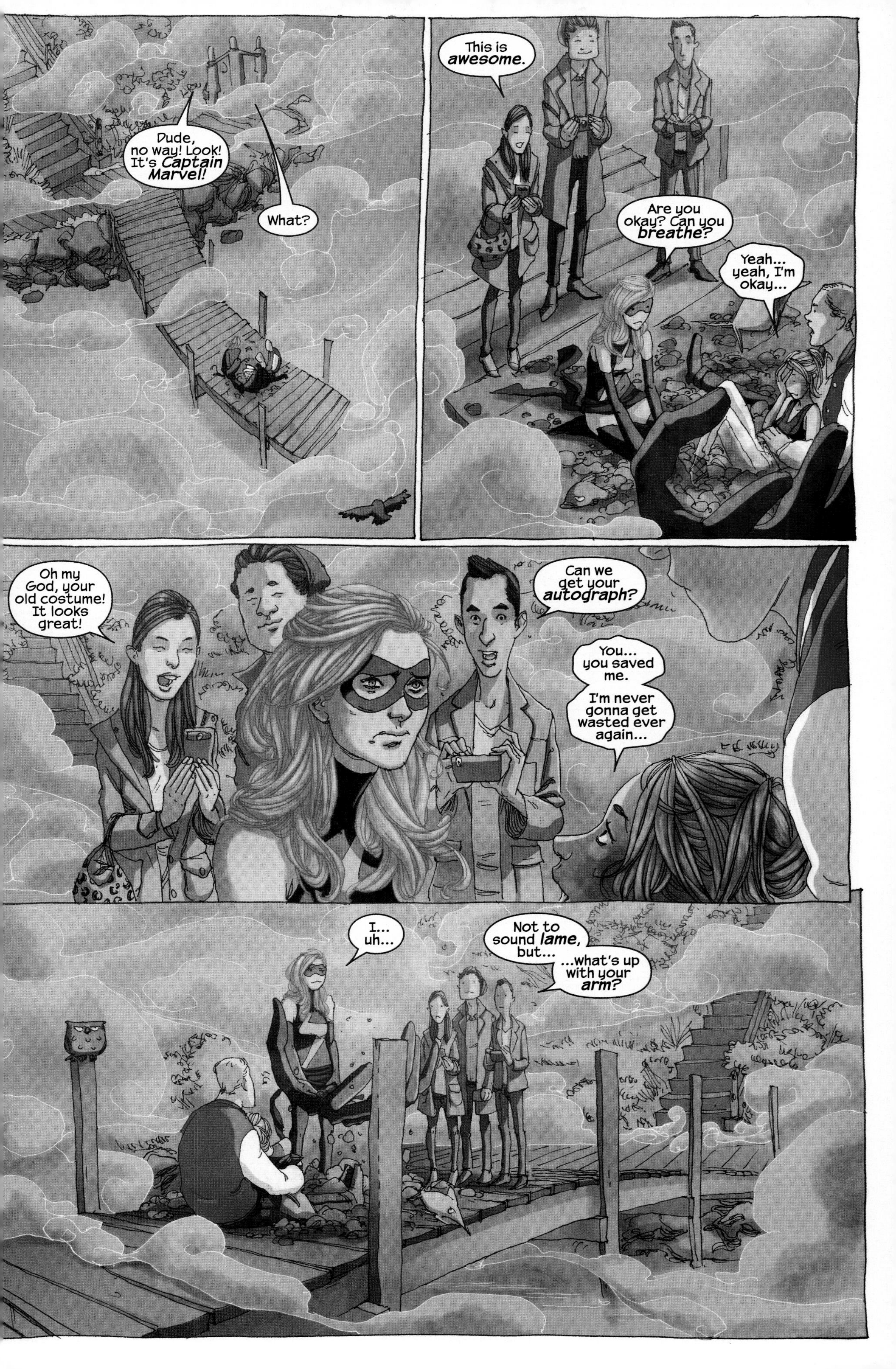

Dude, no way! Look! It's *Captain Marvel!*
What?
This is *awesome.*
Are you okay? Can you *breathe?*
Yeah... yeah, I'm okay...
Oh my God, your old costume! It looks great!
Can we get your *autograph?*
You... you saved me.
I'm never gonna get wasted ever again...
I... uh...
Not to sound *lame,* but...
...what's up with your *arm?*

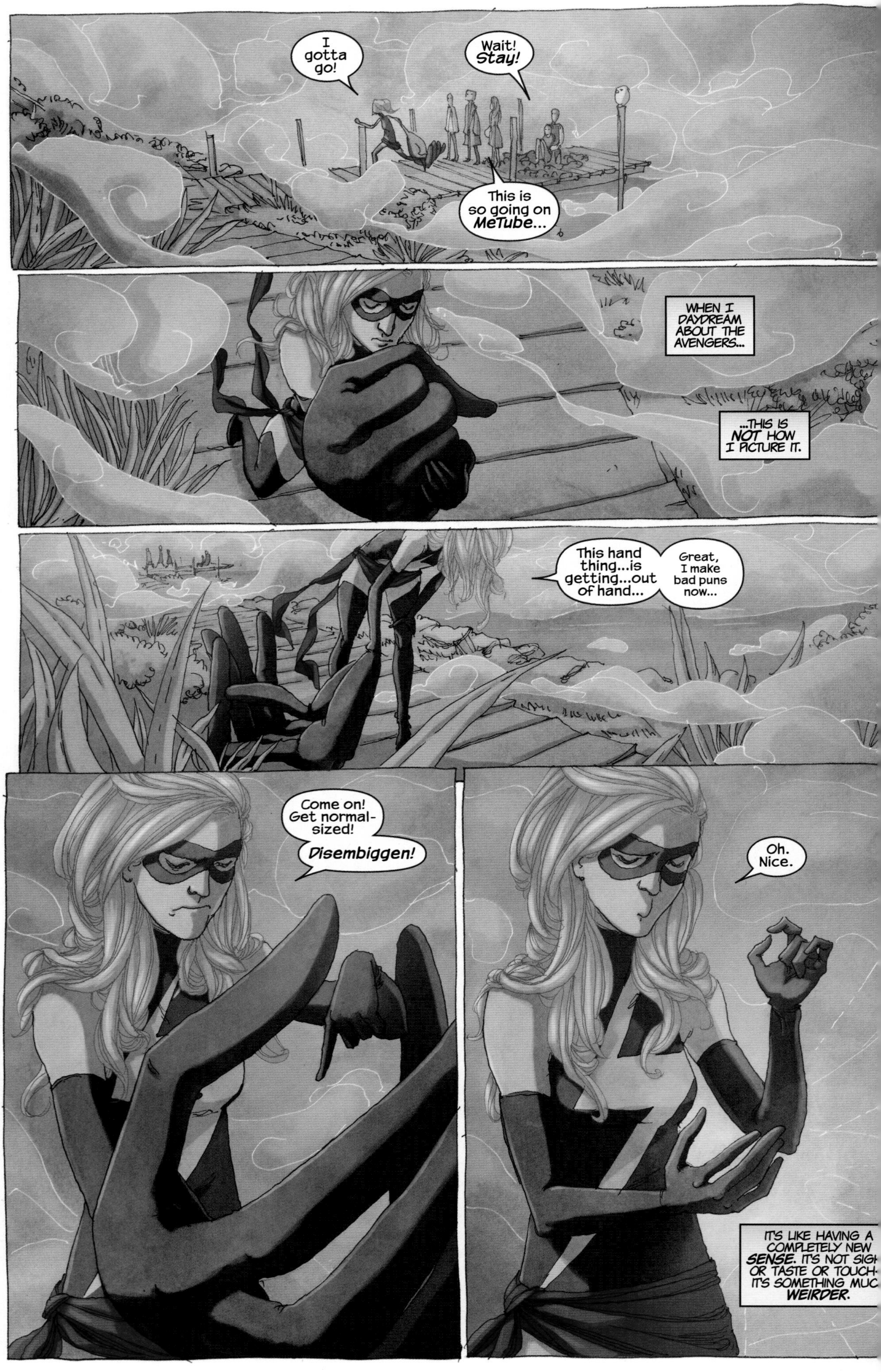

I gotta go!
Wait! *Stay!*
This is so going on *MeTube*...
WHEN I DAYDREAM ABOUT THE AVENGERS...
...THIS IS *NOT* HOW I PICTURE IT.
This hand thing...is getting...out of hand...
Great, I make bad puns now...
Come on! Get normal-sized!
Disembiggen!
Oh. Nice.
IT'S LIKE HAVING A COMPLETELY NEW *SENSE*. IT'S NOT SIGH OR TASTE OR TOUCH- IT'S SOMETHING MUC *WEIRDER*.

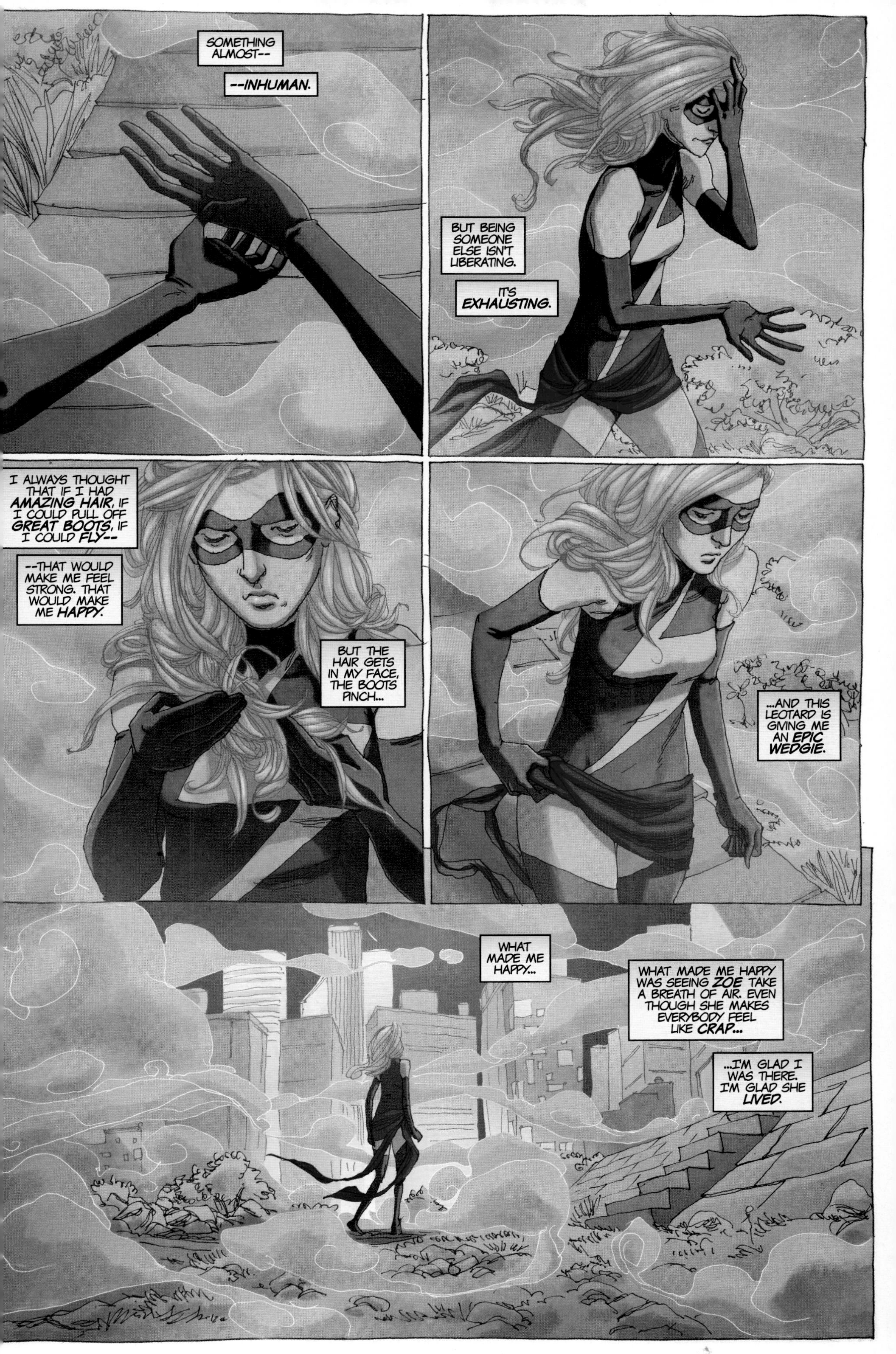
SOMETHING ALMOST--
--INHUMAN.
BUT BEING SOMEONE ELSE ISN'T LIBERATING.
IT'S EXHAUSTING.
I ALWAYS THOUGHT THAT IF I HAD AMAZING HAIR, IF I COULD PULL OFF GREAT BOOTS, IF I COULD FLY--
--THAT WOULD MAKE ME FEEL STRONG. THAT WOULD MAKE ME HAPPY.
BUT THE HAIR GETS IN MY FACE, THE BOOTS PINCH...
...AND THIS LEOTARD IS GIVING ME AN EPIC WEDGIE.
WHAT MADE ME HAPPY...
WHAT MADE ME HAPPY WAS SEEING ZOE TAKE A BREATH OF AIR. EVEN THOUGH SHE MAKES EVERYBODY FEEL LIKE CRAP...
...I'M GLAD I WAS THERE. I'M GLAD SHE LIVED.

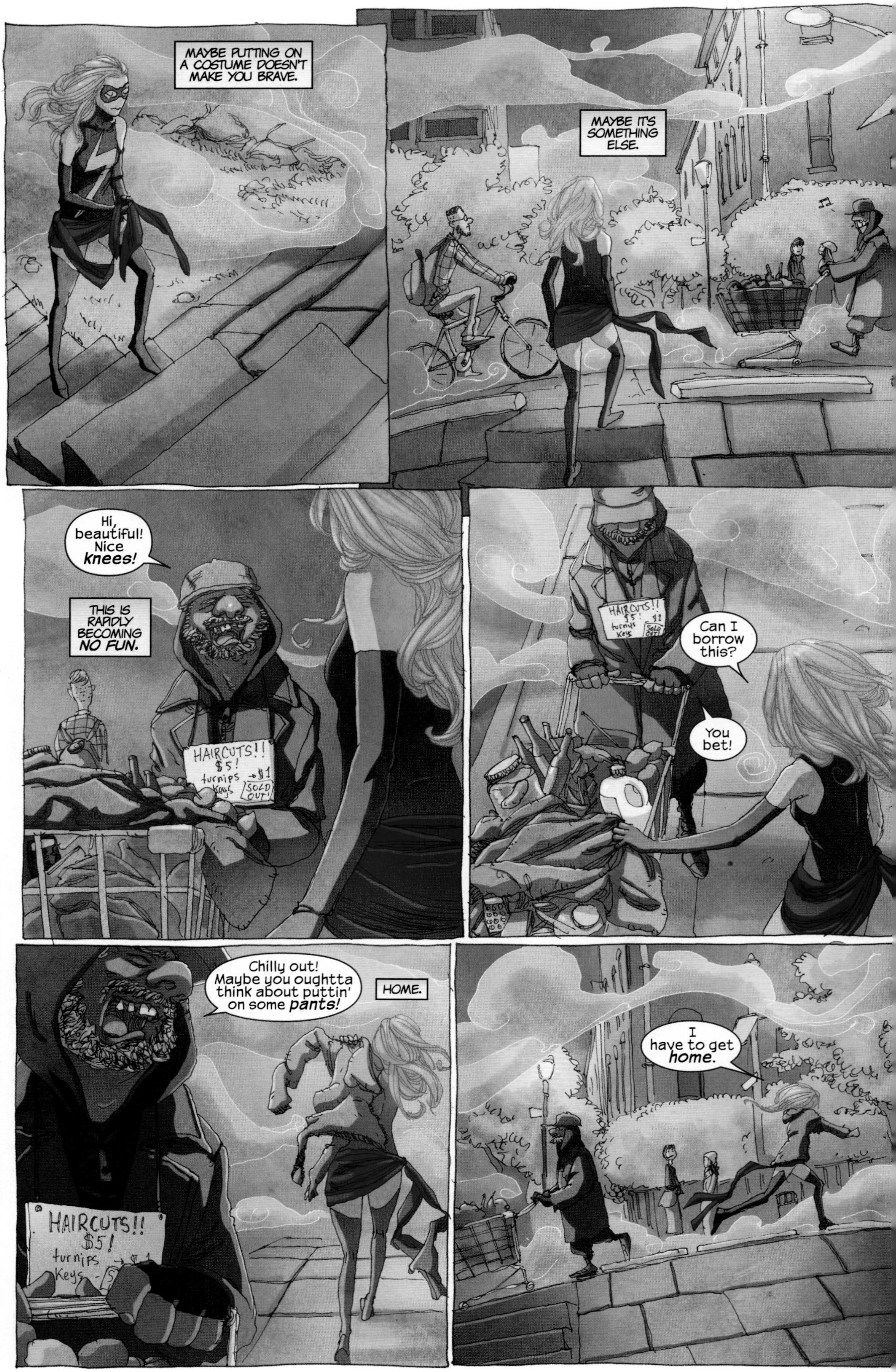
MAYBE PUTTING ON A COSTUME DOESN'T MAKE YOU BRAVE.
MAYBE IT'S SOMETHING ELSE.
Hi, beautiful! Nice *knees!*
THIS IS RAPIDLY BECOMING *NO FUN.*
HAIRCUTS!! $5! turnips → $1 Keys SOLD OUT!
Can I borrow this?
You bet!
Chilly out! Maybe you oughtta think about puttin' on some *pants!*
HOME.
HAIRCUTS!! $5! turnips Keys
I have to get *home.*

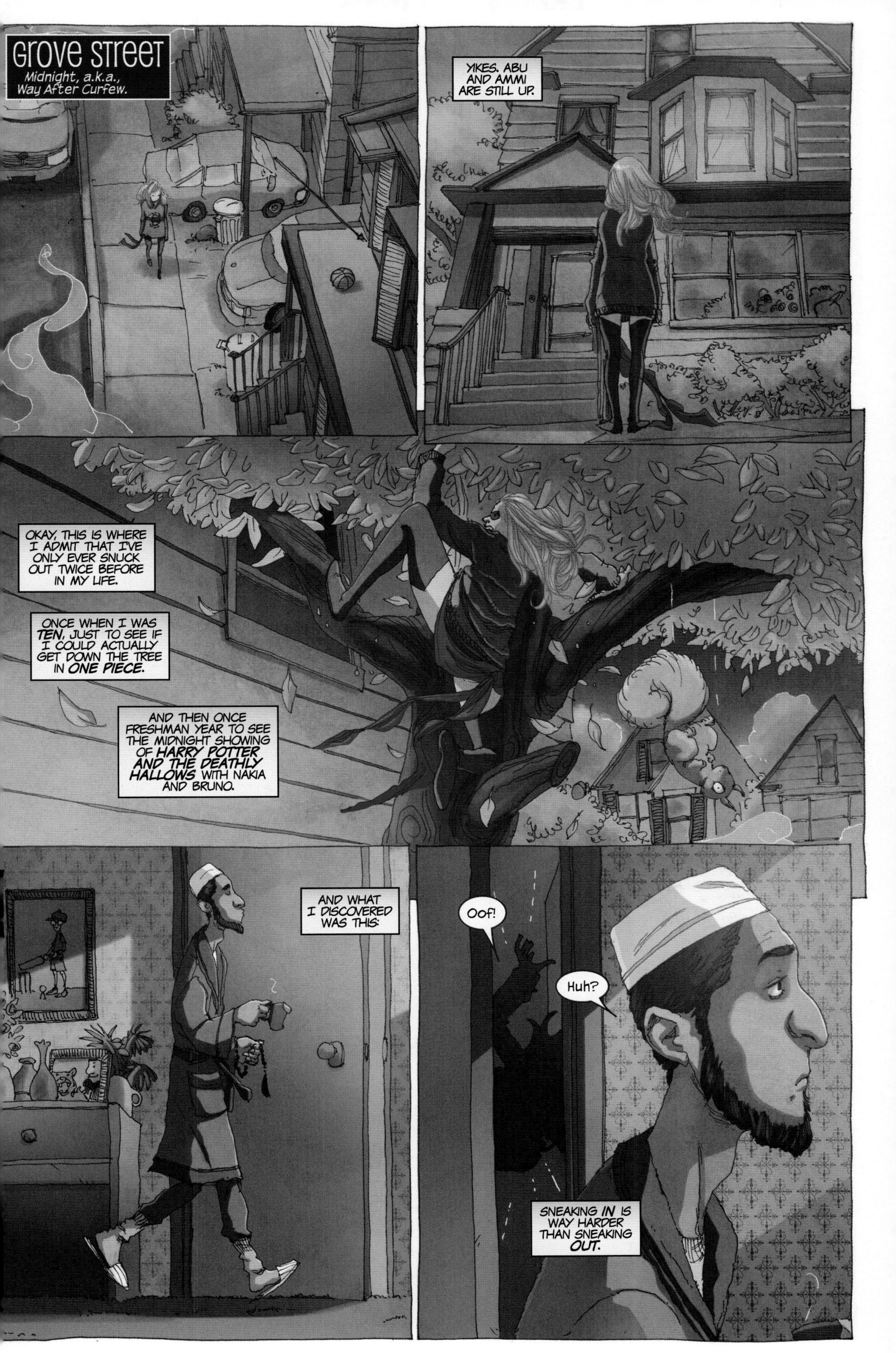
GROVE STREET
Midnight, a.k.a., Way After Curfew.
YIKES. ABU AND AMMI ARE STILL UP.
OKAY, THIS IS WHERE I ADMIT THAT I'VE ONLY EVER SNUCK OUT TWICE BEFORE IN MY LIFE.
ONCE WHEN I WAS TEN, JUST TO SEE IF I COULD ACTUALLY GET DOWN THE TREE IN ONE PIECE.
AND THEN ONCE FRESHMAN YEAR TO SEE THE MIDNIGHT SHOWING OF HARRY POTTER AND THE DEATHLY HALLOWS WITH NAKIA AND BRUNO.
AND WHAT I DISCOVERED WAS THIS:
Oof!
Huh?
SNEAKING IN IS WAY HARDER THAN SNEAKING OUT.

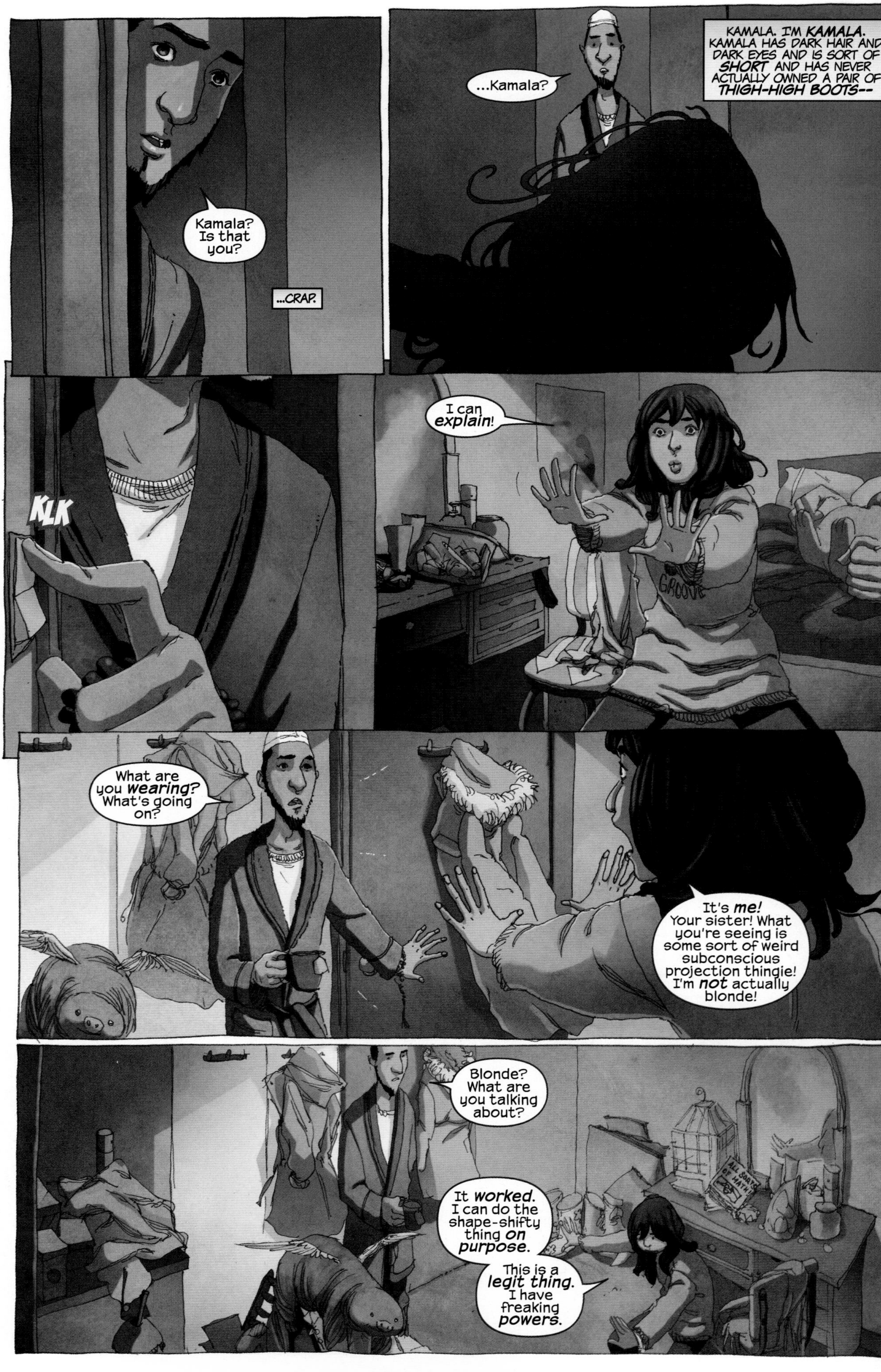
Kamala? Is that you?
...CRAP.
...Kamala?
KAMALA. I'M KAMALA. KAMALA HAS DARK HAIR AND DARK EYES AND IS SORT OF SHORT AND HAS NEVER ACTUALLY OWNED A PAIR OF THIGH-HIGH BOOTS--
KLK
I can explain!
GROOVE
What are you wearing? What's going on?
It's me! Your sister! What you're seeing is some sort of weird subconscious projection thingie! I'm not actually blonde!
Blonde? What are you talking about?
It worked. I can do the shape-shifty thing on purpose.
This is a legit thing. I have freaking powers.

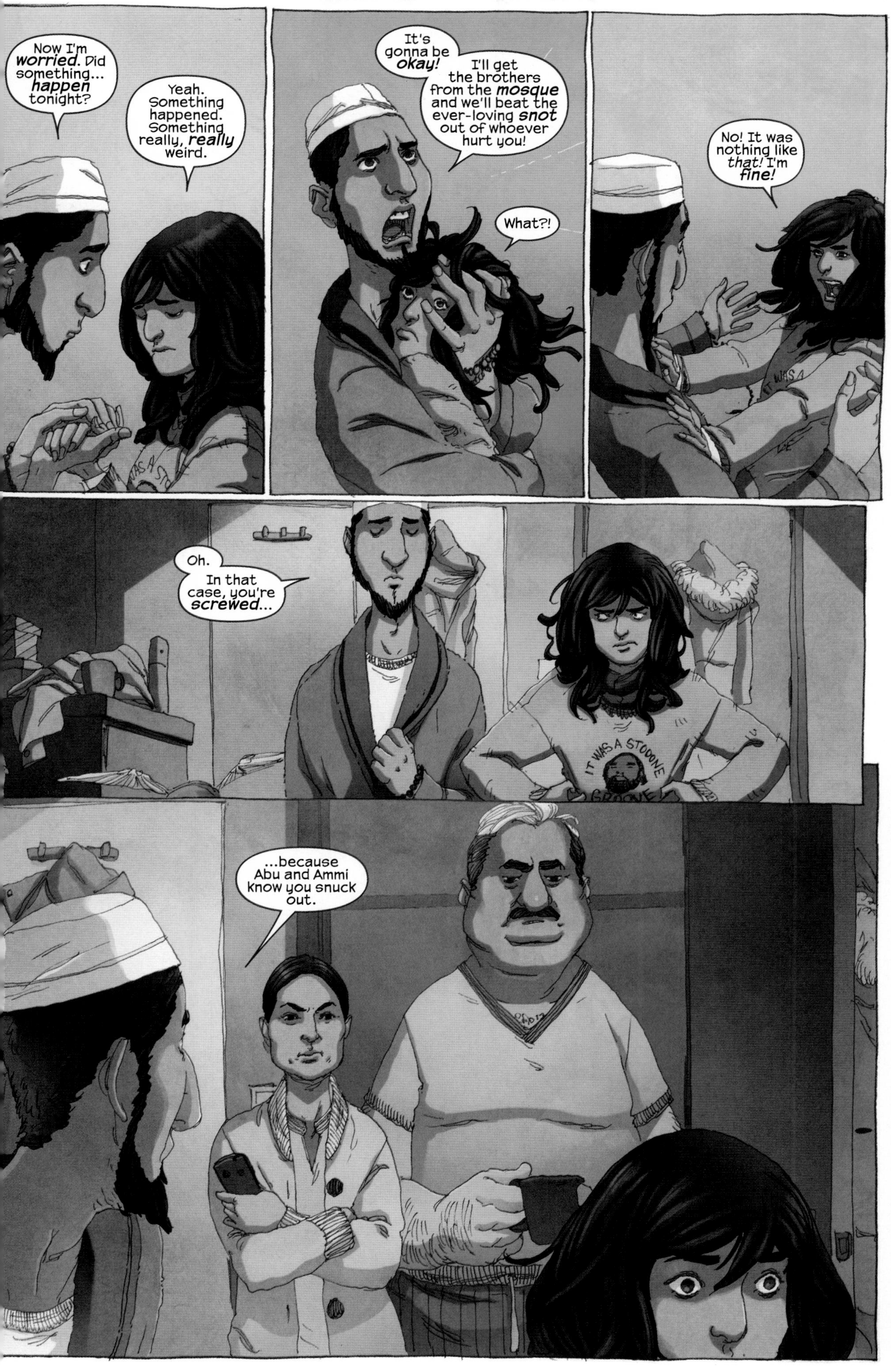
Now I'm *worried*. Did something... *happen* tonight?
Yeah. Something happened. Something really, *really* weird.
It's gonna be *okay!*
I'll get the brothers from the *mosque* and we'll beat the ever-loving *snot* out of whoever hurt you!
What?!
No! It was nothing like *that!* I'm *fine!*
Oh.
In that case, you're *screwed*...
IT WAS A STOOONE GROOVE
...because Abu and Ammi know you snuck out.

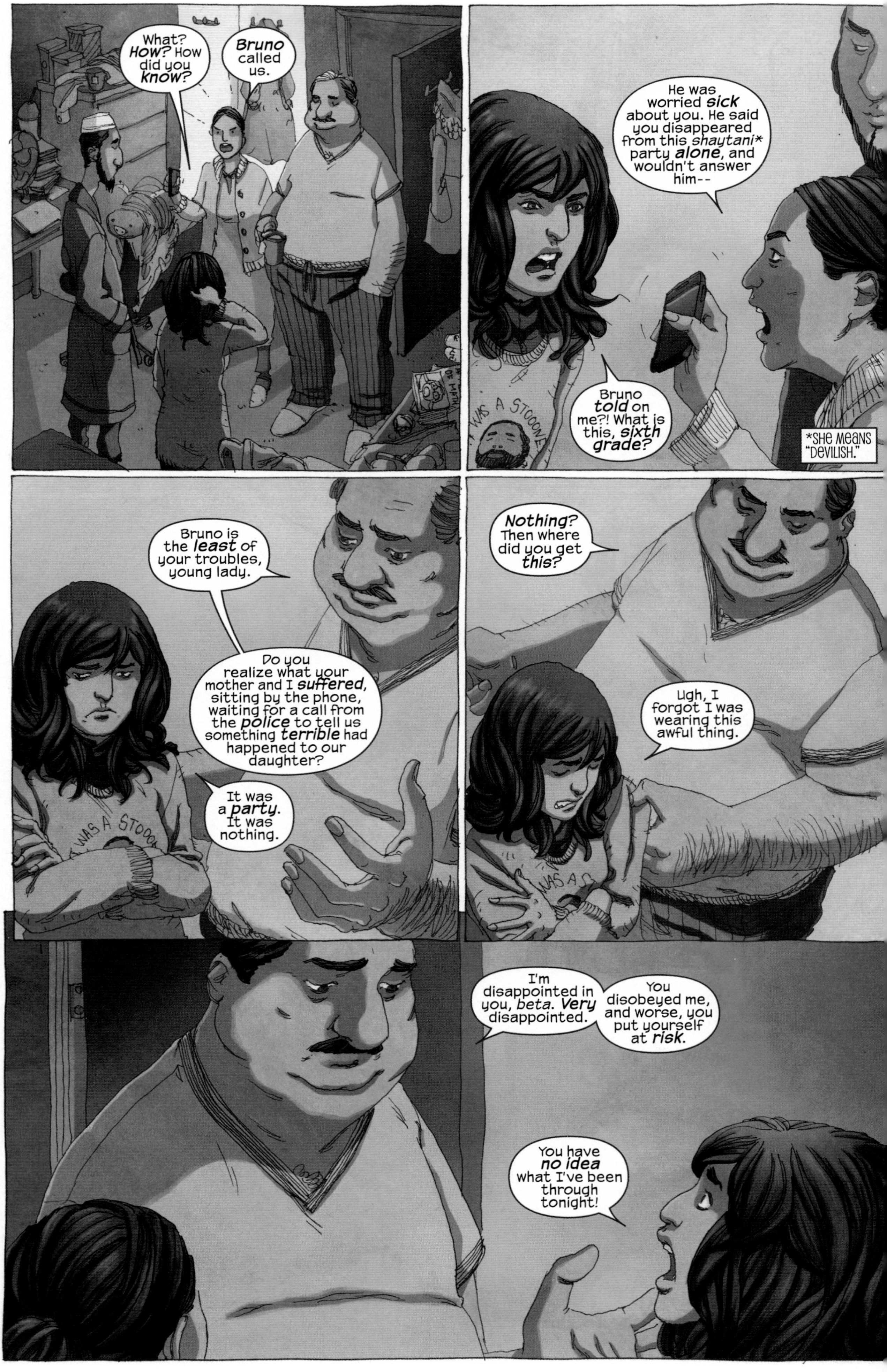
What? HOW? How did you KNOW?
Bruno called us.
He was worried sick about you. He said you disappeared from this shaytani* party alone, and wouldn't answer him--
Bruno told on me?! What is this, sixth grade?
*SHE MEANS "DEVILISH."
Bruno is the least of your troubles, young lady.
Do you realize what your mother and I suffered, sitting by the phone, waiting for a call from the police to tell us something terrible had happened to our daughter?
It was a party. It was nothing.
Nothing? Then where did you get this?
Ugh, I forgot I was wearing this awful thing.
I'm disappointed in you, beta. Very disappointed.
You disobeyed me, and worse, you put yourself at risk.
You have no idea what I've been through tonight!

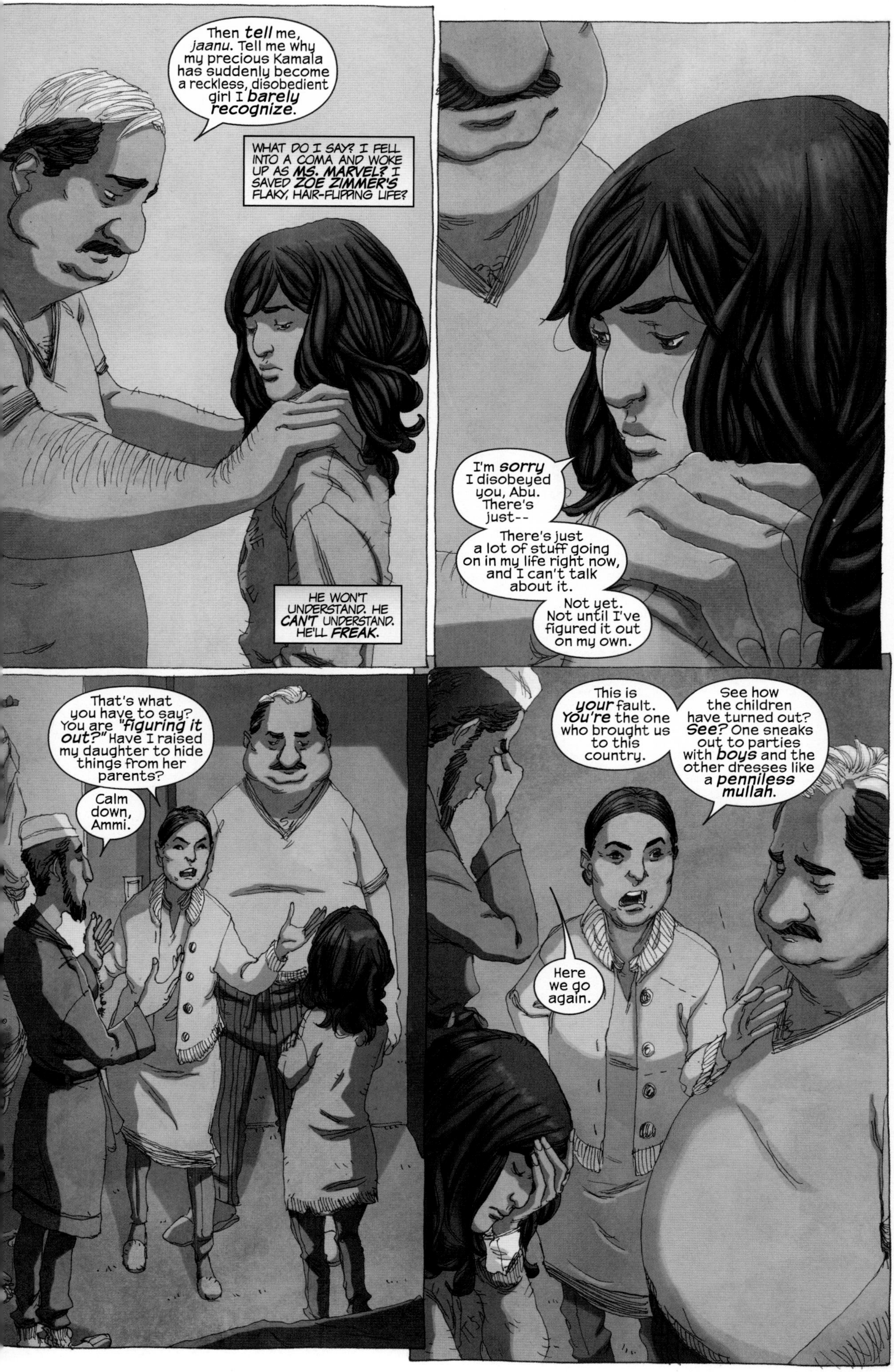
Then tell me, jaanu. Tell me why my precious Kamala has suddenly become a reckless, disobedient girl I barely recognize.
WHAT DO I SAY? I FELL INTO A COMA AND WOKE UP AS MS. MARVEL? I SAVED ZOE ZIMMER'S FLAKY, HAIR-FLIPPING LIFE?
HE WON'T UNDERSTAND. HE CAN'T UNDERSTAND. HE'LL FREAK.
I'm sorry I disobeyed you, Abu. There's just--
There's just a lot of stuff going on in my life right now, and I can't talk about it.
Not yet. Not until I've figured it out on my own.
That's what you have to say? You are "figuring it out?" Have I raised my daughter to hide things from her parents?
Calm down, Ammi.
This is your fault. You're the one who brought us to this country.
See how the children have turned out? See? One sneaks out to parties with boys and the other dresses like a penniless mullah.
Here we go again.

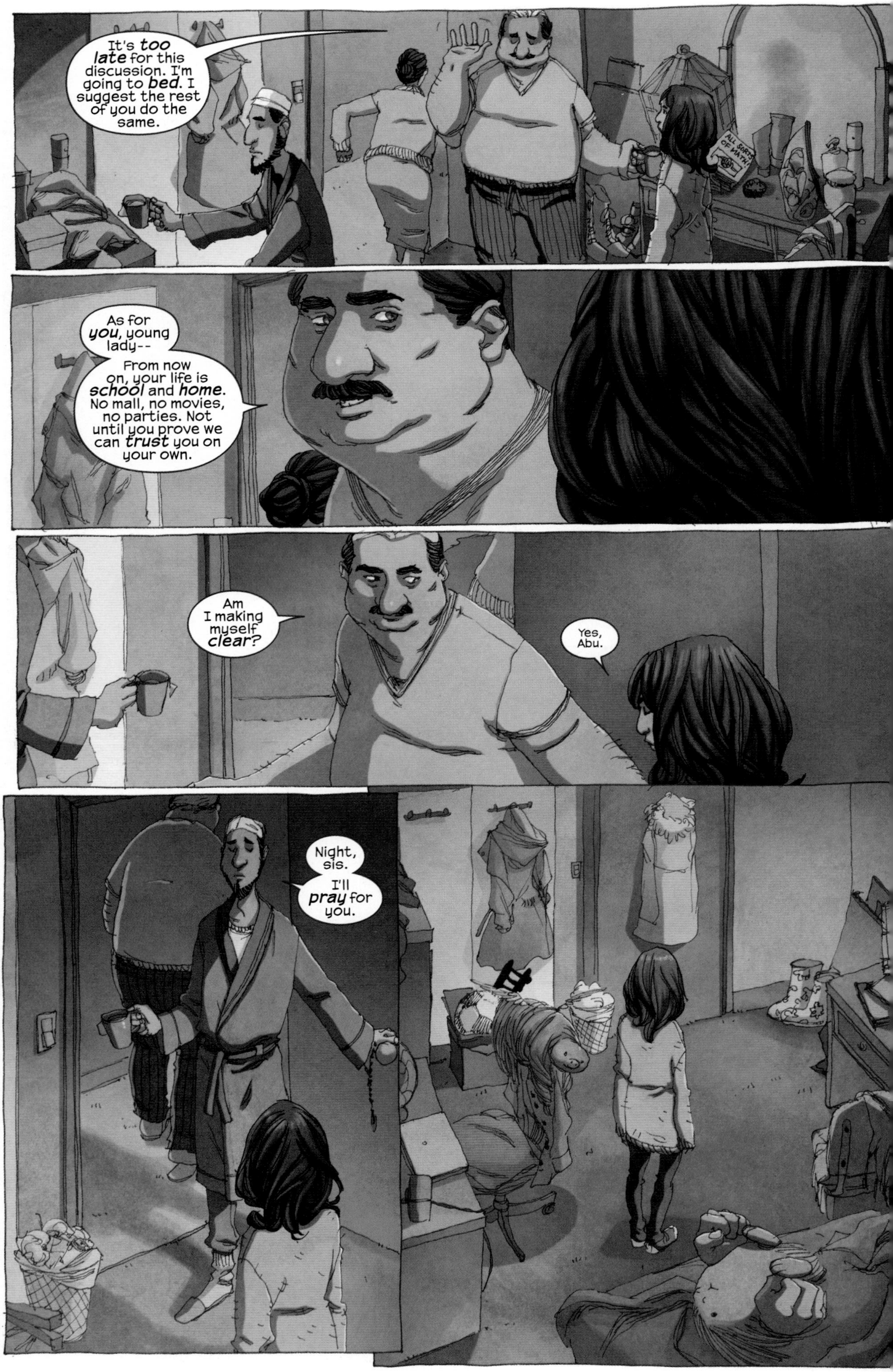

It's too late for this discussion. I'm going to bed. I suggest the rest of you do the same.
ALL SORTS OF MATH!
As for you, young lady--
From now on, your life is school and home. No mall, no movies, no parties. Not until you prove we can trust you on your own.
Am I making myself clear?
Yes, Abu.
Night, sis.
I'll pray for you.

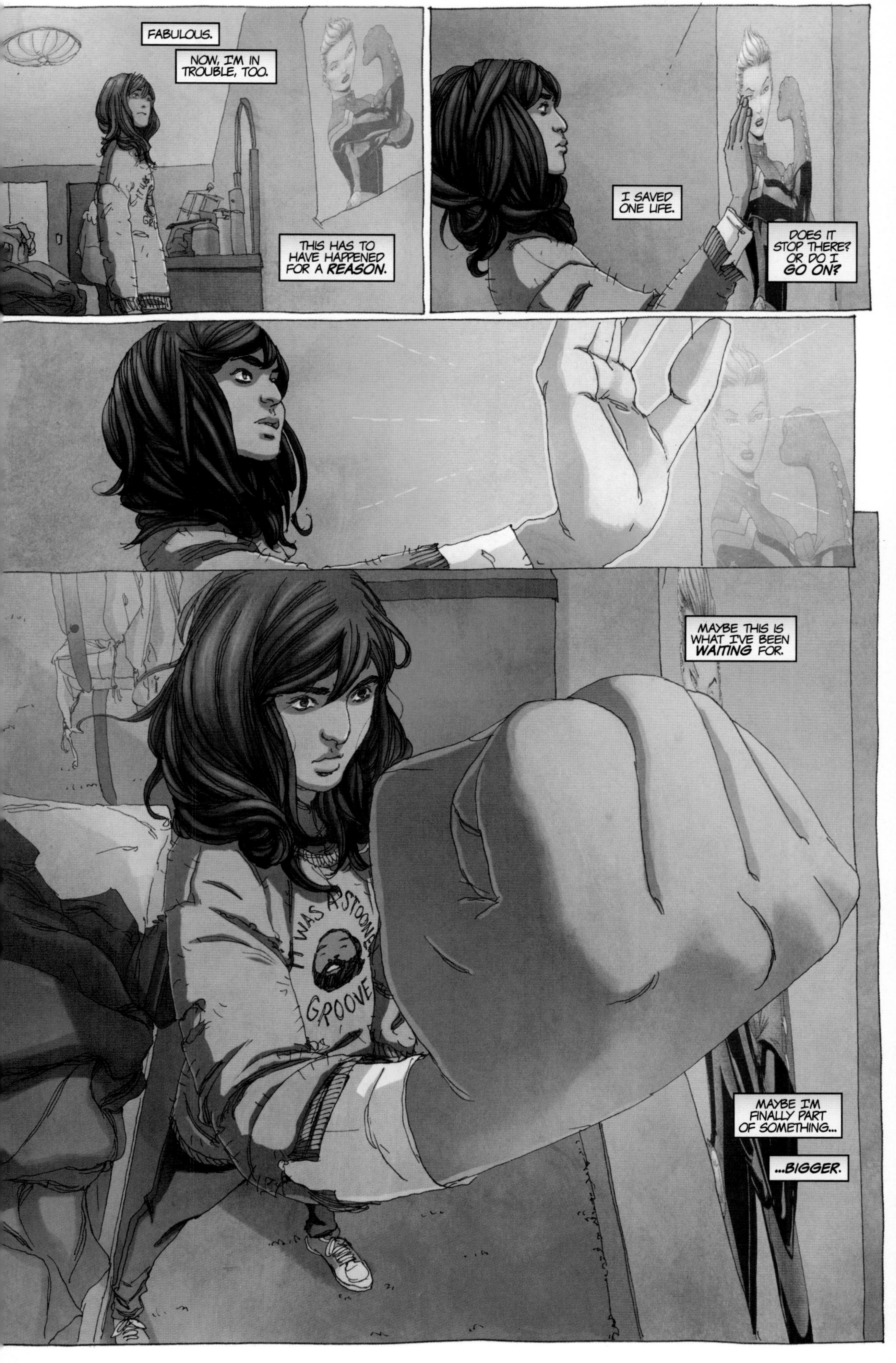
FABULOUS.
NOW, I'M IN TROUBLE, TOO.
THIS HAS TO HAVE HAPPENED FOR A **REASON**.
I SAVED ONE LIFE.
DOES IT STOP THERE? OR DO I **GO ON?**
MAYBE THIS IS WHAT I'VE BEEN **WAITING** FOR.
IT WAS A STOONER GROOVE
MAYBE I'M FINALLY PART OF SOMETHING...
...**BIGGER**.

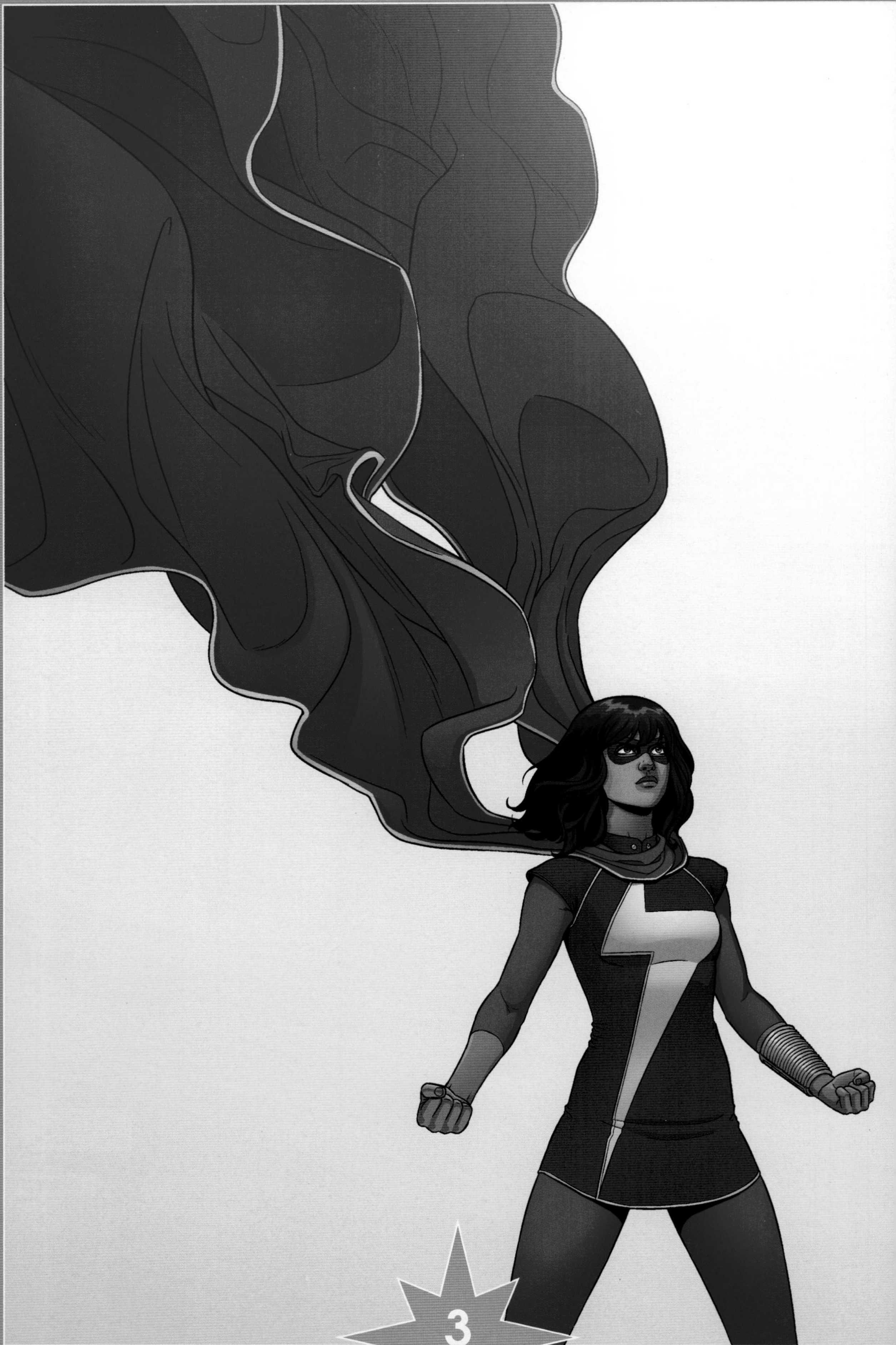
3

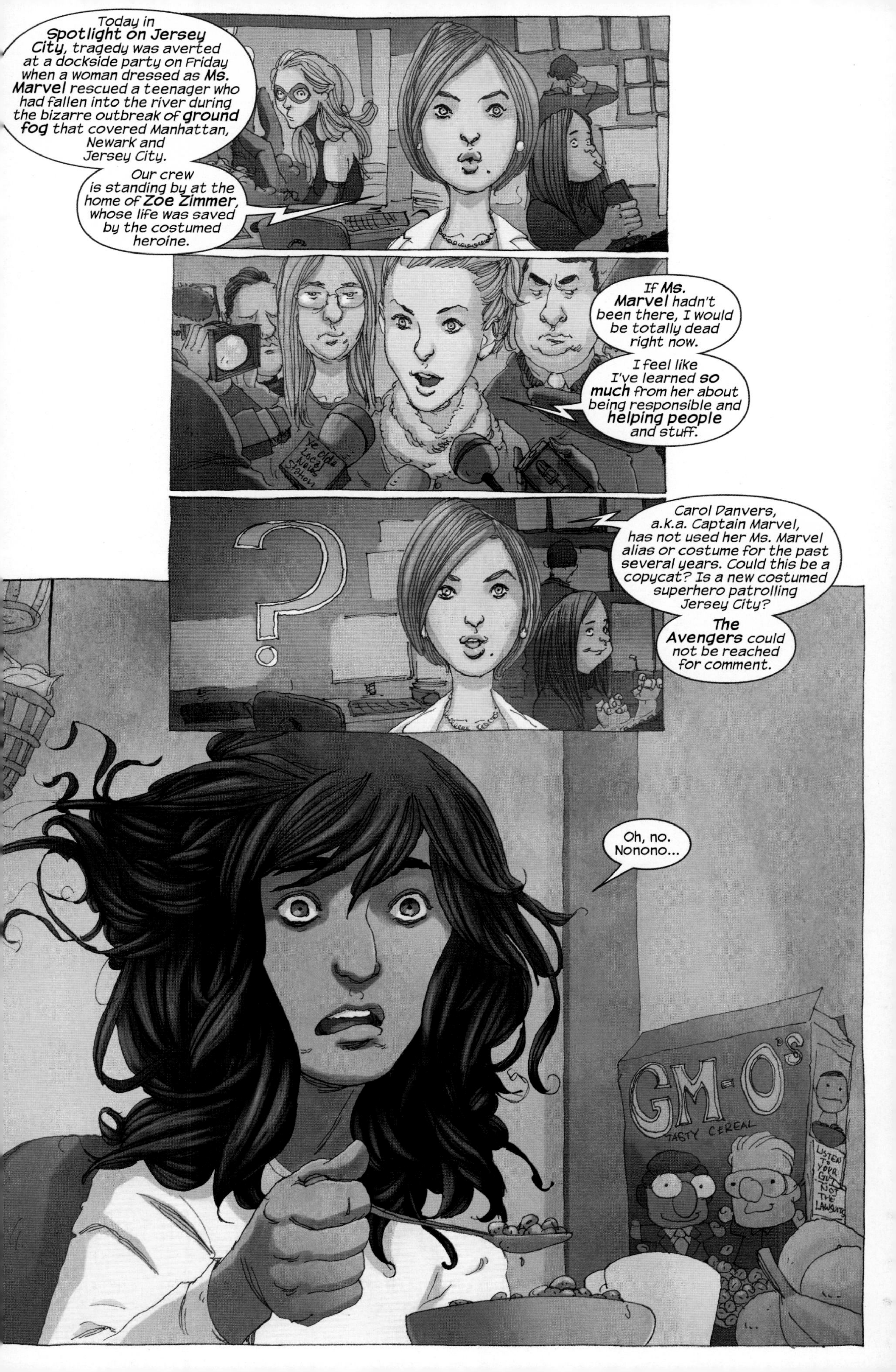

Today in **Spotlight on Jersey City**, tragedy was averted at a dockside party on Friday when a woman dressed as **Ms. Marvel** rescued a teenager who had fallen into the river during the bizarre outbreak of **ground fog** that covered Manhattan, Newark and Jersey City.
Our crew is standing by at the home of **Zoe Zimmer**, whose life was saved by the costumed heroine.
If **Ms. Marvel** hadn't been there, I would be totally dead right now.
I feel like I've learned **so much** from her about being responsible and **helping people** and stuff.
Ye Olde Local News Station
Carol Danvers, a.k.a. Captain Marvel, has not used her Ms. Marvel alias or costume for the past several years. Could this be a copycat? Is a new costumed superhero patrolling Jersey City?
The Avengers could not be reached for comment.
Oh, no. Nonono...
GM-O's
TASTY CEREAL
LISTEN TO YOUR GUT NOT THE LAWSUITS

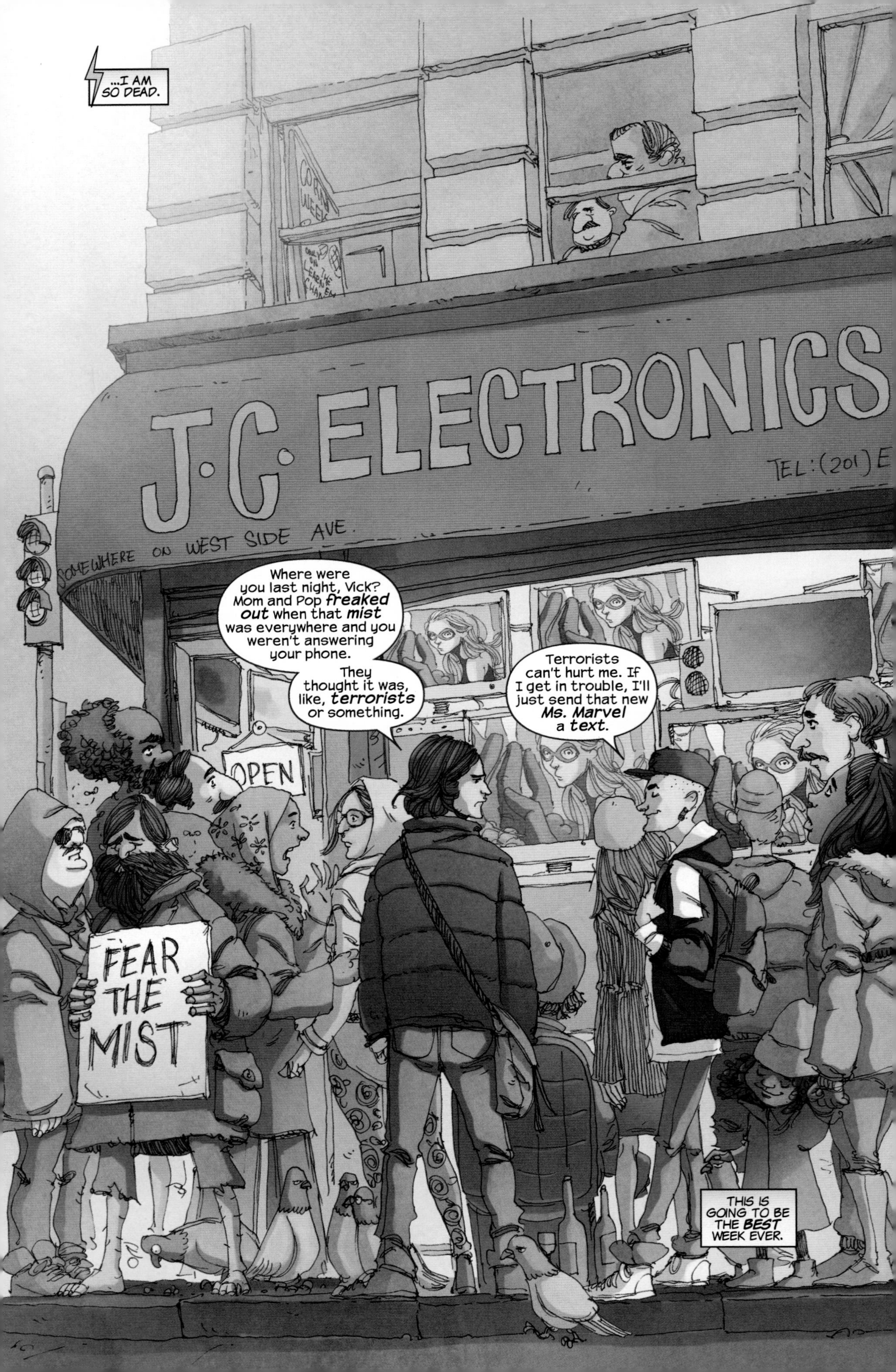
...I AM SO DEAD.
J·C· ELECTRONICS
TEL:(201)E
SOMEWHERE ON WEST SIDE AVE.
Where were you last night, Vick? Mom and Pop freaked out when that mist was everywhere and you weren't answering your phone.
They thought it was, like, terrorists or something.
Terrorists can't hurt me. If I get in trouble, I'll just send that new Ms. Marvel a text.
OPEN
FEAR THE MIST
THIS IS GOING TO BE THE BEST WEEK EVER.

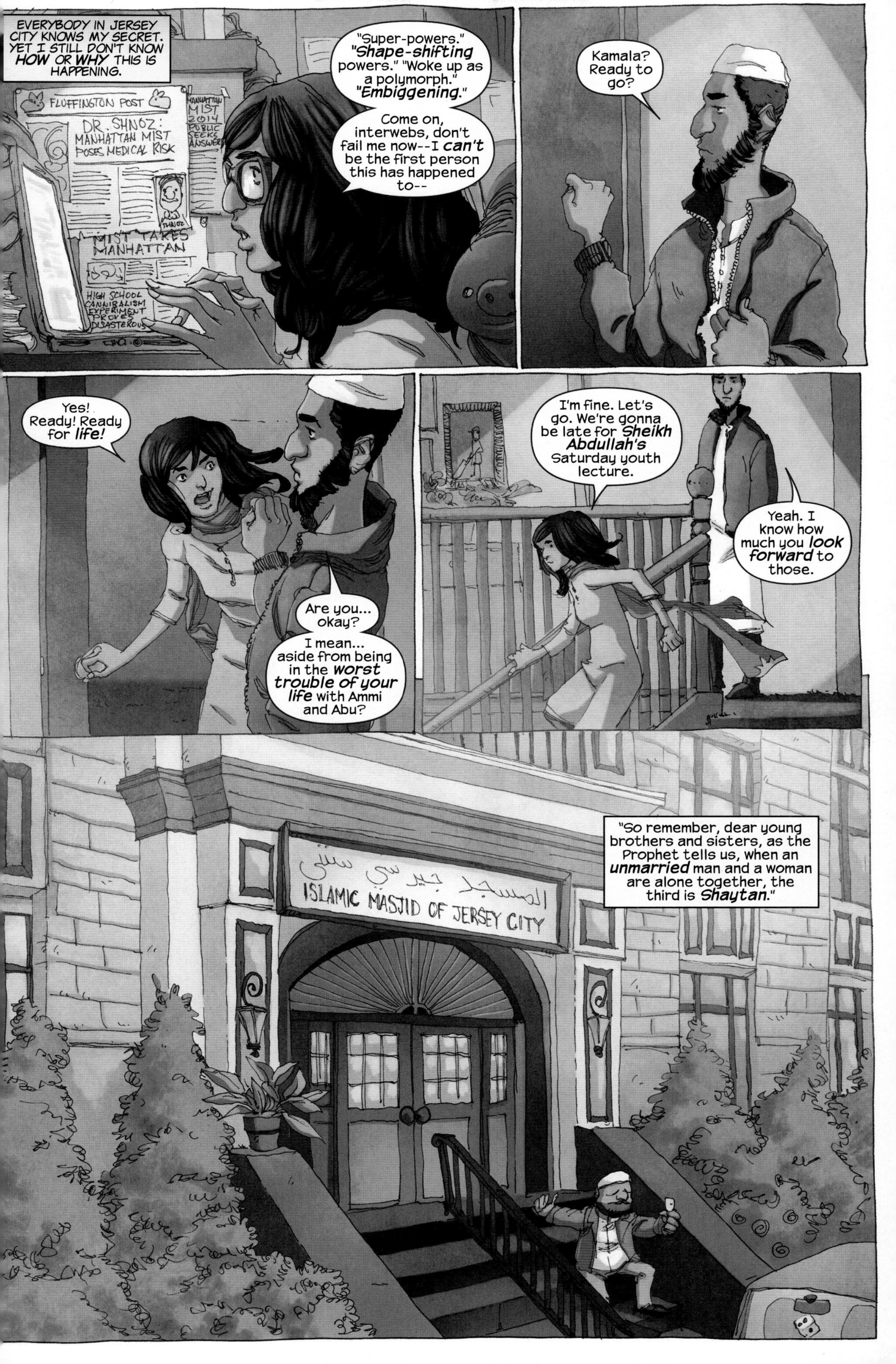

EVERYBODY IN JERSEY CITY KNOWS MY SECRET. YET I STILL DON'T KNOW **HOW** OR **WHY** THIS IS HAPPENING.
FLUFFINGTON POST
DR. SHNOZ: MANHATTAN MIST POSES MEDICAL RISK
MANHATTAN MIST 2014 PUBLIC SEEKS ANSWERS
MIST TAKES MANHATTAN
HIGH SCHOOL CANNIBALISM EXPERIMENT PROVES DISASTEROUS
"Super-powers." "***Shape-shifting*** powers." "Woke up as a polymorph." "***Embiggening***."
Come on, interwebs, don't fail me now--I ***can't*** be the first person this has happened to--
Kamala? Ready to go?
Yes! Ready! Ready for ***life!***
Are you... okay? I mean... aside from being in the ***worst trouble of your life*** with Ammi and Abu?
I'm fine. Let's go. We're gonna be late for ***Sheikh Abdullah's*** Saturday youth lecture.
Yeah. I know how much you ***look forward*** to those.
ISLAMIC MASJID OF JERSEY CITY
"So remember, dear young brothers and sisters, as the Prophet tells us, when an ***unmarried*** man and a woman are alone together, the third is ***Shaytan***."

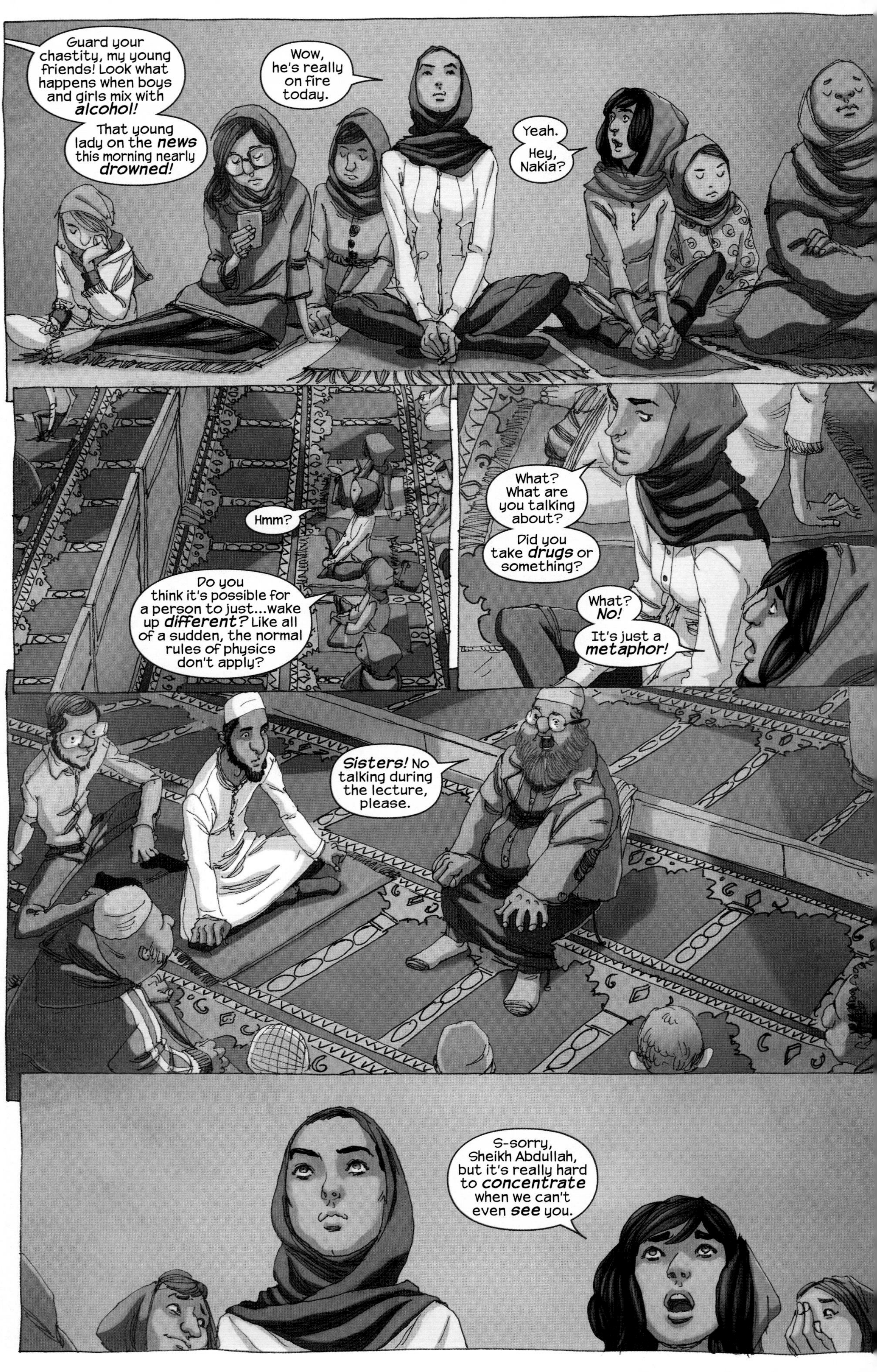
Guard your chastity, my young friends! Look what happens when boys and girls mix with alcohol!
That young lady on the news this morning nearly drowned!
Wow, he's really on fire today.
Yeah.
Hey, Nakia?
Hmm?
Do you think it's possible for a person to just...wake up different? Like all of a sudden, the normal rules of physics don't apply?
What? What are you talking about?
Did you take drugs or something?
What? No!
It's just a metaphor!
Sisters! No talking during the lecture, please.
S-sorry, Sheikh Abdullah, but it's really hard to concentrate when we can't even see you.

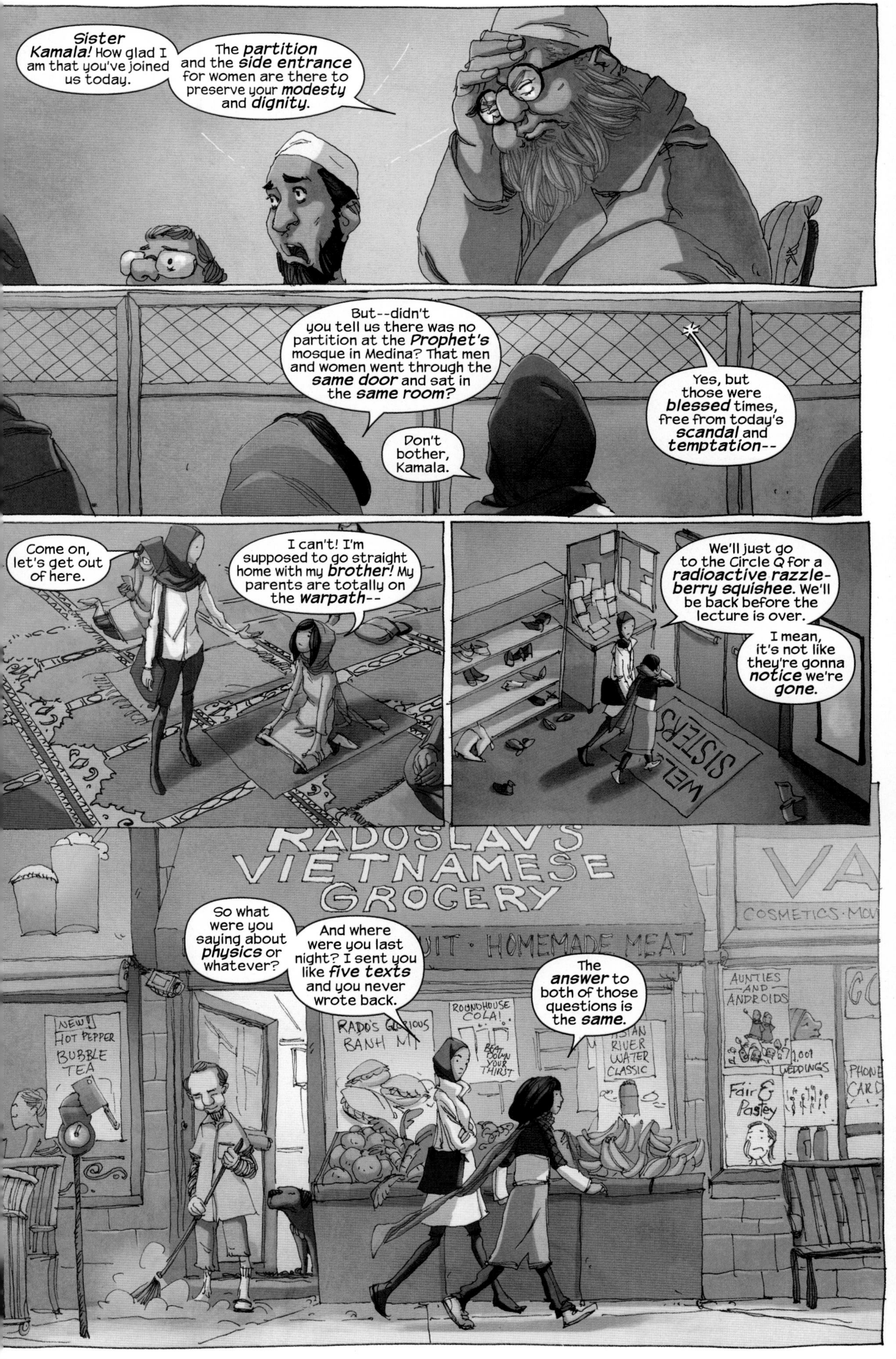

Sister Kamala! How glad I am that you've joined us today.
The partition and the side entrance for women are there to preserve your modesty and dignity.
But--didn't you tell us there was no partition at the Prophet's mosque in Medina? That men and women went through the same door and sat in the same room?
Yes, but those were blessed times, free from today's scandal and temptation--
Don't bother, Kamala.
Come on, let's get out of here.
I can't! I'm supposed to go straight home with my brother! My parents are totally on the warpath--
We'll just go to the Circle Q for a radioactive razzle-berry squishee. We'll be back before the lecture is over.
I mean, it's not like they're gonna notice we're gone.
SISTERS
RADOSLAV'S VIETNAMESE GROCERY
HOMEMADE MEAT
COSMETICS
NEW! HOT PEPPER BUBBLE TEA
RADO'S GLORIOUS BANH MI
ROUNDHOUSE COLA!
BEAT DOWN YOUR THIRST
ASIAN RIVER WATER CLASSIC
AUNTIES AND ANDROIDS
1,001 WEDDINGS
Fair & Pastey
So what were you saying about physics or whatever?
And where were you last night? I sent you like five texts and you never wrote back.
The answer to both of those questions is the same.

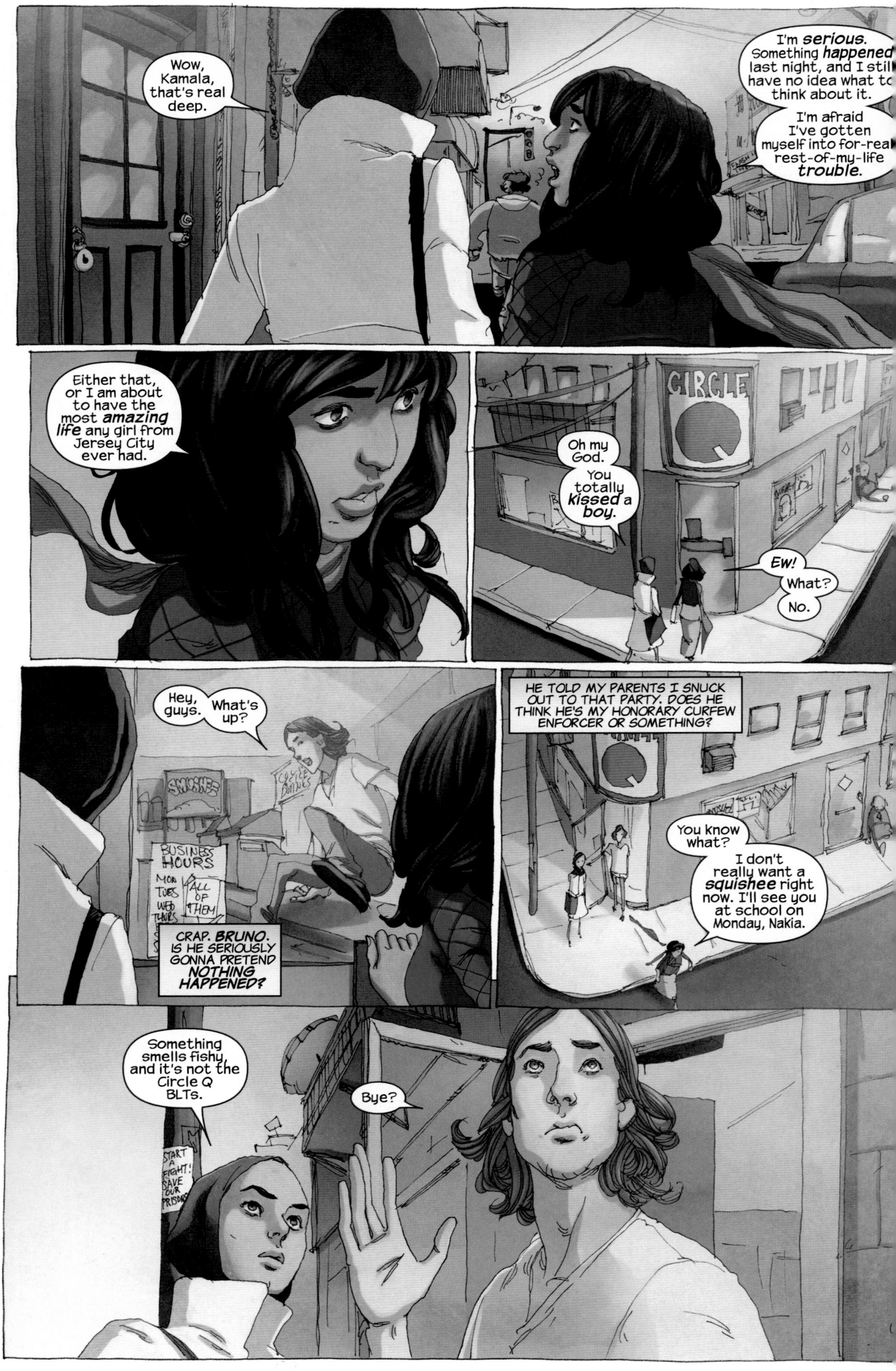

Wow, Kamala, that's real deep.
I'm serious. Something happened last night, and I still have no idea what to think about it.
I'm afraid I've gotten myself into for-real rest-of-my-life trouble.
Either that, or I am about to have the most amazing life any girl from Jersey City ever had.
CIRCLE
Oh my God.
You totally kissed a boy.
Ew!
What?
No.
Hey, guys.
What's up?
BUSINESS HOURS
CRAP. BRUNO. IS HE SERIOUSLY GONNA PRETEND NOTHING HAPPENED?
HE TOLD MY PARENTS I SNUCK OUT TO THAT PARTY. DOES HE THINK HE'S MY HONORARY CURFEW ENFORCER OR SOMETHING?
You know what?
I don't really want a squishee right now. I'll see you at school on Monday, Nakia.
Something smells fishy, and it's not the Circle Q BLTs.
Bye?

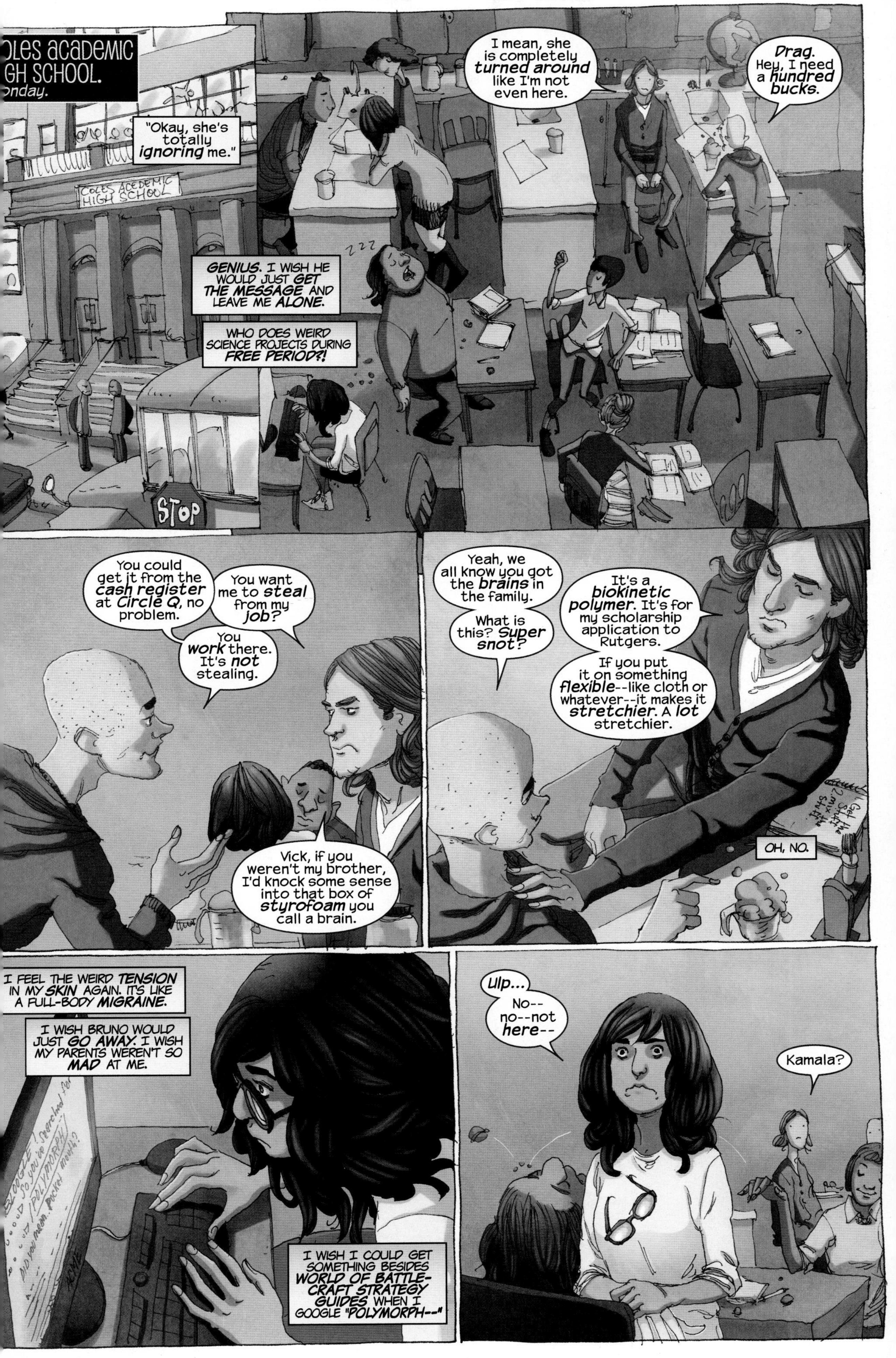
oles academic
gh SCHOOL.
onday.
COLES ACADEMIC HIGH SCHOOL
"Okay, she's totally ignoring me."
I mean, she is completely turned around like I'm not even here.
Drag. Hey, I need a hundred bucks.
GENIUS. I WISH HE WOULD JUST GET THE MESSAGE AND LEAVE ME ALONE.
WHO DOES WEIRD SCIENCE PROJECTS DURING FREE PERIOD?!
ZZZ
STOP
You could get it from the cash register at Circle Q, no problem.
You want me to steal from my job?
You work there. It's not stealing.
Vick, if you weren't my brother, I'd knock some sense into that box of styrofoam you call a brain.
Yeah, we all know you got the brains in the family.
What is this? Super snot?
It's a biokinetic polymer. It's for my scholarship application to Rutgers.
If you put it on something flexible--like cloth or whatever--it makes it stretchier. A lot stretchier.
OH, NO.
I FEEL THE WEIRD TENSION IN MY SKIN AGAIN. IT'S LIKE A FULL-BODY MIGRAINE.
I WISH BRUNO WOULD JUST GO AWAY. I WISH MY PARENTS WEREN'T SO MAD AT ME.
I WISH I COULD GET SOMETHING BESIDES WORLD OF BATTLE-CRAFT STRATEGY GUIDES WHEN I GOOGLE "POLYMORPH--"
Ulp...
No--no--not here--
Kamala?

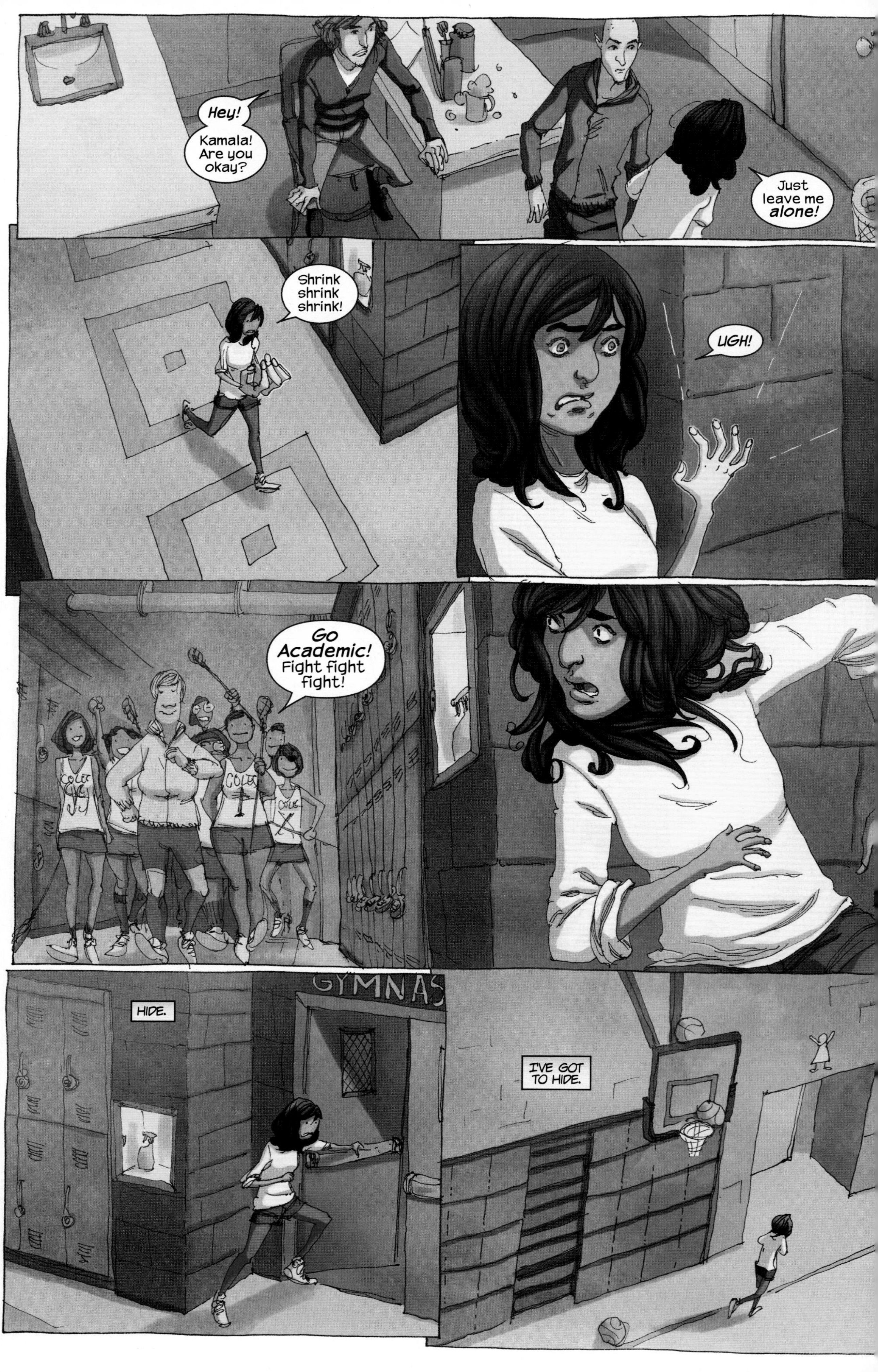
Hey!
Kamala! Are you okay?
Just leave me alone!
Shrink shrink shrink!
UGH!
Go Academic! Fight fight fight!
GYMNAS
HIDE.
I'VE GOT TO HIDE.

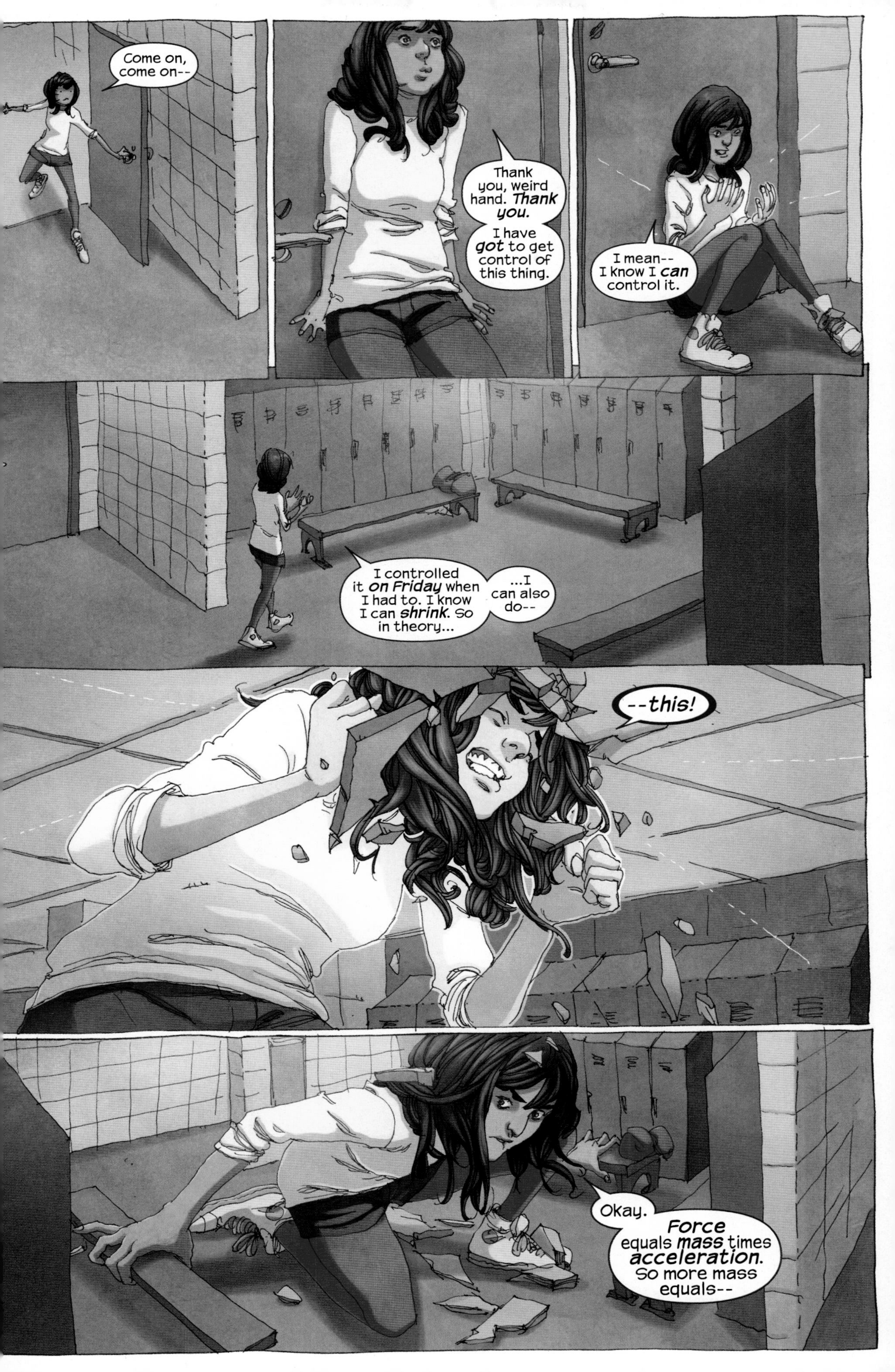
Come on, come on--
Thank you, weird hand. Thank you.
I have got to get control of this thing.
I mean-- I know I can control it.
I controlled it on Friday when I had to. I know I can shrink. So in theory...
...I can also do--
--this!
Okay.
Force equals mass times acceleration. So more mass equals--

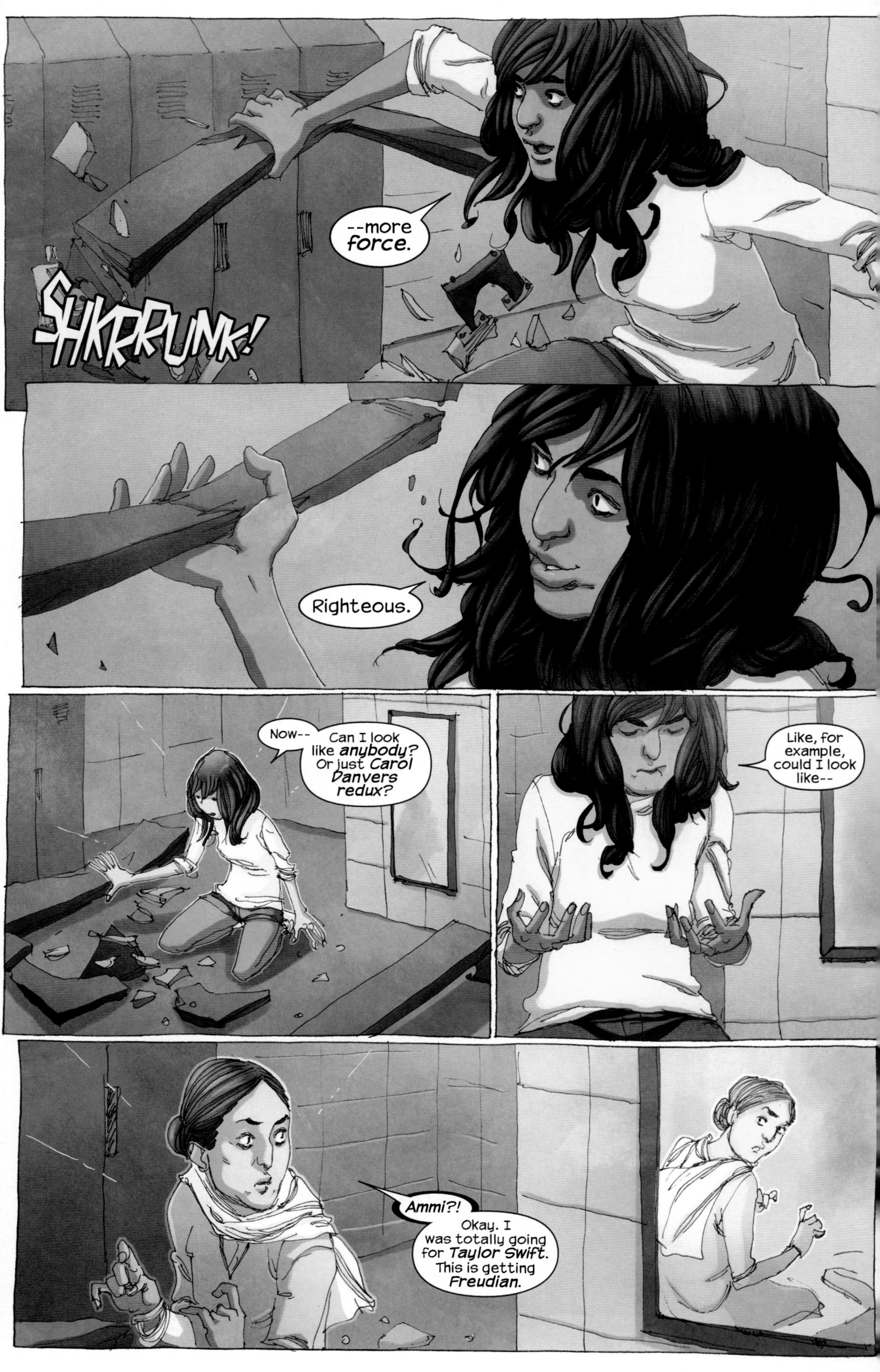
--more force.
SHKRRUNK!
Righteous.
Now--
Can I look like anybody? Or just Carol Danvers redux?
Like, for example, could I look like--
Ammi?!
Okay. I was totally going for Taylor Swift. This is getting Freudian.

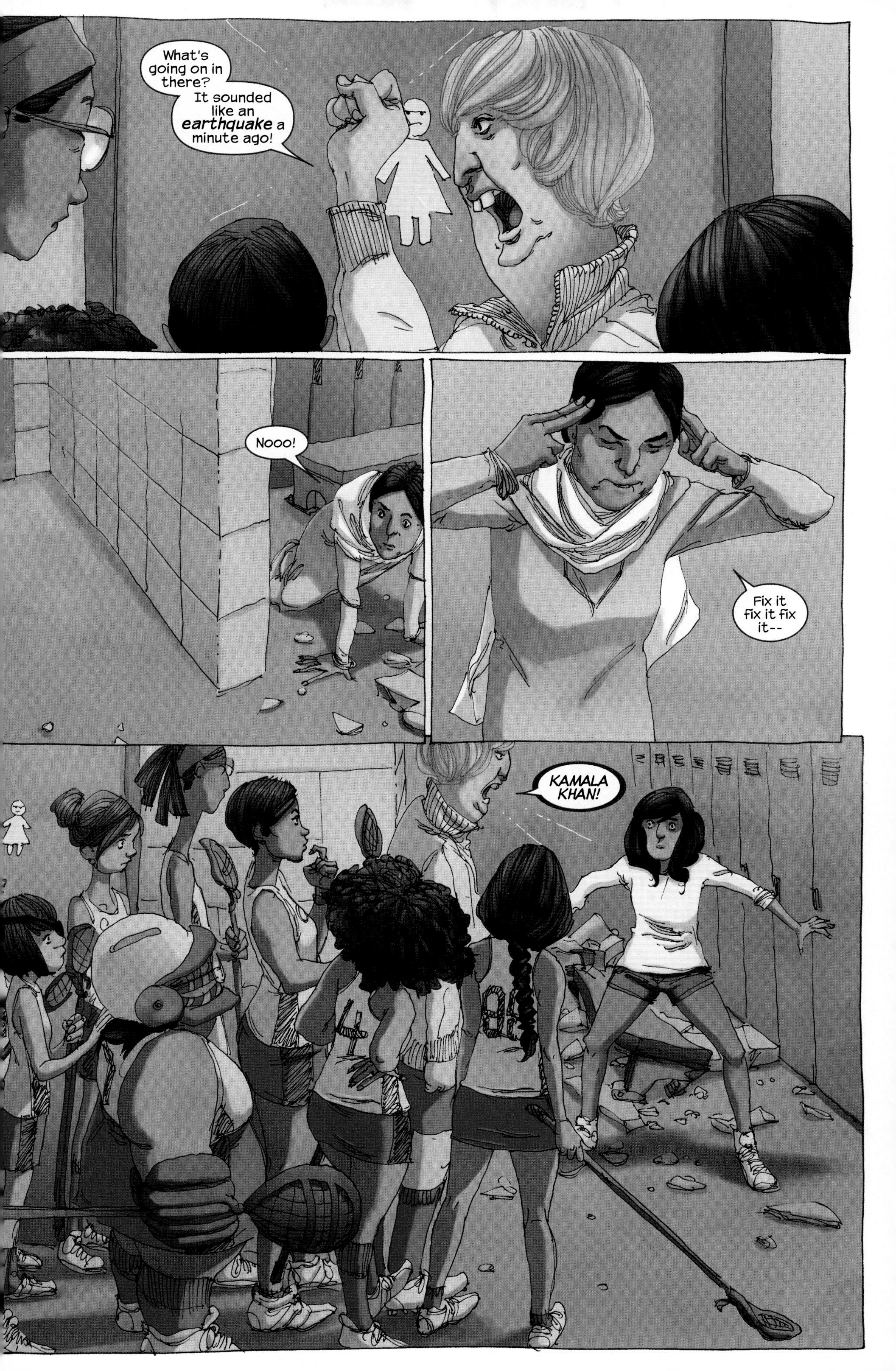
What's going on in there? It sounded like an *earthquake* a minute ago!
Nooo!
Fix it fix it fix it--
KAMALA KHAN!

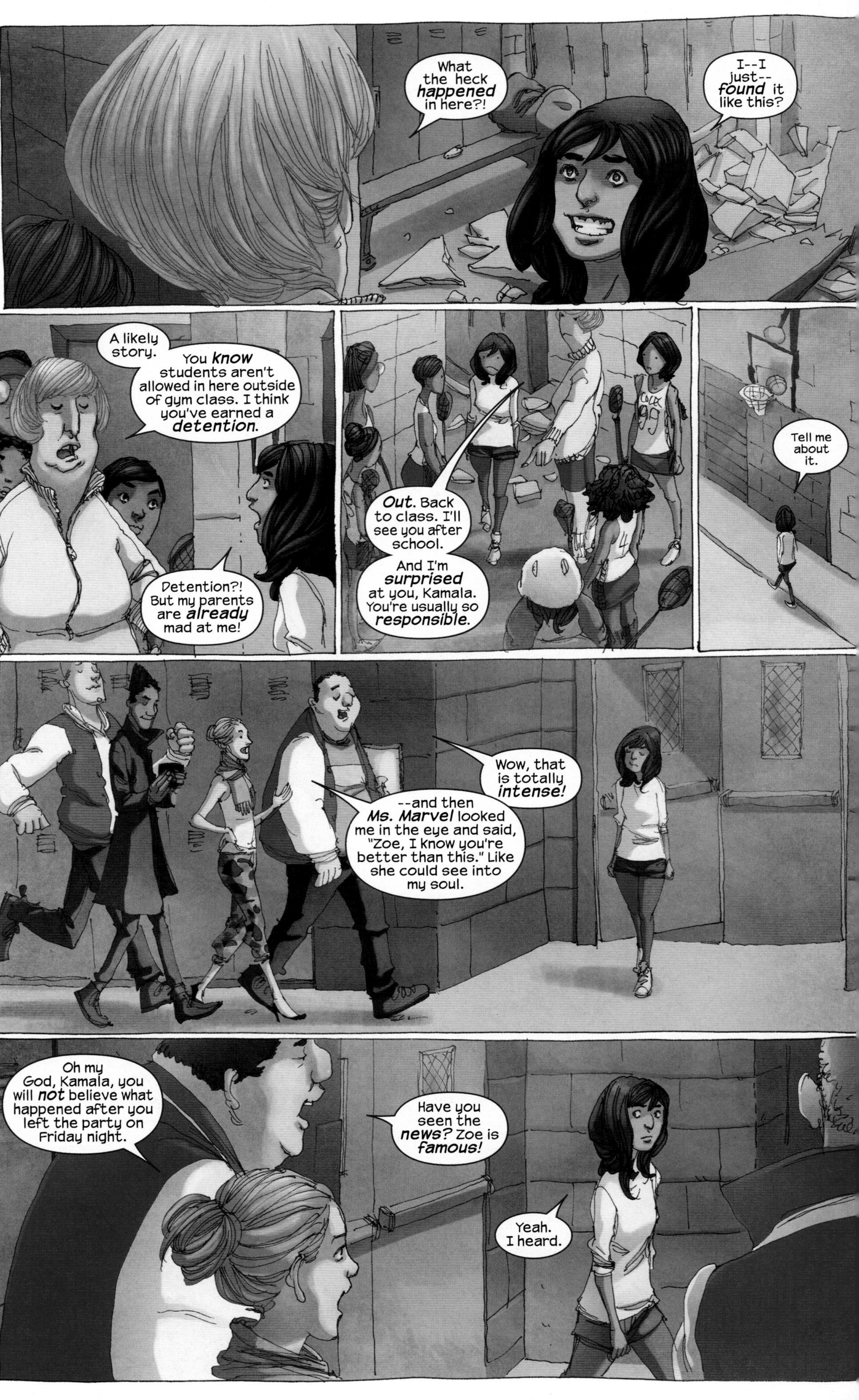
What the heck happened in here?!
I--I just--found it like this?
A likely story.
You know students aren't allowed in here outside of gym class. I think you've earned a detention.
Detention?! But my parents are already mad at me!
Out. Back to class. I'll see you after school.
And I'm surprised at you, Kamala. You're usually so responsible.
Tell me about it.
--and then Ms. Marvel looked me in the eye and said, "Zoe, I know you're better than this." Like she could see into my soul.
Wow, that is totally intense!
Oh my God, Kamala, you will not believe what happened after you left the party on Friday night.
Have you seen the news? Zoe is famous!
Yeah. I heard.

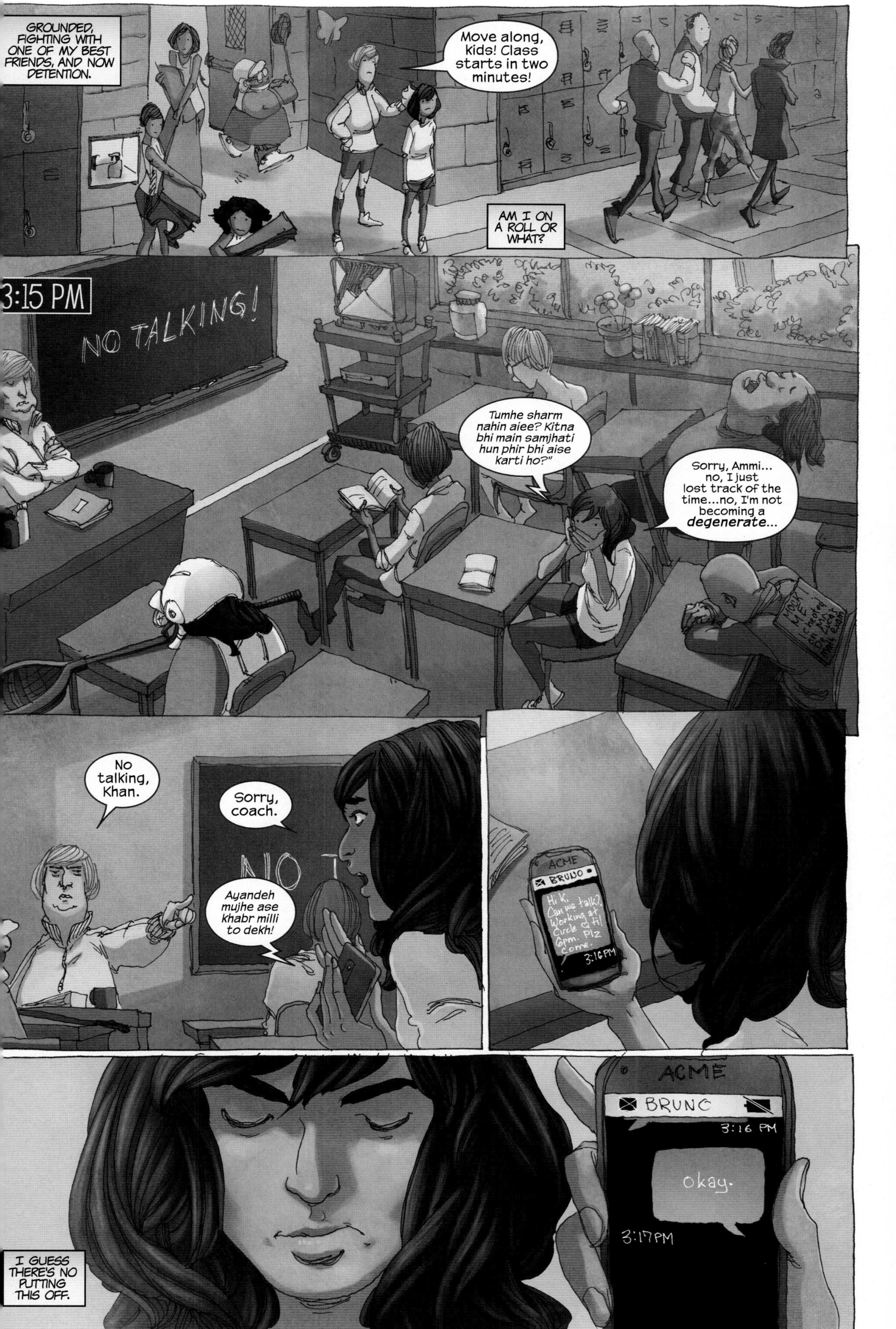

GROUNDED, FIGHTING WITH ONE OF MY BEST FRIENDS, AND NOW DETENTION.
Move along, kids! Class starts in two minutes!
AM I ON A ROLL OR WHAT?
3:15 PM
NO TALKING!
Tumhe sharm nahin aiee? Kitna bhi main samjhati hun phir bhi aise karti ho?"
Sorry, Ammi... no, I just lost track of the time...no, I'm not becoming a *degenerate*...
No talking, Khan.
Sorry, coach.
Ayandeh mujhe ase khabr milli to dekh!
ACME
BRUNO
Hi K. Can we talk? Working at Circle Q til 6pm. Plz come.
3:16PM
ACME
BRUNO
3:16 PM
okay.
3:17PM
I GUESS THERE'S NO PUTTING THIS OFF.

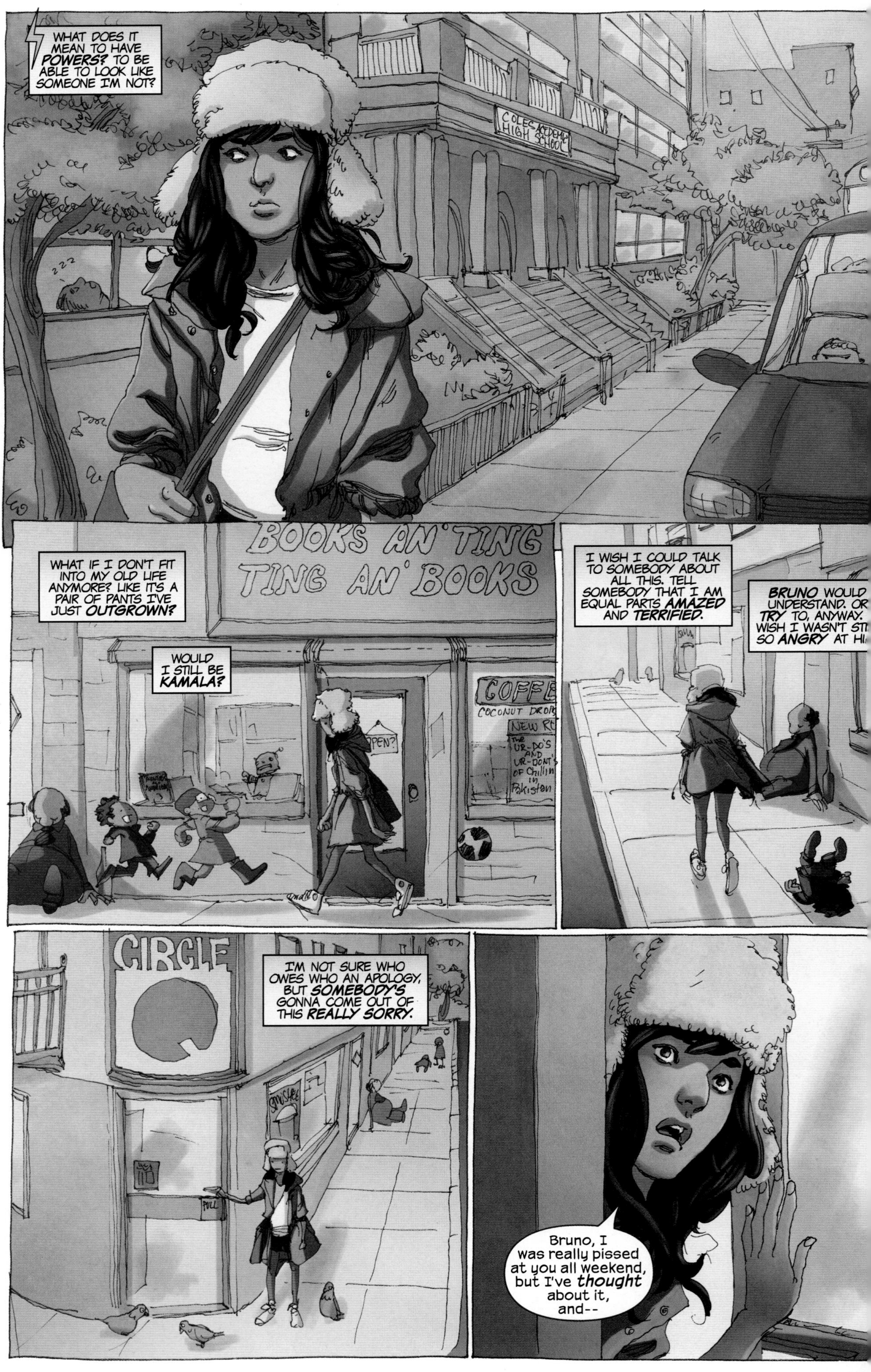
WHAT DOES IT MEAN TO HAVE POWERS? TO BE ABLE TO LOOK LIKE SOMEONE I'M NOT?
COLES ACADEMIC HIGH SCHOOL
BOOKS AN' TING
TING AN' BOOKS
WHAT IF I DON'T FIT INTO MY OLD LIFE ANYMORE? LIKE IT'S A PAIR OF PANTS I'VE JUST OUTGROWN?
WOULD I STILL BE KAMALA?
OPEN?
COFFE
COCONUT DROP
I WISH I COULD TALK TO SOMEBODY ABOUT ALL THIS. TELL SOMEBODY THAT I AM EQUAL PARTS AMAZED AND TERRIFIED.
BRUNO WOULD UNDERSTAND. OR TRY TO, ANYWAY. WISH I WASN'T STI SO ANGRY AT HI
CIRCLE
I'M NOT SURE WHO OWES WHO AN APOLOGY, BUT SOMEBODY'S GONNA COME OUT OF THIS REALLY SORRY.
PULL
Bruno, I was really pissed at you all weekend, but I've thought about it, and--

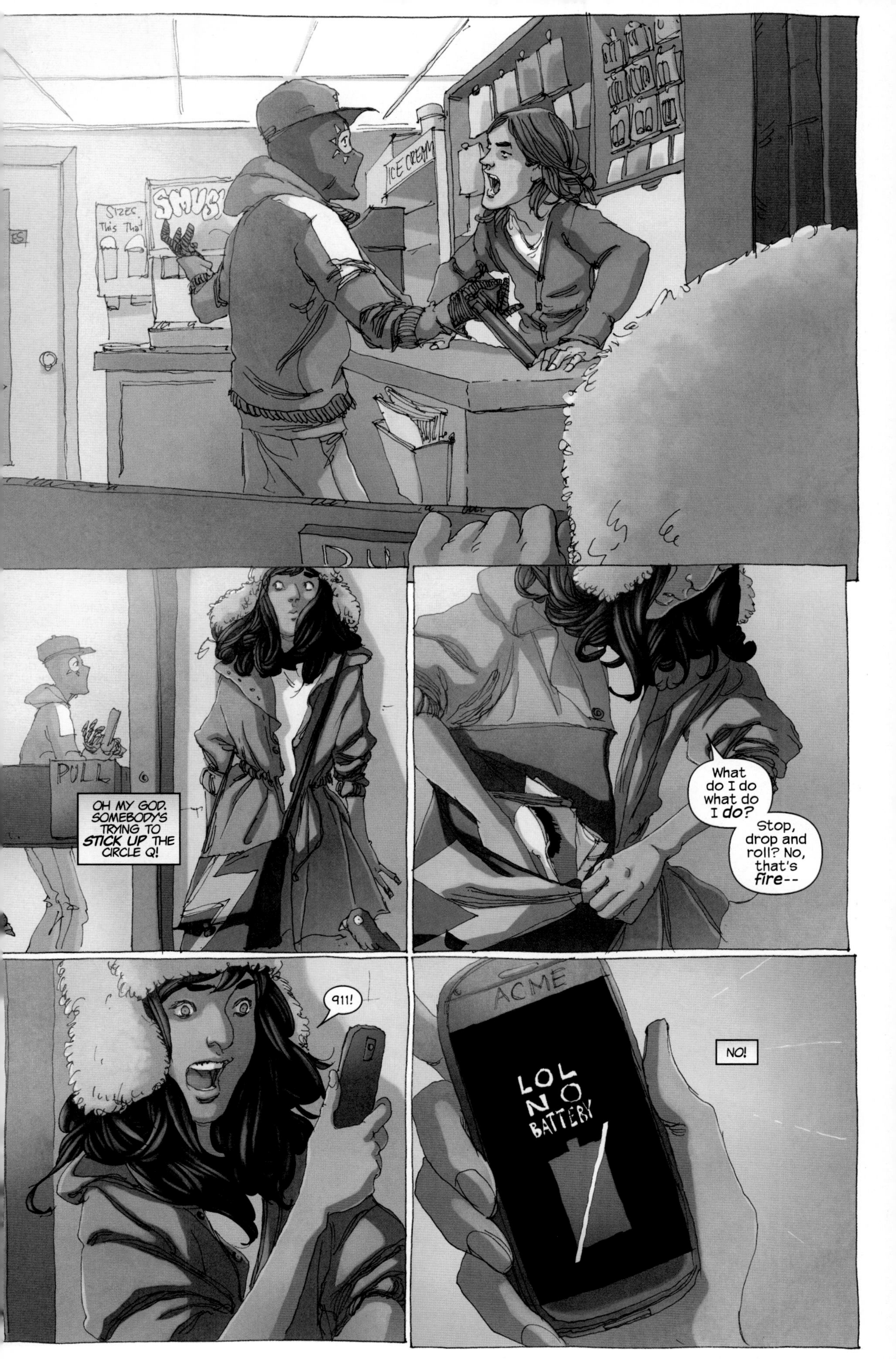
SIZES
This That
SMUS
ICE CREAM
PULL
OH MY GOD. SOMEBODY'S TRYING TO STICK UP THE CIRCLE Q!
What do I do what do I do?
Stop, drop and roll? No, that's fire--
911!
ACME
LOL NO BATTERY
NO!

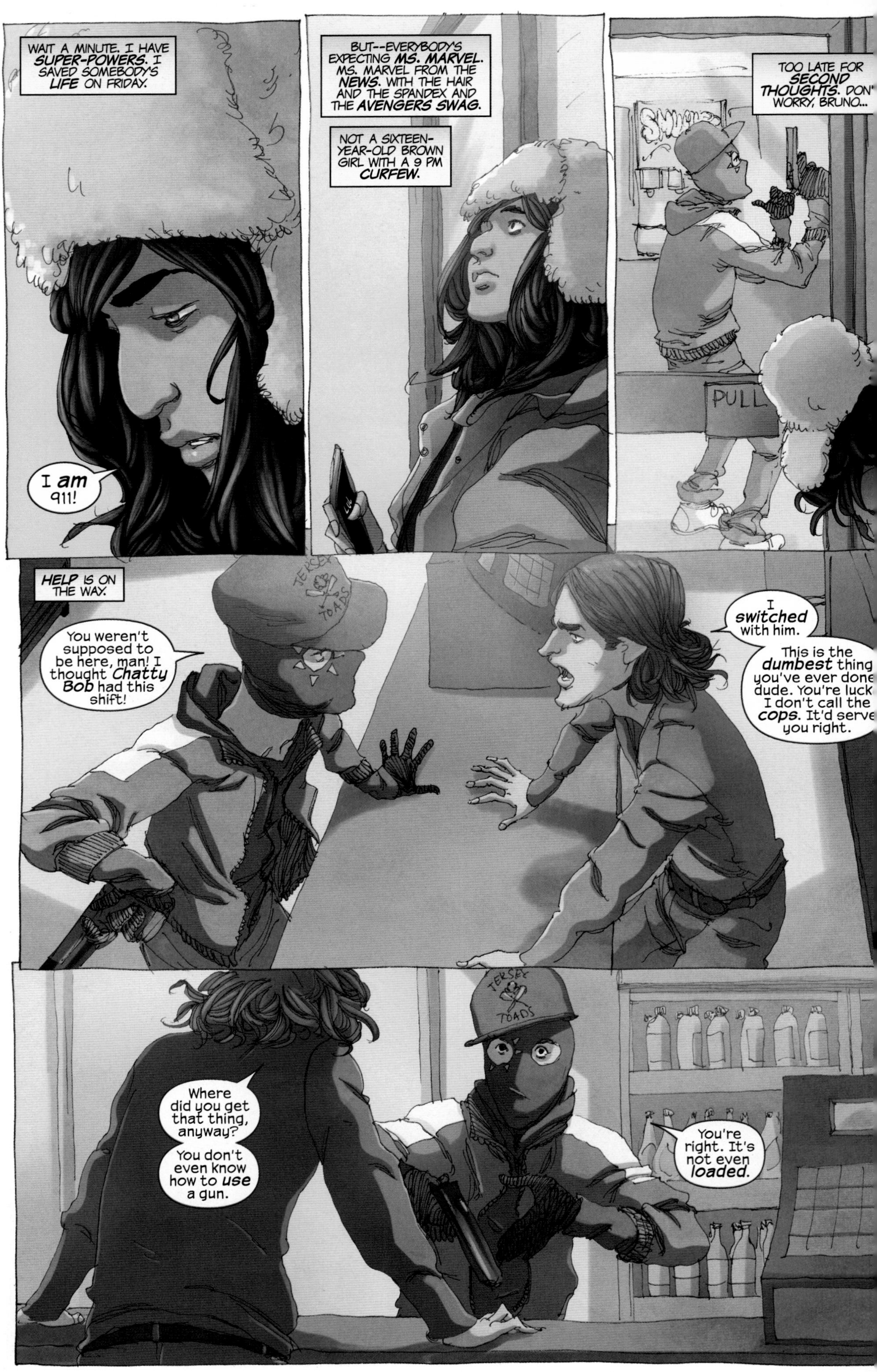
WAIT A MINUTE. I HAVE SUPER-POWERS. I SAVED SOMEBODY'S LIFE ON FRIDAY.
I am 911!
BUT--EVERYBODY'S EXPECTING MS. MARVEL. MS. MARVEL FROM THE NEWS. WITH THE HAIR AND THE SPANDEX AND THE AVENGERS SWAG.
NOT A SIXTEEN-YEAR-OLD BROWN GIRL WITH A 9 PM CURFEW.
TOO LATE FOR SECOND THOUGHTS. DON' WORRY, BRUNO...
PULL
HELP IS ON THE WAY.
JERSEY TOADS
You weren't supposed to be here, man! I thought Chatty Bob had this shift!
I switched with him.
This is the dumbest thing you've ever done dude. You're luck I don't call the cops. It'd serve you right.
JERSEY TOADS
Where did you get that thing, anyway?
You don't even know how to use a gun.
You're right. It's not even loaded.

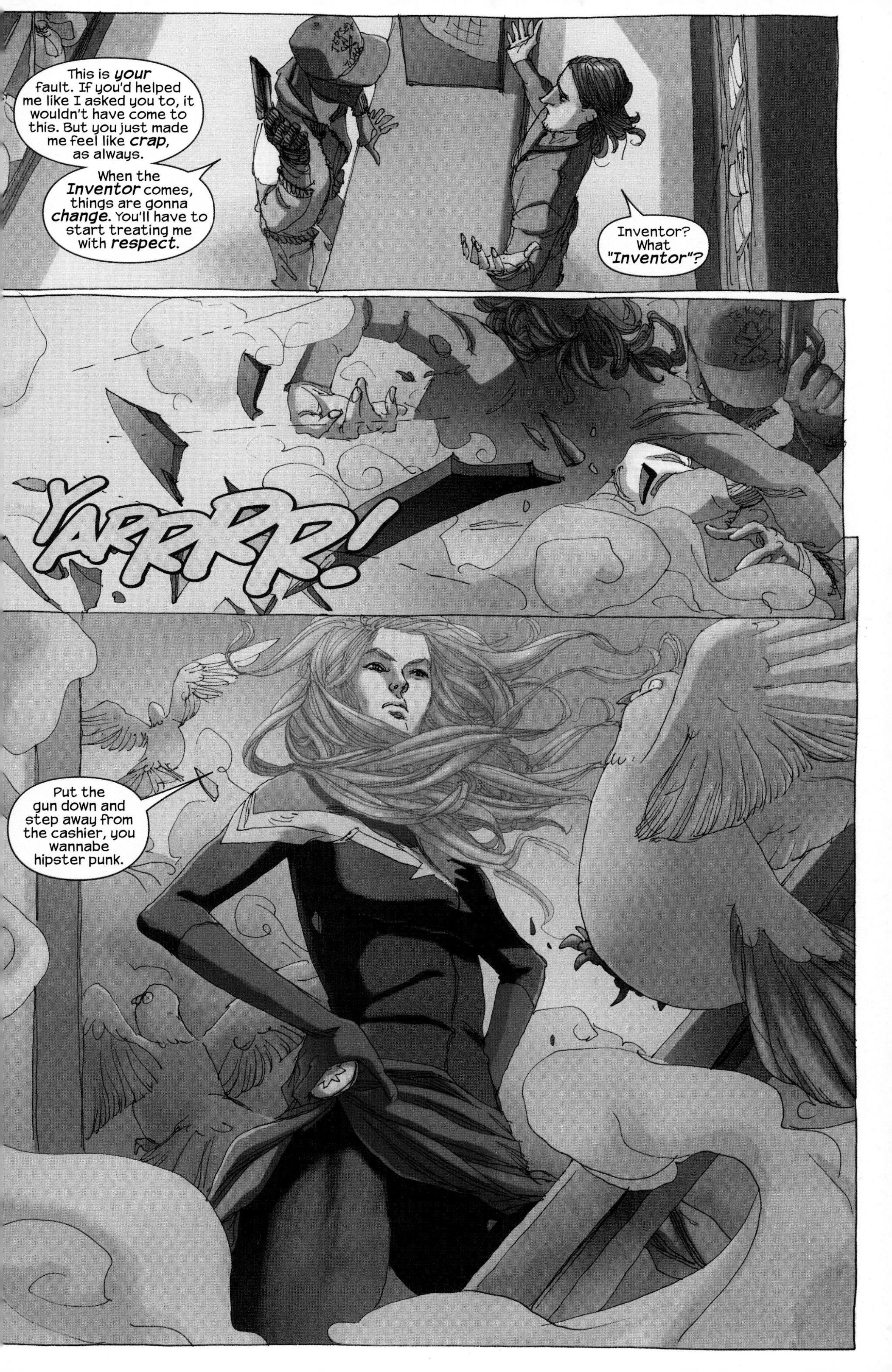
This is *your* fault. If you'd helped me like I asked you to, it wouldn't have come to this. But you just made me feel like *crap*, as always.
When the *Inventor* comes, things are gonna *change*. You'll have to start treating me with *respect*.
Inventor? What "*Inventor*"?
YARRRR!
Put the gun down and step away from the cashier, you wannabe hipster punk.

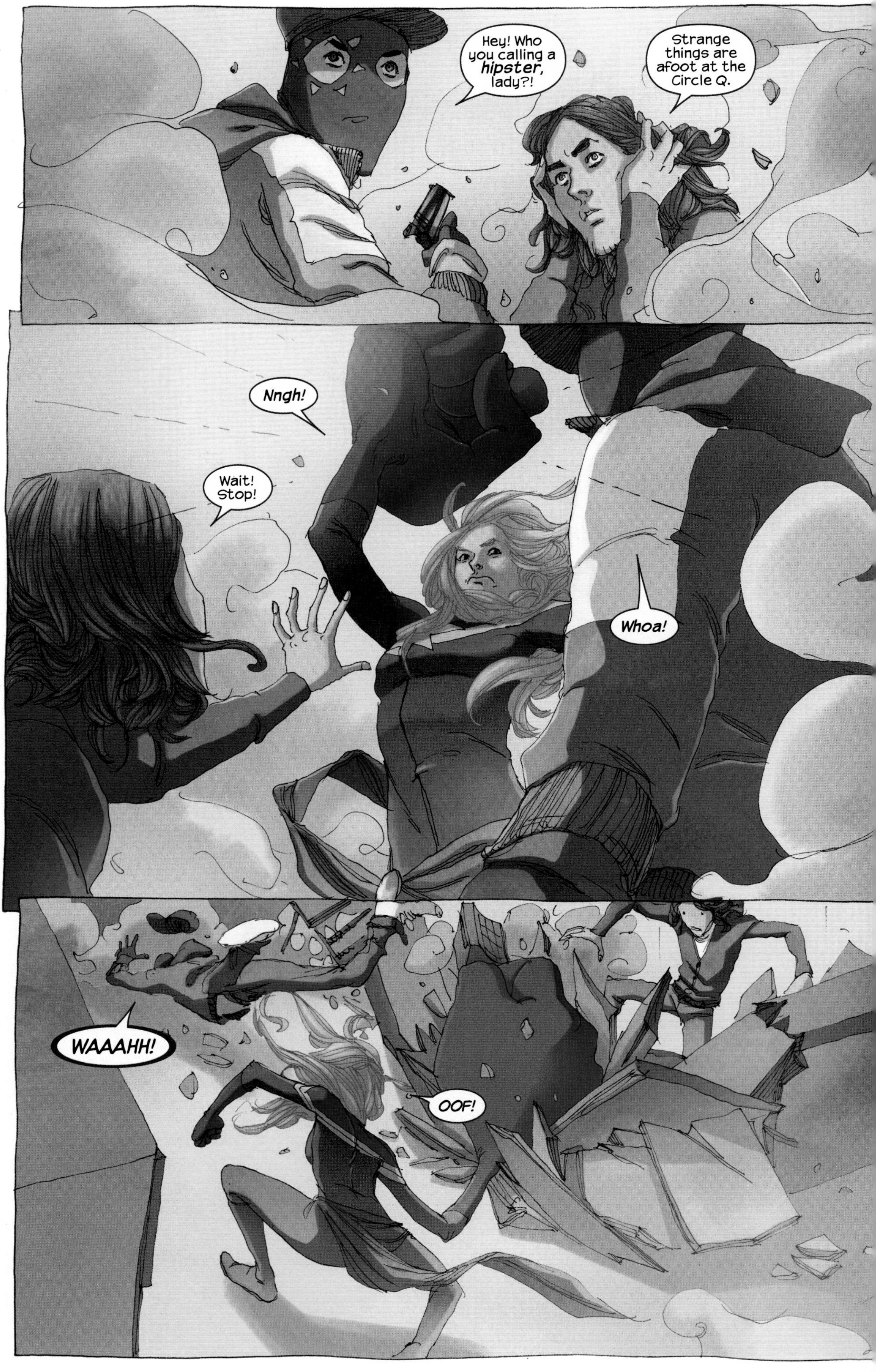
Hey! Who you calling a *hipster*, lady?!
Strange things are afoot at the Circle Q.
Nngh!
Wait! Stop!
Whoa!
WAAAHH!
OOF!

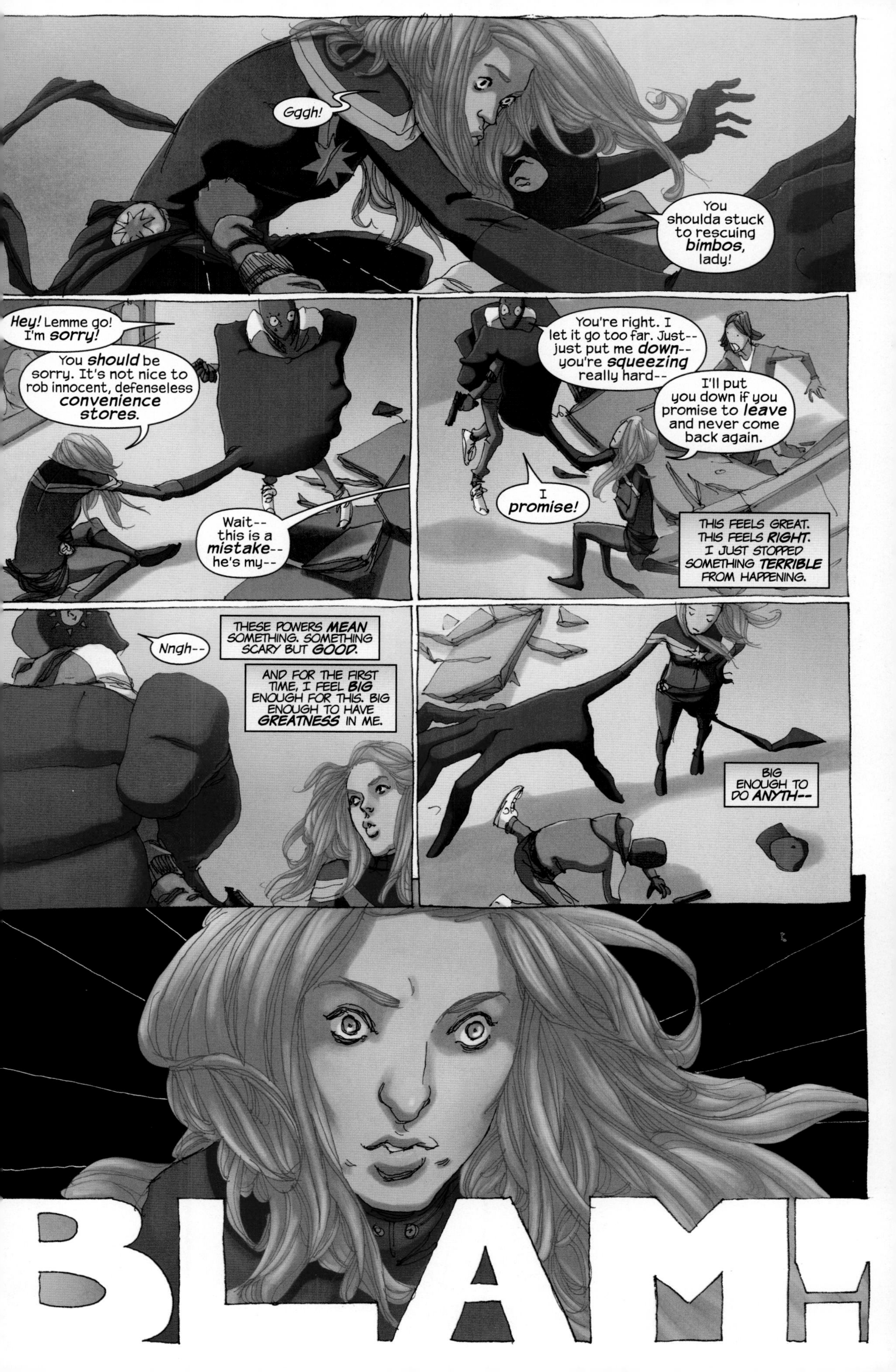

Gggh!
You shoulda stuck to rescuing bimbos, lady!
Hey! Lemme go! I'm sorry!
You should be sorry. It's not nice to rob innocent, defenseless convenience stores.
Wait-- this is a mistake-- he's my--
You're right. I let it go too far. Just-- just put me down-- you're squeezing really hard--
I'll put you down if you promise to leave and never come back again.
I promise!
THIS FEELS GREAT. THIS FEELS RIGHT. I JUST STOPPED SOMETHING TERRIBLE FROM HAPPENING.
Nngh--
THESE POWERS MEAN SOMETHING. SOMETHING SCARY BUT GOOD.
AND FOR THE FIRST TIME, I FEEL BIG ENOUGH FOR THIS. BIG ENOUGH TO HAVE GREATNESS IN ME.
BIG ENOUGH TO DO ANYTH--
BLAMM

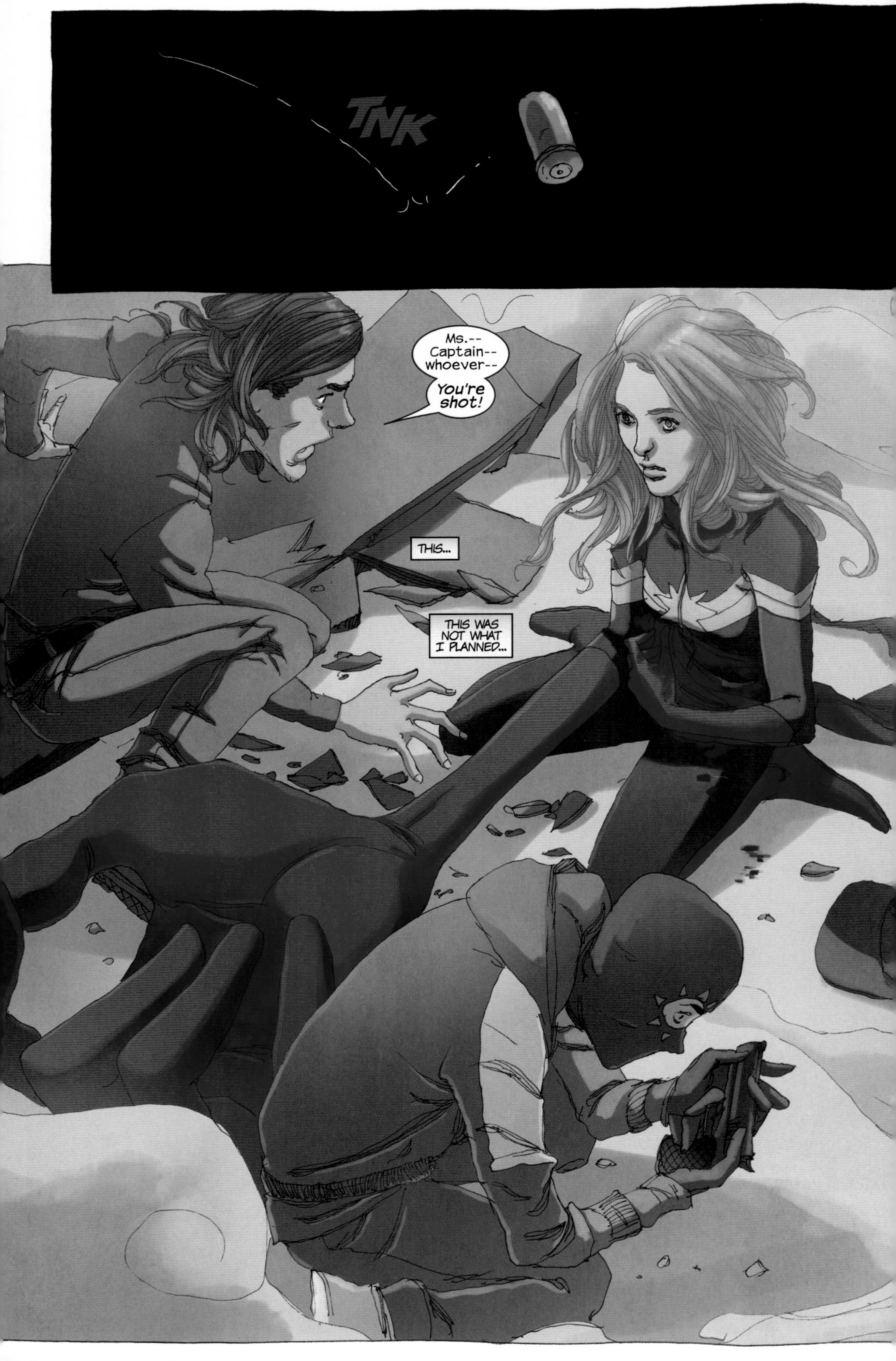
TNK
Ms.-- Captain-- whoever--
You're shot!
THIS...
THIS WAS NOT WHAT I PLANNED...

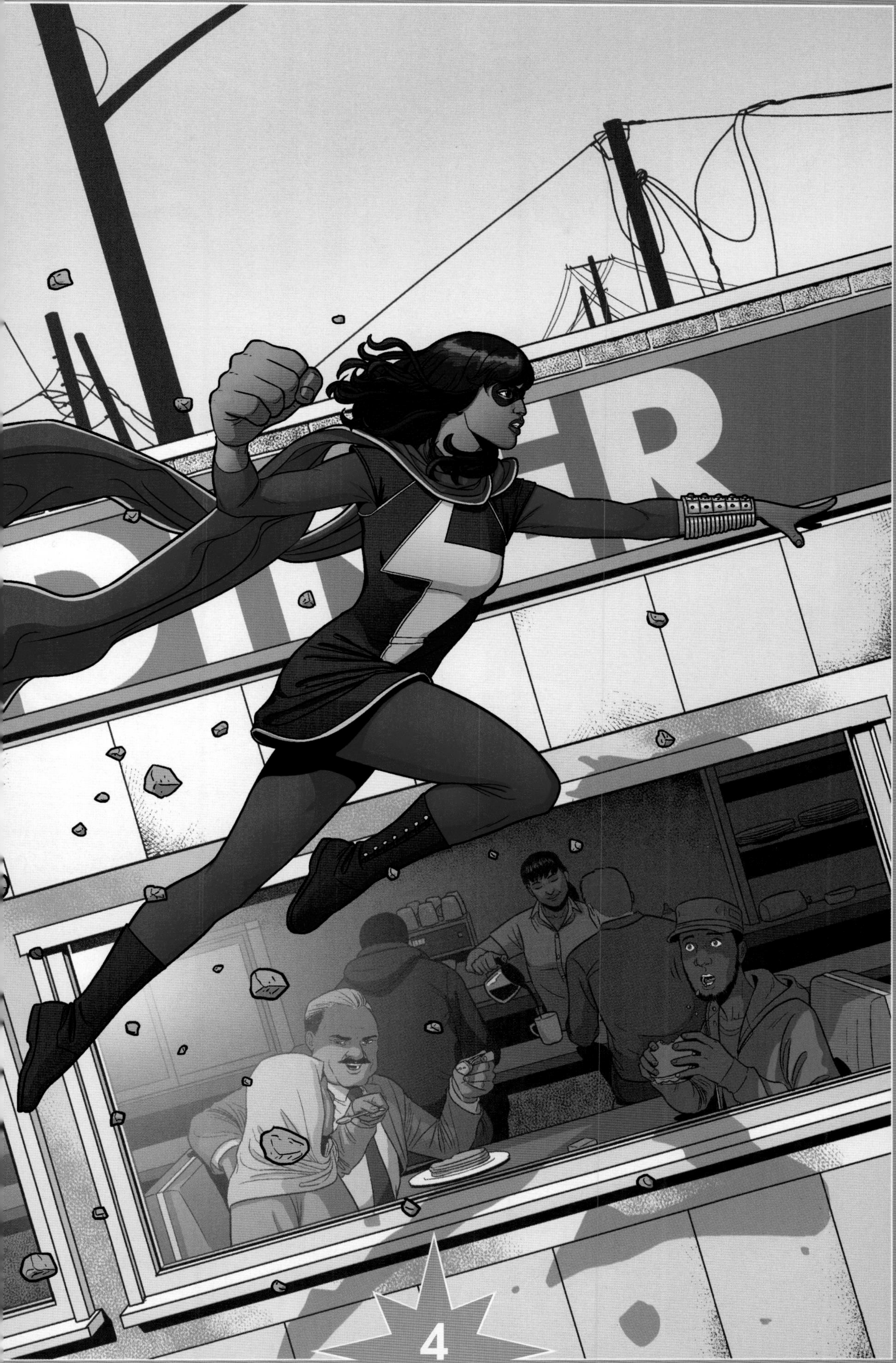

4

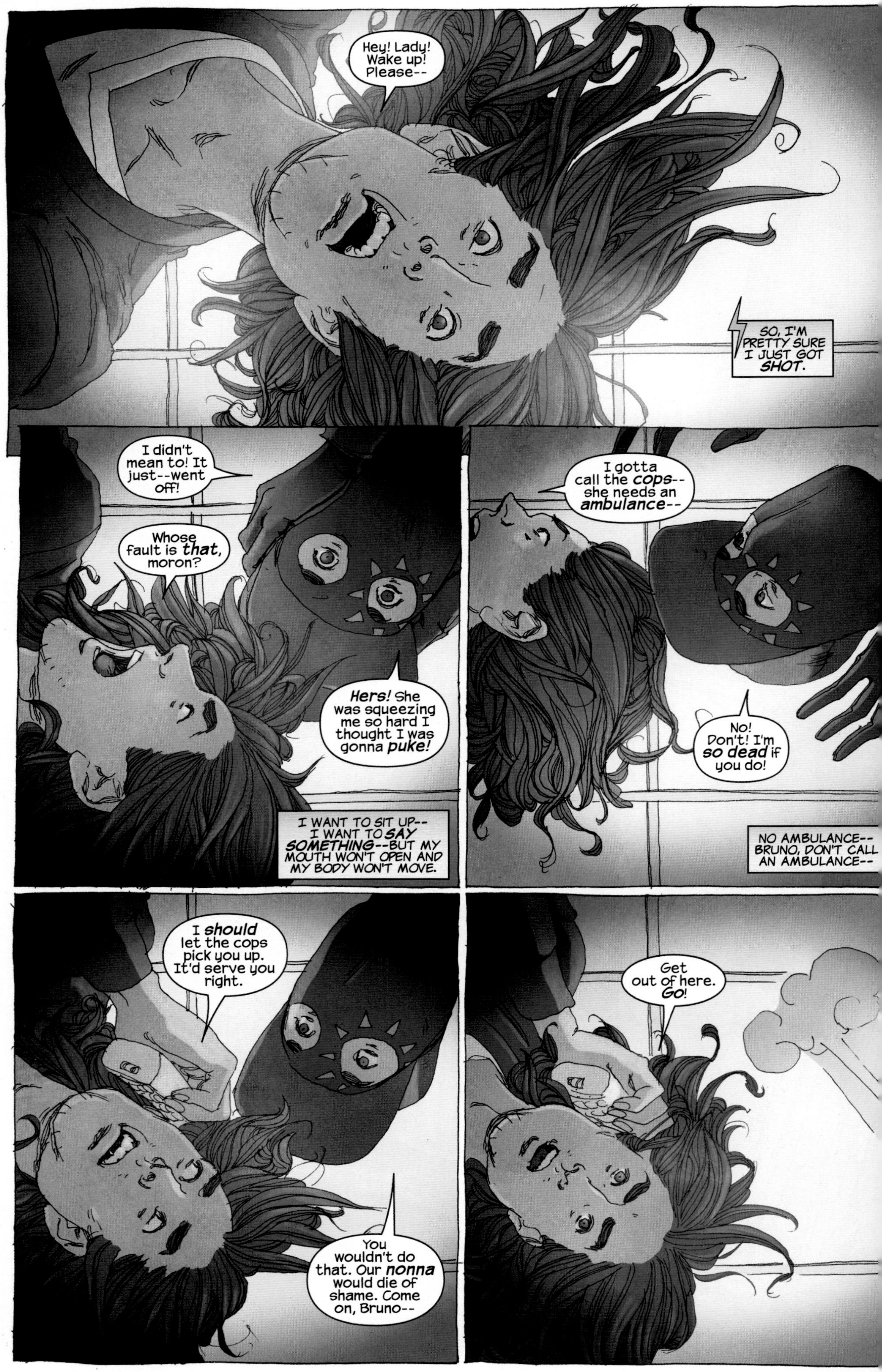
Hey! Lady! Wake up! Please--
SO, I'M PRETTY SURE I JUST GOT SHOT.
I didn't mean to! It just--went off!
Whose fault is that, moron?
Hers! She was squeezing me so hard I thought I was gonna puke!
I WANT TO SIT UP-- I WANT TO SAY SOMETHING--BUT MY MOUTH WON'T OPEN AND MY BODY WON'T MOVE.
I gotta call the cops-- she needs an ambulance--
No! Don't! I'm so dead if you do!
NO AMBULANCE-- BRUNO, DON'T CALL AN AMBULANCE--
I should let the cops pick you up. It'd serve you right.
You wouldn't do that. Our nonna would die of shame. Come on, Bruno--
Get out of here. GO!

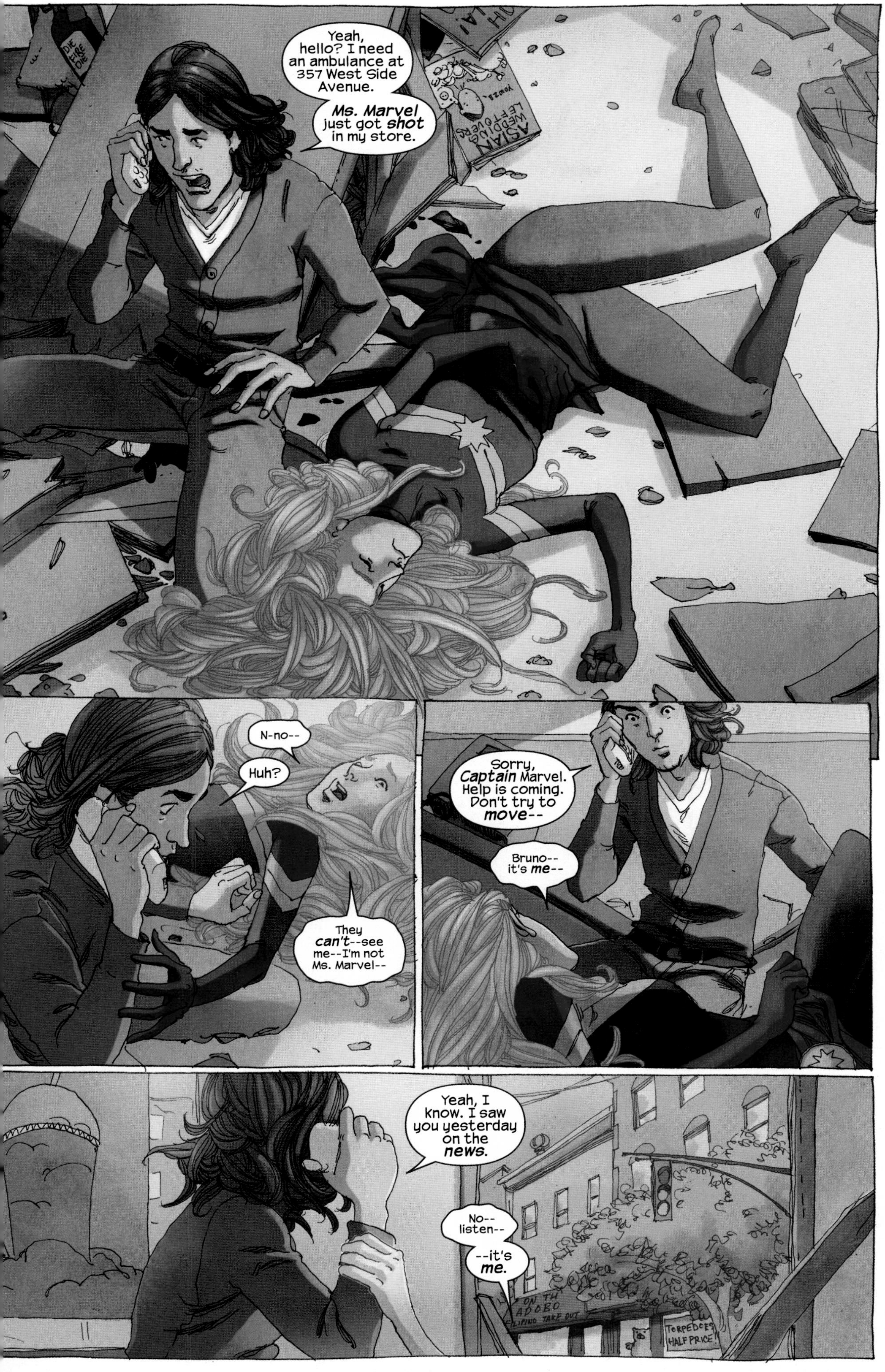
DIE FIRE DIE
Yeah, hello? I need an ambulance at 357 West Side Avenue.
Ms. Marvel just got ***shot*** in my store.
N-no--
Huh?
They ***can't***--see me--I'm not Ms. Marvel--
Sorry, *Captain* Marvel. Help is coming. Don't try to ***move***--
Bruno--it's ***me***--
Yeah, I know. I saw you yesterday on the ***news***.
No--listen--
--it's ***me***.

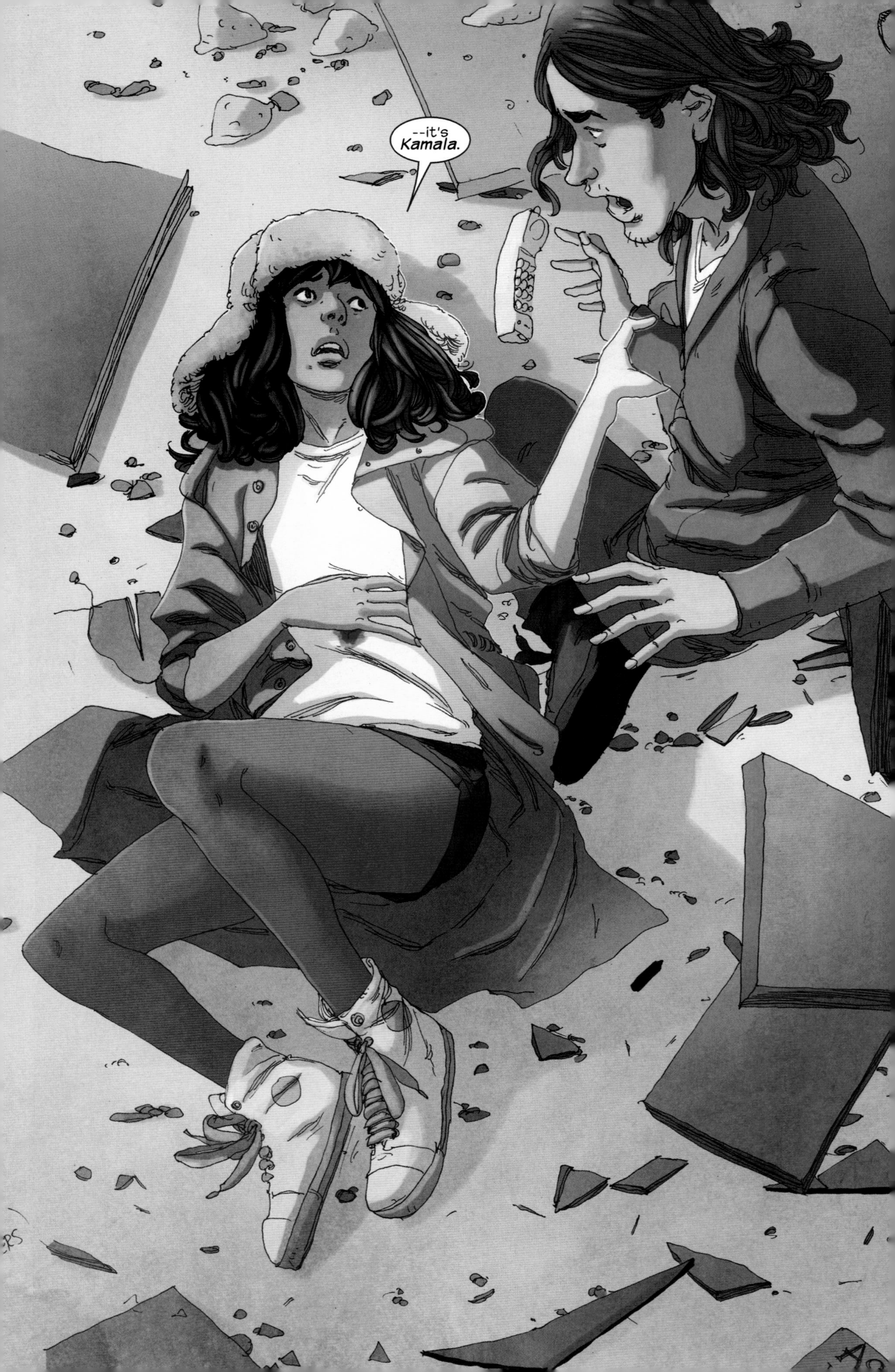
--it's Kamala.

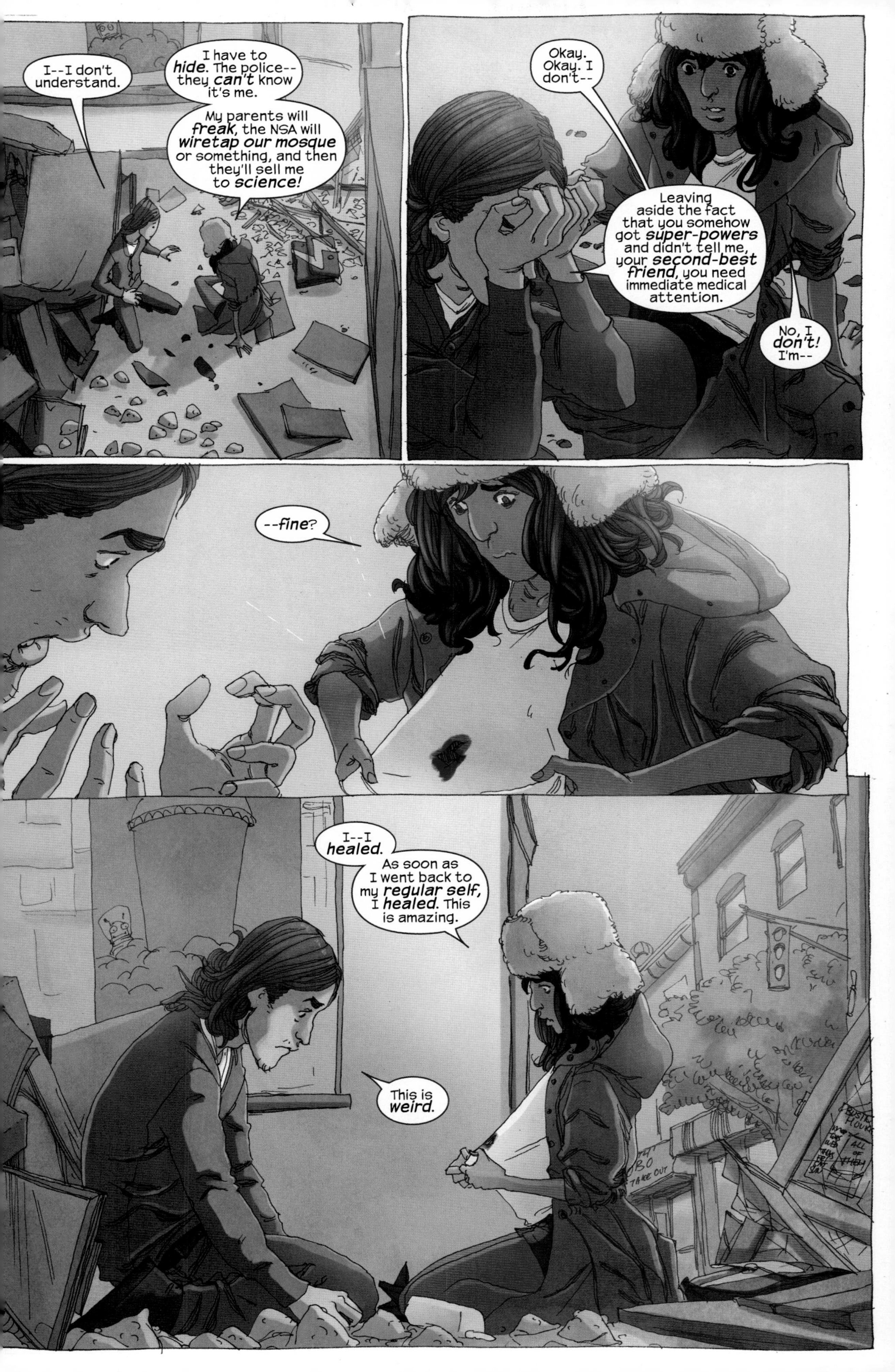
I--I don't understand.
I have to hide. The police--they can't know it's me.
My parents will freak, the NSA will wiretap our mosque or something, and then they'll sell me to science!
Okay. Okay. I don't--
Leaving aside the fact that you somehow got super-powers and didn't tell me, your second-best friend, you need immediate medical attention.
No, I don't! I'm--
--fine?
I--I healed.
As soon as I went back to my regular self, I healed. This is amazing.
This is weird.

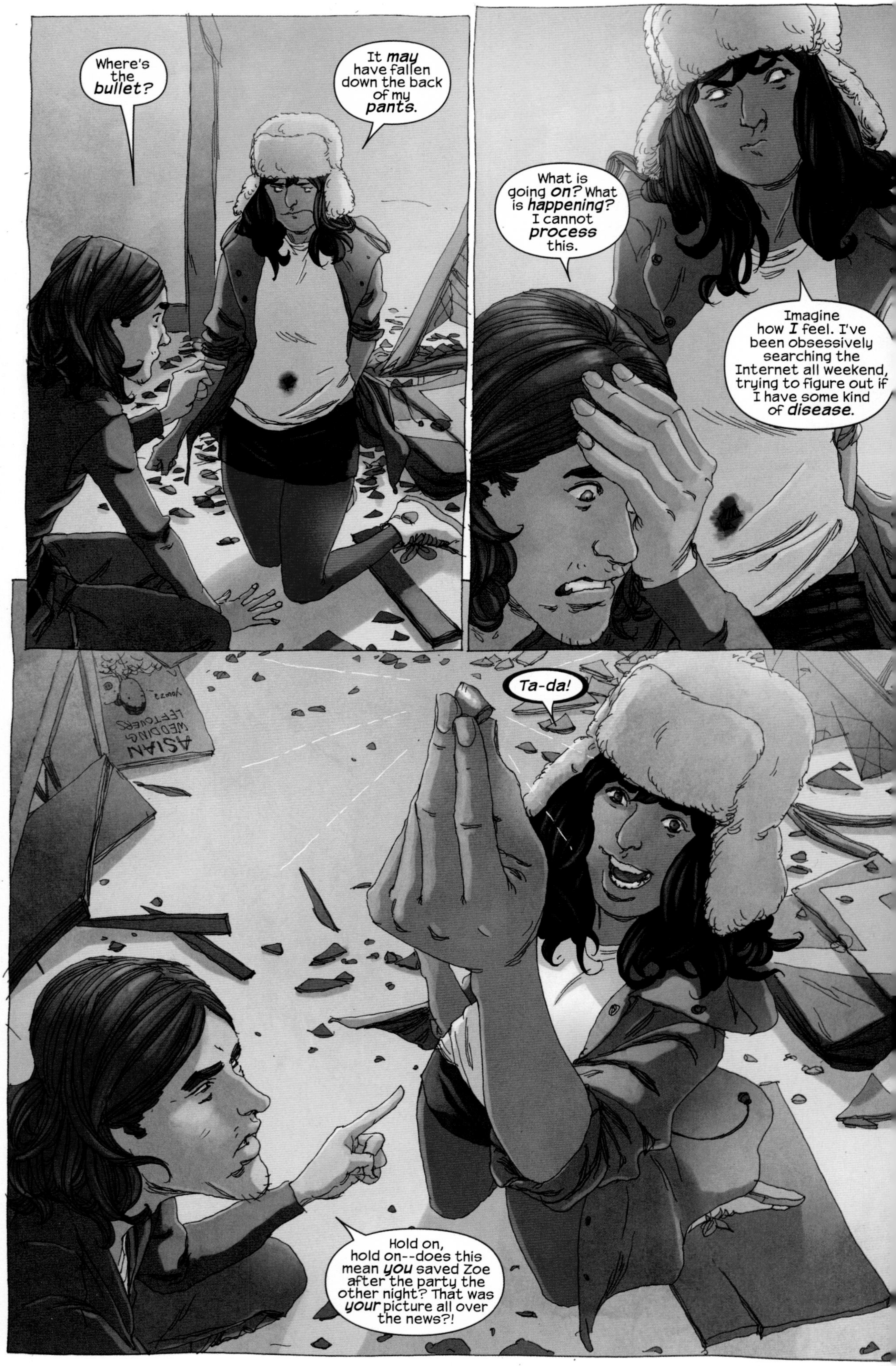
Where's the bullet?
It may have fallen down the back of my pants.
What is going on? What is happening? I cannot process this.
Imagine how I feel. I've been obsessively searching the Internet all weekend, trying to figure out if I have some kind of disease.
ASIAN WEDDING LEFTOVERS
Ta-da!
Hold on, hold on--does this mean you saved Zoe after the party the other night? That was your picture all over the news?!

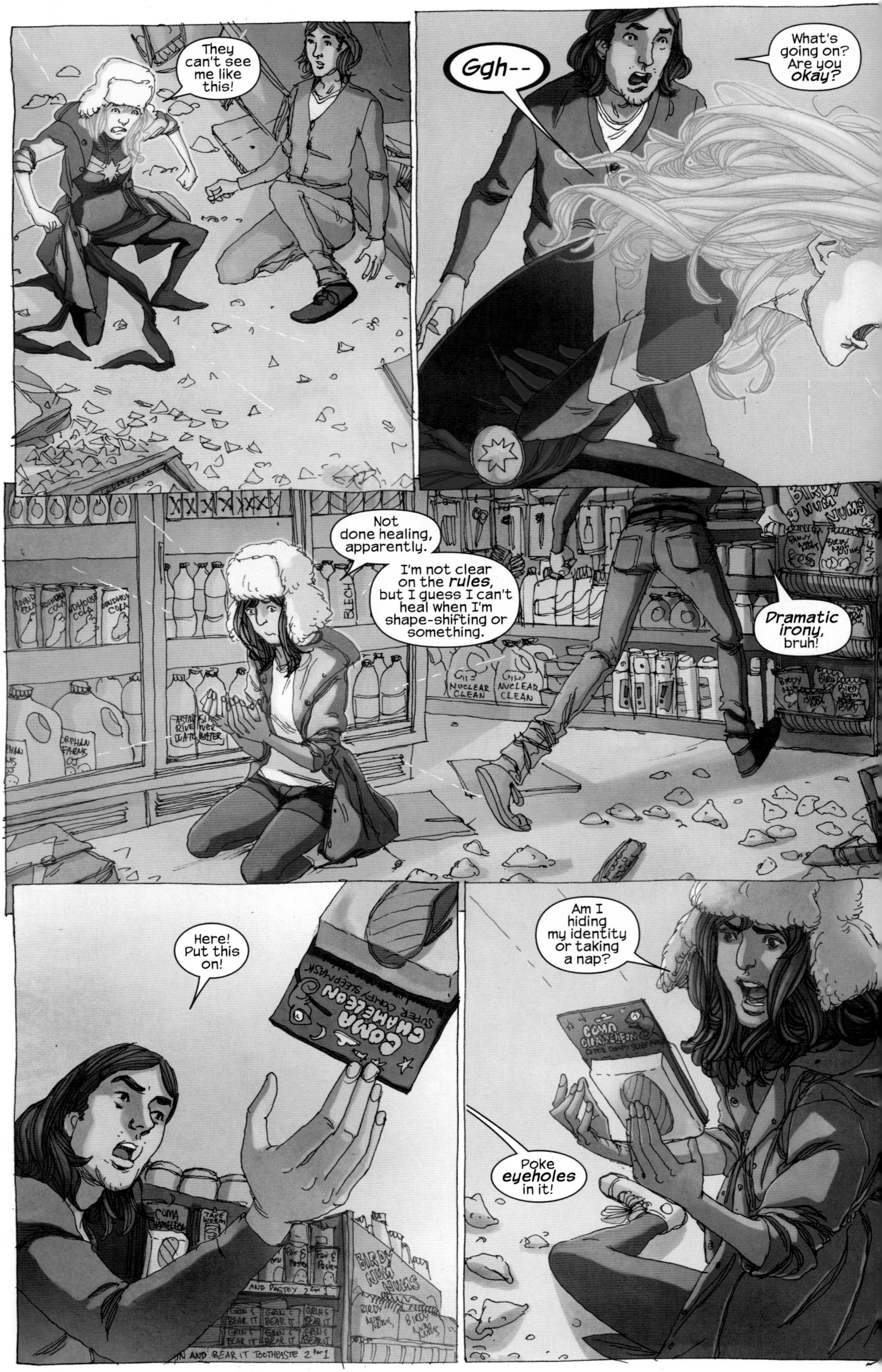
They can't see me like this!
Ggh--
What's going on? Are you *okay?*
Not done healing, apparently.
I'm not clear on the *rules,* but I guess I can't heal when I'm shape-shifting or something.
BLECH
NUCLEAR CLEAN
NUCLEAR CLEAN
Dramatic irony, bruh!
Here! Put this on!
COMA CHAMELEON
SUPER COMFY SLEEPMASK
Am I hiding my identity or taking a nap?
Poke *eyeholes* in it!

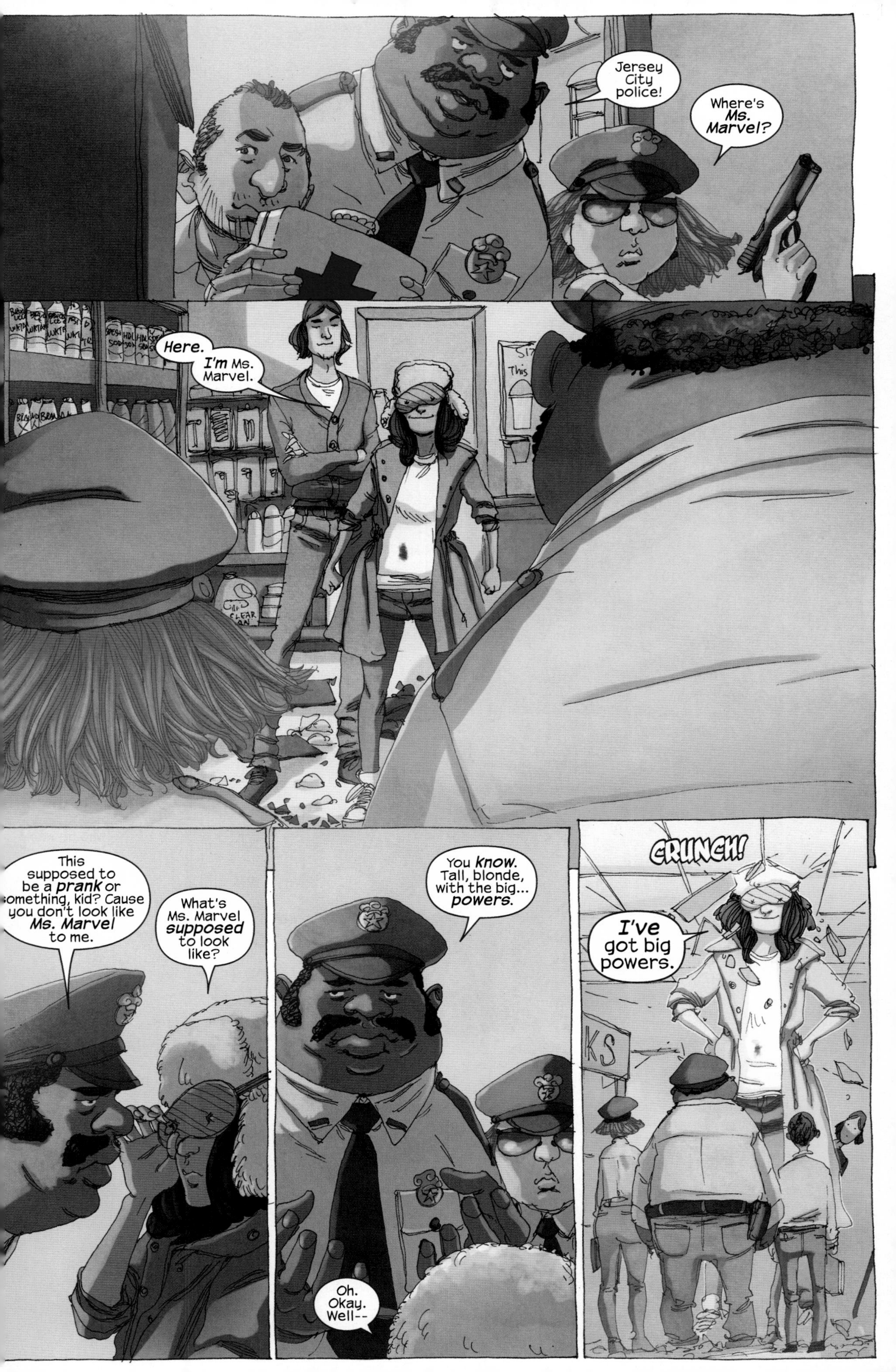
Jersey City police!
Where's Ms. Marvel?
Here. I'm Ms. Marvel.
This supposed to be a prank or something, kid? Cause you don't look like Ms. Marvel to me.
What's Ms. Marvel supposed to look like?
You know. Tall, blonde, with the big... powers.
Oh. Okay. Well--
CRUNCH!
I've got big powers.

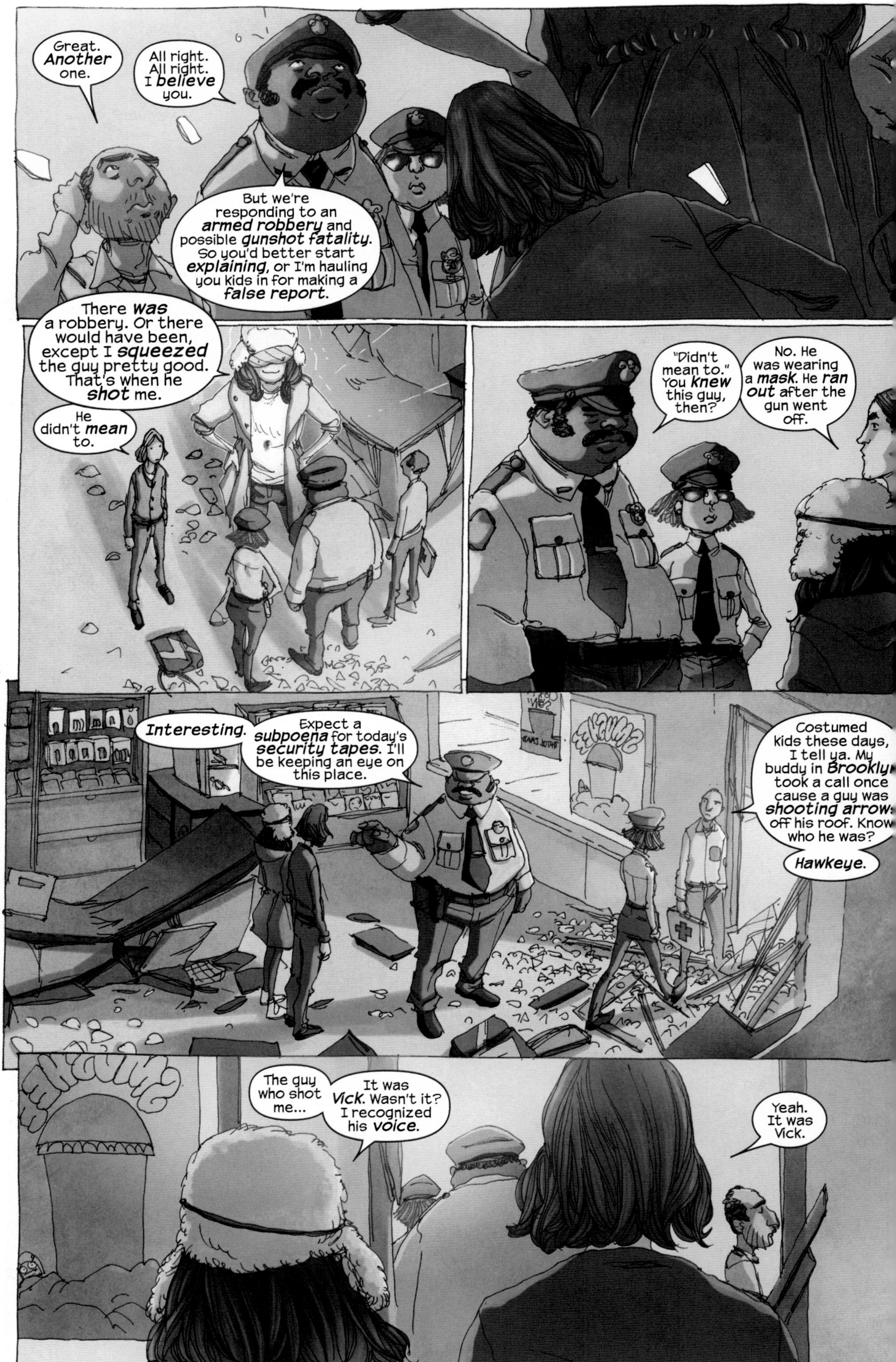
Great. Another one.
All right. All right. I believe you.
But we're responding to an armed robbery and possible gunshot fatality. So you'd better start explaining, or I'm hauling you kids in for making a false report.
There was a robbery. Or there would have been, except I squeezed the guy pretty good. That's when he shot me.
He didn't mean to.
"Didn't mean to." You knew this guy, then?
No. He was wearing a mask. He ran out after the gun went off.
Interesting.
Expect a subpoena for today's security tapes. I'll be keeping an eye on this place.
Costumed kids these days, I tell ya. My buddy in Brookly took a call once cause a guy was shooting arrow off his roof. Know who he was?
Hawkeye.
The guy who shot me...
It was Vick. Wasn't it? I recognized his voice.
Yeah. It was Vick.

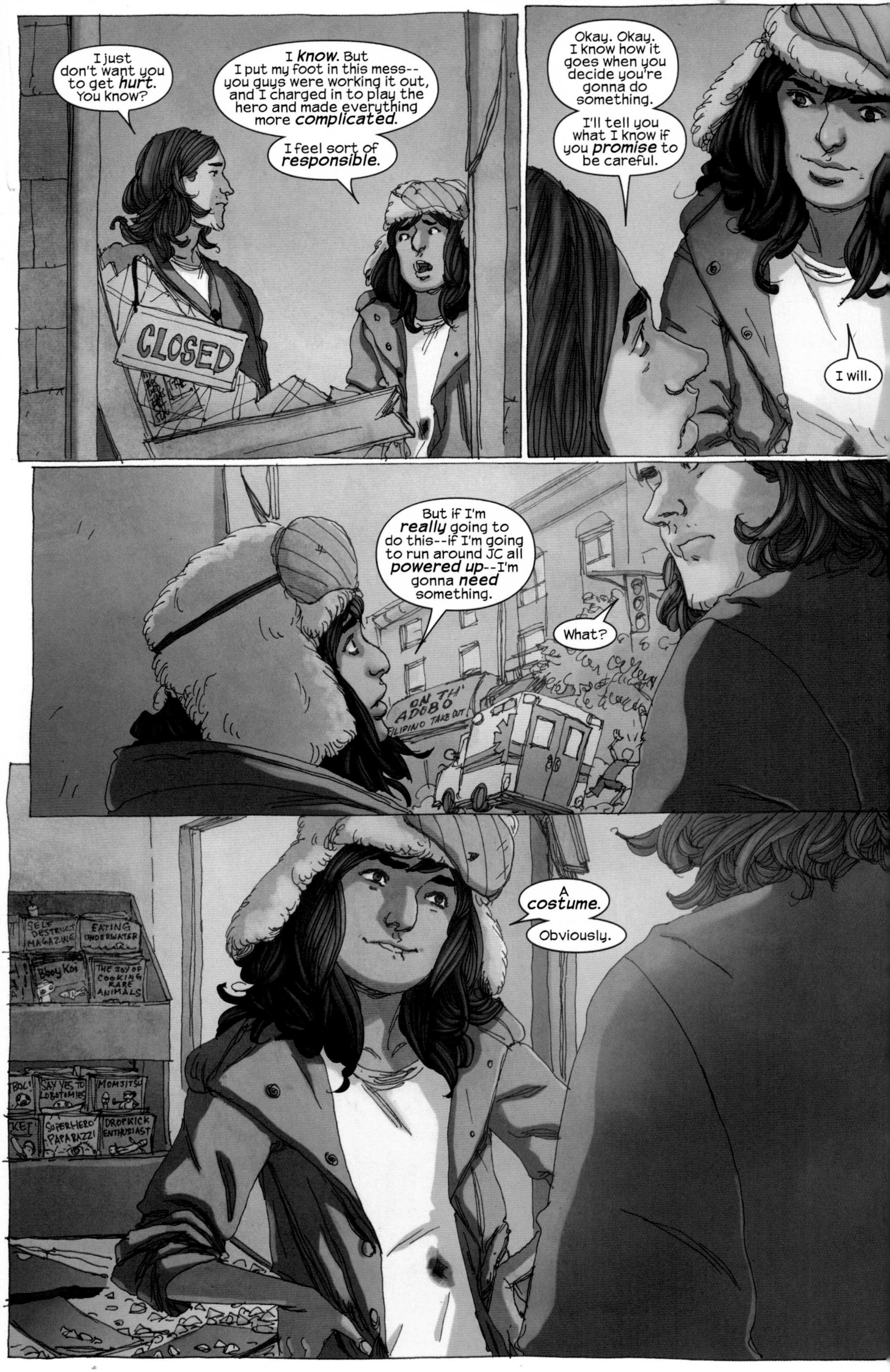
I just don't want you to get *hurt*. You know?
I *know*. But I put my foot in this mess--you guys were working it out, and I charged in to play the hero and made everything more *complicated*.
I feel sort of *responsible*.
CLOSED
Okay. Okay. I know how it goes when you decide you're gonna do something.
I'll tell you what I know if you *promise* to be careful.
I will.
But if I'm *really* going to do this--if I'm going to run around JC all *powered up*--I'm gonna *need* something.
What?
ON TH' ADOBO
FILIPINO TAKE OUT
A *costume.*
Obviously.
SELF DESTRUCT MAGAZINE
EATING UNDERWATER
THE JOY OF COOKING RARE ANIMALS
SAY YES TO LOBOTOMIES
MOMJITSU
SUPERHERO PAPARAZZI
DROPKICK ENTHUSIAST

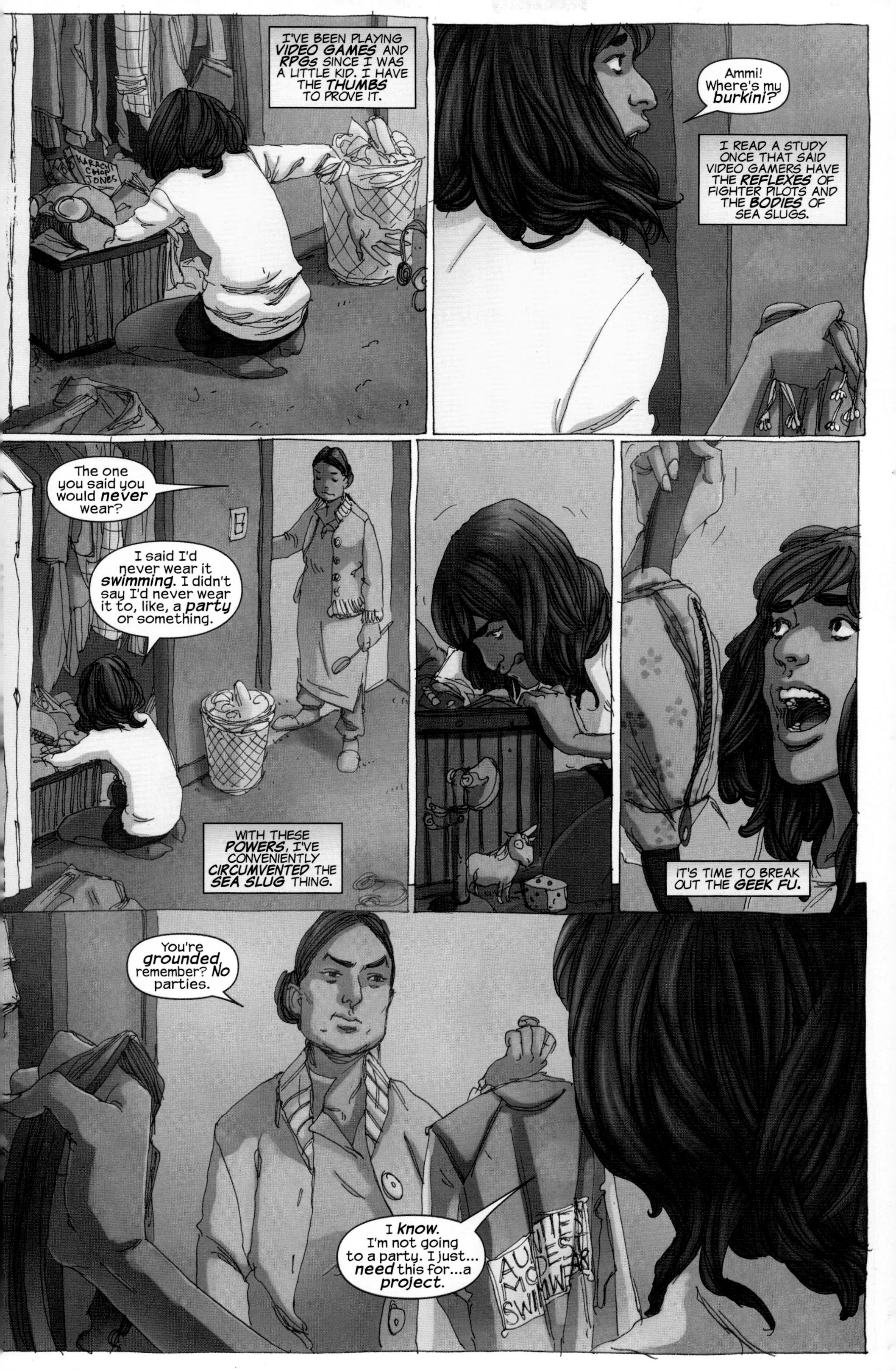
I'VE BEEN PLAYING VIDEO GAMES AND RPGs SINCE I WAS A LITTLE KID. I HAVE THE THUMBS TO PROVE IT.
KARACHI CHOP JONES
Ammi! Where's my burkini?
I READ A STUDY ONCE THAT SAID VIDEO GAMERS HAVE THE REFLEXES OF FIGHTER PILOTS AND THE BODIES OF SEA SLUGS.
The one you said you would never wear?
I said I'd never wear it swimming. I didn't say I'd never wear it to, like, a party or something.
WITH THESE POWERS, I'VE CONVENIENTLY CIRCUMVENTED THE SEA SLUG THING.
IT'S TIME TO BREAK OUT THE GEEK FU.
You're grounded, remember? No parties.
I know. I'm not going to a party. I just... need this for...a project.

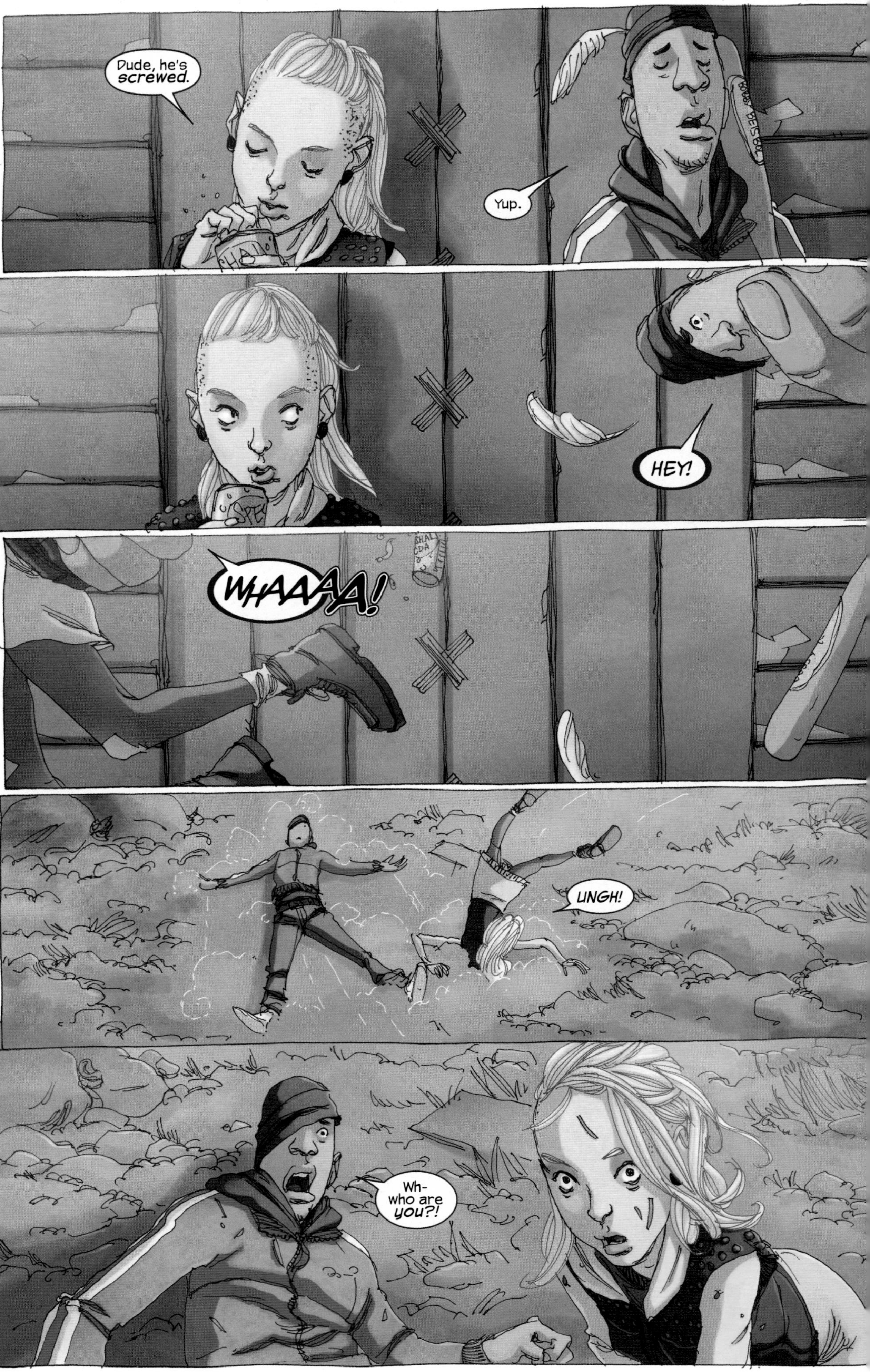
Dude, he's screwed.
Yup.
HEY!
WHAAAA!
UNGH!
Wh- who are you?!

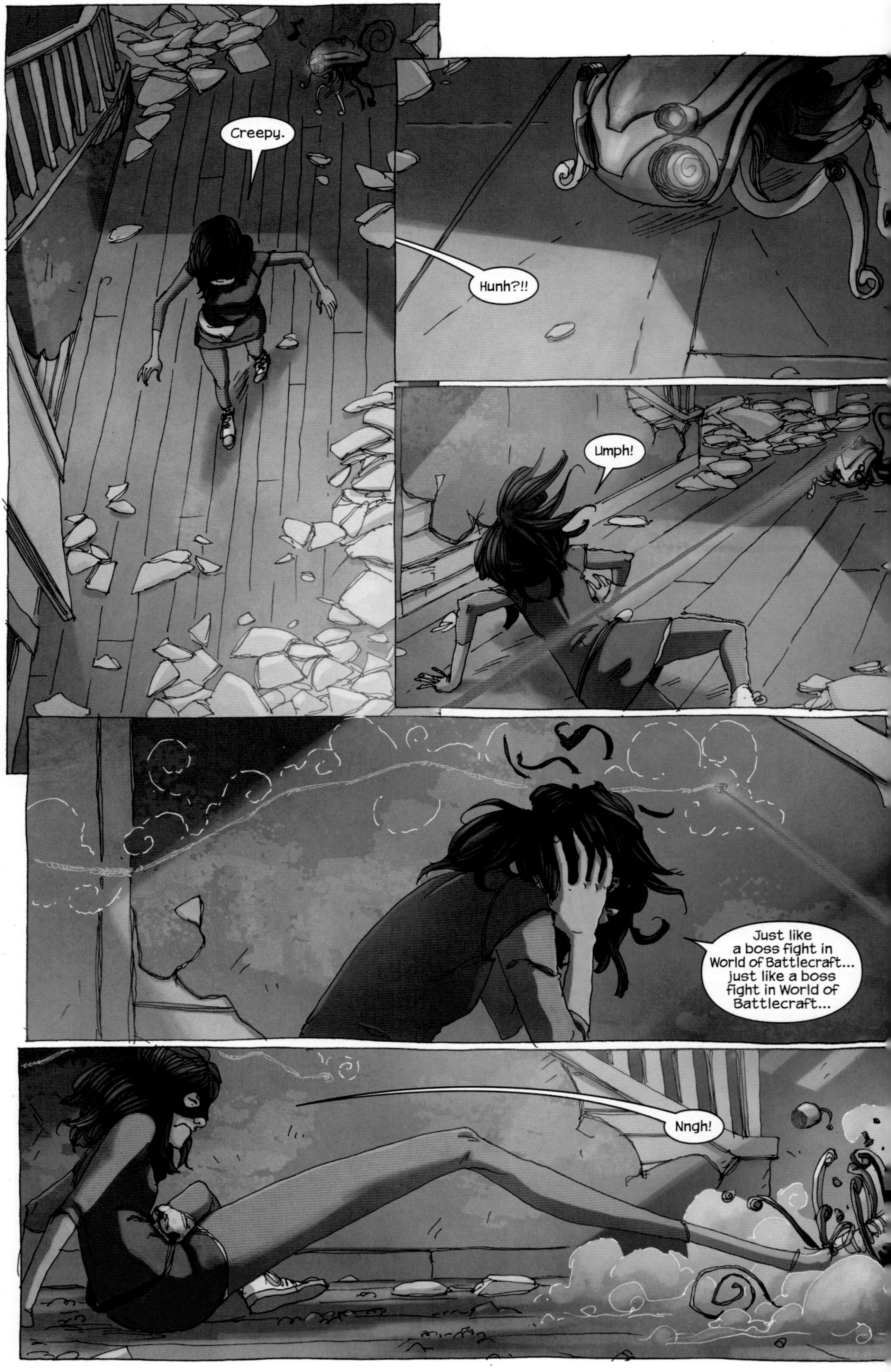
Creepy.
Hunh?!!
Umph!
Just like a boss fight in World of Battlecraft... just like a boss fight in World of Battlecraft...
Nngh!

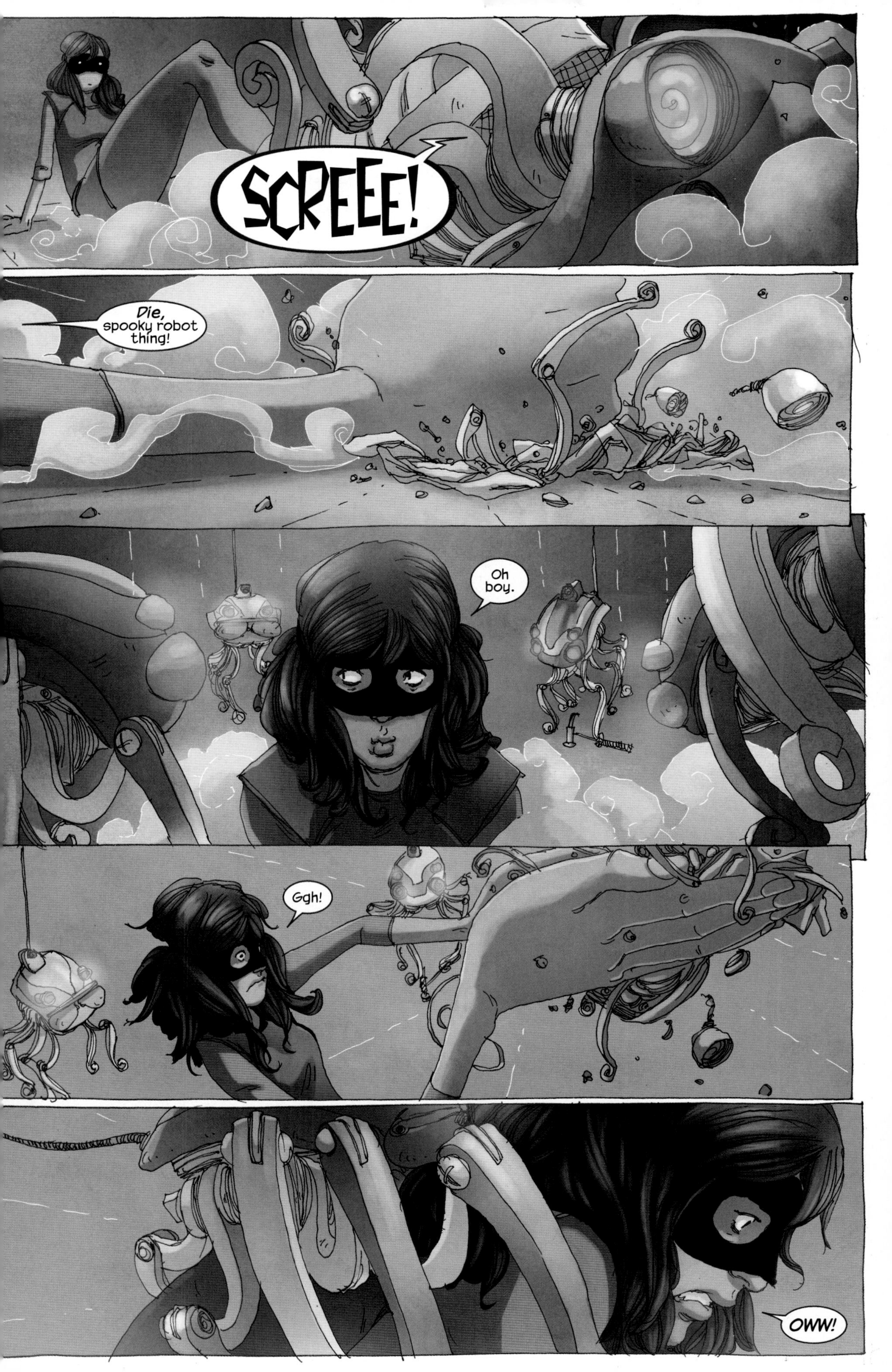
SCREEE!
Die, spooky robot thing!
Oh boy.
Ggh!
OWW!

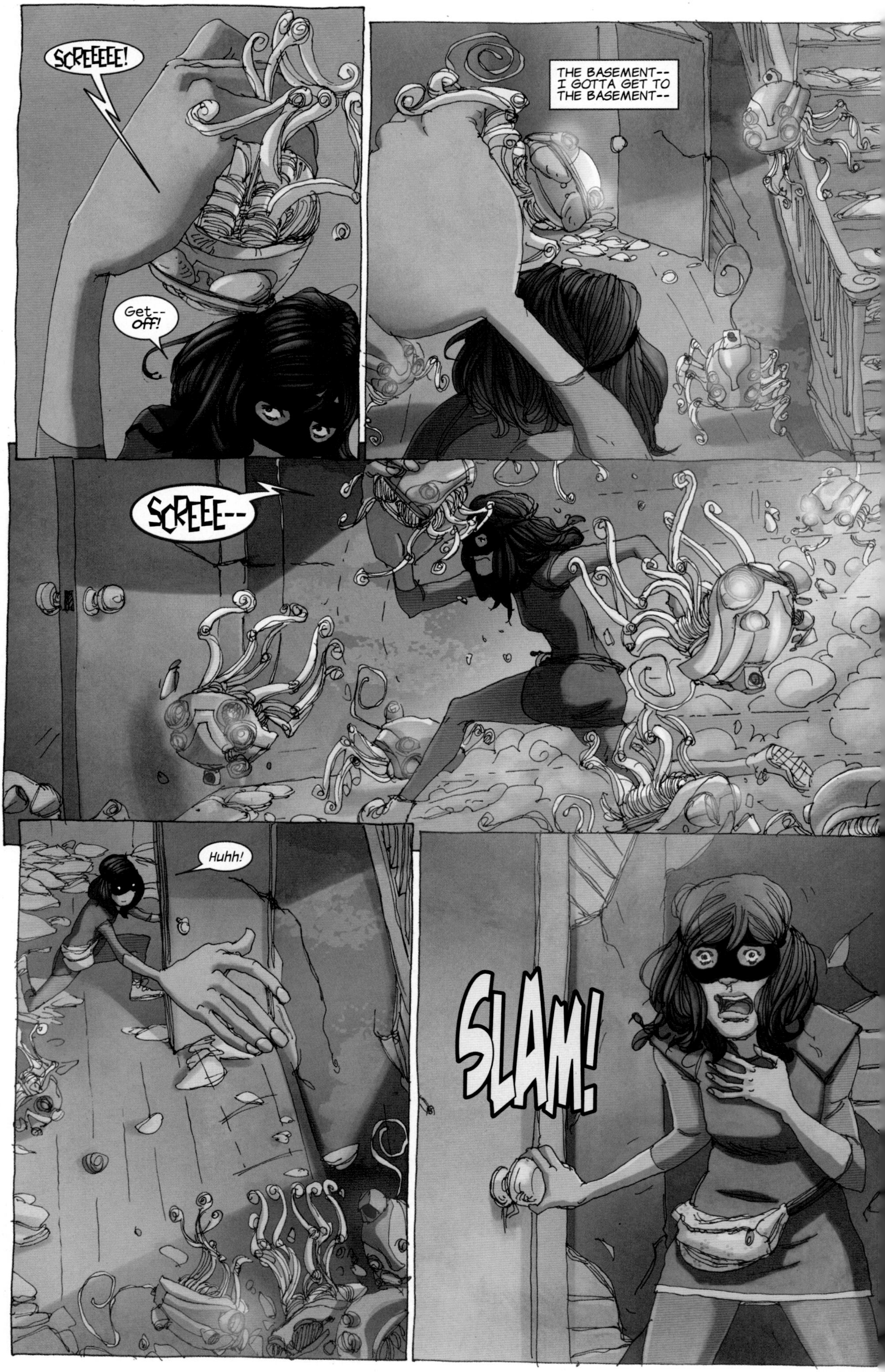
SCREEEEE!
Get-- off!
THE BASEMENT-- I GOTTA GET TO THE BASEMENT--
SCREEE--
Huhh!
SLAM!

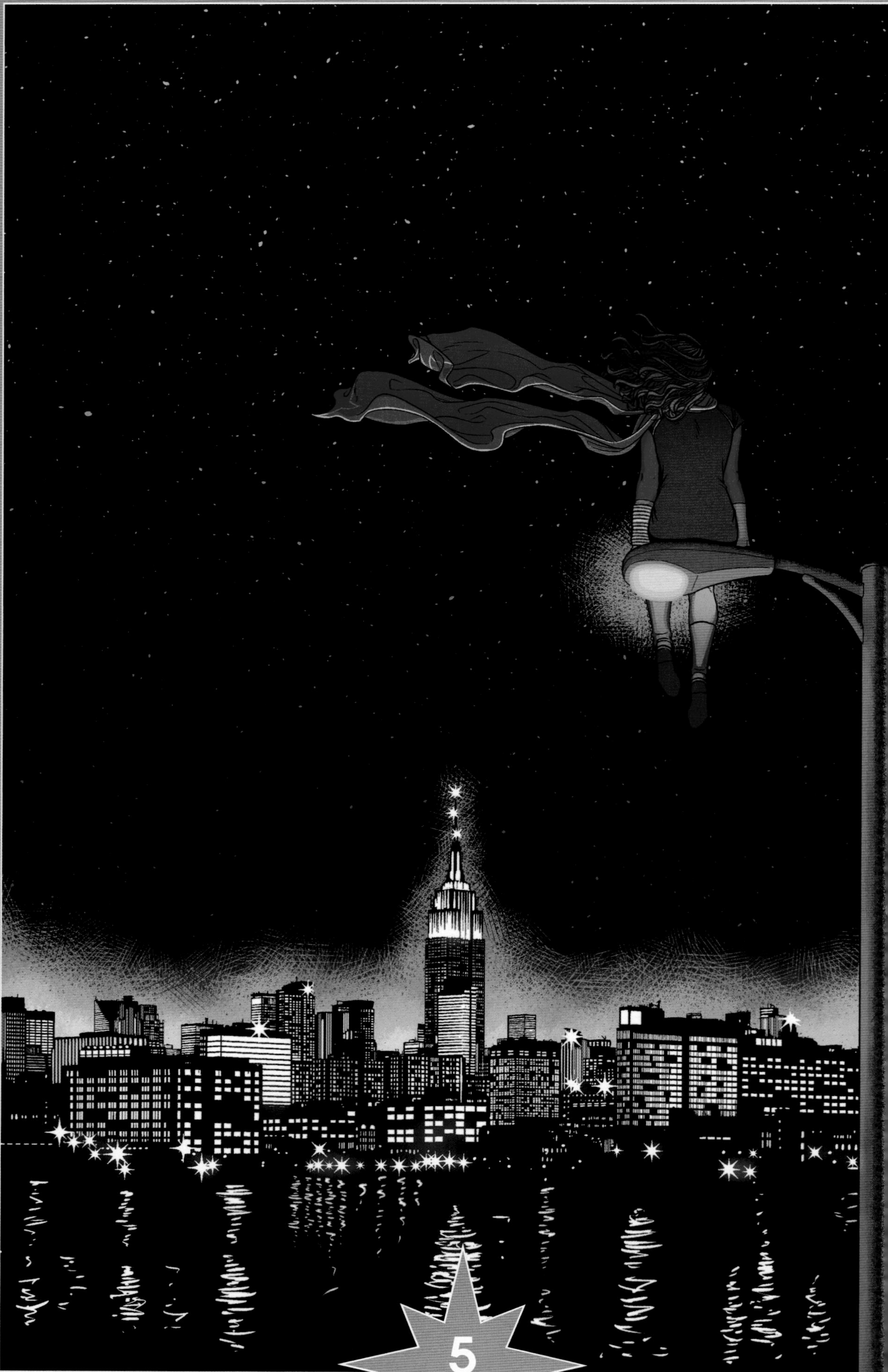
5

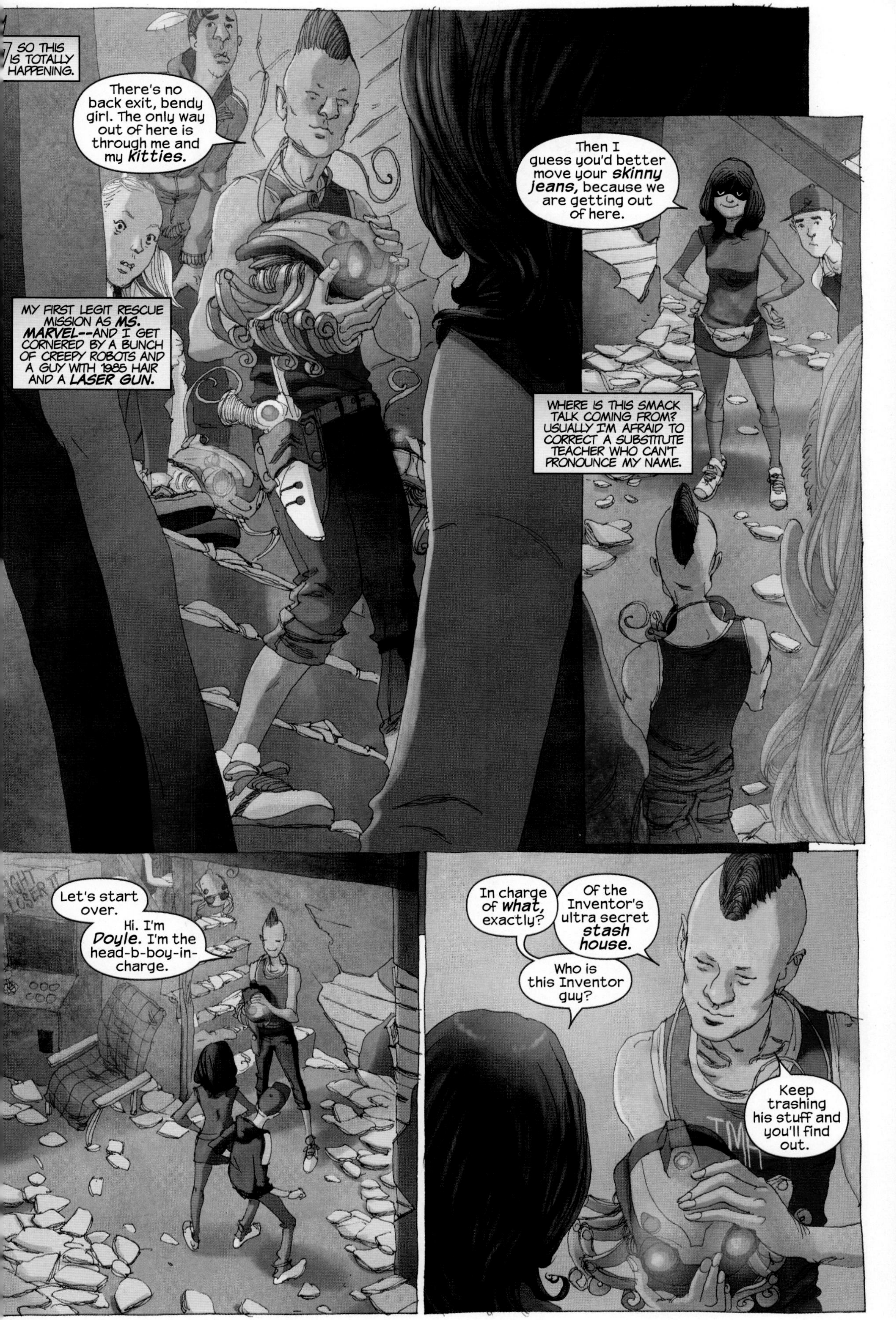
SO THIS IS TOTALLY HAPPENING.
There's no back exit, bendy girl. The only way out of here is through me and my kitties.
MY FIRST LEGIT RESCUE MISSION AS MS. MARVEL--AND I GET CORNERED BY A BUNCH OF CREEPY ROBOTS AND A GUY WITH 1985 HAIR AND A LASER GUN.
Then I guess you'd better move your skinny jeans, because we are getting out of here.
WHERE IS THIS SMACK TALK COMING FROM? USUALLY I'M AFRAID TO CORRECT A SUBSTITUTE TEACHER WHO CAN'T PRONOUNCE MY NAME.
Let's start over.
Hi. I'm Doyle. I'm the head-b-boy-in-charge.
In charge of what, exactly?
Of the Inventor's ultra secret stash house.
Who is this Inventor guy?
Keep trashing his stuff and you'll find out.

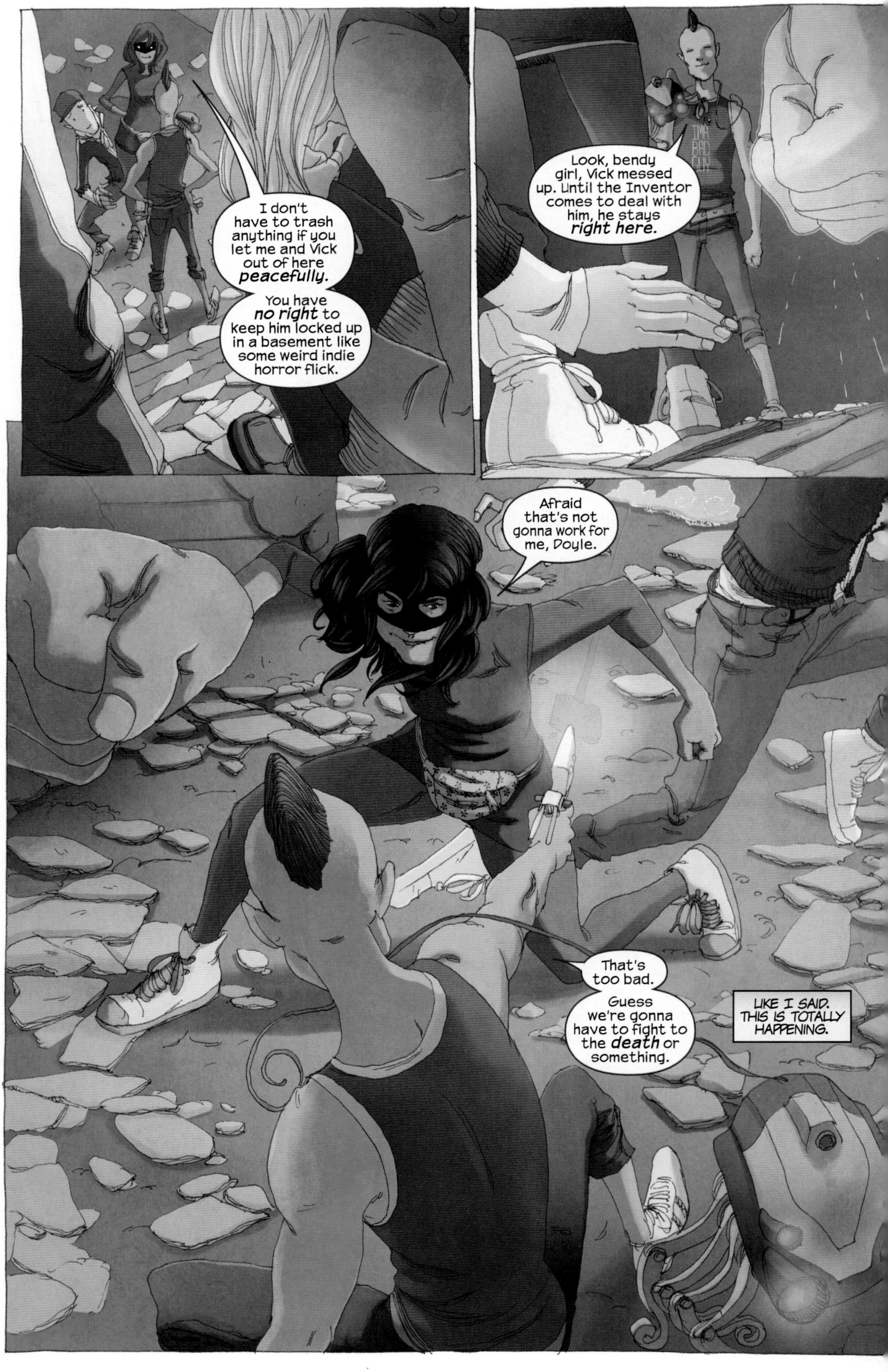
I don't have to trash anything if you let me and Vick out of here *peacefully.*
You have *no right* to keep him locked up in a basement like some weird indie horror flick.
Look, bendy girl, Vick messed up. Until the Inventor comes to deal with him, he stays *right here.*
IMA BAD GUY
Afraid that's not gonna work for me, Doyle.
That's too bad.
Guess we're gonna have to fight to the *death* or something.
LIKE I SAID. THIS IS TOTALLY HAPPENING.

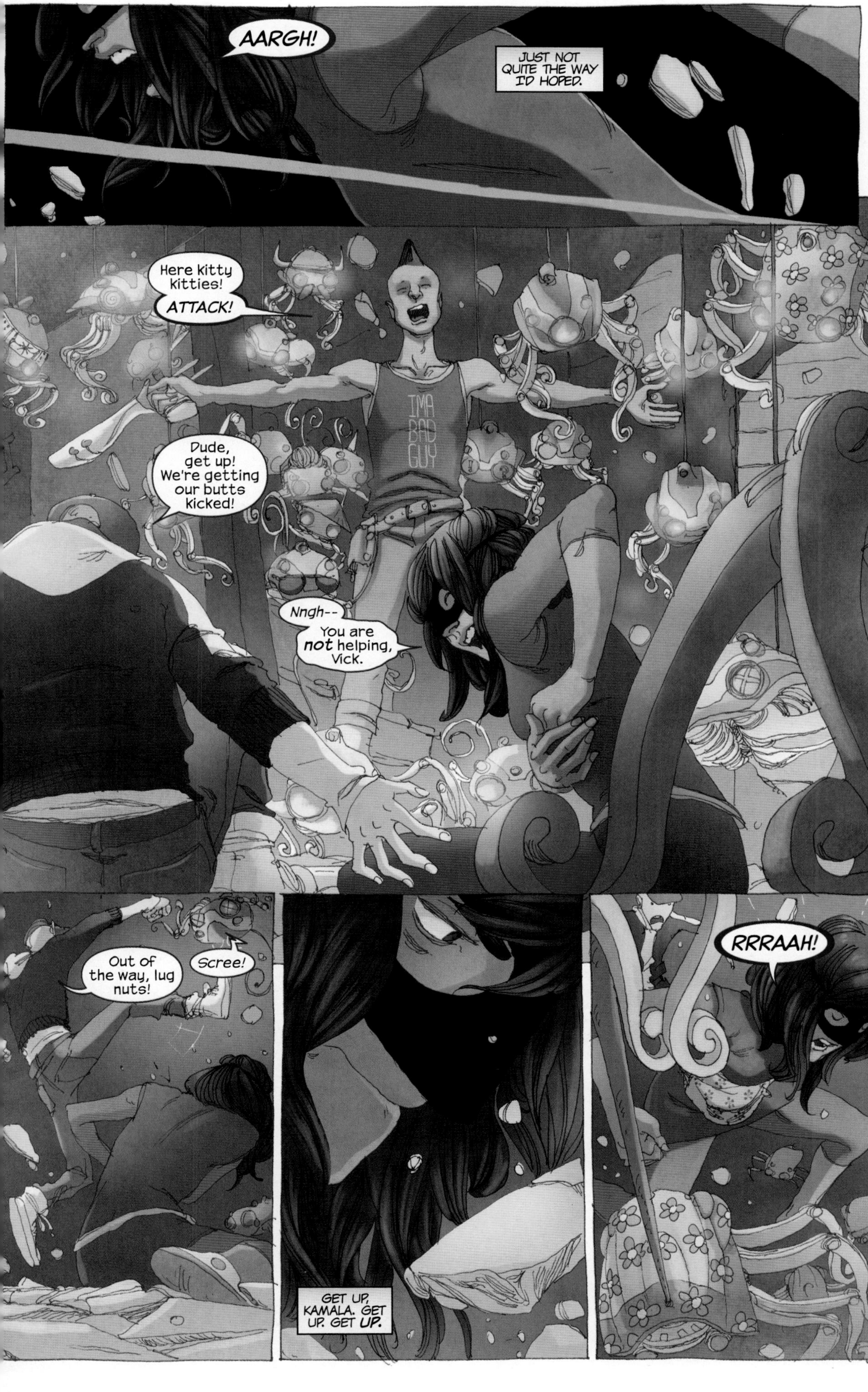
AARGH!
JUST NOT QUITE THE WAY I'D HOPED.
Here kitty kitties!
ATTACK!
IMA BAD GUY
Dude, get up! We're getting our butts kicked!
Nngh--
You are *not* helping, Vick.
Out of the way, lug nuts!
Scree!
GET UP, KAMALA. GET UP. GET *UP*.
RRRAAH!

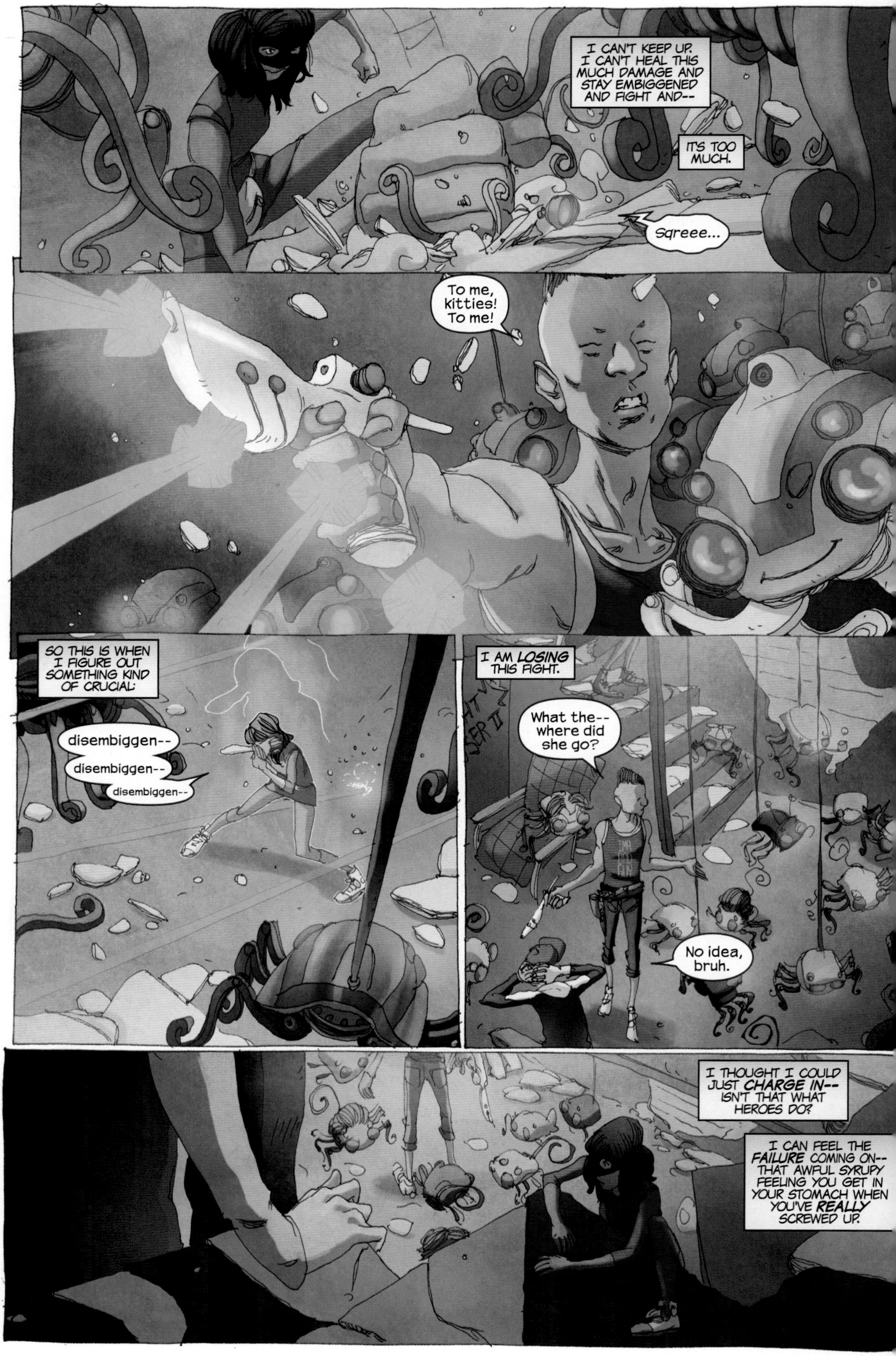
I CAN'T KEEP UP. I CAN'T HEAL THIS MUCH DAMAGE AND STAY EMBIGGENED AND FIGHT AND--
IT'S TOO MUCH.
Sqreee...
To me, kitties! To me!
SO THIS IS WHEN I FIGURE OUT SOMETHING KIND OF CRUCIAL:
disembiggen--
disembiggen--
disembiggen--
I AM LOSING THIS FIGHT.
What the-- where did she go?
No idea, bruh.
I THOUGHT I COULD JUST CHARGE IN-- ISN'T THAT WHAT HEROES DO?
I CAN FEEL THE FAILURE COMING ON-- THAT AWFUL SYRUPY FEELING YOU GET IN YOUR STOMACH WHEN YOU'VE REALLY SCREWED UP.

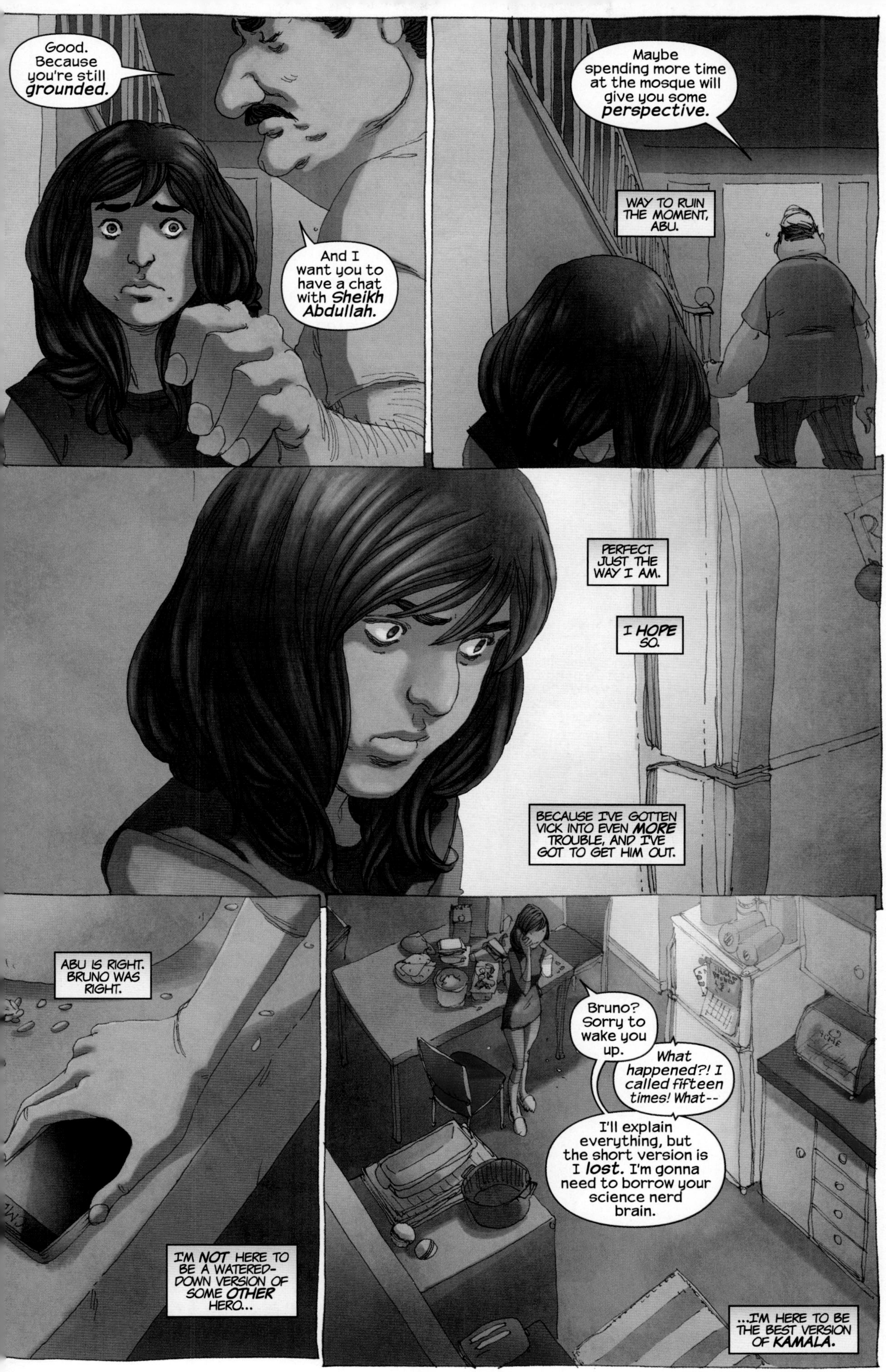

Good. Because you're still **grounded.**
And I want you to have a chat with ***Sheikh Abdullah.***
Maybe spending more time at the mosque will give you some ***perspective.***
WAY TO RUIN THE MOMENT, ABU.
PERFECT JUST THE WAY I AM.
I ***HOPE*** SO.
BECAUSE I'VE GOTTEN VICK INTO EVEN ***MORE*** TROUBLE, AND I'VE GOT TO GET HIM OUT.
ABU IS RIGHT. BRUNO WAS RIGHT.
I'M ***NOT*** HERE TO BE A WATERED-DOWN VERSION OF SOME ***OTHER*** HERO...
Bruno? Sorry to wake you up.
What happened?! I called fifteen times! What--
I'll explain everything, but the short version is I ***lost.*** I'm gonna need to borrow your science nerd brain.
...I'M HERE TO BE THE BEST VERSION OF ***KAMALA.***

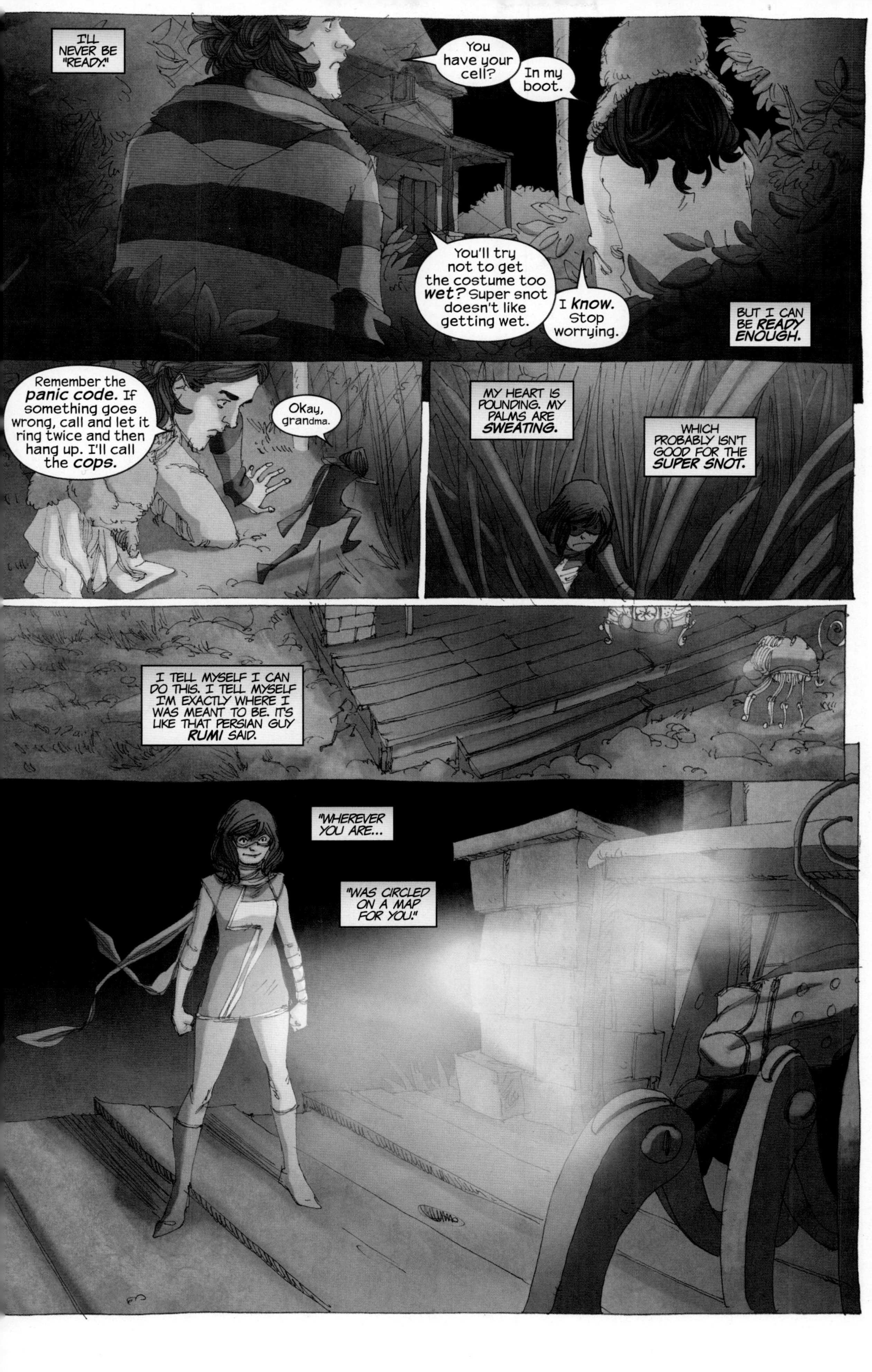
I'LL NEVER BE "READY."
You have your cell?
In my boot.
You'll try not to get the costume too wet? Super snot doesn't like getting wet.
I know. Stop worrying.
BUT I CAN BE READY ENOUGH.
Remember the panic code. If something goes wrong, call and let it ring twice and then hang up. I'll call the cops.
Okay, grandma.
MY HEART IS POUNDING. MY PALMS ARE SWEATING.
WHICH PROBABLY ISN'T GOOD FOR THE SUPER SNOT.
I TELL MYSELF I CAN DO THIS. I TELL MYSELF I'M EXACTLY WHERE I WAS MEANT TO BE. IT'S LIKE THAT PERSIAN GUY RUMI SAID.
"WHEREVER YOU ARE...
"WAS CIRCLED ON A MAP FOR YOU."

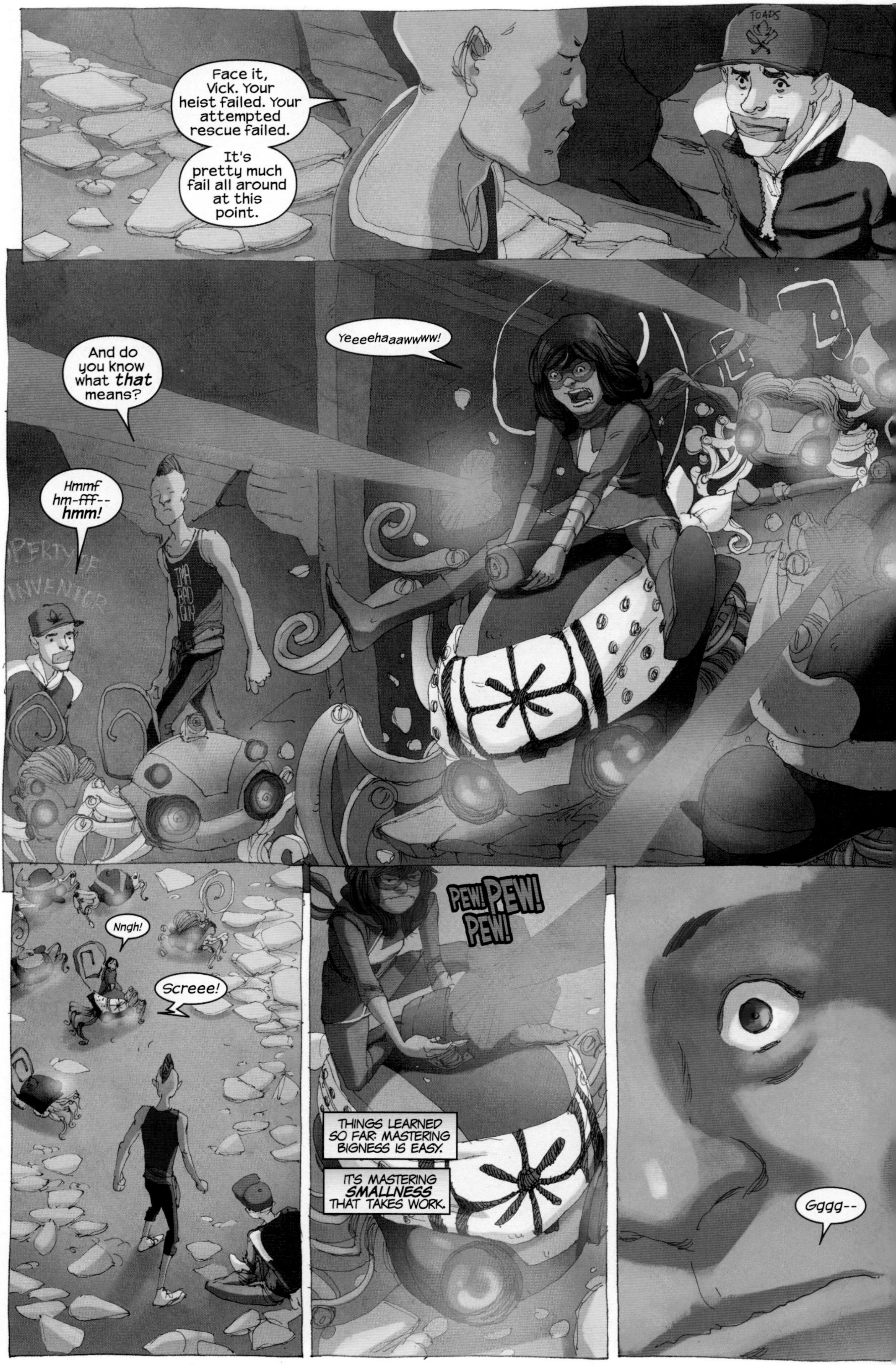

Face it, Vick. Your heist failed. Your attempted rescue failed.
It's pretty much fail all around at this point.
And do you know what *that* means?
Yeeeehaaawwww!
Hmmf hm-fff-- **hmm!**
Nngh!
Screee!
PEW! PEW! PEW!
THINGS LEARNED SO FAR: MASTERING BIGNESS IS EASY.
IT'S MASTERING ***SMALLNESS*** THAT TAKES WORK.
Gggg--

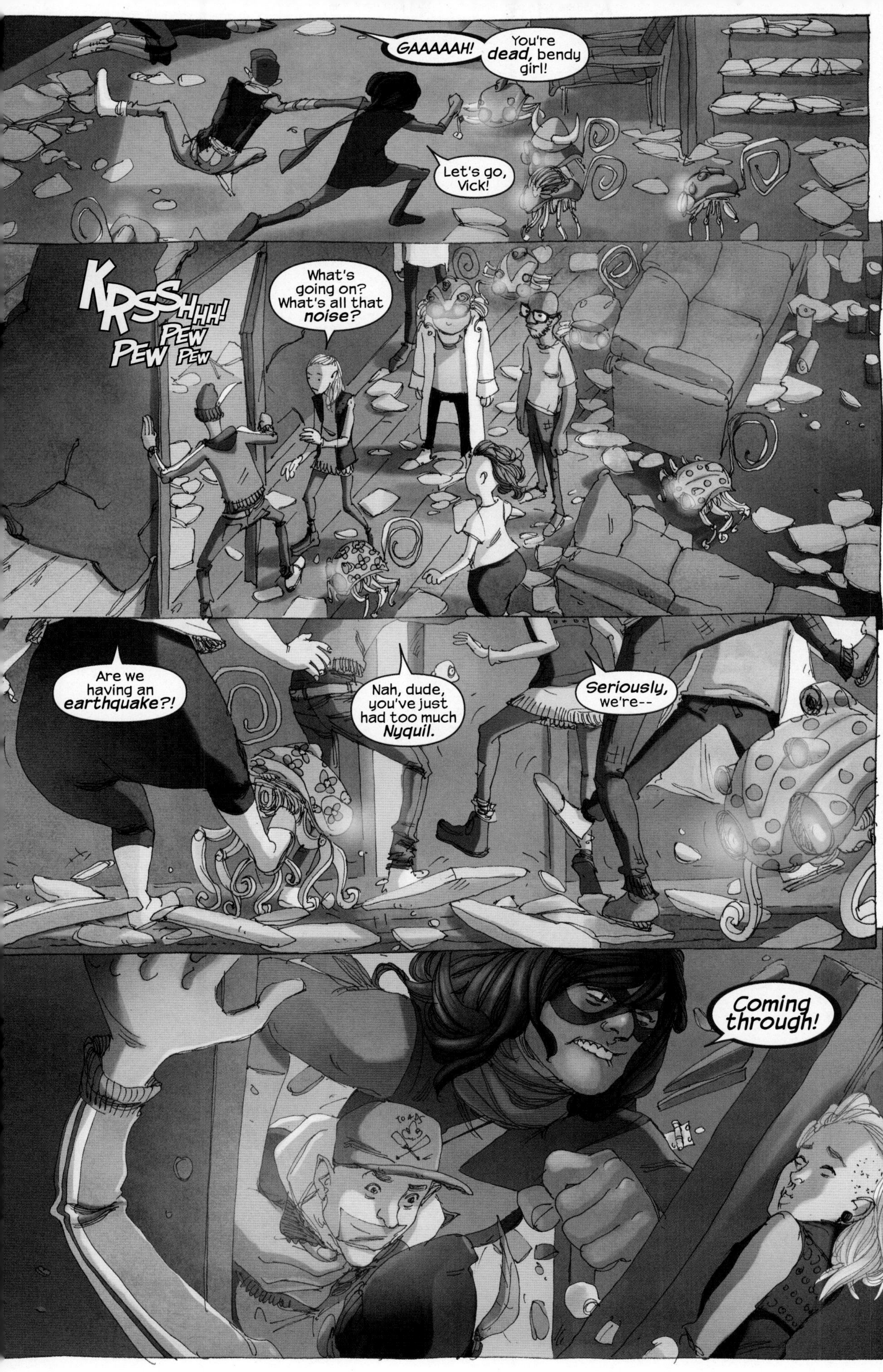
GAAAAAH!
You're dead, bendy girl!
Let's go, Vick!
KRSSHHH! PEW PEW PEW PEW
What's going on? What's all that noise?
Are we having an earthquake?!
Nah, dude, you've just had too much Nyquil.
Seriously, we're--
Coming through!

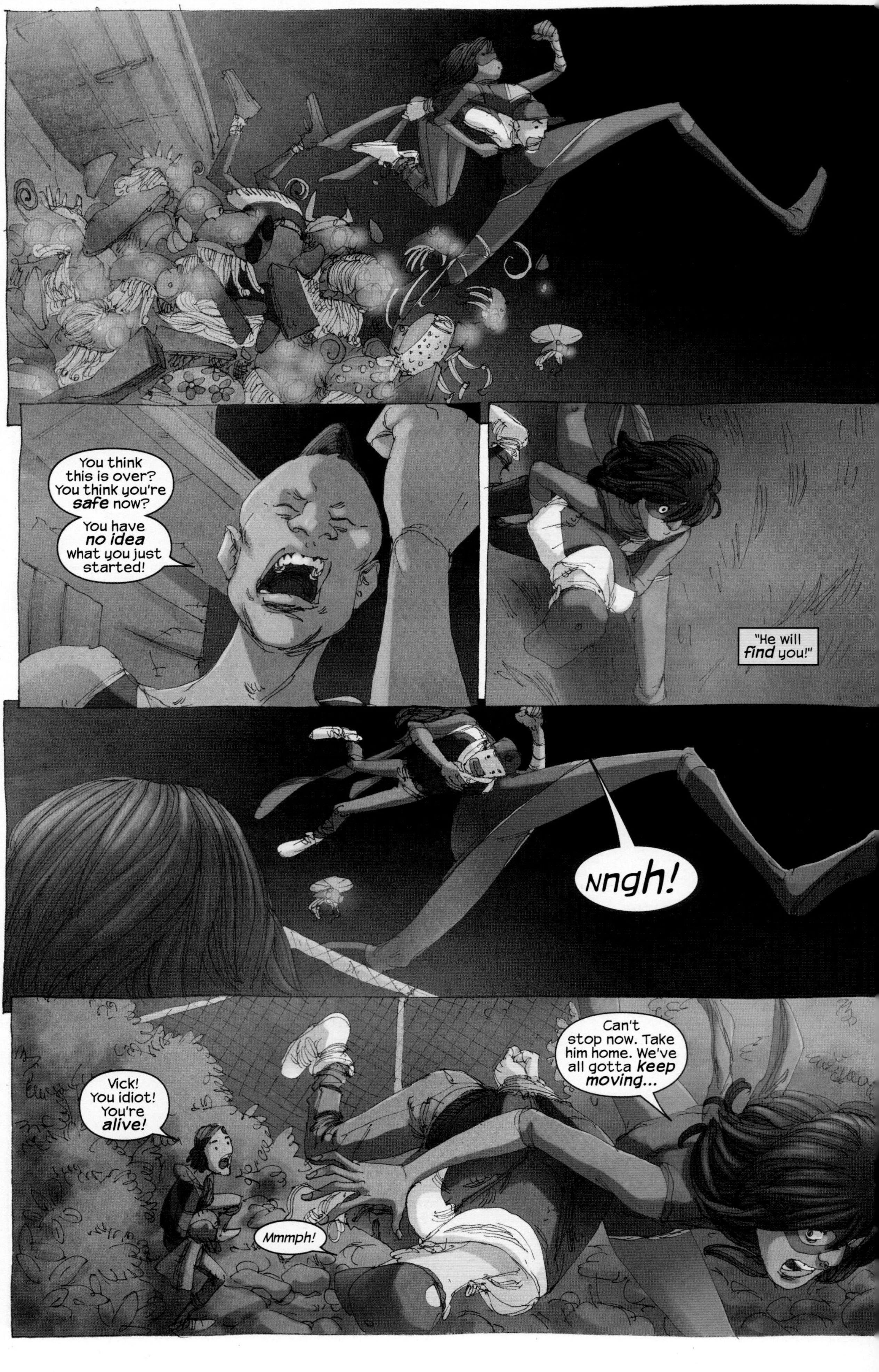
You think this is over? You think you're safe now?
You have no idea what you just started!
"He will find you!"
Nngh!
Vick! You idiot! You're alive!
Mmmph!
Can't stop now. Take him home. We've all gotta keep moving...

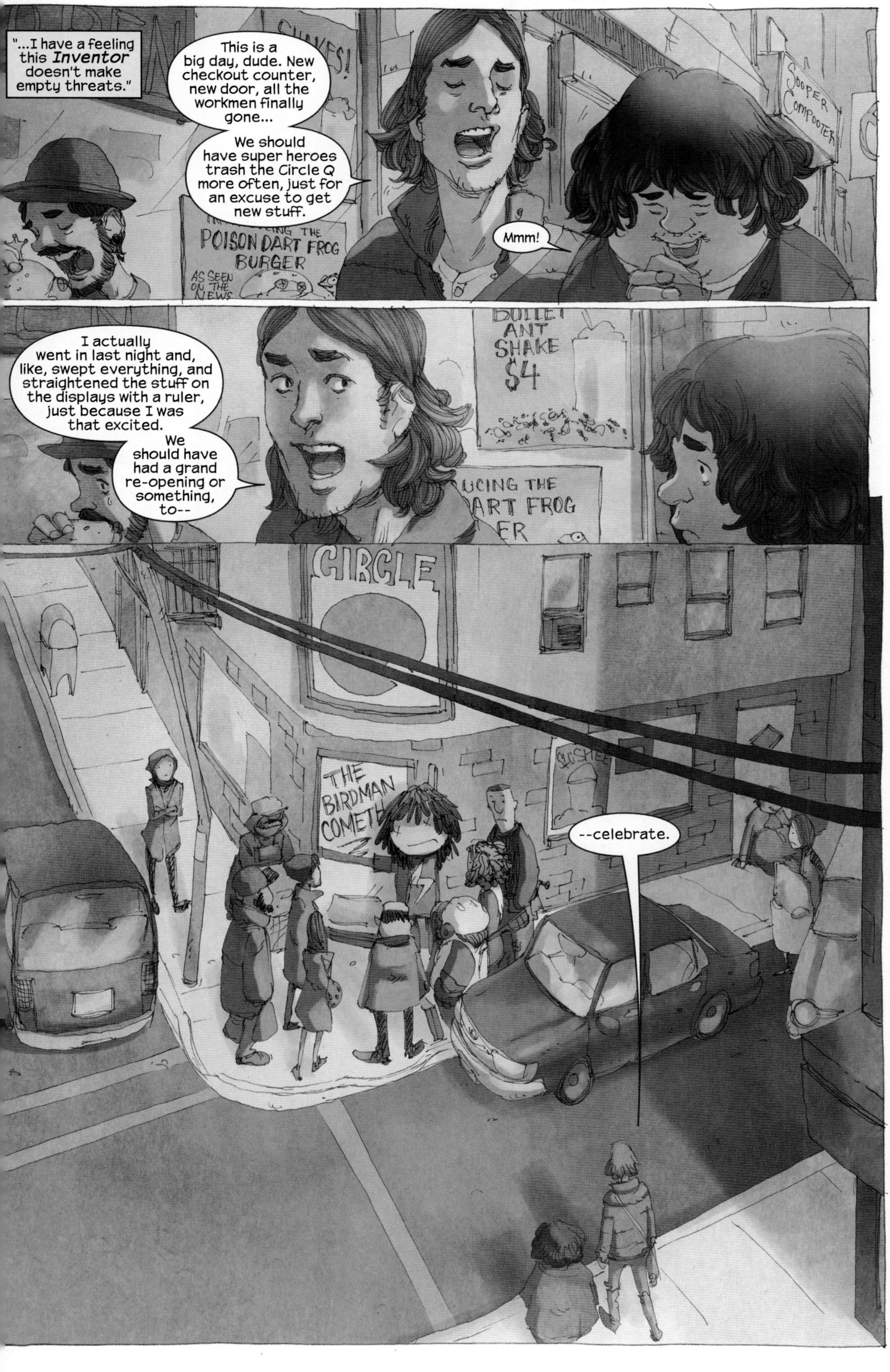
"...I have a feeling this *Inventor* doesn't make empty threats."
SHAKES!
This is a big day, dude. New checkout counter, new door, all the workmen finally gone...
We should have super heroes trash the Circle Q more often, just for an excuse to get new stuff.
Sooper Compooter
POISON DART FROG BURGER
AS SEEN ON THE NEWS
Mmm!
I actually went in last night and, like, swept everything, and straightened the stuff on the displays with a ruler, just because I was that excited.
We should have had a grand re-opening or something, to--
ANT SHAKE $4
CIRCLE
THE BIRDMAN COMETH
--celebrate.

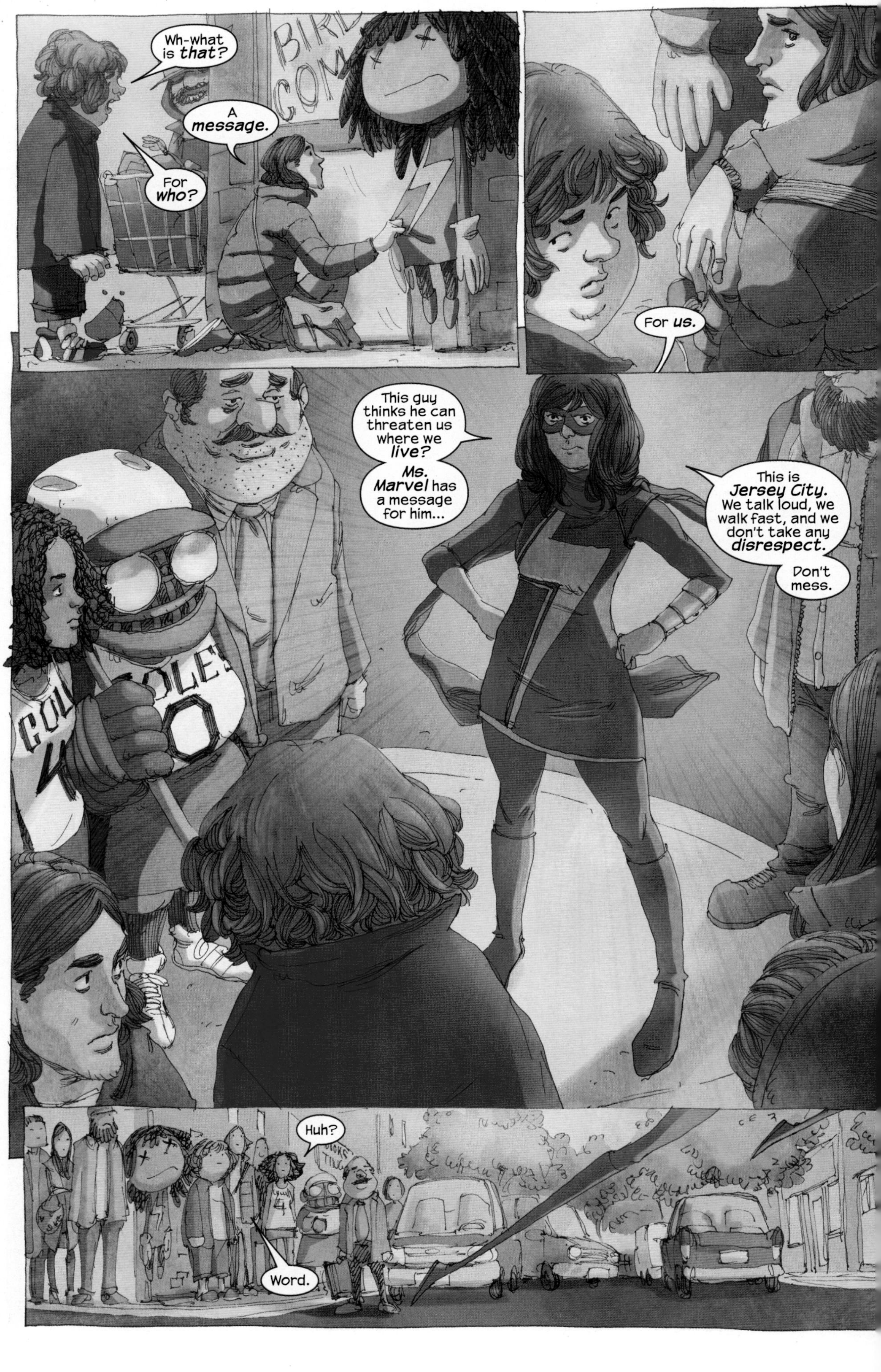
Wh-what is *that?*
A *message.*
For *who?*
For *us.*
This guy thinks he can threaten us where we *live?*
Ms. Marvel has a message for him...
This is *Jersey City.* We talk loud, we walk fast, and we don't take any *disrespect.*
Don't mess.
Huh?
Word.

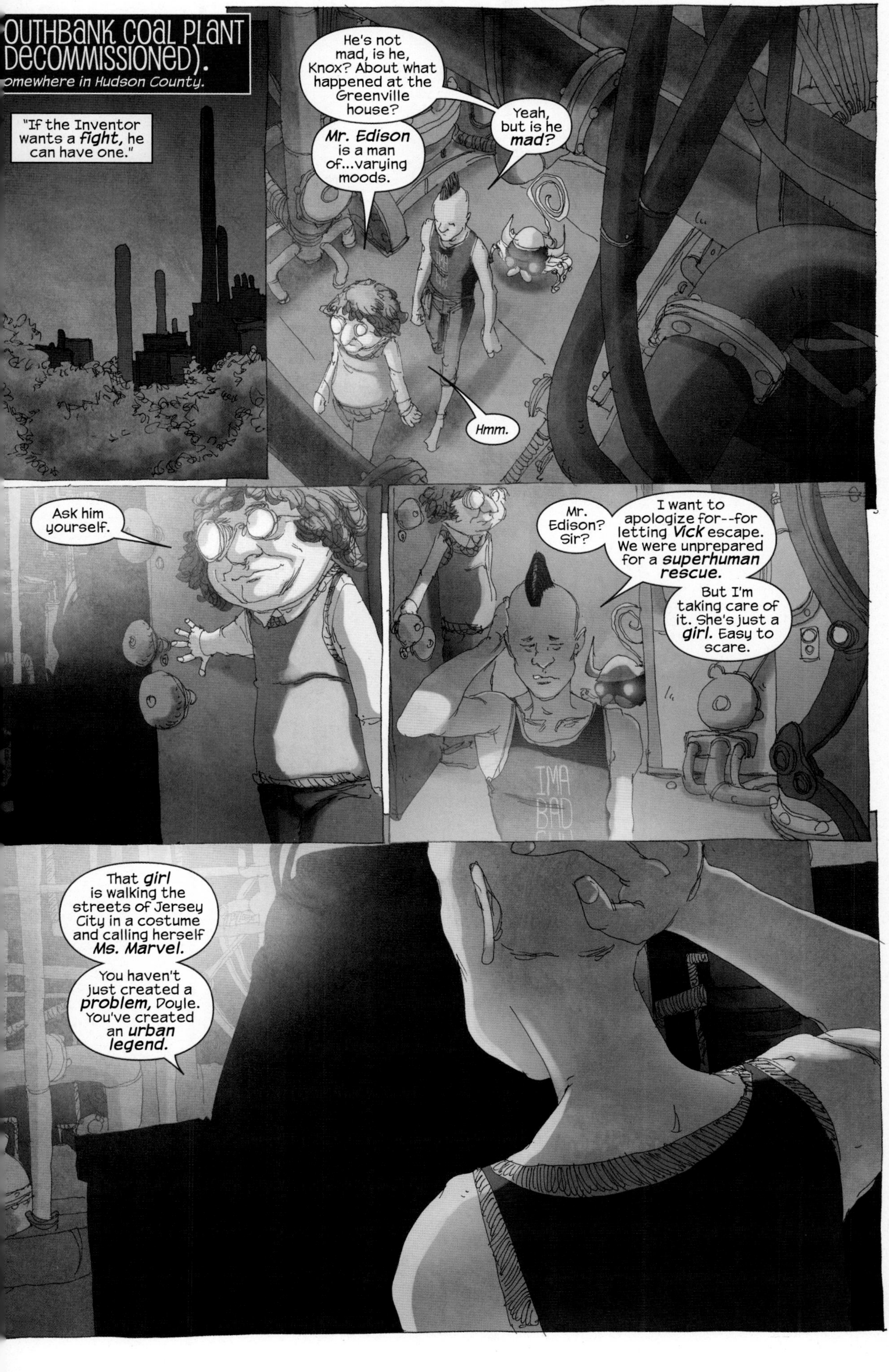
OUTHBANK COAL PLANT DECOMMISSIONED).
omewhere in Hudson County.
"If the Inventor wants a fight, he can have one."
He's not mad, is he, Knox? About what happened at the Greenville house?
Mr. Edison is a man of...varying moods.
Yeah, but is he mad?
Hmm.
Ask him yourself.
Mr. Edison? Sir?
I want to apologize for--for letting Vick escape. We were unprepared for a superhuman rescue.
But I'm taking care of it. She's just a girl. Easy to scare.
IMA BAD
That girl is walking the streets of Jersey City in a costume and calling herself Ms. Marvel.
You haven't just created a problem, Doyle. You've created an urban legend.

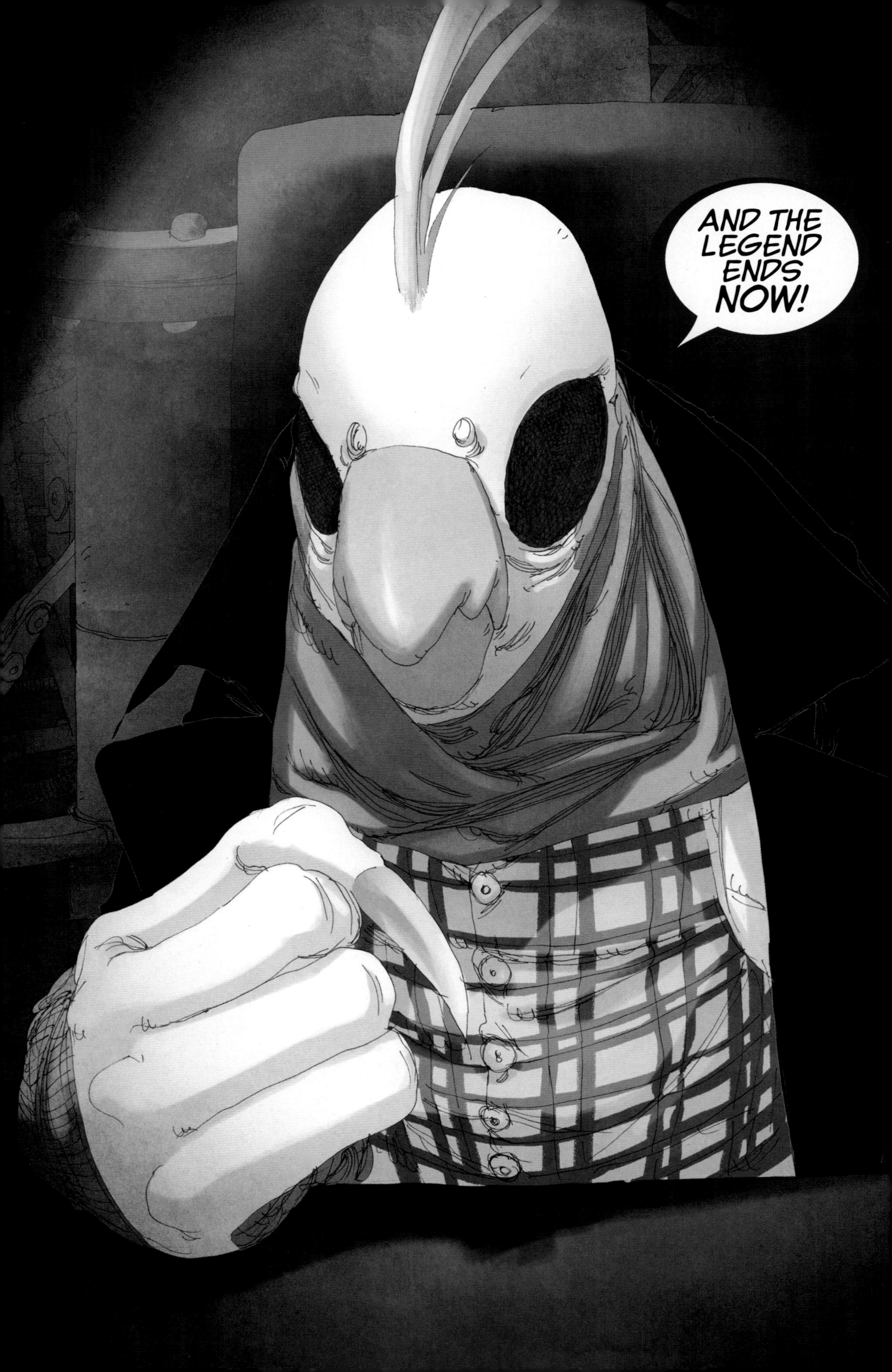
AND THE LEGEND ENDS NOW!

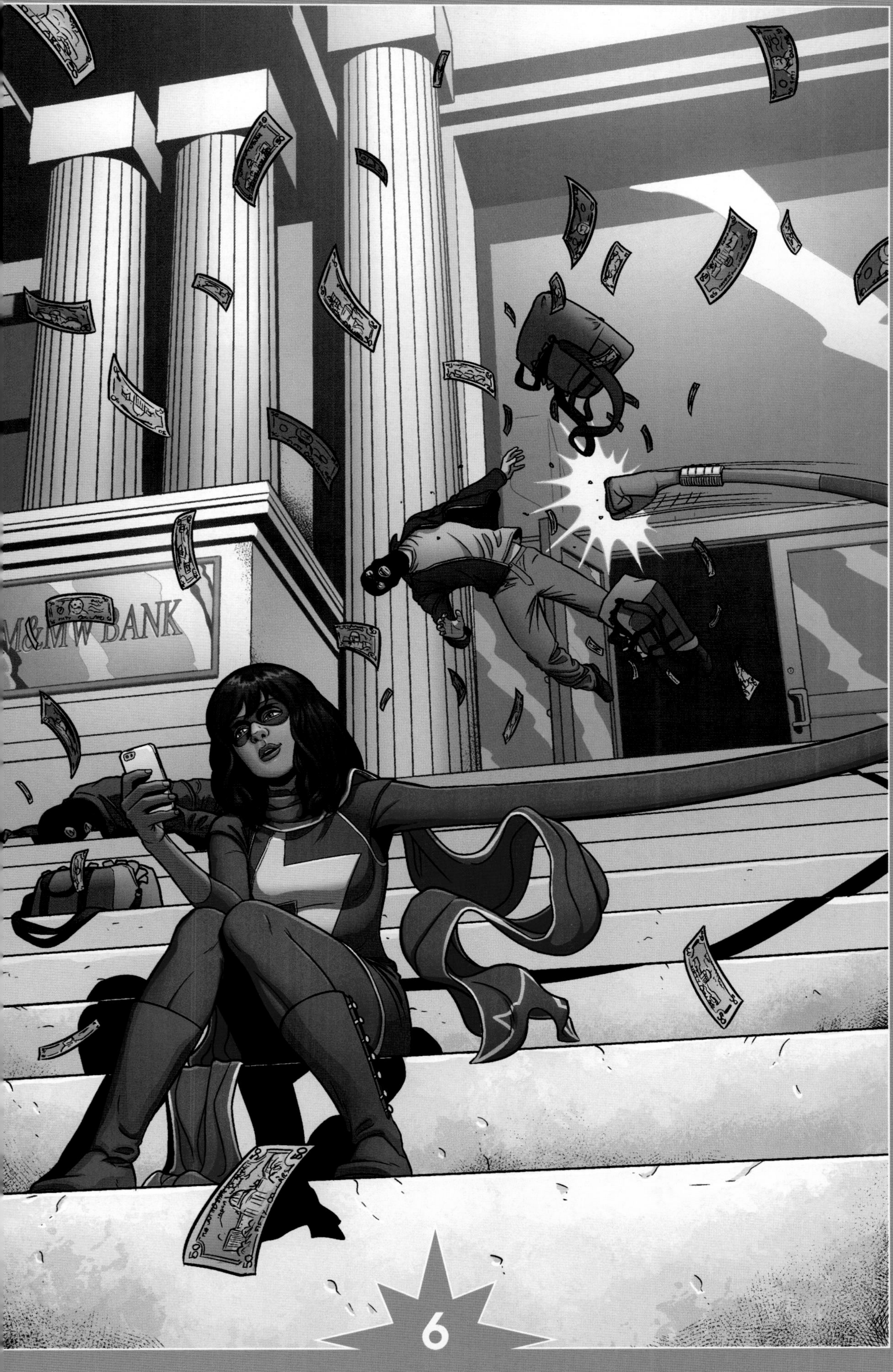
M&MW BANK
6

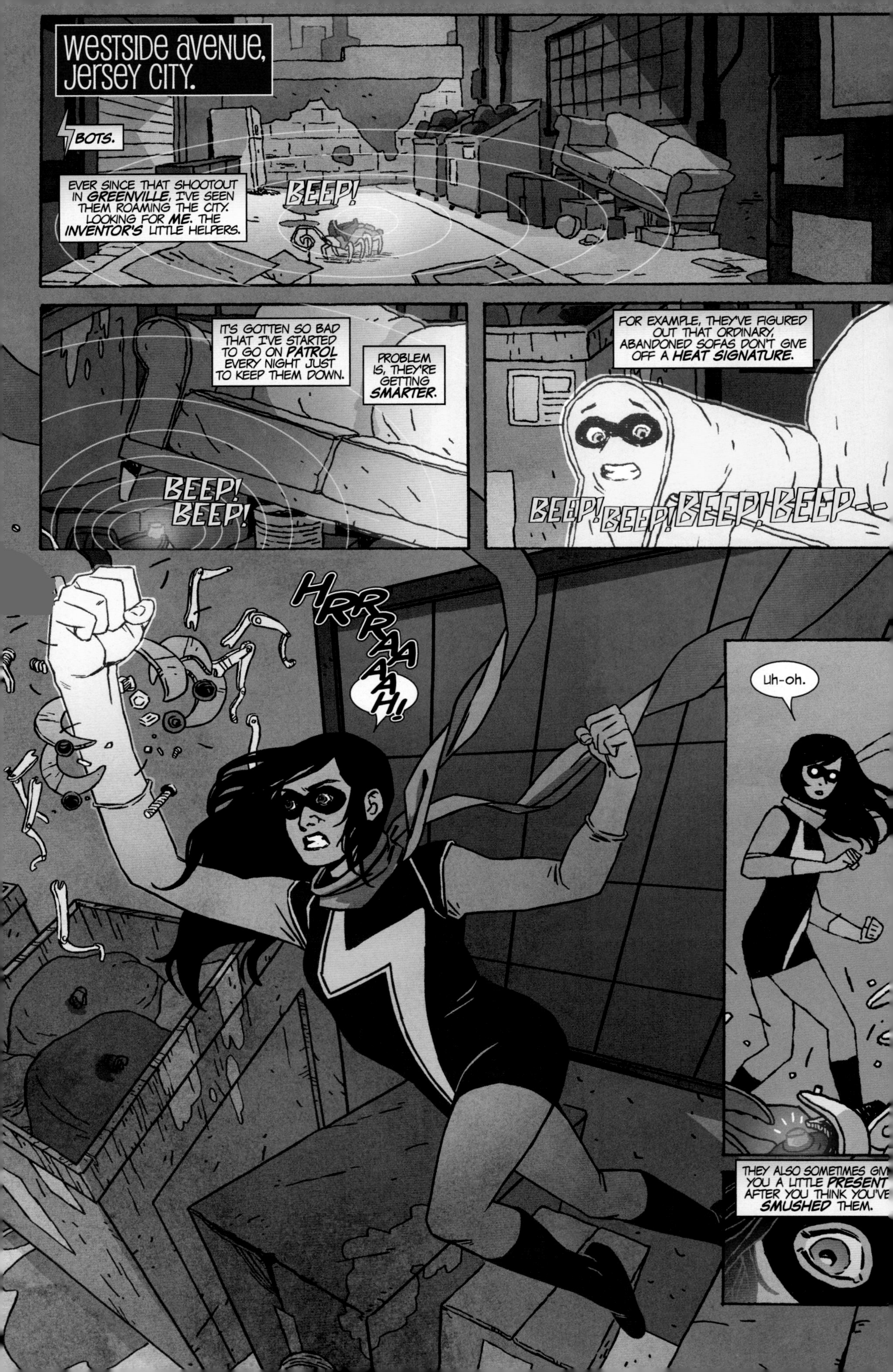
WESTSIDE AVENUE, JERSEY CITY.
BOTS.
EVER SINCE THAT SHOOTOUT IN GREENVILLE, I'VE SEEN THEM ROAMING THE CITY. LOOKING FOR ME. THE INVENTOR'S LITTLE HELPERS.
BEEP!
IT'S GOTTEN SO BAD THAT I'VE STARTED TO GO ON PATROL EVERY NIGHT JUST TO KEEP THEM DOWN.
PROBLEM IS, THEY'RE GETTING SMARTER.
BEEP! BEEP!
FOR EXAMPLE, THEY'VE FIGURED OUT THAT ORDINARY, ABANDONED SOFAS DON'T GIVE OFF A HEAT SIGNATURE.
BEEP! BEEP! BEEP! BEEP--
HRRRAAAAAH!
Uh-oh.
THEY ALSO SOMETIMES GIV YOU A LITTLE PRESENT AFTER YOU THINK YOU'VE SMUSHED THEM.

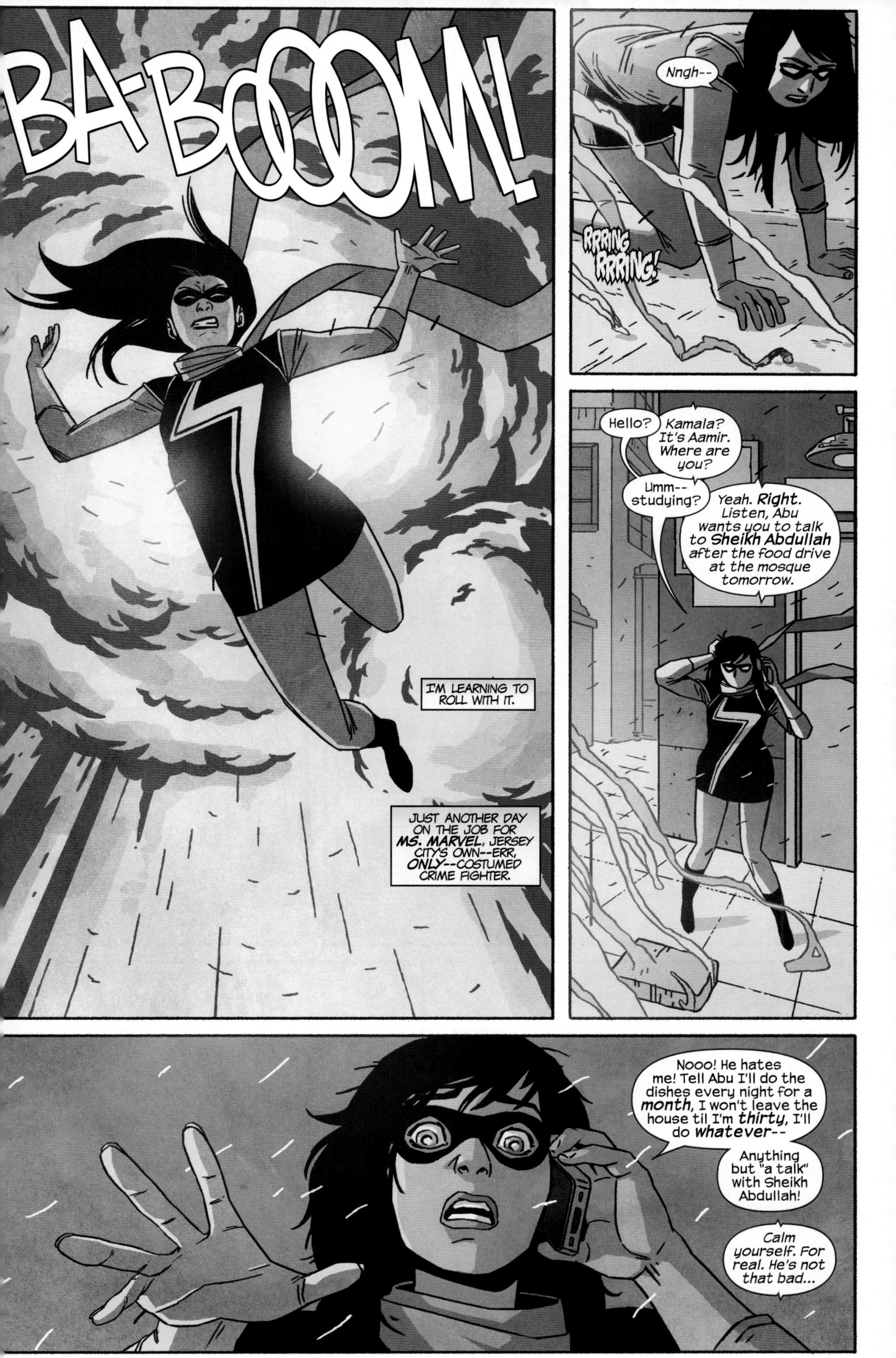
BA-BOOOOM!
I'M LEARNING TO ROLL WITH IT.
JUST ANOTHER DAY ON THE JOB FOR MS. MARVEL, JERSEY CITY'S OWN--ERR, ONLY--COSTUMED CRIME FIGHTER.
Nngh--
RRRING RRRING!
Hello?
Kamala? It's Aamir. Where are you?
Umm-- studying?
Yeah. Right. Listen, Abu wants you to talk to Sheikh Abdullah after the food drive at the mosque tomorrow.
Nooo! He hates me! Tell Abu I'll do the dishes every night for a month, I won't leave the house til I'm thirty, I'll do whatever--
Anything but "a talk" with Sheikh Abdullah!
Calm yourself. For real. He's not that bad...

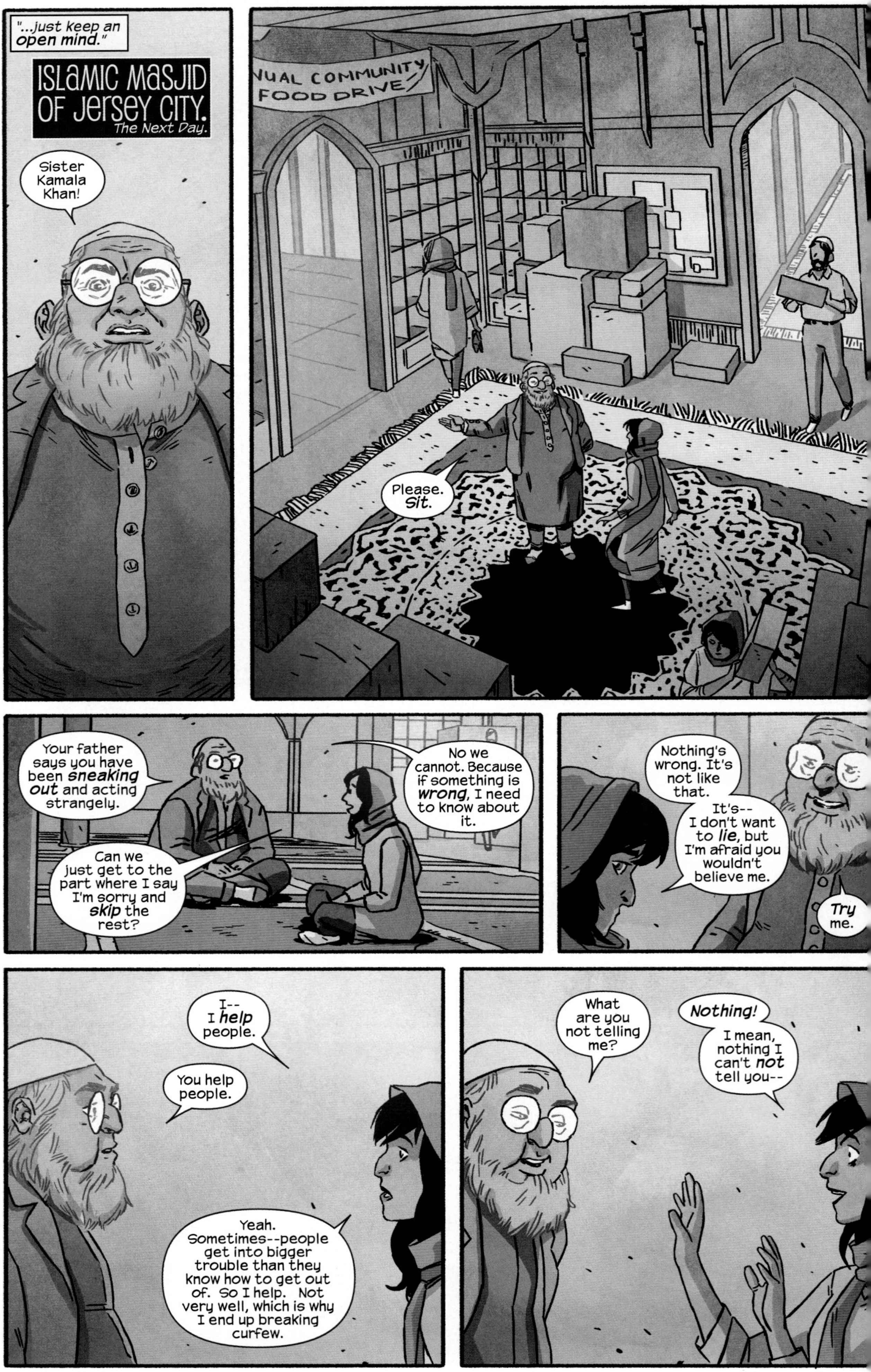
"...just keep an open mind."
ISLAMIC MASJID OF JERSEY CITY. The Next Day.
Sister Kamala Khan!
NUAL COMMUNITY FOOD DRIVE
Please. Sit.
Your father says you have been sneaking out and acting strangely.
Can we just get to the part where I say I'm sorry and skip the rest?
No we cannot. Because if something is wrong, I need to know about it.
Nothing's wrong. It's not like that.
It's-- I don't want to lie, but I'm afraid you wouldn't believe me.
Try me.
I-- I help people.
You help people.
Yeah. Sometimes--people get into bigger trouble than they know how to get out of. So I help. Not very well, which is why I end up breaking curfew.
What are you not telling me?
Nothing!
I mean, nothing I can't not tell you--

I don't **mean** to disobey Abu and Ammi. It's just that sometimes I **have to** in order to do the right thing.

I see.

Well, if you're not very **good** at it--**helping** people, that is-- perhaps you need a **teacher**.

A **teacher**?

Wait--you're **not** going to tell me to be a good girl, focus on my studies, and do istaghfar * or something?

If I told you that, you'd **ignore** me. I know how **headstrong** you are.

So instead, I will tell you to do what you are doing with as much **honor** and **skill** as you can.

*Repentance.

I can't believe it. I thought you were going to warn me about **Satan** and **boys**.

I've been giving **youth lectures** at this mosque for ten years. If I still have to warn you about Satan and boys, I should lose my job.

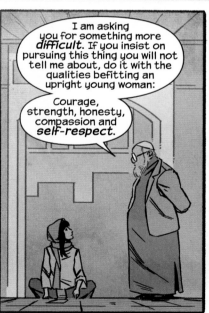

I am asking you for something more **difficult**. If you insist on pursuing this thing you will not tell me about, do it with the qualities befitting an upright young woman:

Courage, strength, honesty, compassion and **self-respect**.

Do we have a **deal**?

Yeah. I mean **yes**, hazrat sahib. Thank you, hazrat sahib.

But--about finding a **teacher**. How am I supposed to find someone to teach me how to--you know-- be better? At **helping**?

As the ancient saying goes:

"When the student is ready...

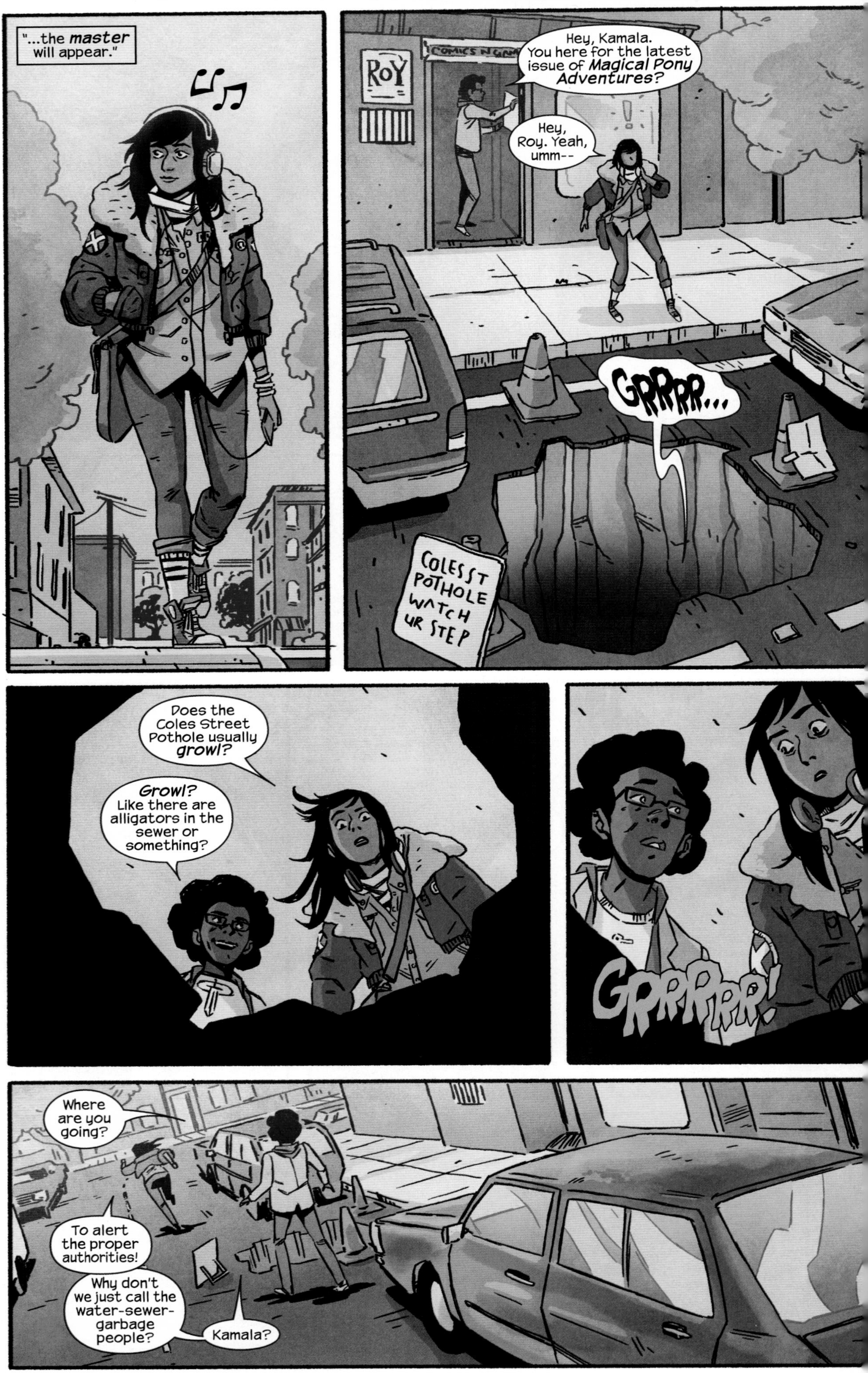
"...the *master* will appear."
Hey, Kamala. You here for the latest issue of *Magical Pony Adventures?*
Hey, Roy. Yeah, umm--
ROY
GRRRR...
COLES ST POTHOLE WATCH UR STEP
Does the Coles Street Pothole usually *growl?*
Growl? Like there are alligators in the sewer or something?
GRRRRRR!
Where are you going?
To alert the proper authorities!
Why don't we just call the water-sewer-garbage people?
Kamala?

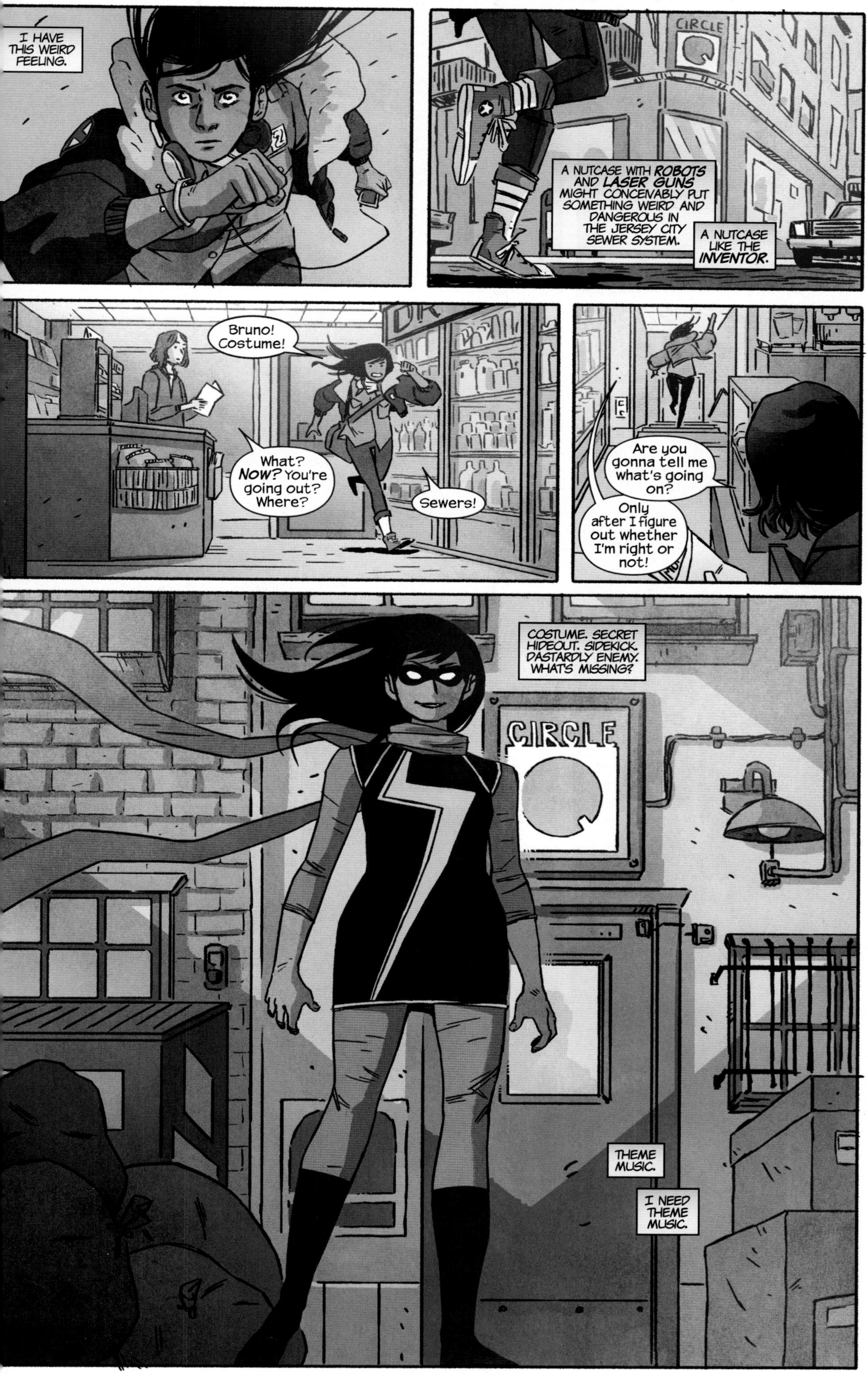

I HAVE THIS WEIRD FEELING.
A NUTCASE WITH ROBOTS AND LASER GUNS MIGHT CONCENVABLY PUT SOMETHING WEIRD AND DANGEROUS IN THE JERSEY CITY SEWER SYSTEM.
A NUTCASE LIKE THE INVENTOR.
CIRCLE
Bruno! Costume!
What? NOW? You're going out? Where?
Sewers!
Are you gonna tell me what's going on?
Only after I figure out whether I'm right or not!
COSTUME. SECRET HIDEOUT. SIDEKICK. DASTARDLY ENEMY. WHAT'S MISSING?
CIRCLE
THEME MUSIC.
I NEED THEME MUSIC.

IT'S DARK. IT'S HUMID. AND THERE'S A STRANGE SMELL--LIKE STUFF *DECOMPOSING* AND OTHER STUFF *LIVING* IN THE DECOMPOSING STUFF.

BUT NO ALLIGATORS.

I'M STARTING TO FEEL A LITTLE BIT SILLY.

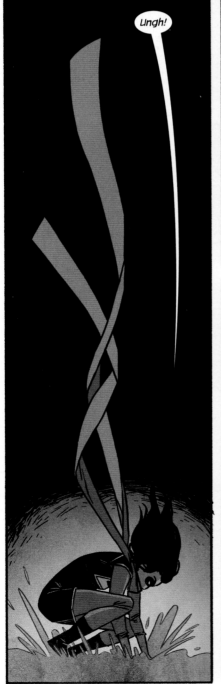

Ungh!

THE INVENTOR SEEMS PRETTY CRAZY, BUT HE CAN'T BE *THAT--*

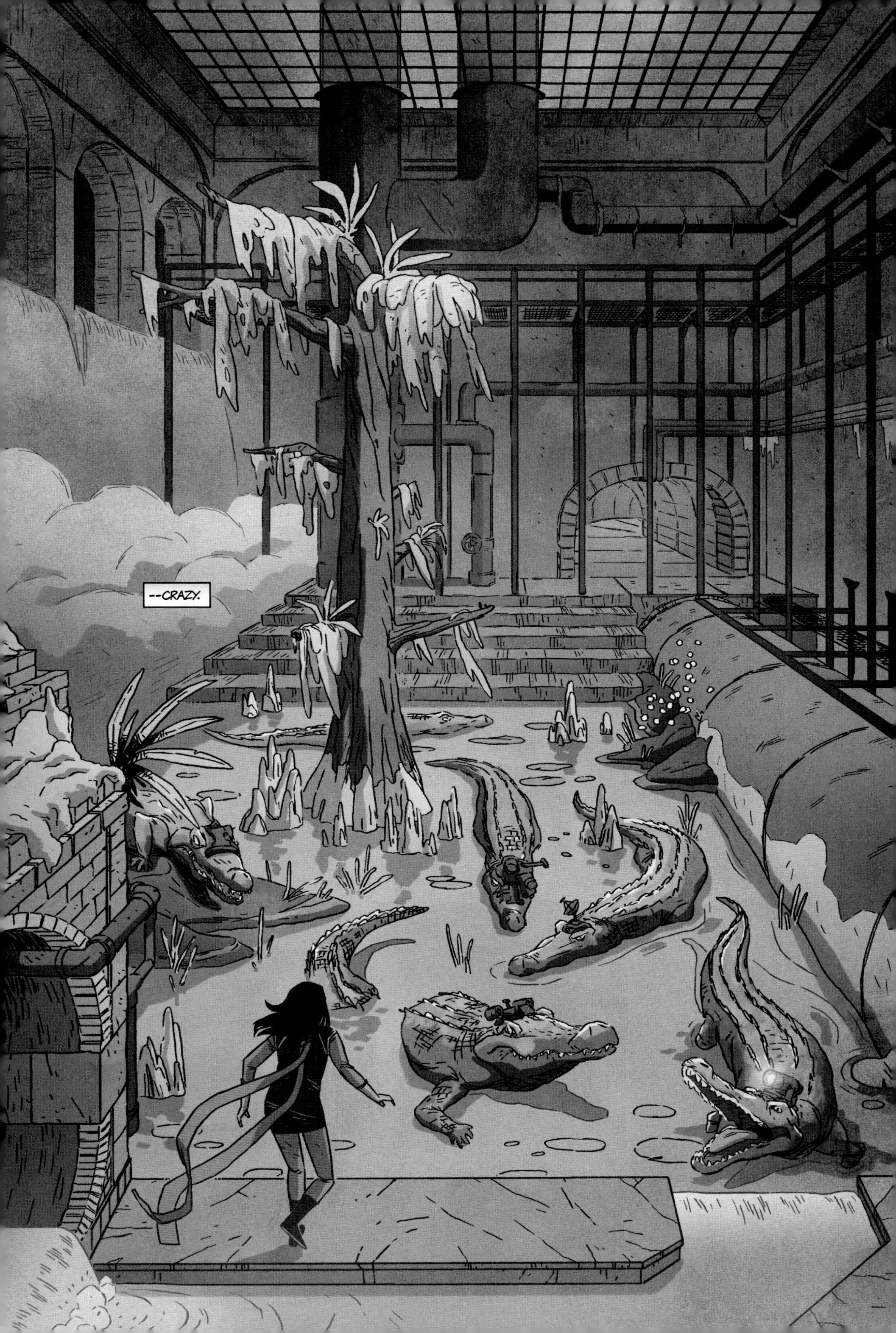
--CRAZY.

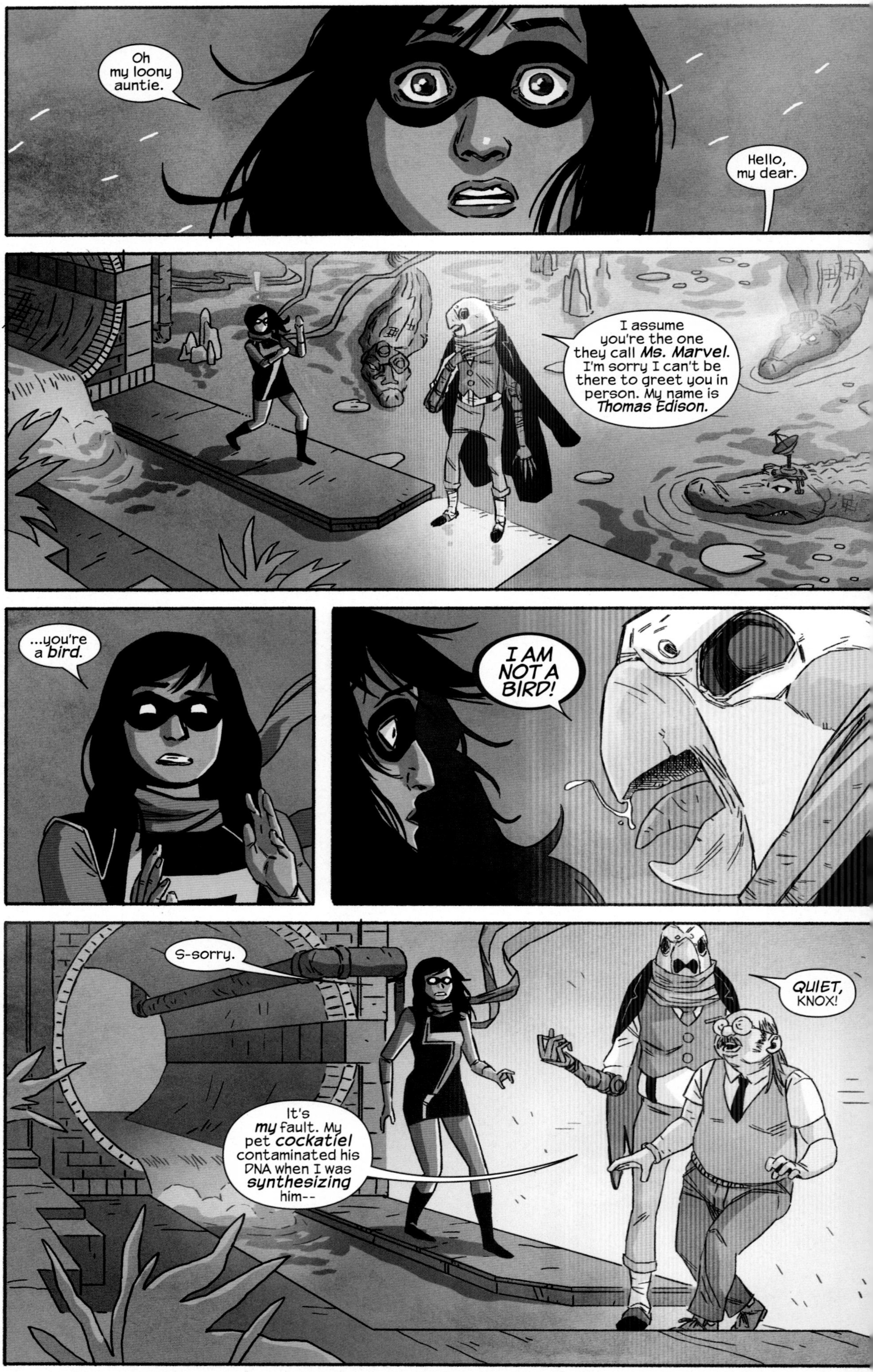

Oh my loony auntie.
Hello, my dear.
I assume you're the one they call Ms. Marvel. I'm sorry I can't be there to greet you in person. My name is Thomas Edison.
...you're a bird.
I AM NOT A BIRD!
S-sorry.
QUIET, KNOX!
It's my fault. My pet cockatiel contaminated his DNA when I was synthesizing him--

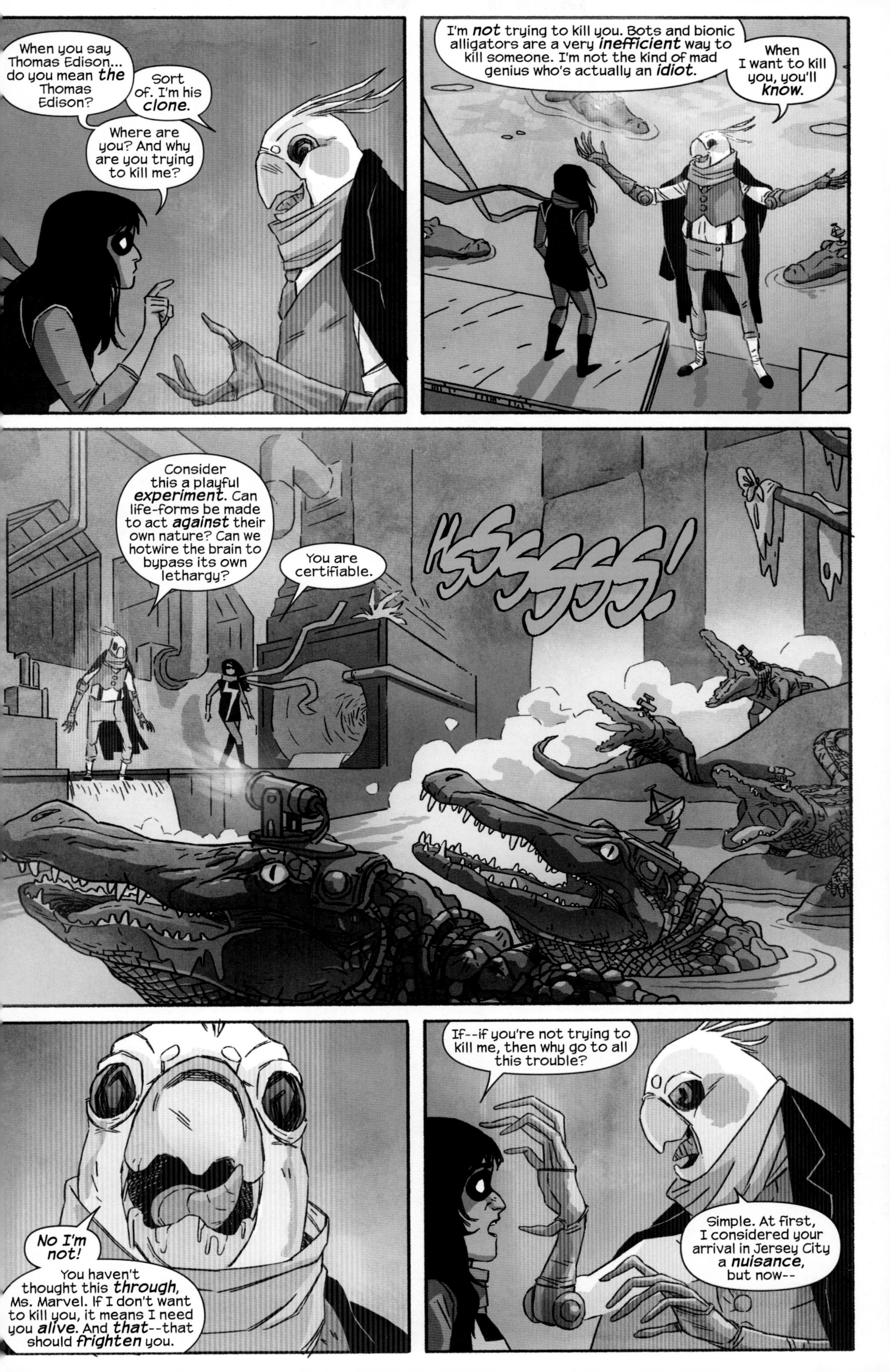
When you say Thomas Edison... do you mean the Thomas Edison?
Sort of. I'm his clone.
Where are you? And why are you trying to kill me?
I'm not trying to kill you. Bots and bionic alligators are a very inefficient way to kill someone. I'm not the kind of mad genius who's actually an idiot.
When I want to kill you, you'll know.
Consider this a playful experiment. Can life-forms be made to act against their own nature? Can we hotwire the brain to bypass its own lethargy?
You are certifiable.
HSSSSSS!
No I'm not!
You haven't thought this through, Ms. Marvel. If I don't want to kill you, it means I need you alive. And that--that should frighten you.
If--if you're not trying to kill me, then why go to all this trouble?
Simple. At first, I considered your arrival in Jersey City a nuisance, but now--

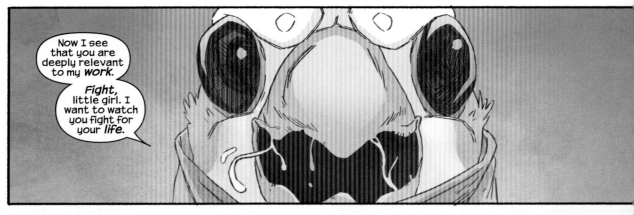

Now I see that you are deeply relevant to my *work*.

Fight, little girl. I want to watch you fight for your *life.*

Sir! Infrared has detected someone else approaching the holding tank!

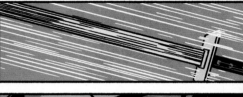

Someone? What do you mean, *"someone?"* This place was supposed to be locked down!

GREAT. MORE BAD GUYS? WITH *SWORDS?*

HOW MUCH WORSE CAN THIS DAY POSSIBLY GET?

GET READY TO *LOSE,* WEIRD SHORT DUDE. I'VE GOT +10 HEALS.

POWER ATTACK!

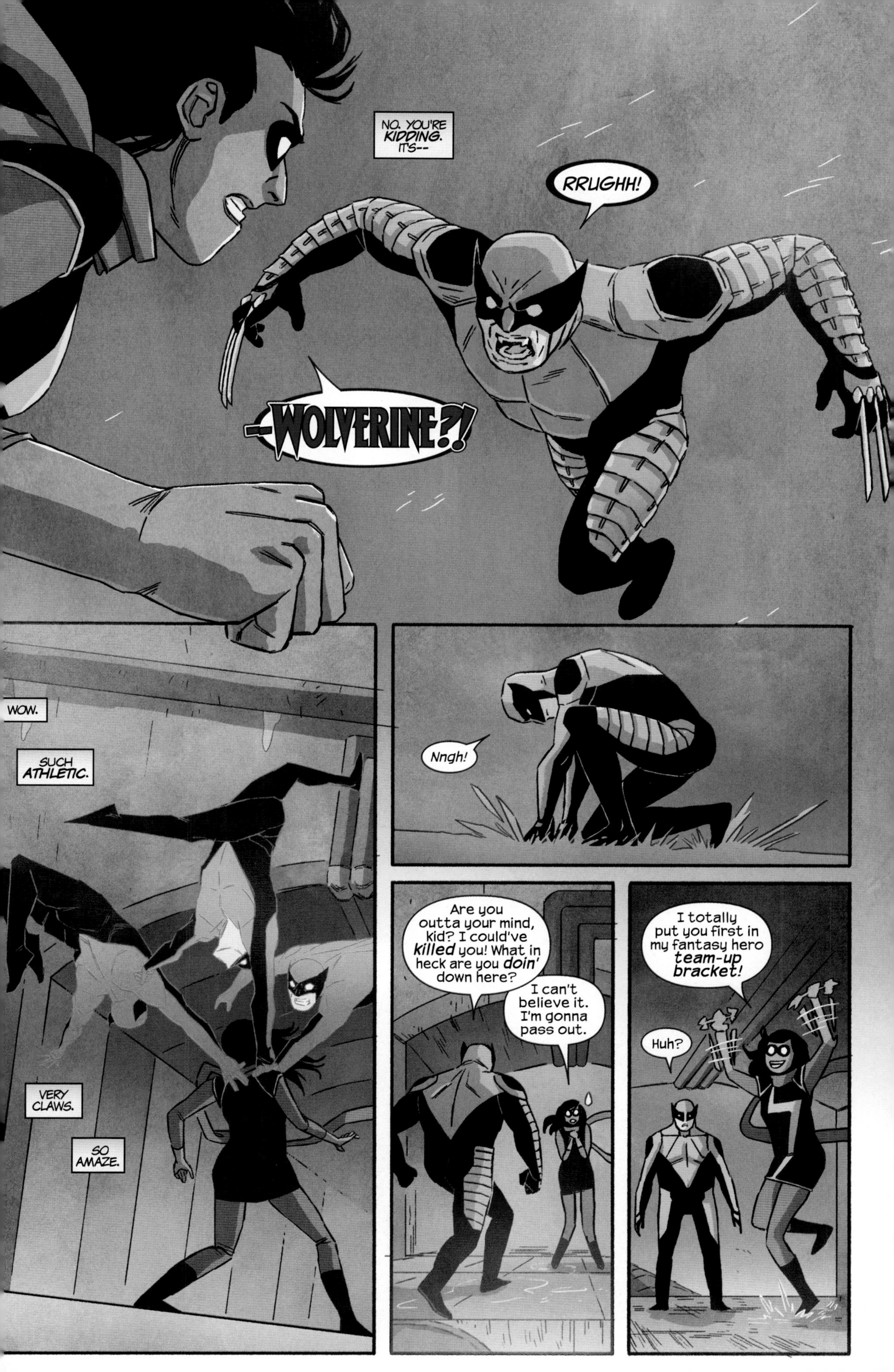
NO. YOU'RE KIDDING. IT'S--
RRUGHH!
--WOLVERINE?!
WOW.
SUCH ATHLETIC.
VERY CLAWS.
SO AMAZE.
Nngh!
Are you outta your mind, kid? I could've killed you! What in heck are you doin' down here?
I can't believe it. I'm gonna pass out.
I totally put you first in my fantasy hero team-up bracket!
Huh?

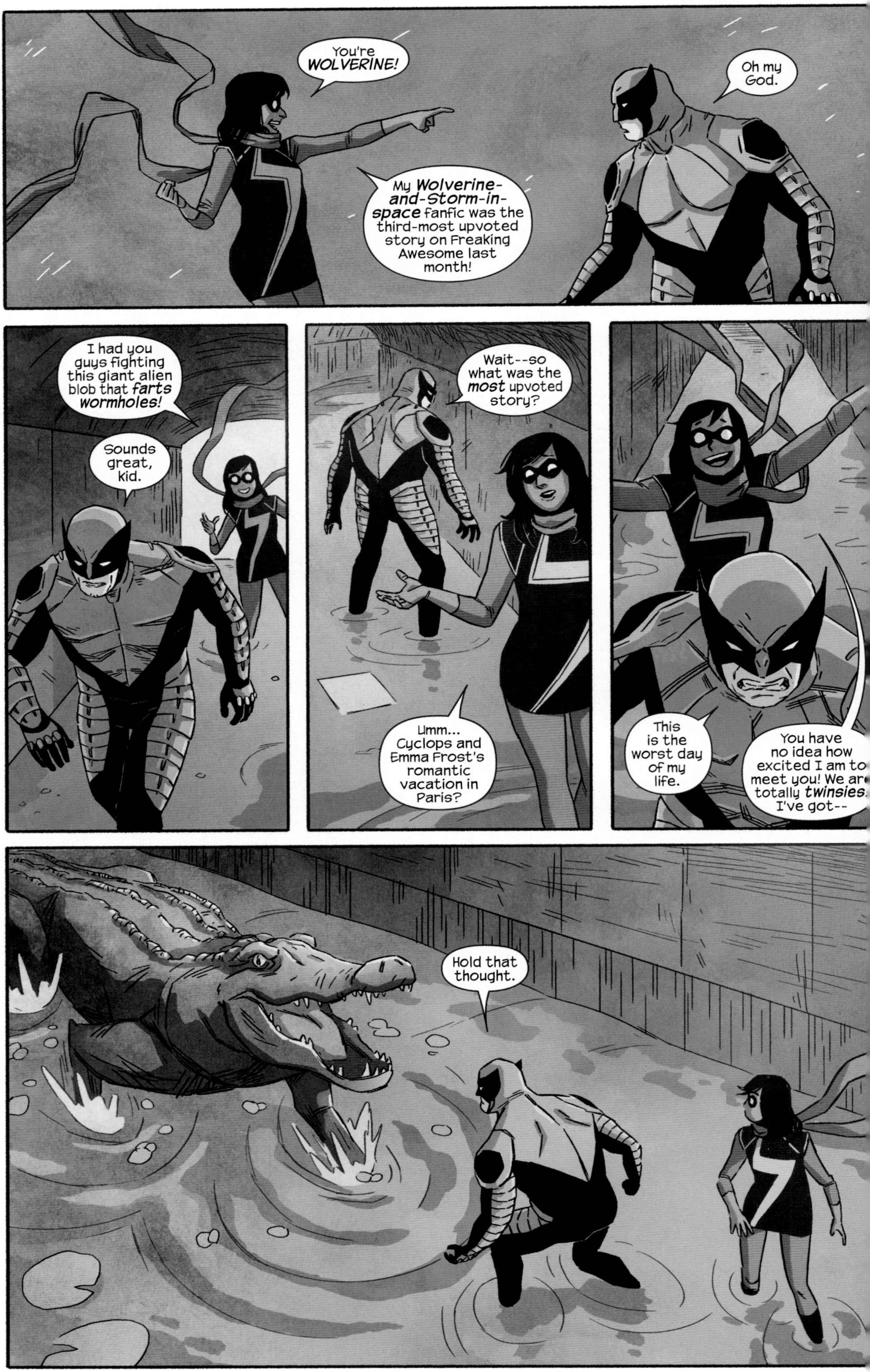
You're *WOLVERINE!*
My *Wolverine-and-Storm-in-space* fanfic was the third-most upvoted story on Freaking Awesome last month!
Oh my God.
I had you guys fighting this giant alien blob that *farts wormholes!*
Sounds great, kid.
Wait--so what was the *most* upvoted story?
Umm... Cyclops and Emma Frost's romantic vacation in Paris?
This is the worst day of my life.
You have no idea how excited I am to meet you! We ar totally *twinsies* I've got--
Hold that thought.

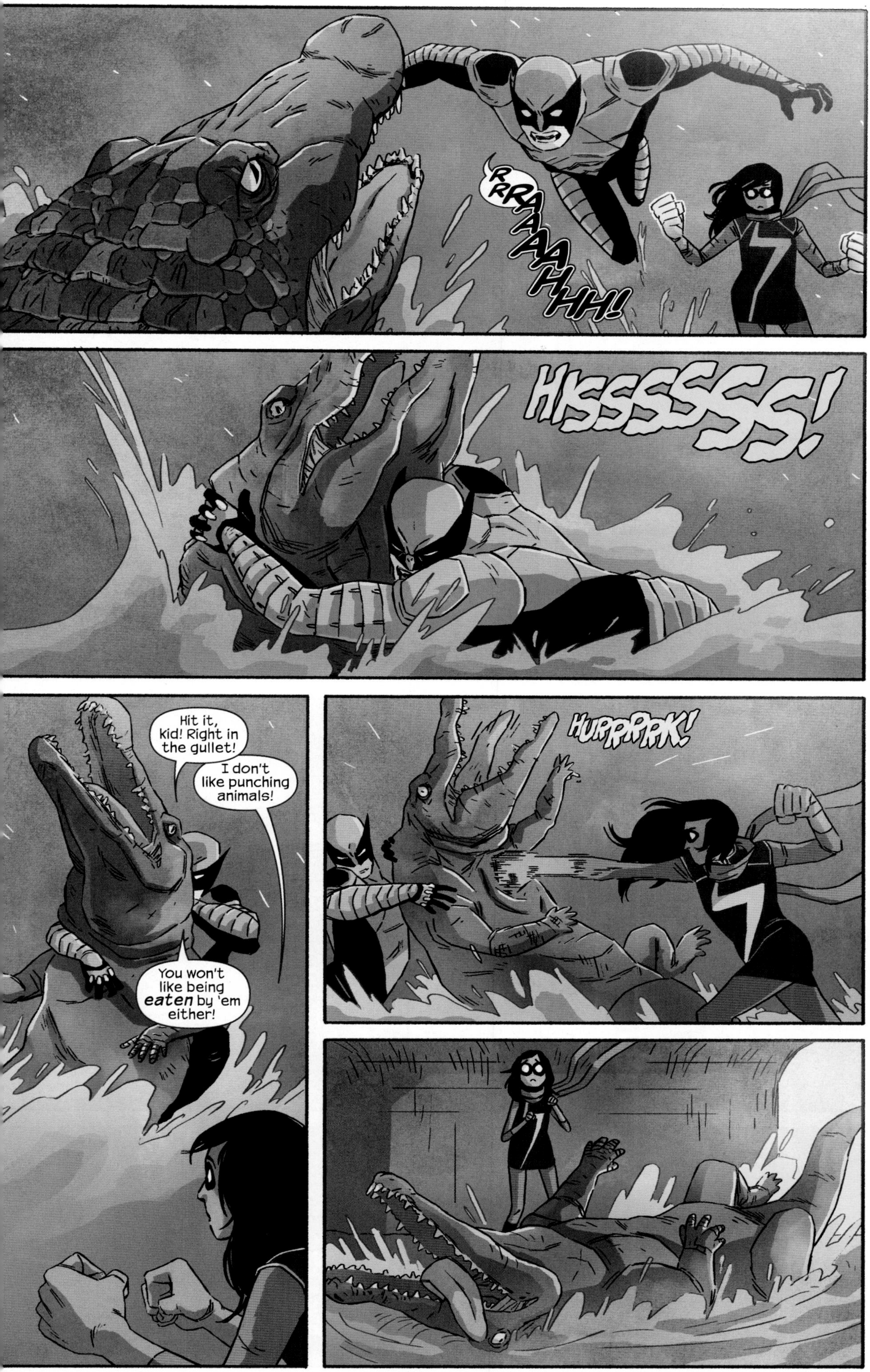
RRRAAAHHH!
HISSSSSS!
Hit it, kid! Right in the gullet!
I don't like punching animals!
You won't like being eaten by 'em either!
HURRRRK!

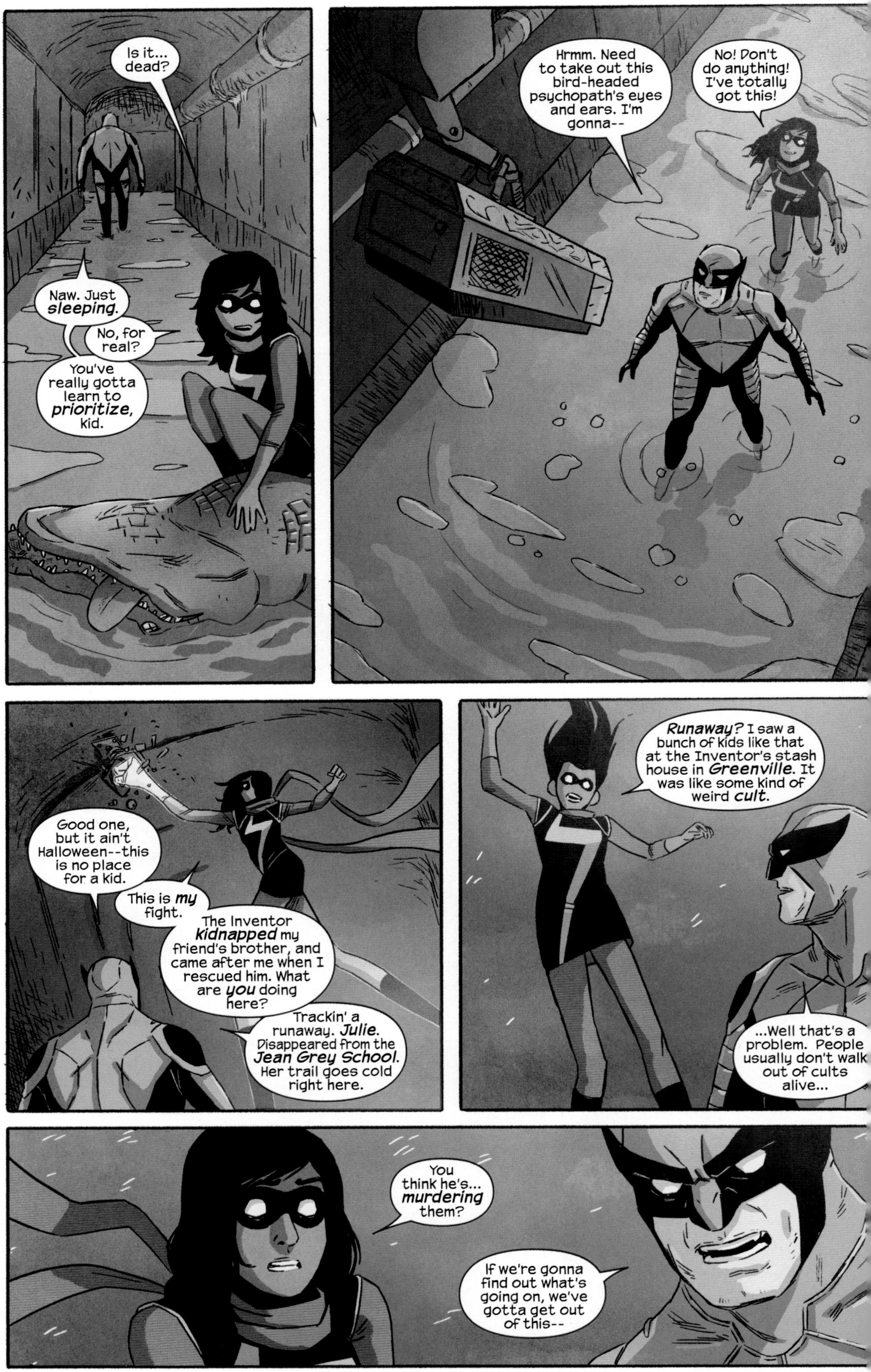

Is it... dead?
Naw. Just *sleeping*.
No, for real?
You've really gotta learn to *prioritize*, kid.
Hrmm. Need to take out this bird-headed psychopath's eyes and ears. I'm gonna--
No! Don't do anything! I've totally got this!
Good one, but it ain't Halloween--this is no place for a kid.
This is *my* fight.
The Inventor *kidnapped* my friend's brother, and came after me when I rescued him. What are *you* doing here?
Trackin' a runaway. *Julie*. Disappeared from the *Jean Grey School*. Her trail goes cold right here.
Runaway? I saw a bunch of kids like that at the Inventor's stash house in *Greenville*. It was like some kind of weird *cult*.
...Well that's a problem. People usually don't walk out of cults alive...
You think he's... *murdering* them?
If we're gonna find out what's going on, we've gotta get out of this--

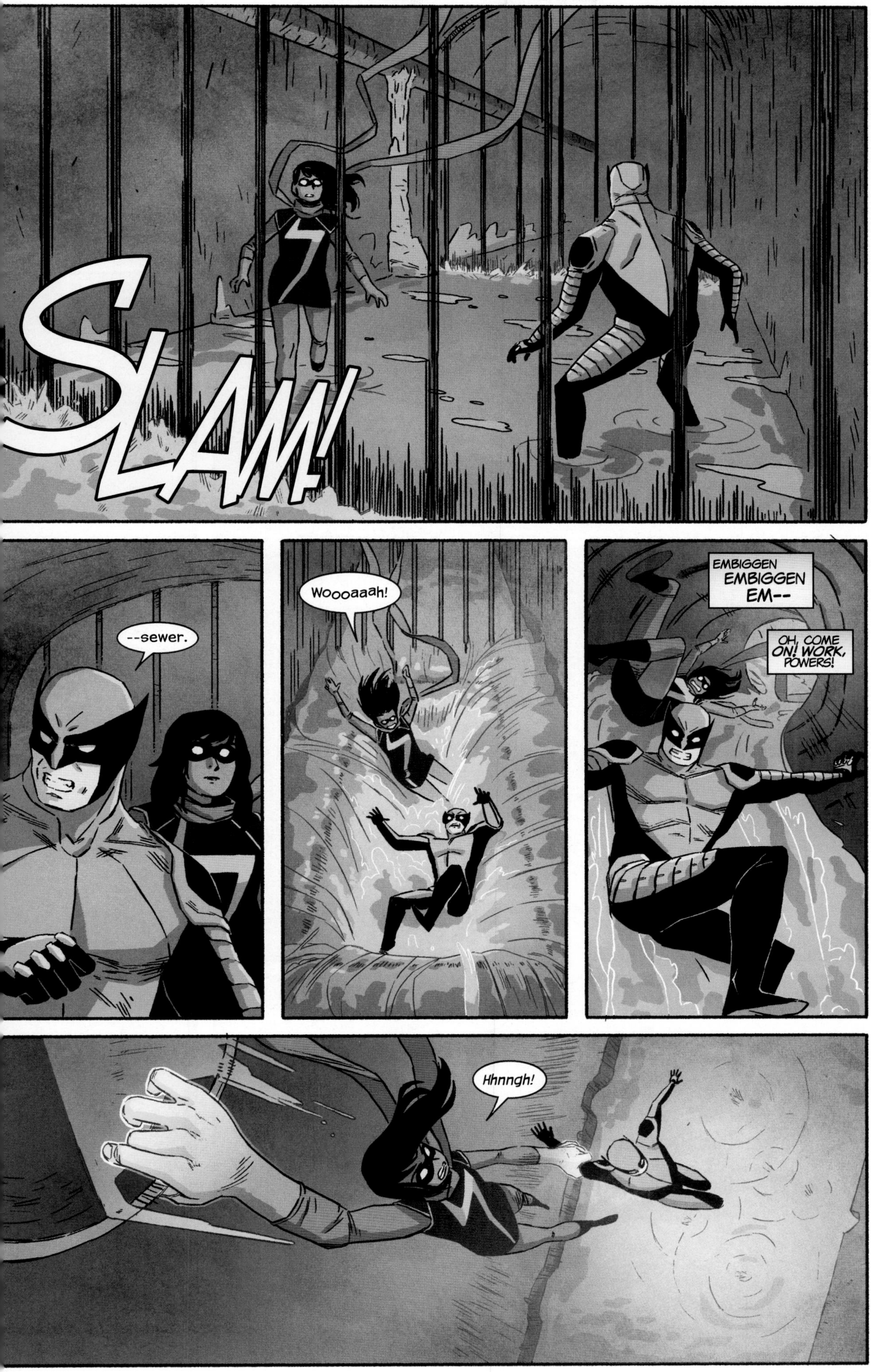
SLAM!
--sewer.
Woooaaah!
EMBIGGEN EMBIGGEN EM--
OH, COME ON! WORK, POWERS!
Hhnngh!

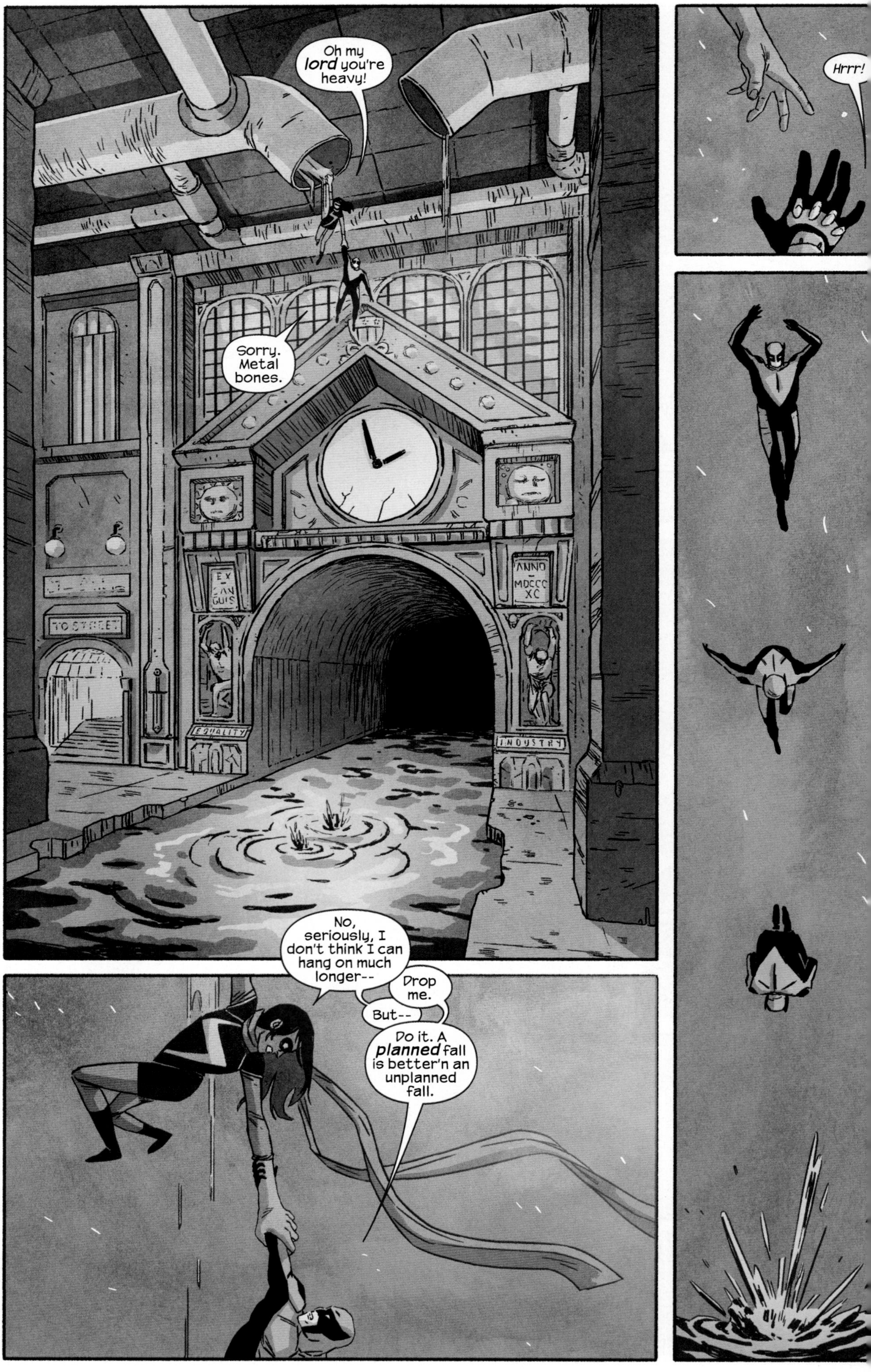
Oh my *lord* you're heavy!
Sorry. Metal bones.
EX SANGUIS
ANNO MDCCCXC
TO STREET
EQUALITY
INDUSTRY
No, seriously, I don't think I can hang on much longer--
Drop me.
But--
Do it. A *planned* fall is better'n an unplanned fall.
Hrrr!

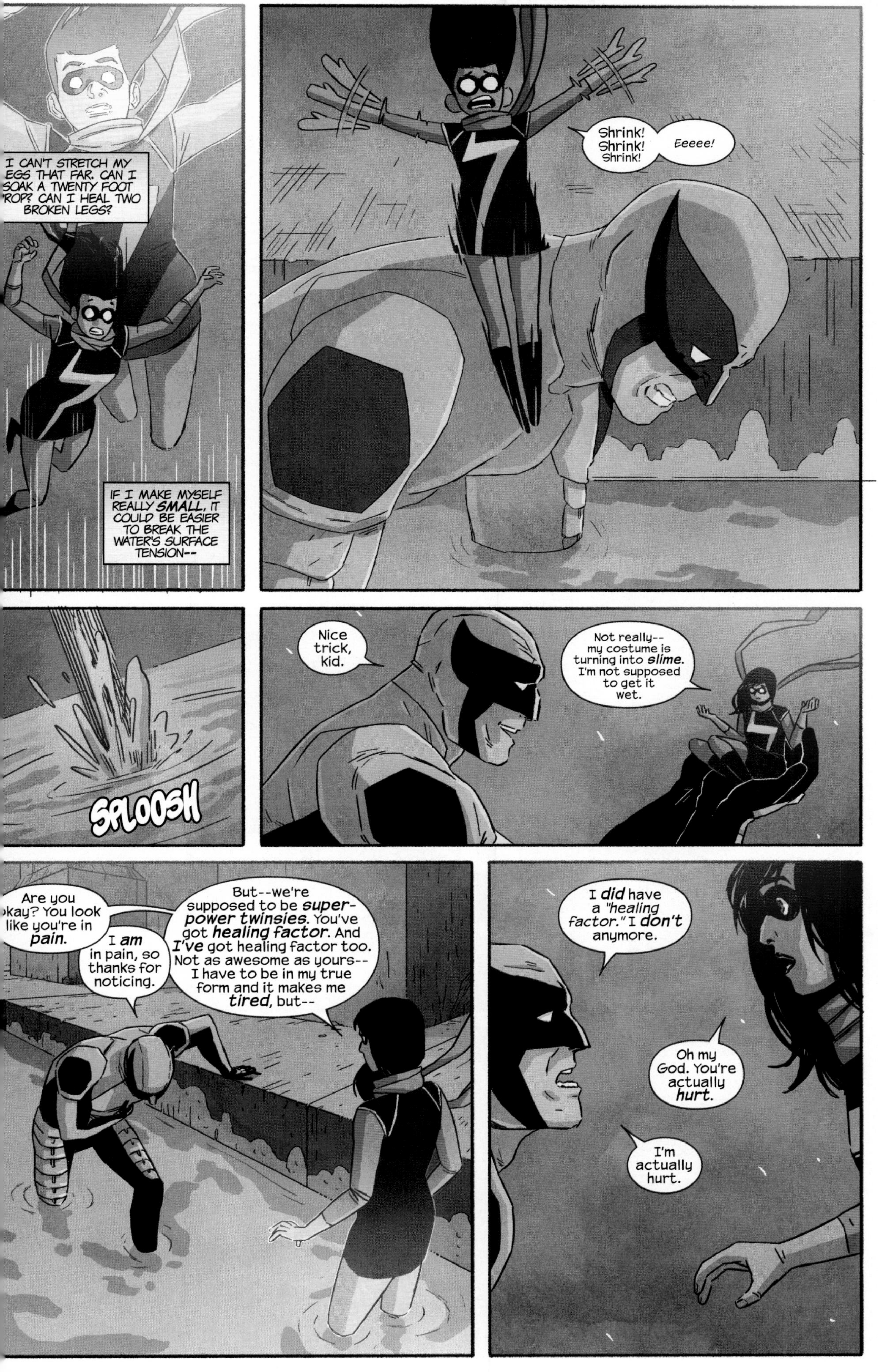

I CAN'T STRETCH MY
EGS THAT FAR. CAN I
SOAK A TWENTY FOOT
ROP? CAN I HEAL TWO
BROKEN LEGS?
IF I MAKE MYSELF REALLY SMALL, IT COULD BE EASIER TO BREAK THE WATER'S SURFACE TENSION--
Shrink! Shrink! Shrink!
Eeeee!
SPLOOSH
Nice trick, kid.
Not really-- my costume is turning into slime. I'm not supposed to get it wet.
Are you
kay? You look
like you're in
pain.
I am in pain, so thanks for noticing.
But--we're supposed to be super-power twinsies. You've got healing factor. And I've got healing factor too. Not as awesome as yours-- I have to be in my true form and it makes me tired, but--
I did have a "healing factor." I don't anymore.
Oh my God. You're actually hurt.
I'm actually hurt.

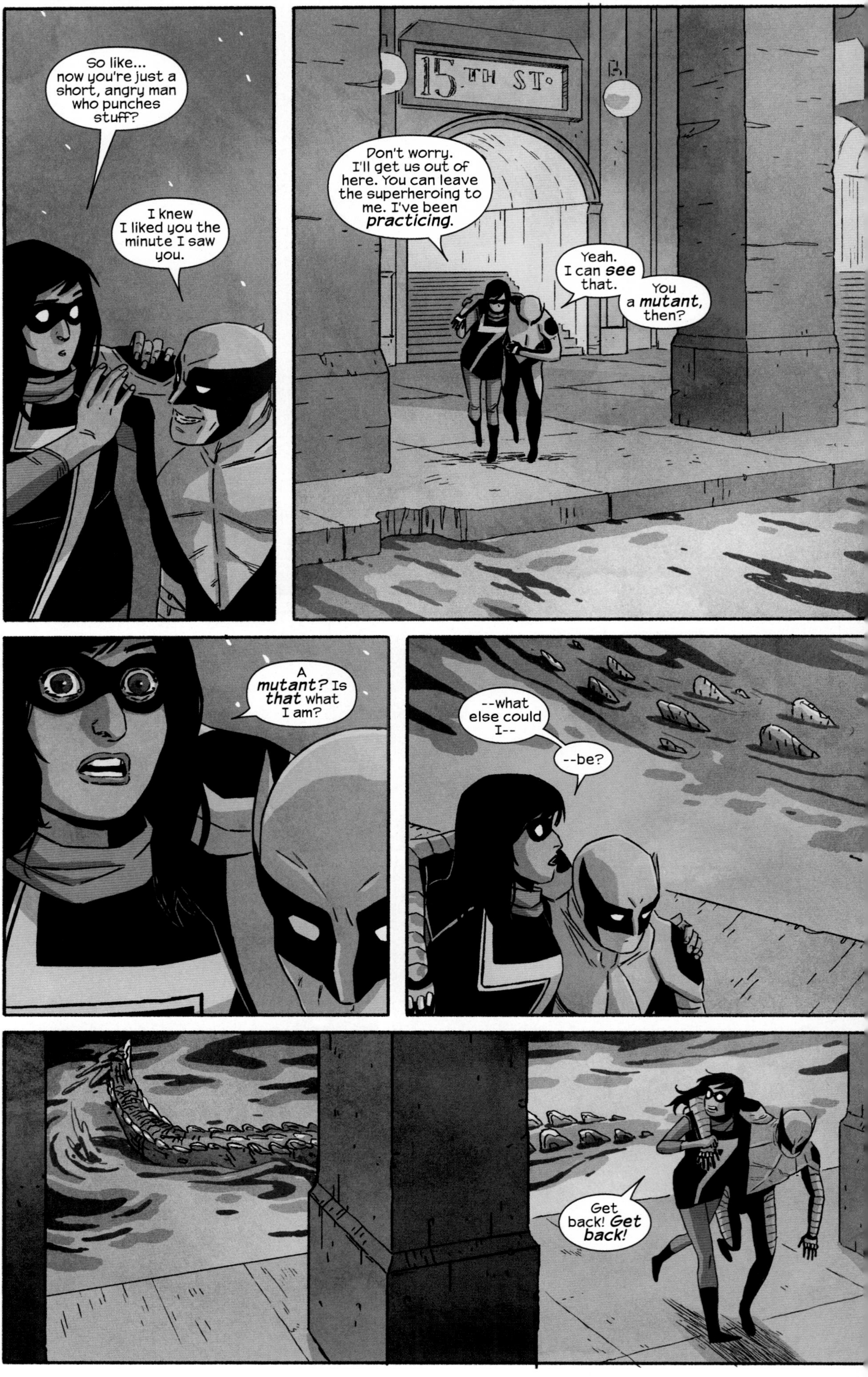
So like... now you're just a short, angry man who punches stuff?
I knew I liked you the minute I saw you.
15TH ST.
Don't worry. I'll get us out of here. You can leave the superheroing to me. I've been *practicing*.
Yeah. I can *see* that.
You a *mutant*, then?
A *mutant?* Is *that* what I am?
--what else could I--
--be?
Get back! *Get back!*

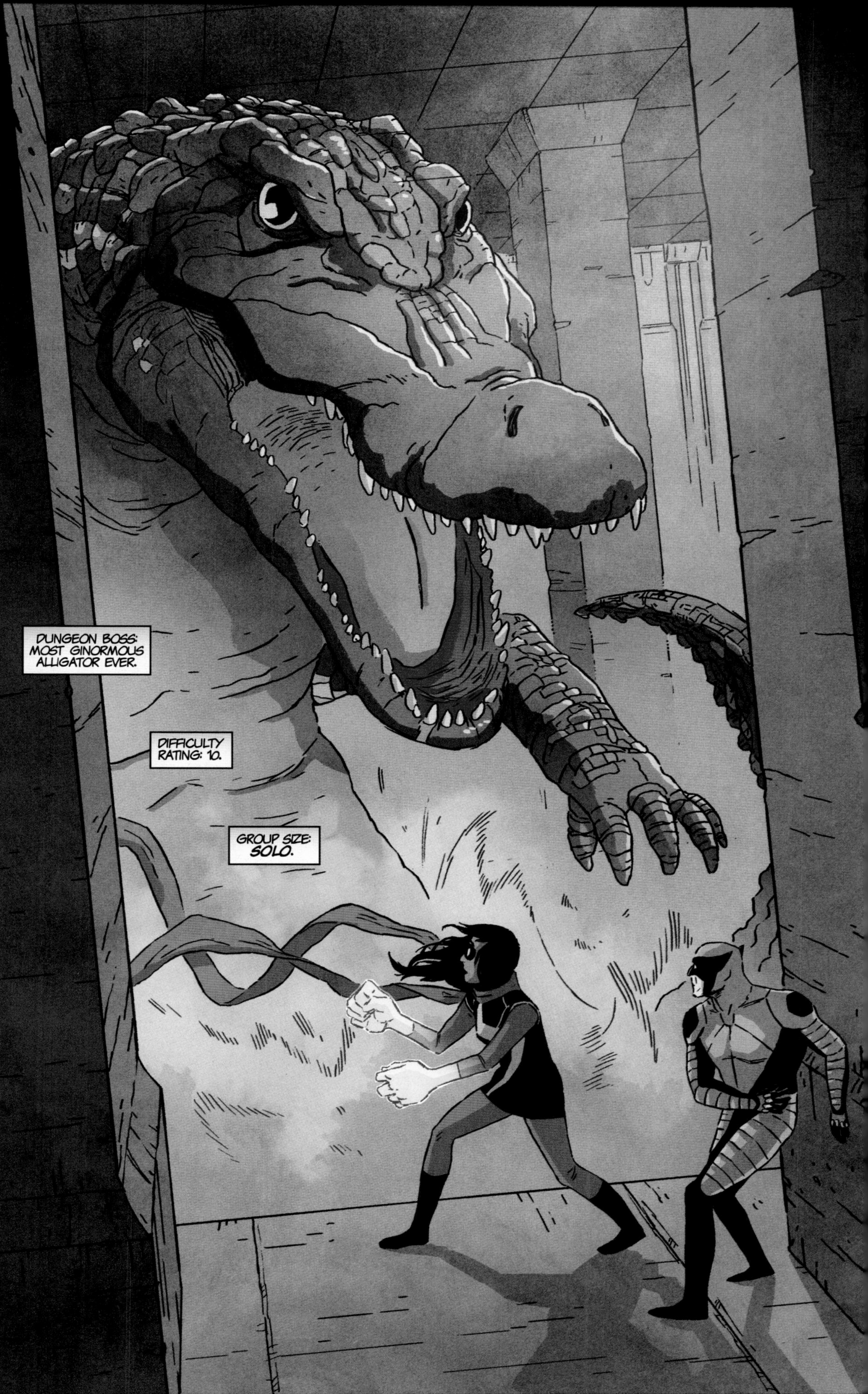
DUNGEON BOSS: MOST GINORMOUS ALLIGATOR EVER.
DIFFICULTY RATING: 10.
GROUP SIZE: SOLO.

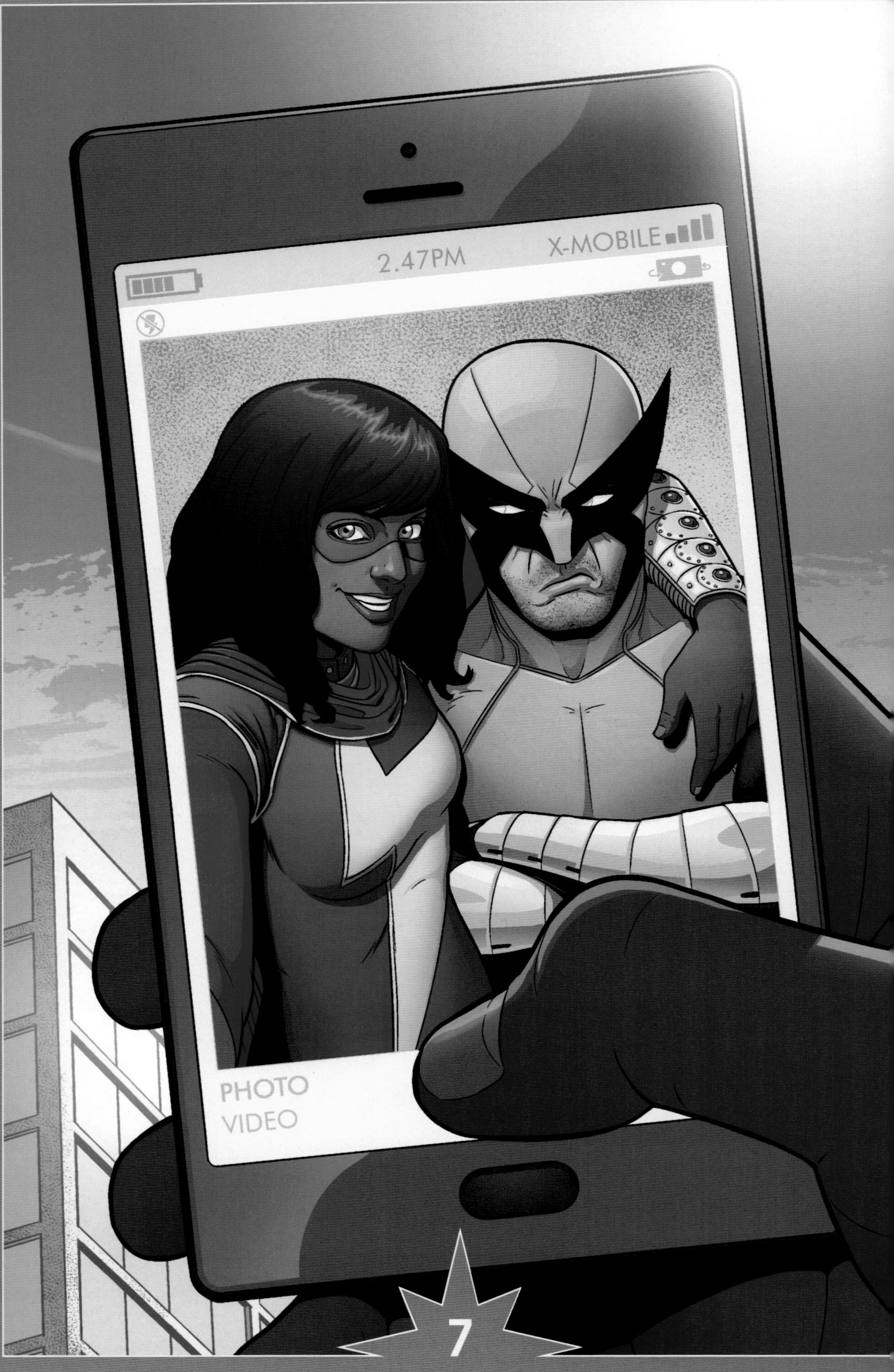
2.47PM
X-MOBILE
PHOTO
VIDEO
7

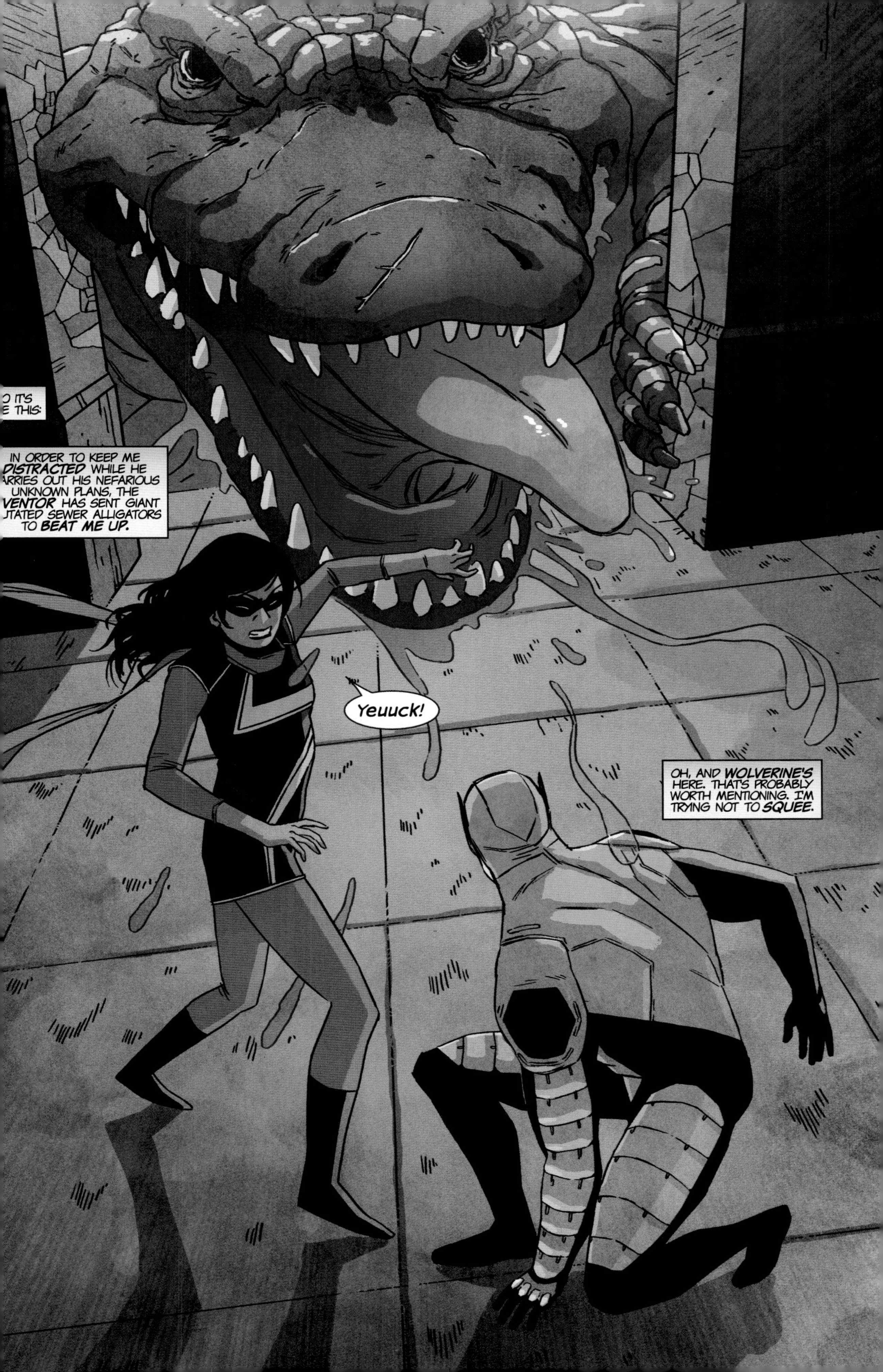
O IT'S
E THIS:
IN ORDER TO KEEP ME DISTRACTED WHILE HE ARRIES OUT HIS NEFARIOUS UNKNOWN PLANS, THE VENTOR HAS SENT GIANT UTATED SEWER ALLIGATORS TO BEAT ME UP.
Yeuuck!
OH, AND WOLVERINE'S HERE. THAT'S PROBABLY WORTH MENTIONING. I'M TRYING NOT TO SQUEE.

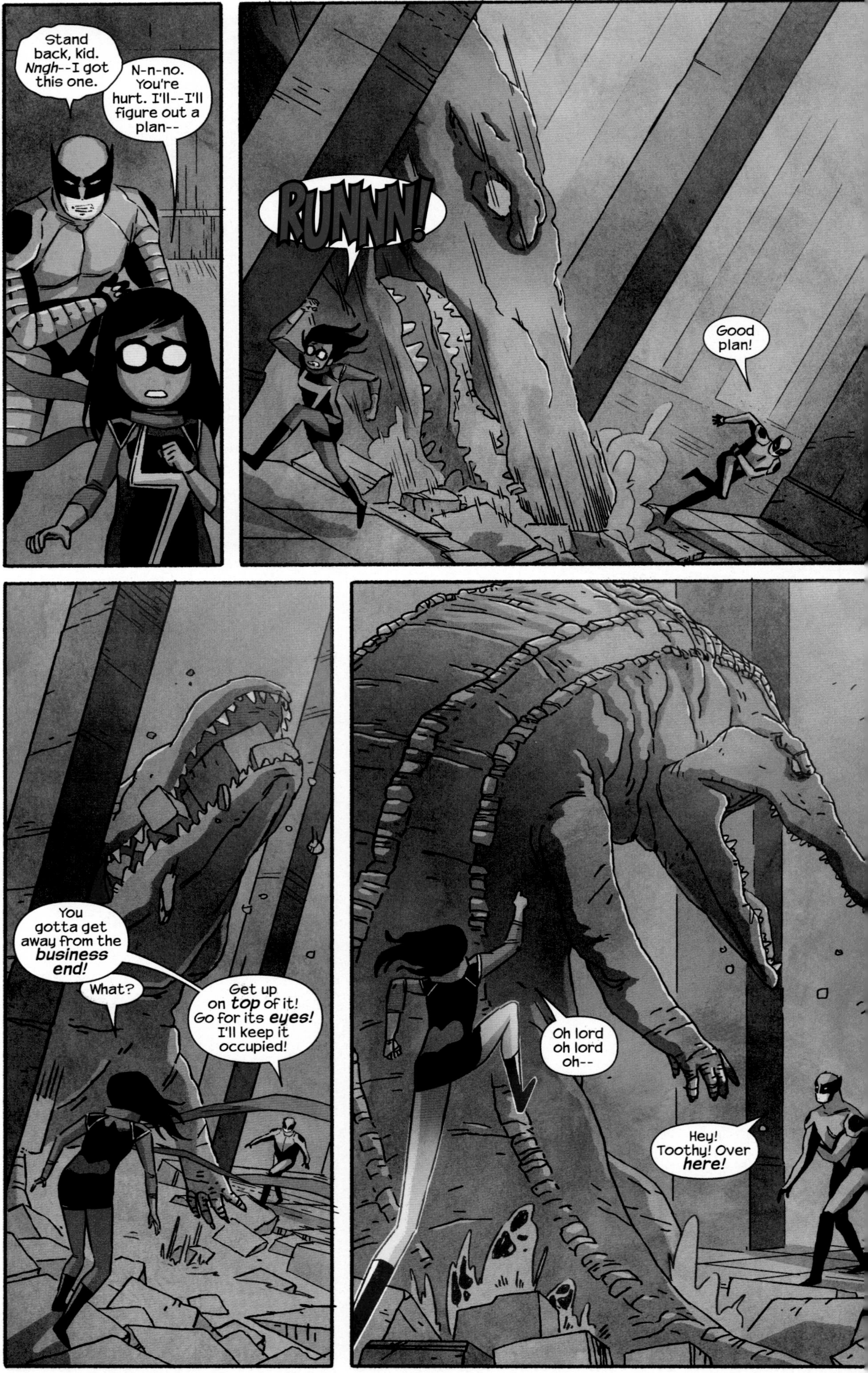
Stand back, kid. *Nngh*--I got this one.
N-n-no. You're hurt. I'll--I'll figure out a plan--
RUNNN!
Good plan!
You gotta get away from the *business end!*
What?
Get up on *top* of it! Go for its *eyes!* I'll keep it occupied!
Oh lord oh lord oh--
Hey! Toothy! Over *here!*

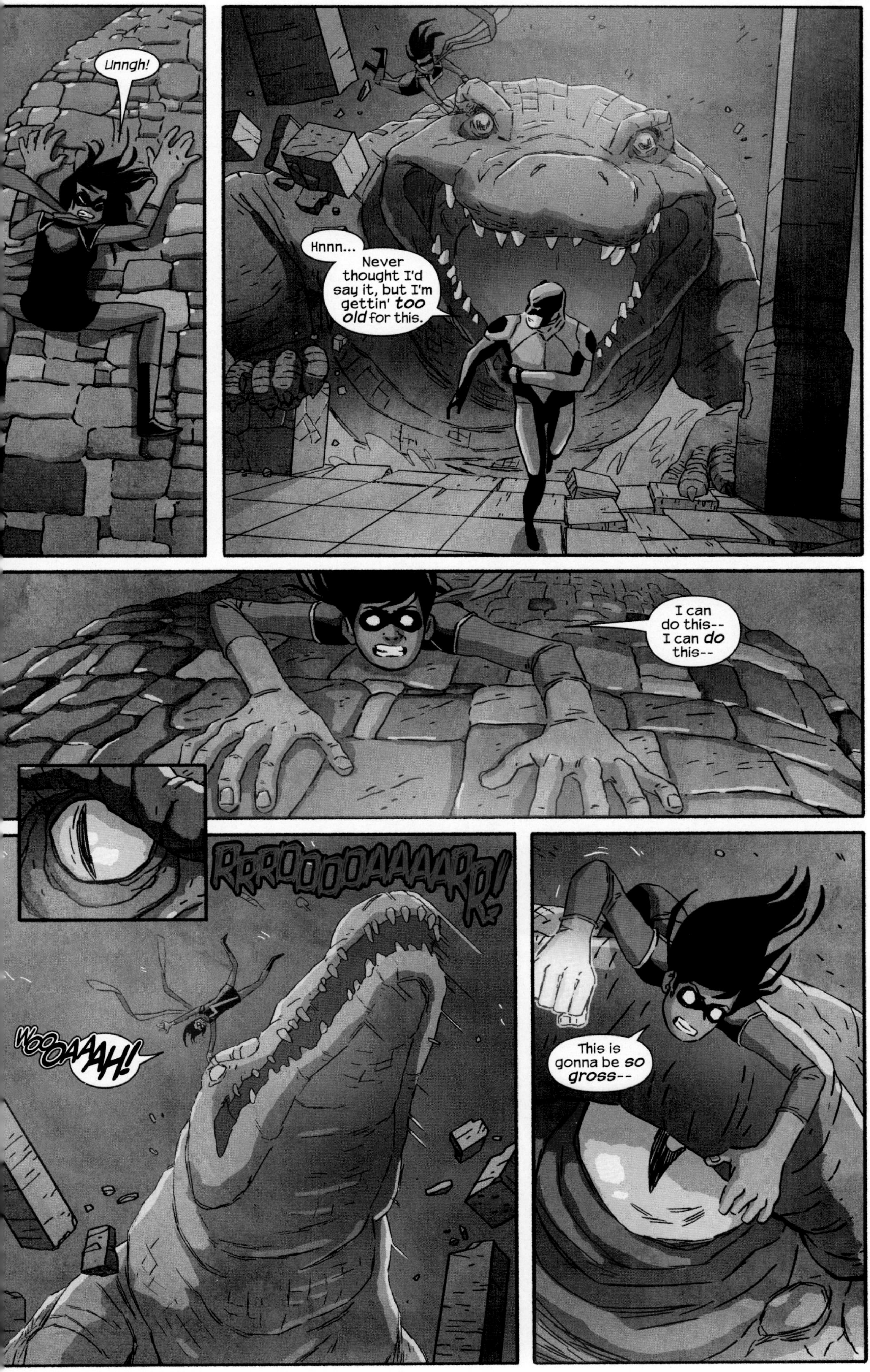
Unngh!
Hnnn... Never thought I'd say it, but I'm gettin' too old for this.
I can do this-- I can do this--
RRROOOOAAAARR!
WOOOAAAH!
This is gonna be so gross--

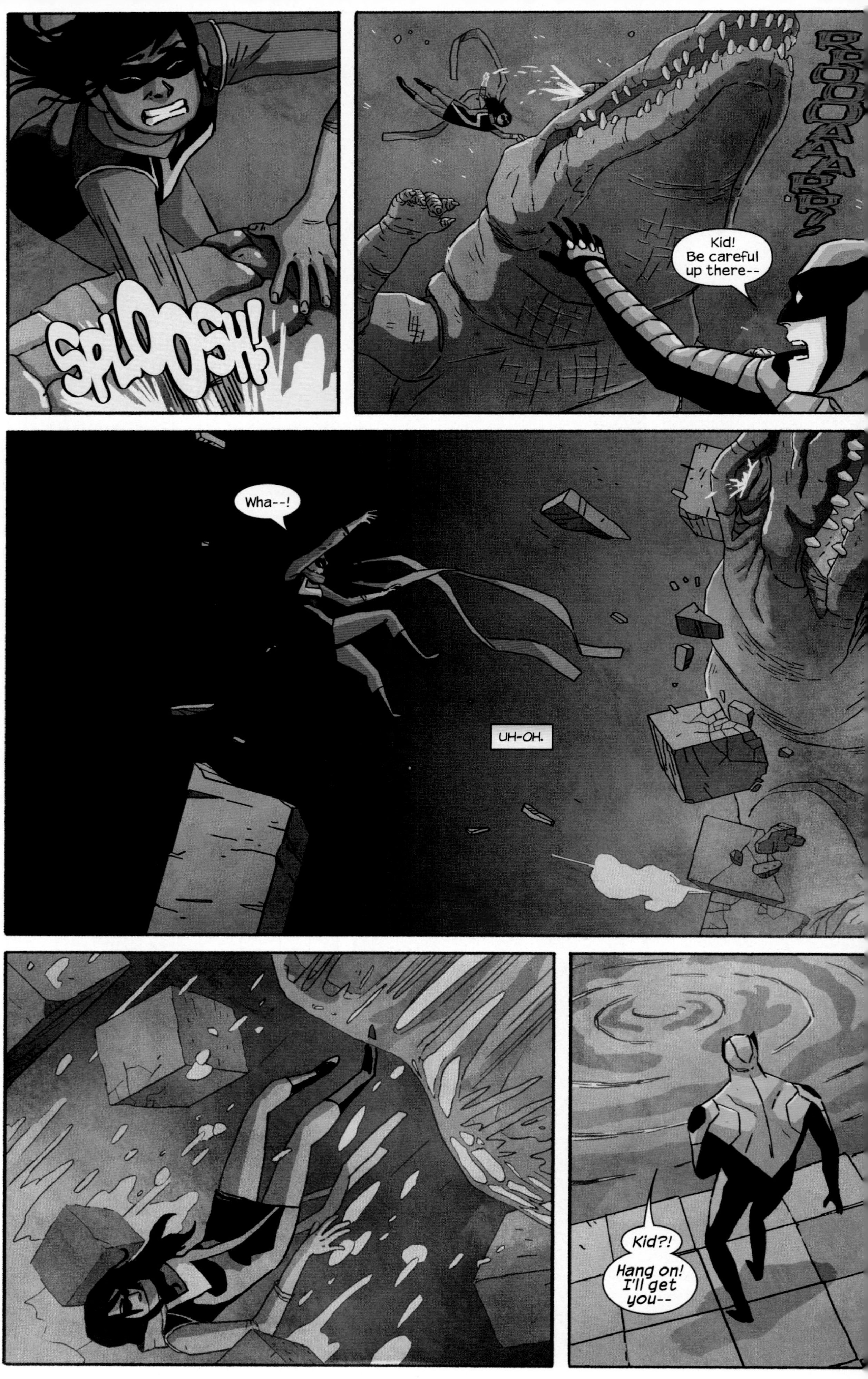
SPLOOSH!
RRROOOAAARR!
Kid! Be careful up there--
Wha--!
UH-OH.
Kid?!
Hang on! I'll get you--

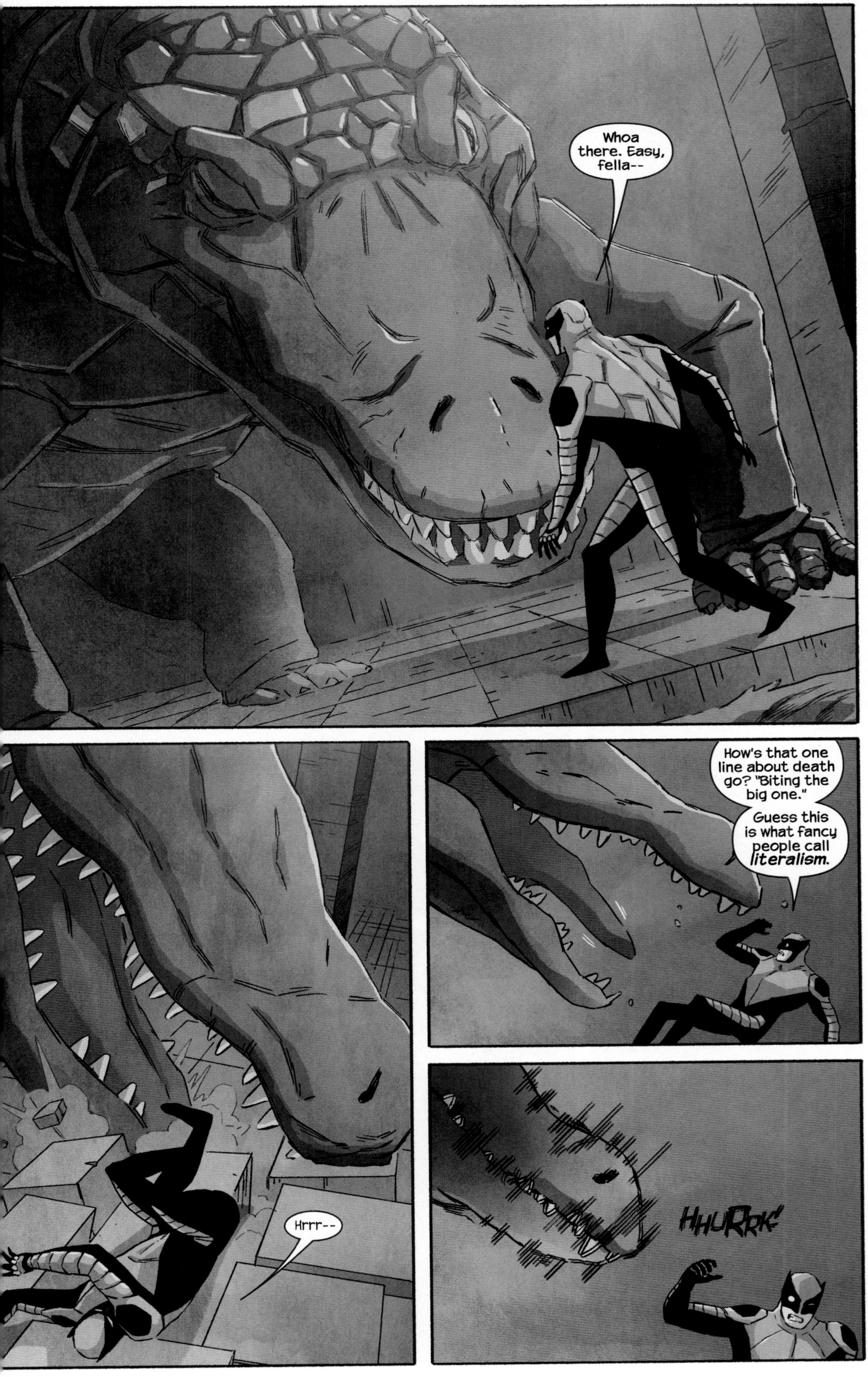
Whoa there. Easy, fella--
How's that one line about death go? "Biting the big one."
Guess this is what fancy people call *literalism*.
Hrrr--
HHURRK!

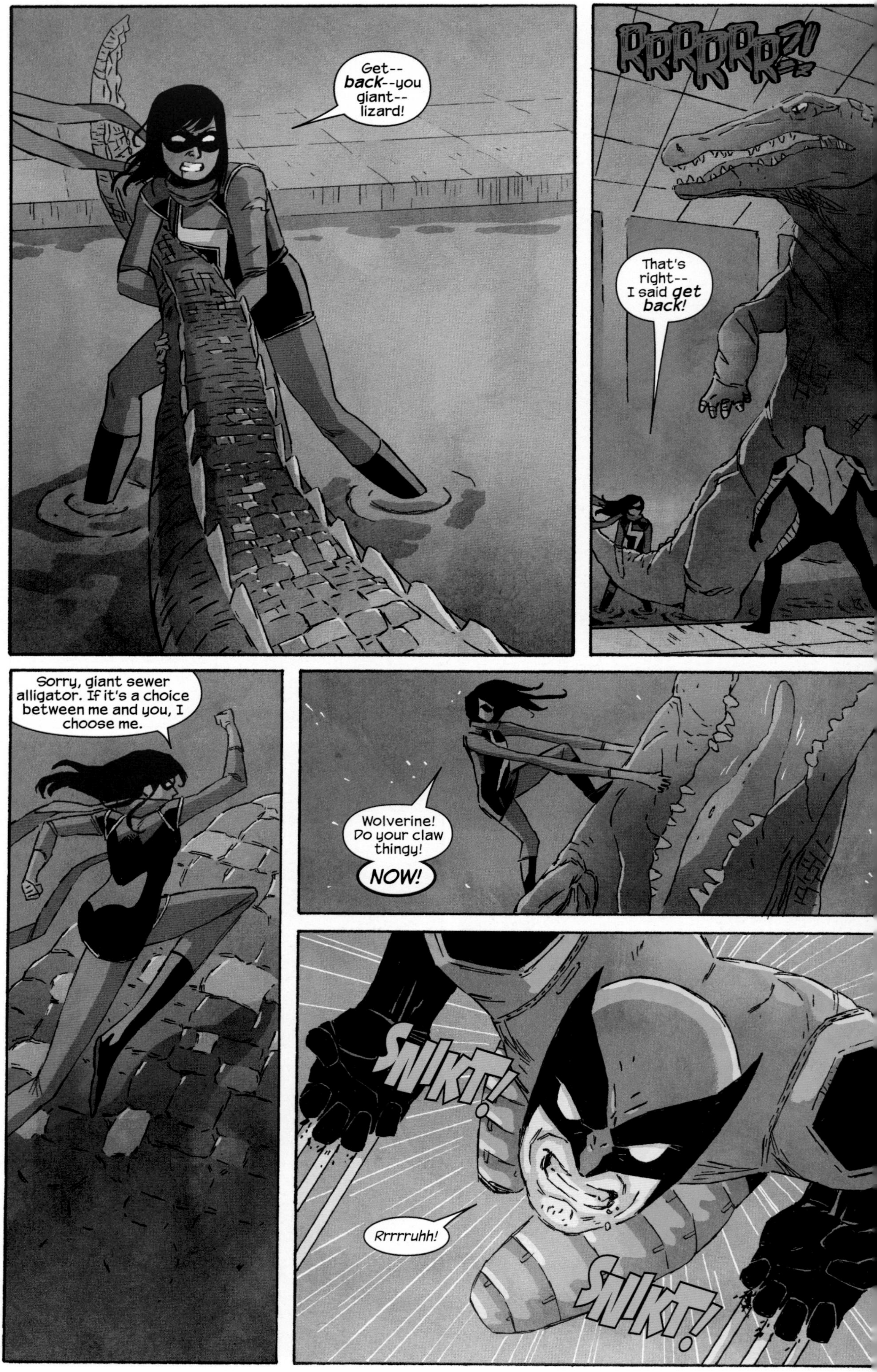
Get-- back--you giant-- lizard!
RRRRRRR!
That's right-- I said get back!
Sorry, giant sewer alligator. If it's a choice between me and you, I choose me.
Wolverine! Do your claw thingy!
NOW!
SNIKT!
Rrrrruhh!
SNIKT!

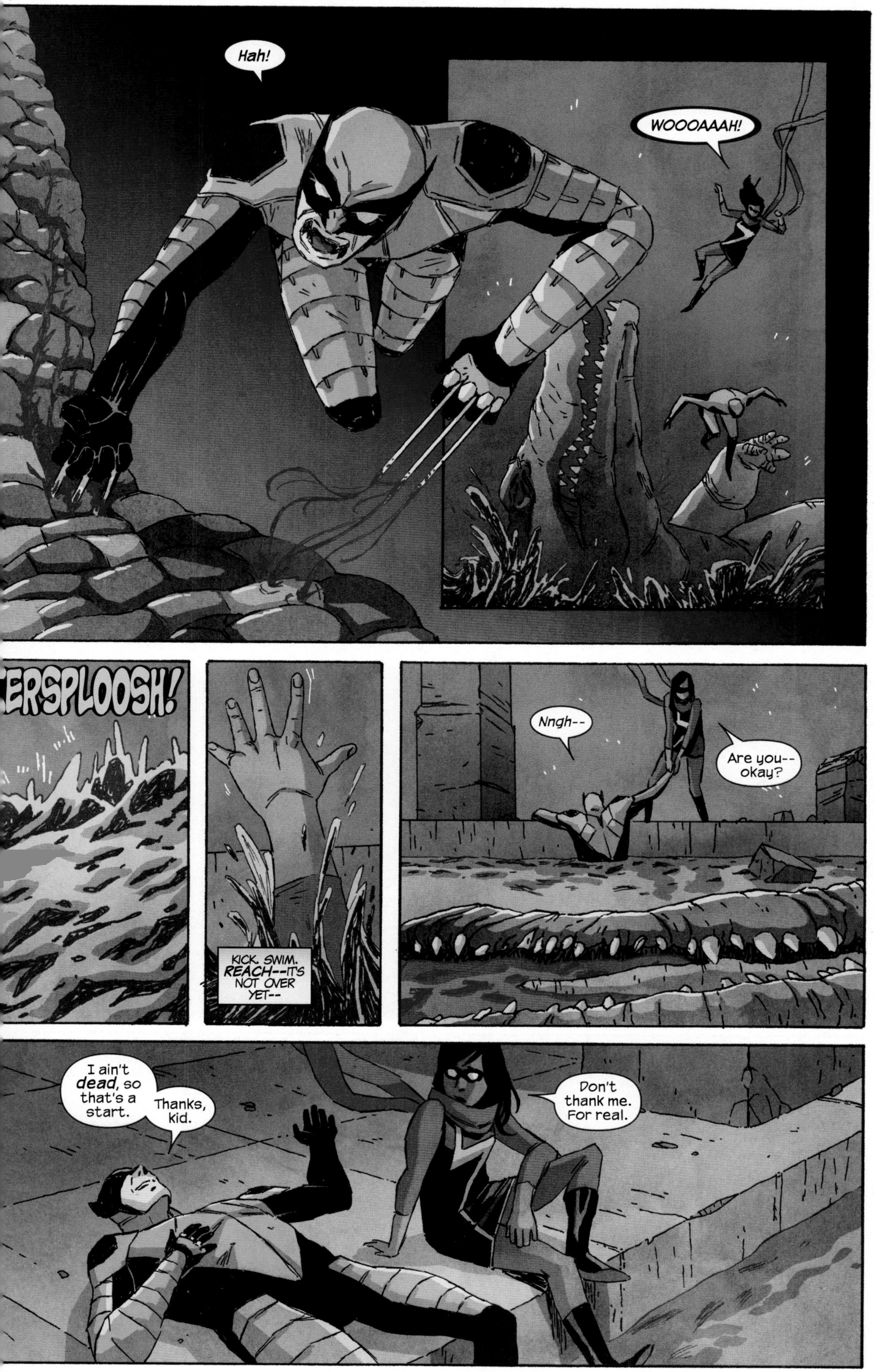
Hah!
WOOOAAAH!
ERSPLOOSH!
KICK. SWIM. REACH--IT'S NOT OVER YET--
Nngh--
Are you-- okay?
I ain't dead, so that's a start.
Thanks, kid.
Don't thank me. For real.

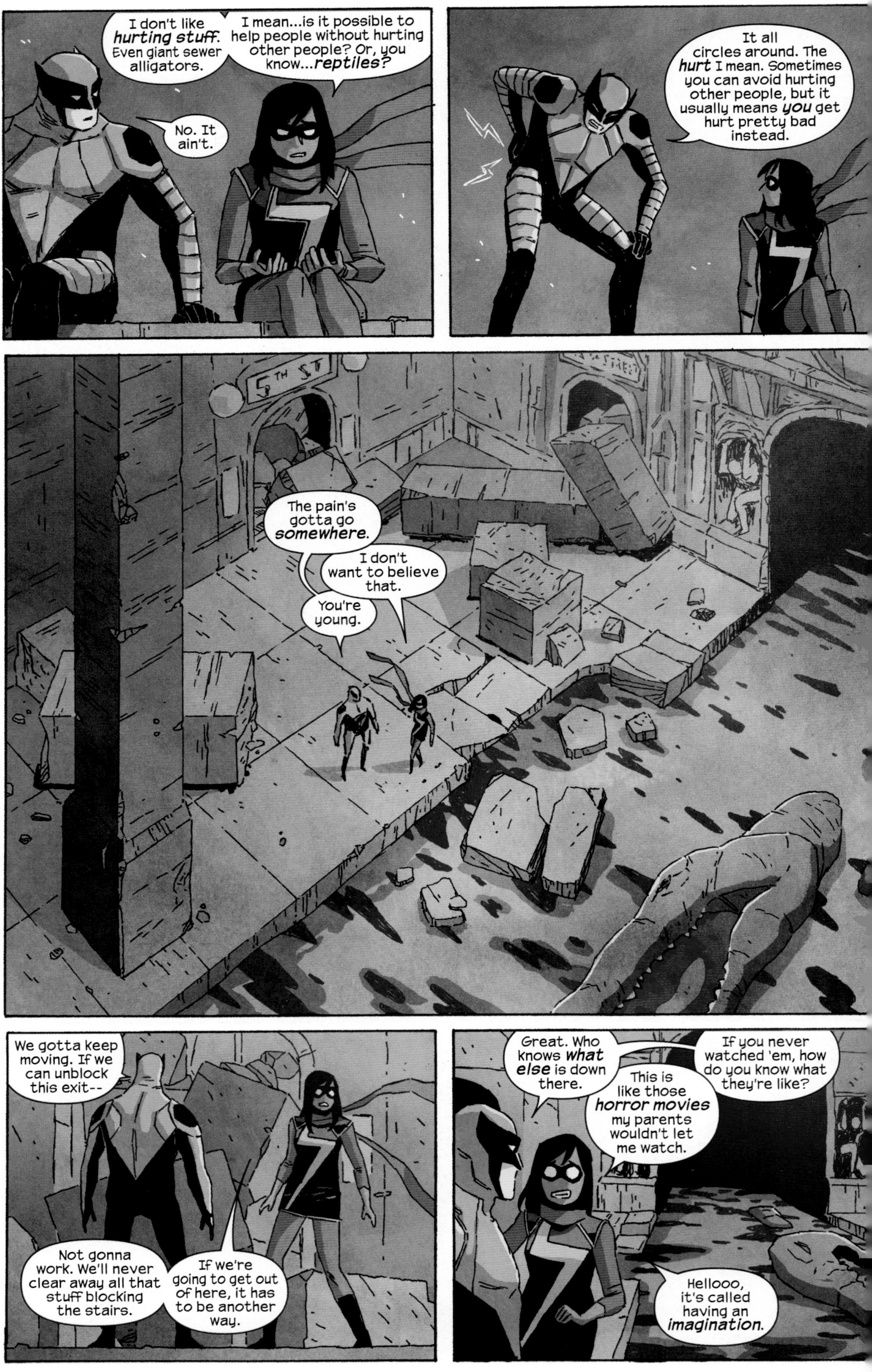

I don't like hurting stuff. Even giant sewer alligators.
I mean...is it possible to help people without hurting other people? Or, you know...reptiles?
No. It ain't.
It all circles around. The hurt I mean. Sometimes you can avoid hurting other people, but it usually means you get hurt pretty bad instead.
5TH ST
The pain's gotta go somewhere.
I don't want to believe that.
You're young.
We gotta keep moving. If we can unblock this exit--
Not gonna work. We'll never clear away all that stuff blocking the stairs.
If we're going to get out of here, it has to be another way.
Great. Who knows what else is down there.
This is like those horror movies my parents wouldn't let me watch.
If you never watched 'em, how do you know what they're like?
Hellooo, it's called having an imagination.

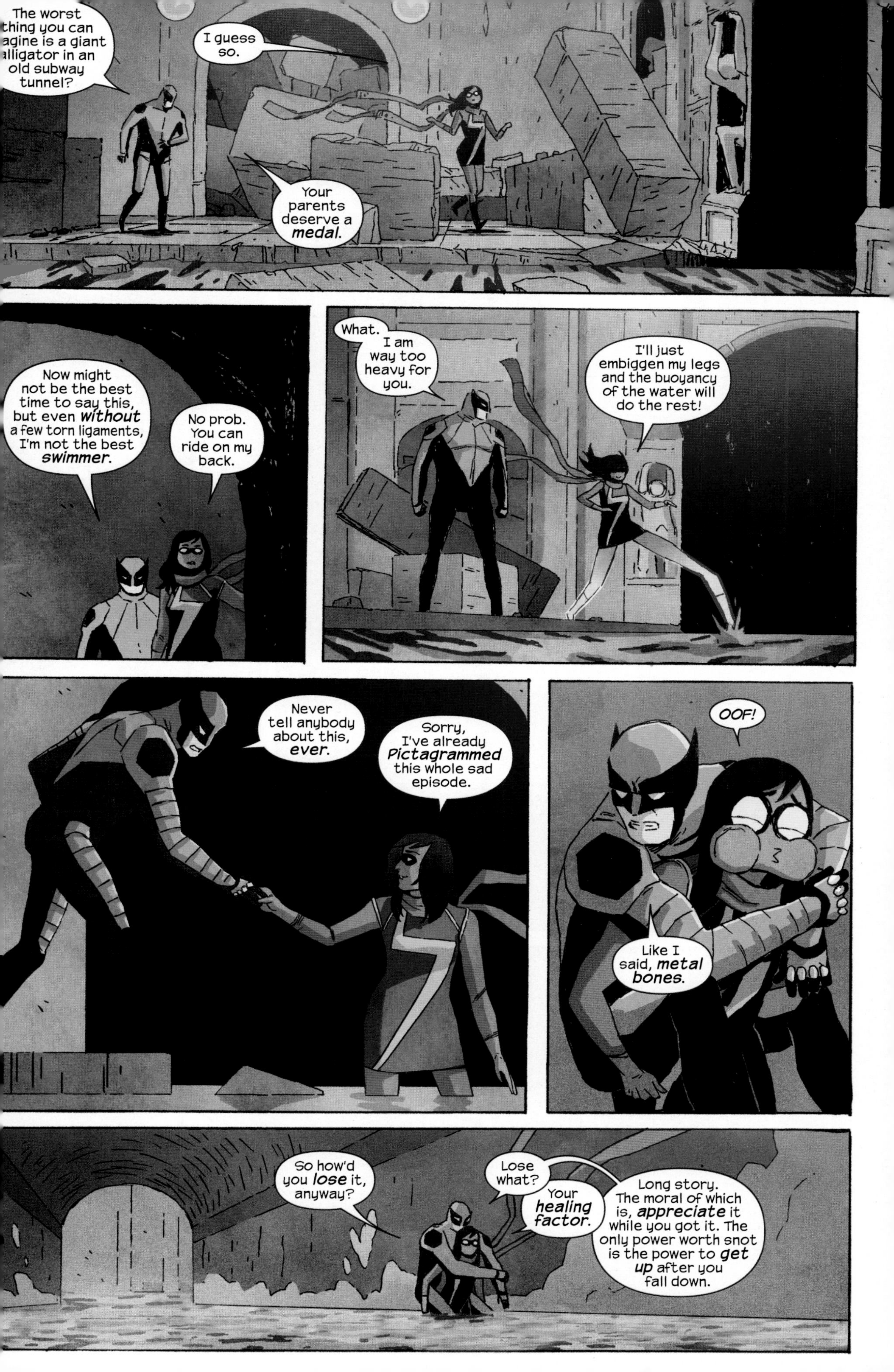
The worst thing you can agine is a giant lligator in an old subway tunnel?
I guess so.
Your parents deserve a *medal*.
Now might not be the best time to say this, but even *without* a few torn ligaments, I'm not the best *swimmer*.
No prob. You can ride on my back.
What. I am way too heavy for you.
I'll just embiggen my legs and the buoyancy of the water will do the rest!
Never tell anybody about this, *ever*.
Sorry, I've already *Pictagrammed* this whole sad episode.
OOF!
Like I said, *metal bones*.
So how'd you *lose* it, anyway?
Lose what?
Your *healing factor*.
Long story. The moral of which is, *appreciate* it while you got it. The only power worth snot is the power to *get up* after you fall down.

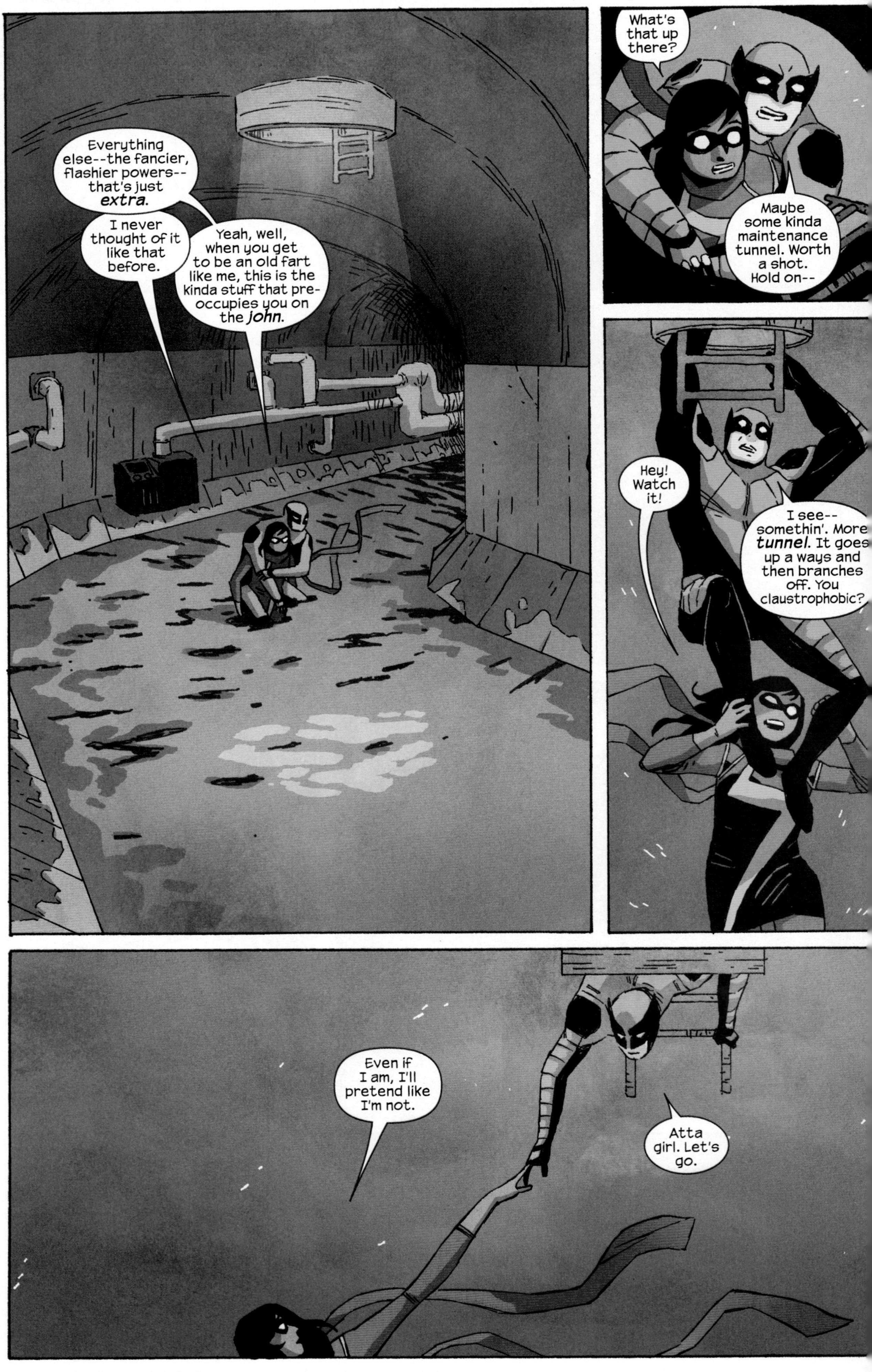

Everything else--the fancier, flashier powers--that's just *extra*.
I never thought of it like that before.
Yeah, well, when you get to be an old fart like me, this is the kinda stuff that pre-occupies you on the *john*.
What's that up there?
Maybe some kinda maintenance tunnel. Worth a shot. Hold on--
Hey! Watch it!
I see--somethin'. More *tunnel*. It goes up a ways and then branches off. You claustrophobic?
Even if I am, I'll pretend like I'm not.
Atta girl. Let's go.

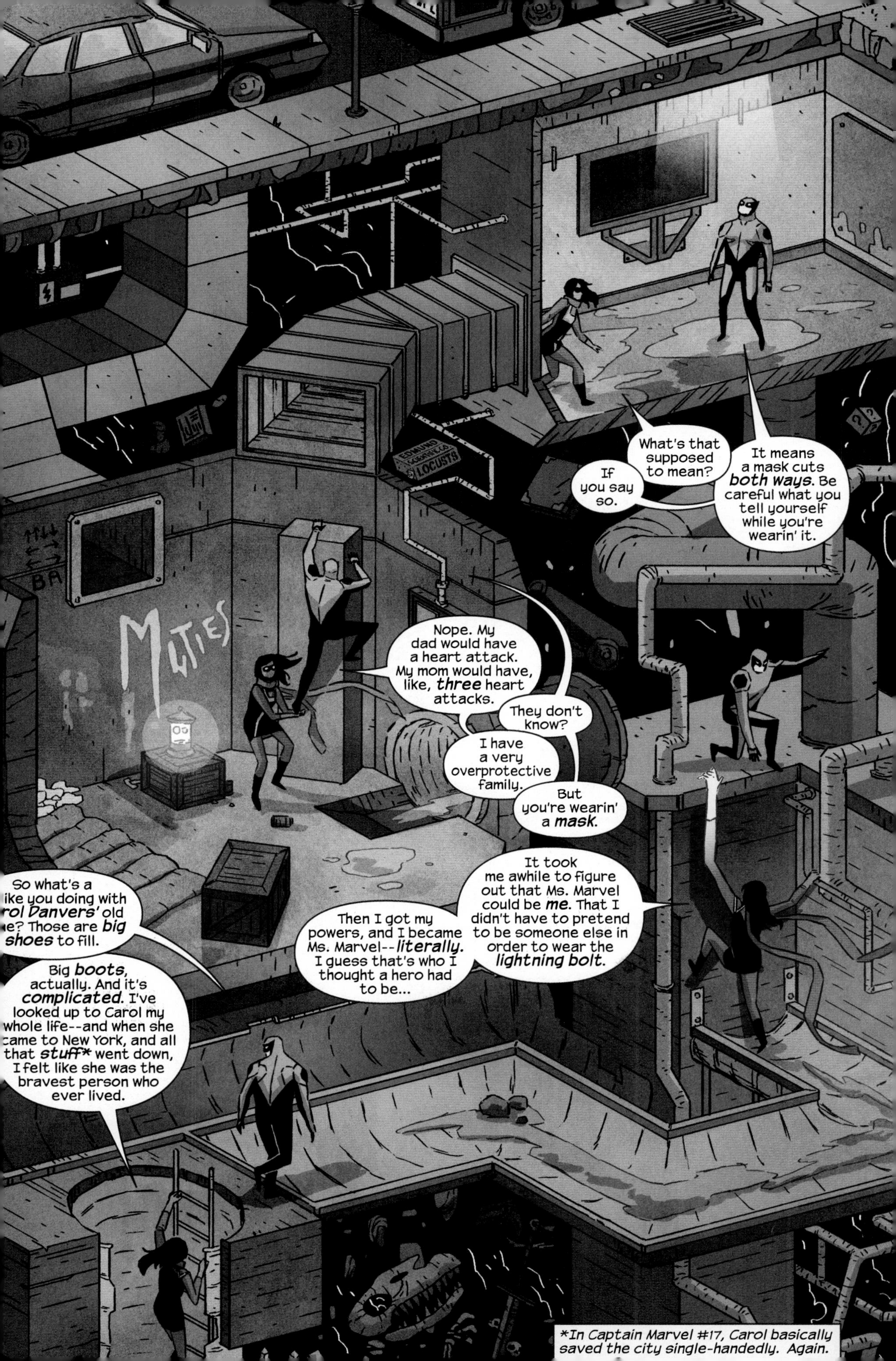
So what's a
ike you doing with
rol Danvers' old
e? Those are big shoes to fill.
Big boots, actually. And it's complicated. I've looked up to Carol my whole life--and when she came to New York, and all that stuff* went down, I felt like she was the bravest person who ever lived.
Then I got my powers, and I became Ms. Marvel--literally. I guess that's who I thought a hero had to be...
It took me awhile to figure out that Ms. Marvel could be me. That I didn't have to pretend to be someone else in order to wear the lightning bolt.
But you're wearin' a mask.
I have a very overprotective family.
They don't know?
Nope. My dad would have a heart attack. My mom would have, like, three heart attacks.
What's that supposed to mean?
It means a mask cuts both ways. Be careful what you tell yourself while you're wearin' it.
If you say so.
MUTIES
EDMUND SCIENTIFIC CO. LOCUSTS
*In Captain Marvel #17, Carol basically saved the city single-handedly. Again.

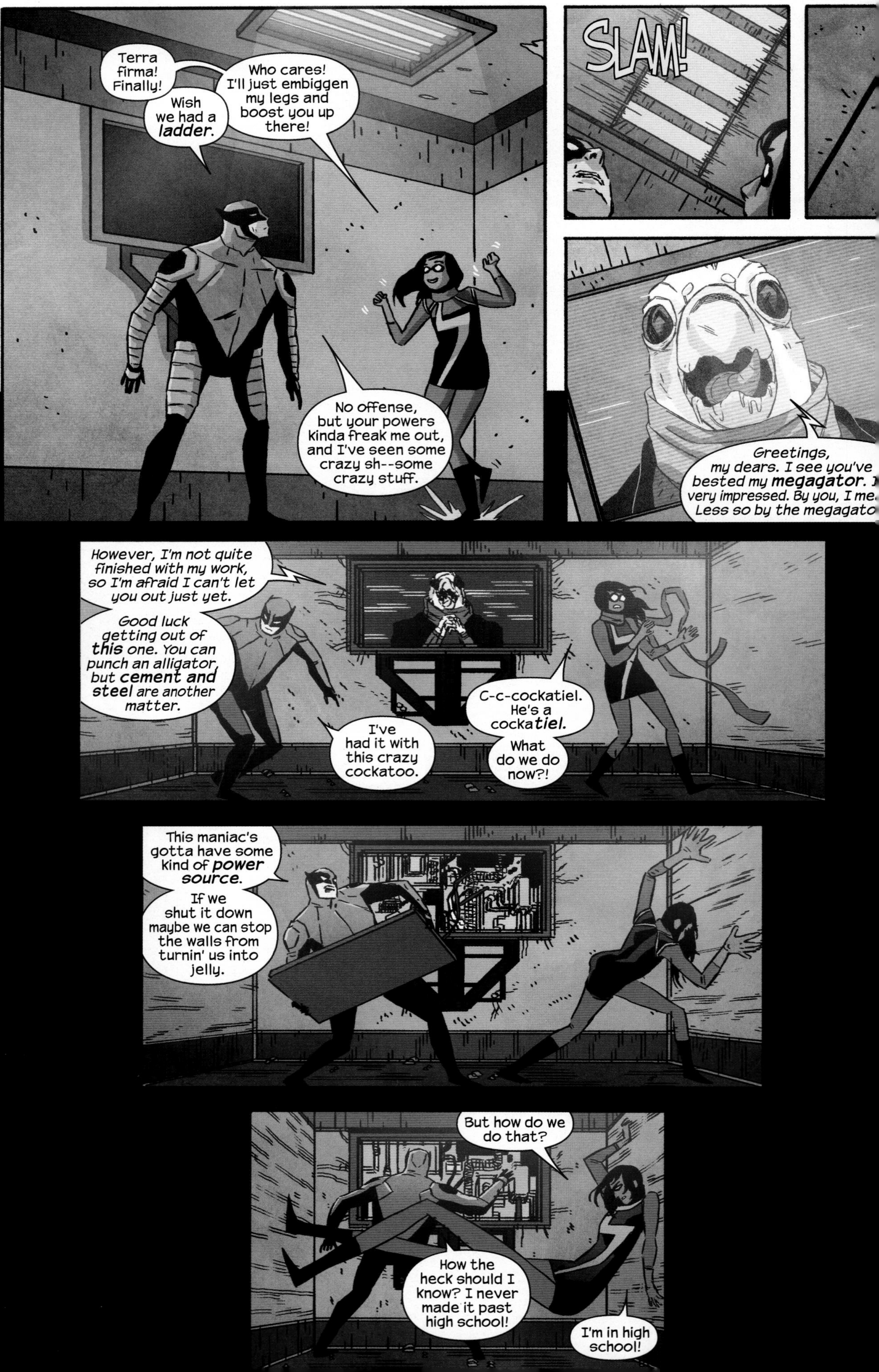
Terra firma! Finally!
Who cares! I'll just embiggen my legs and boost you up there!
Wish we had a *ladder*.
No offense, but your powers kinda freak me out, and I've seen some crazy sh--some crazy stuff.
SLAM!
Greetings, my dears. I see you've bested my **megagator**. I
very impressed. By you, I me
Less so by the megagato
However, I'm not quite finished with my work, so I'm afraid I can't let you out just yet.
Good luck getting out of **this** one. You can punch an alligator, but **cement and steel** are another matter.
I've had it with this crazy cockatoo.
C-c-cockatiel. He's a cocka*tiel*.
What do we do now?!
This maniac's gotta have some kind of *power source*.
If we shut it down maybe we can stop the walls from turnin' us into jelly.
But how do we do that?
How the heck should I know? I never made it past high school!
I'm in high school!

Rrrrrghhh!

Are you okay?

Nngh--

Yeah. Just give me a second.

No. Let *me* do it.

It's gonna hurt. It *always* hurts. That's how this works.

You just gotta trust yourself to come through it.

Hrruhh!

IT'S LIKE BEING SNAPPED WITH A RUBBER BAND, EXCEPT A THOUSAND TIMES *WORSE,* AND ALL OVER--

I CAN FEEL MY *HEALING FACTOR* KICK IN, SUCKING ENERGY OUT OF MY MUSCLES, MY *EVERYTHING--* IT'S ALMOST *WORSE* THAN GETTING HURT.

I BREATHE. I TRUST MYSELF.

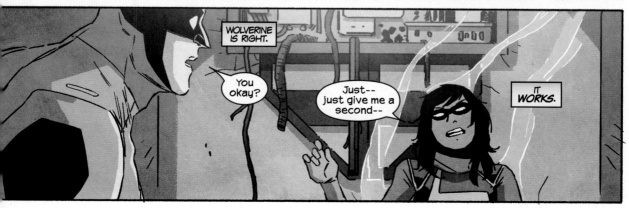

WOLVERINE IS RIGHT.

You okay?

Just-- just give me a second--

IT *WORKS.*

Okay. I'm better-ish now.

It takes a lot out of me, you know? And I get really *hungry*. I could use a *gyro* right now. A *big* one.

When we get outta here, I will buy you the world's biggest gyro. But we gotta keep moving.

Think you can shrink down and follow those cables back into the wall? They've gotta be hooked up to *something*.

Find the *power source*. Right.

Be careful. Holler if you need--I'm gonna find another way in.

Oh no.

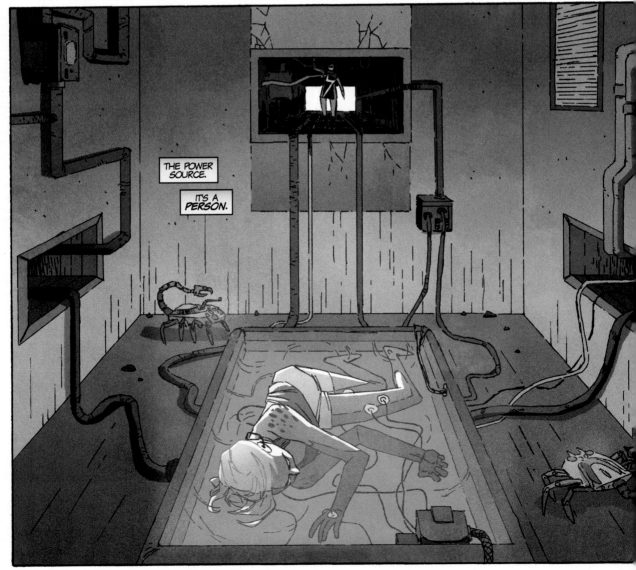

THE POWER SOURCE.

IT'S A *PERSON*.

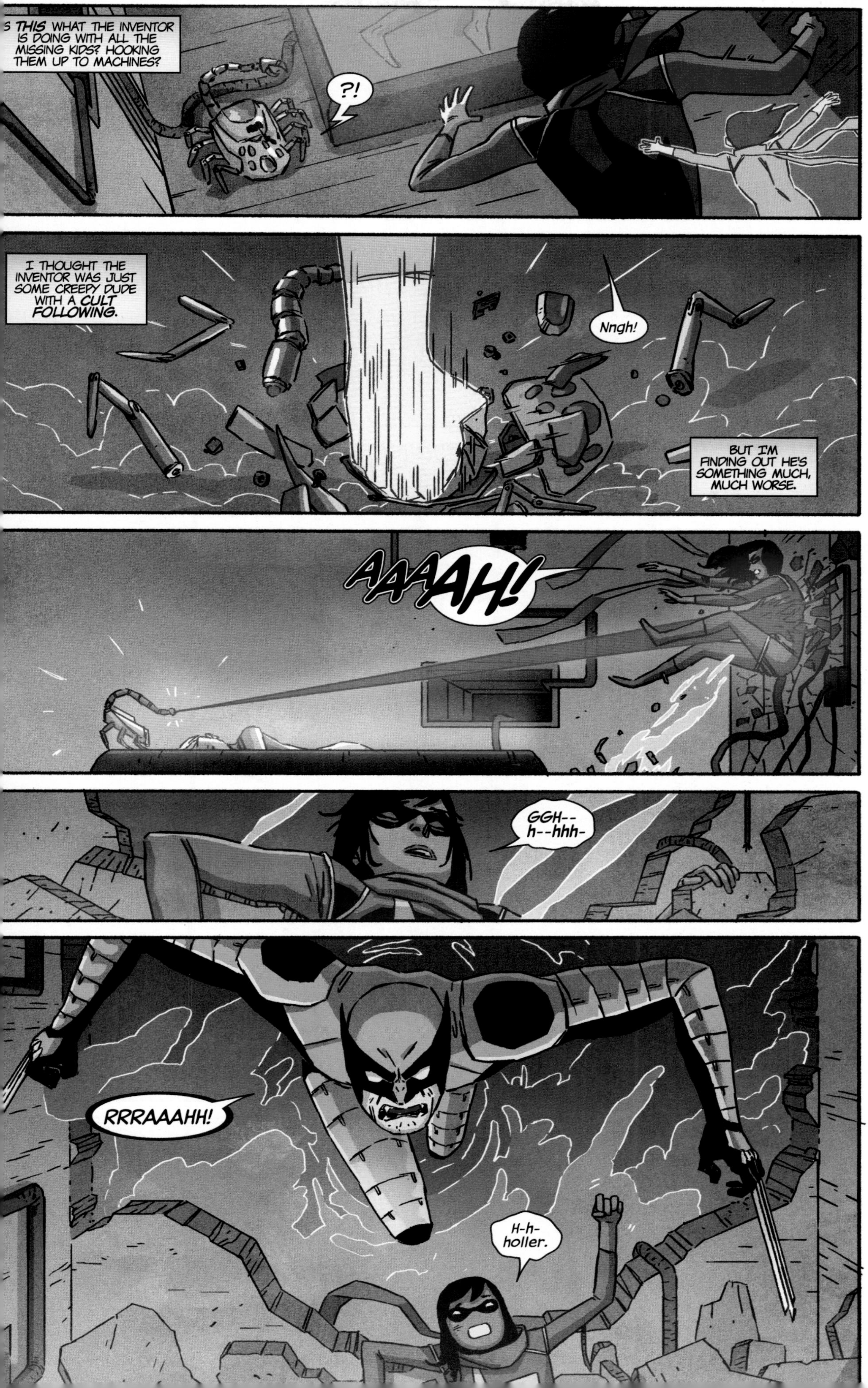
IS THIS WHAT THE INVENTOR IS DOING WITH ALL THE MISSING KIDS? HOOKING THEM UP TO MACHINES?
?!
I THOUGHT THE INVENTOR WAS JUST SOME CREEPY DUDE WITH A CULT FOLLOWING.
Nngh!
BUT I'M FINDING OUT HE'S SOMETHING MUCH, MUCH WORSE.
AAAAH!
GGH-- h--hhh-
RRRAAAHH!
H-h-holler.

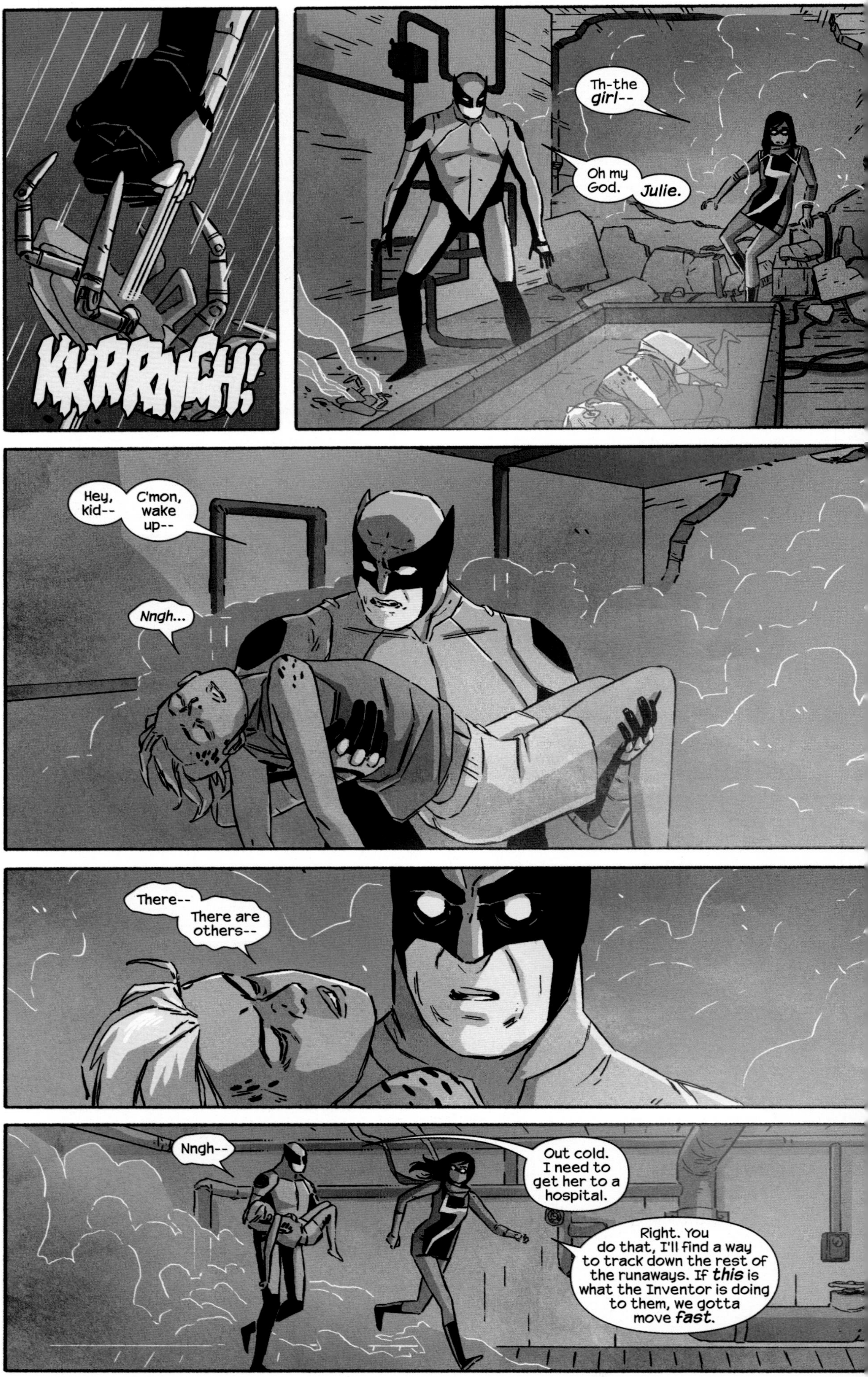
KKRRNCH!
Th-the *girl*--
Oh my God.
Julie.
Hey, kid--
C'mon, wake up--
Nngh...
There--
There are others--
Nngh--
Out cold. I need to get her to a hospital.
Right. You do that, I'll find a way to track down the rest of the runaways. If *this* is what the Inventor is doing to them, we gotta move *fast*.

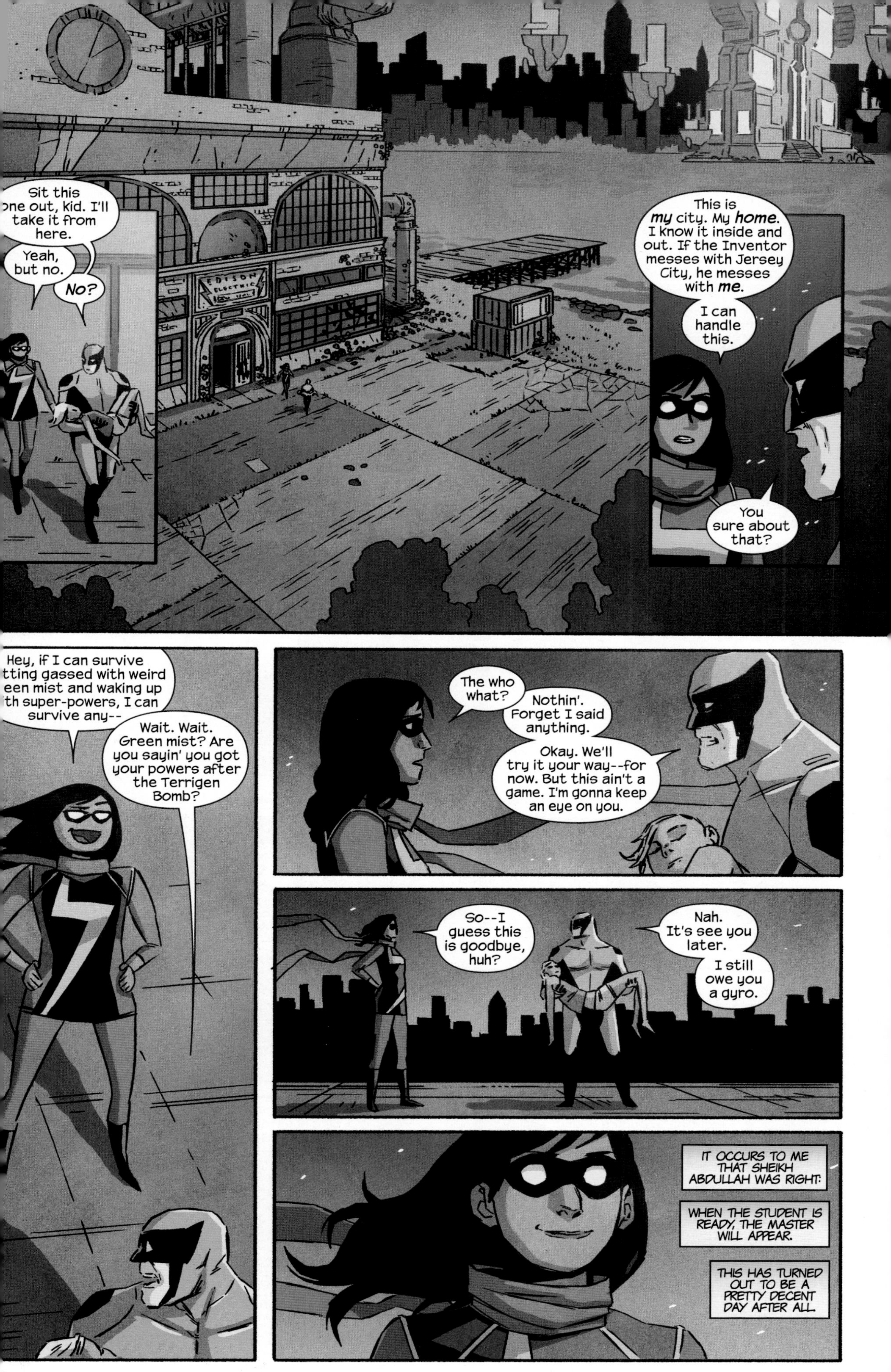

Sit this one out, kid. I'll take it from here.
Yeah, but no.
No?
This is my city. My home. I know it inside and out. If the Inventor messes with Jersey City, he messes with me.
I can handle this.
You sure about that?
Hey, if I can survive tting gassed with weird een mist and waking up th super-powers, I can survive any--
Wait. Wait. Green mist? Are you sayin' you got your powers after the Terrigen Bomb?
The who what?
Nothin'. Forget I said anything.
Okay. We'll try it your way--for now. But this ain't a game. I'm gonna keep an eye on you.
So--I guess this is goodbye, huh?
Nah. It's see you later.
I still owe you a gyro.
IT OCCURS TO ME THAT SHEIKH ABDULLAH WAS RIGHT:
WHEN THE STUDENT IS READY, THE MASTER WILL APPEAR.
THIS HAS TURNED OUT TO BE A PRETTY DECENT DAY AFTER ALL.

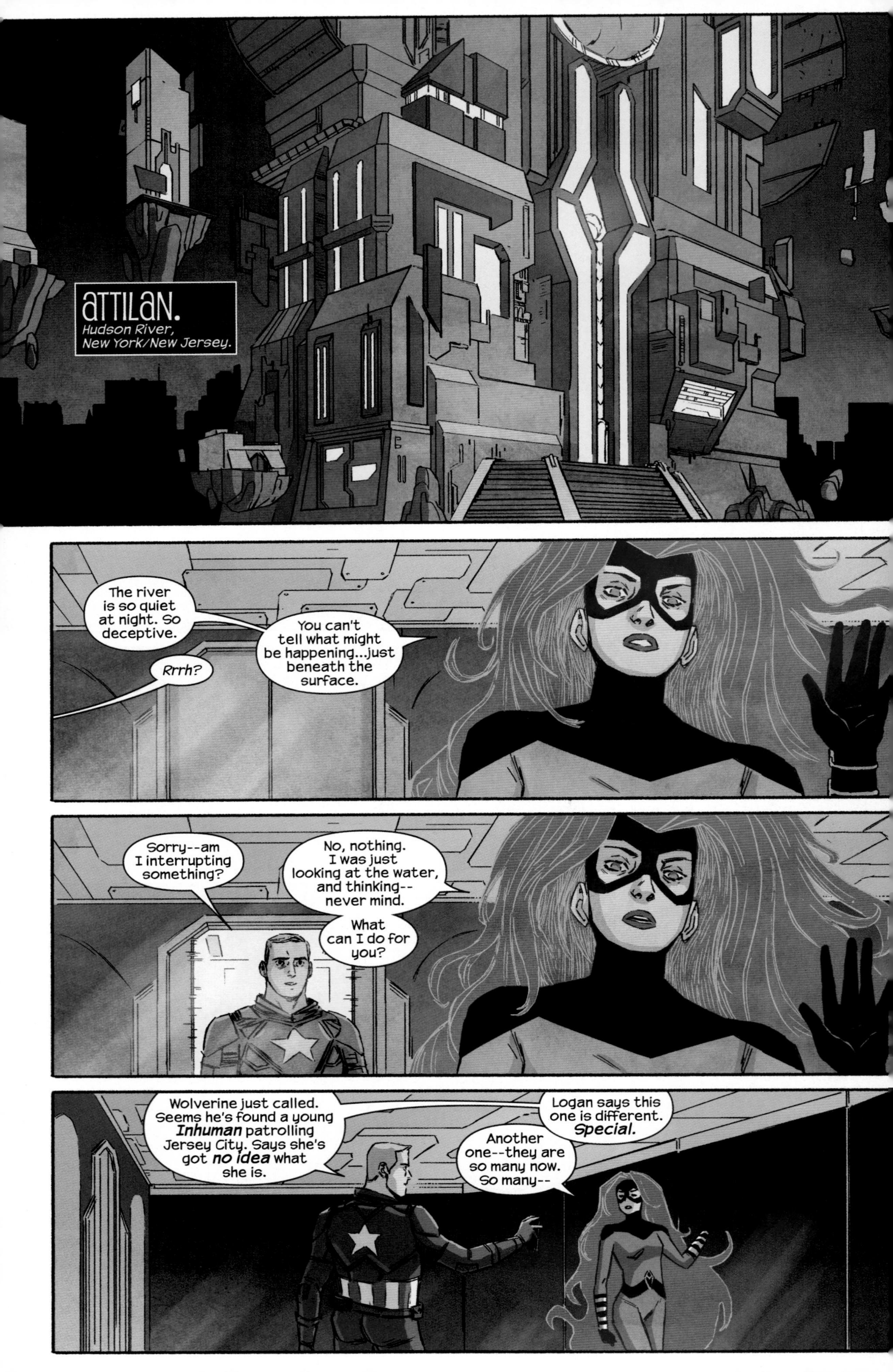
ATTILAN.
Hudson River, New York/New Jersey.
The river is so quiet at night. So deceptive.
You can't tell what might be happening...just beneath the surface.
Rrrh?
Sorry--am I interrupting something?
No, nothing. I was just looking at the water, and thinking-- never mind.
What can I do for you?
Wolverine just called. Seems he's found a young *Inhuman* patrolling Jersey City. Says she's got *no idea* what she is.
Logan says this one is different. *Special.*
Another one--they are so many now. So many--

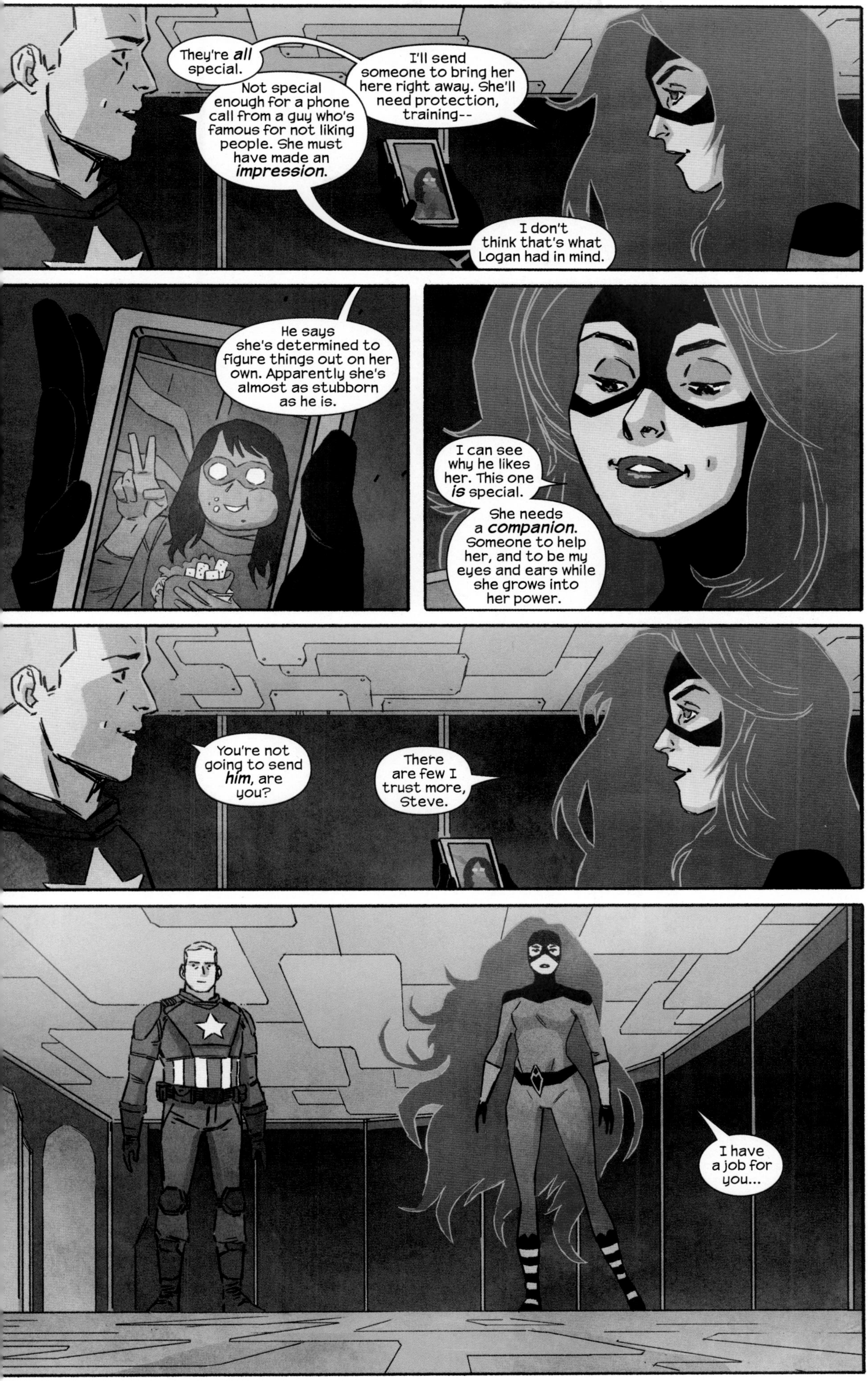

They're all special.
I'll send someone to bring her here right away. She'll need protection, training--
Not special enough for a phone call from a guy who's famous for not liking people. She must have made an impression.
I don't think that's what Logan had in mind.
He says she's determined to figure things out on her own. Apparently she's almost as stubborn as he is.
I can see why he likes her. This one is special.
She needs a companion. Someone to help her, and to be my eyes and ears while she grows into her power.
You're not going to send him, are you?
There are few I trust more, Steve.
I have a job for you...

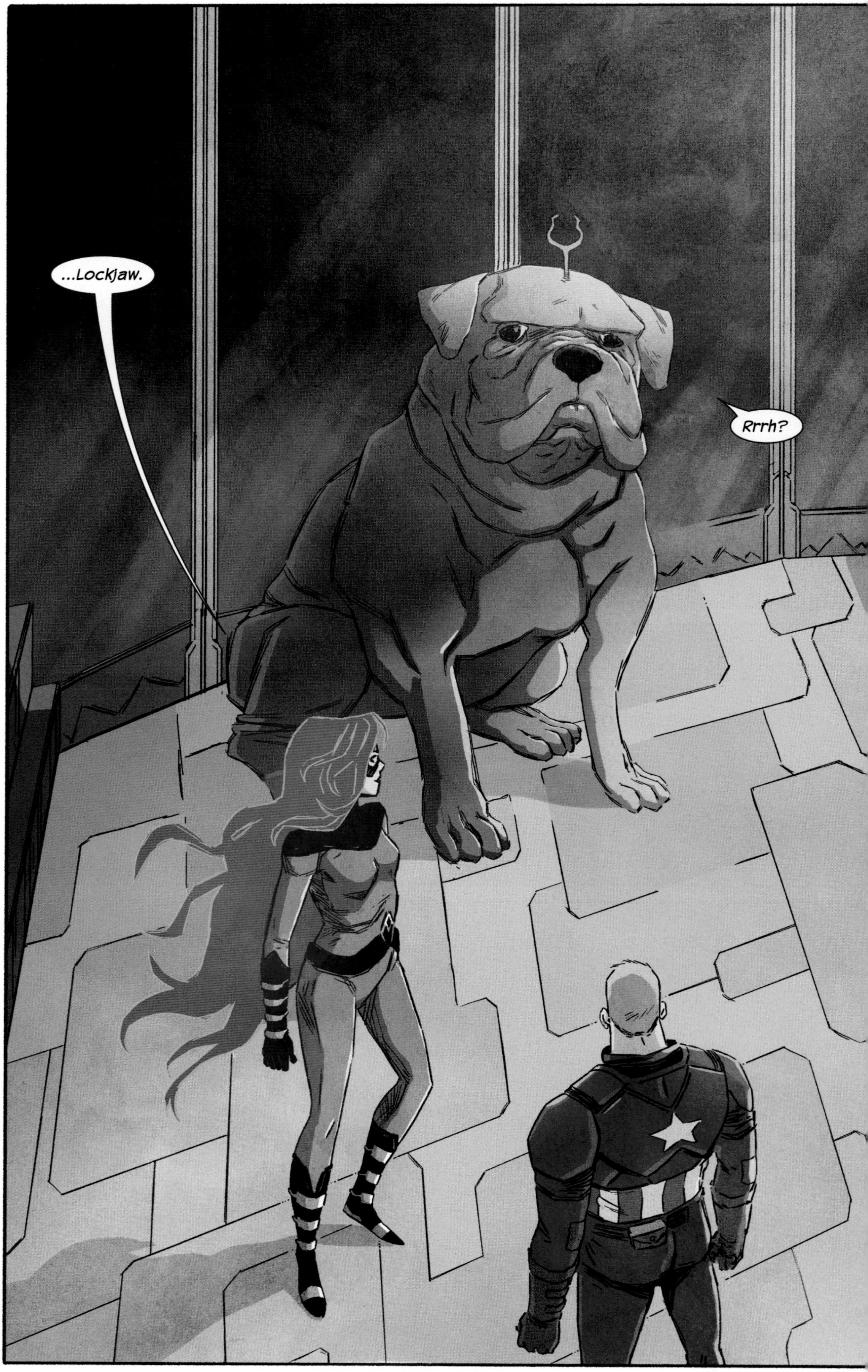
...Lockjaw.
Rrrh?

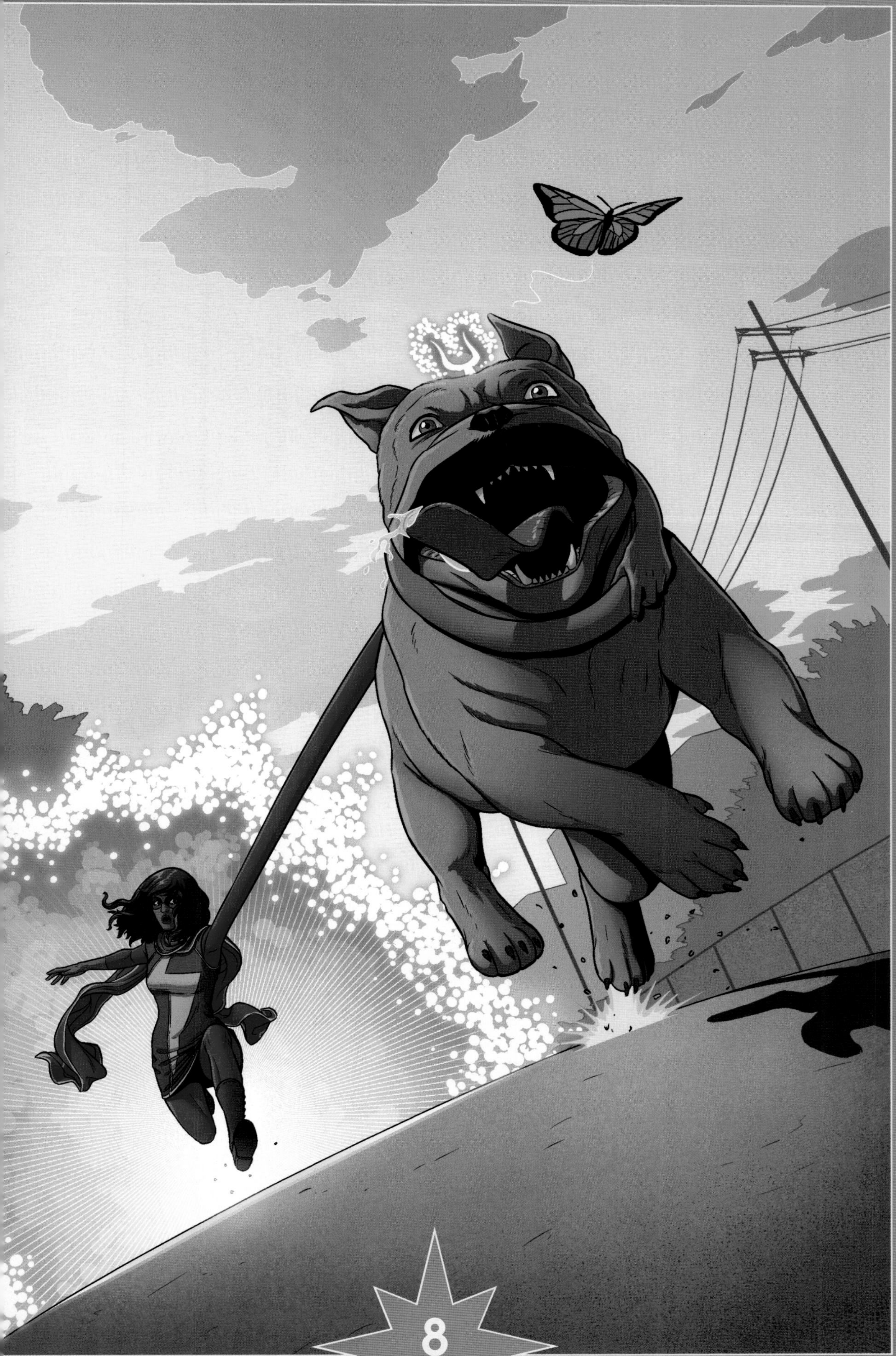
8

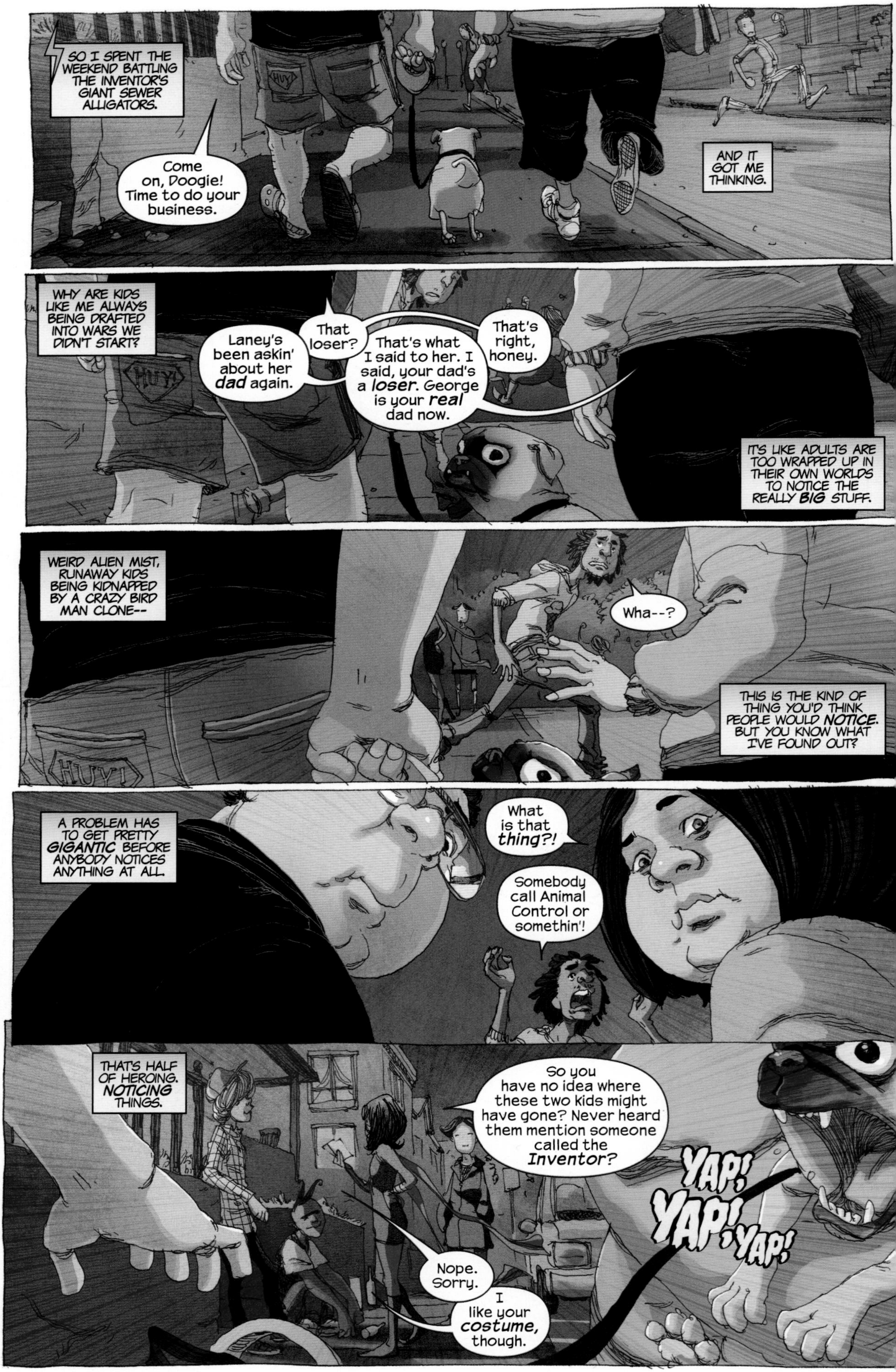

SO I SPENT THE WEEKEND BATTLING THE INVENTOR'S GIANT SEWER ALLIGATORS.
Come on, Doogie! Time to do your business.
AND IT GOT ME THINKING.
WHY ARE KIDS LIKE ME ALWAYS BEING DRAFTED INTO WARS WE DIDN'T START?
Laney's been askin' about her dad again.
That loser?
That's what I said to her. I said, your dad's a loser. George is your real dad now.
That's right, honey.
IT'S LIKE ADULTS ARE TOO WRAPPED UP IN THEIR OWN WORLDS TO NOTICE THE REALLY BIG STUFF.
WEIRD ALIEN MIST, RUNAWAY KIDS BEING KIDNAPPED BY A CRAZY BIRD MAN CLONE--
Wha--?
THIS IS THE KIND OF THING YOU'D THINK PEOPLE WOULD NOTICE. BUT YOU KNOW WHAT I'VE FOUND OUT?
A PROBLEM HAS TO GET PRETTY GIGANTIC BEFORE ANYBODY NOTICES ANYTHING AT ALL.
What is that thing?!
Somebody call Animal Control or somethin'!
THAT'S HALF OF HEROING. NOTICING THINGS.
So you have no idea where these two kids might have gone? Never heard them mention someone called the Inventor?
YAP! YAP! YAP!
Nope. Sorry.
I like your costume, though.

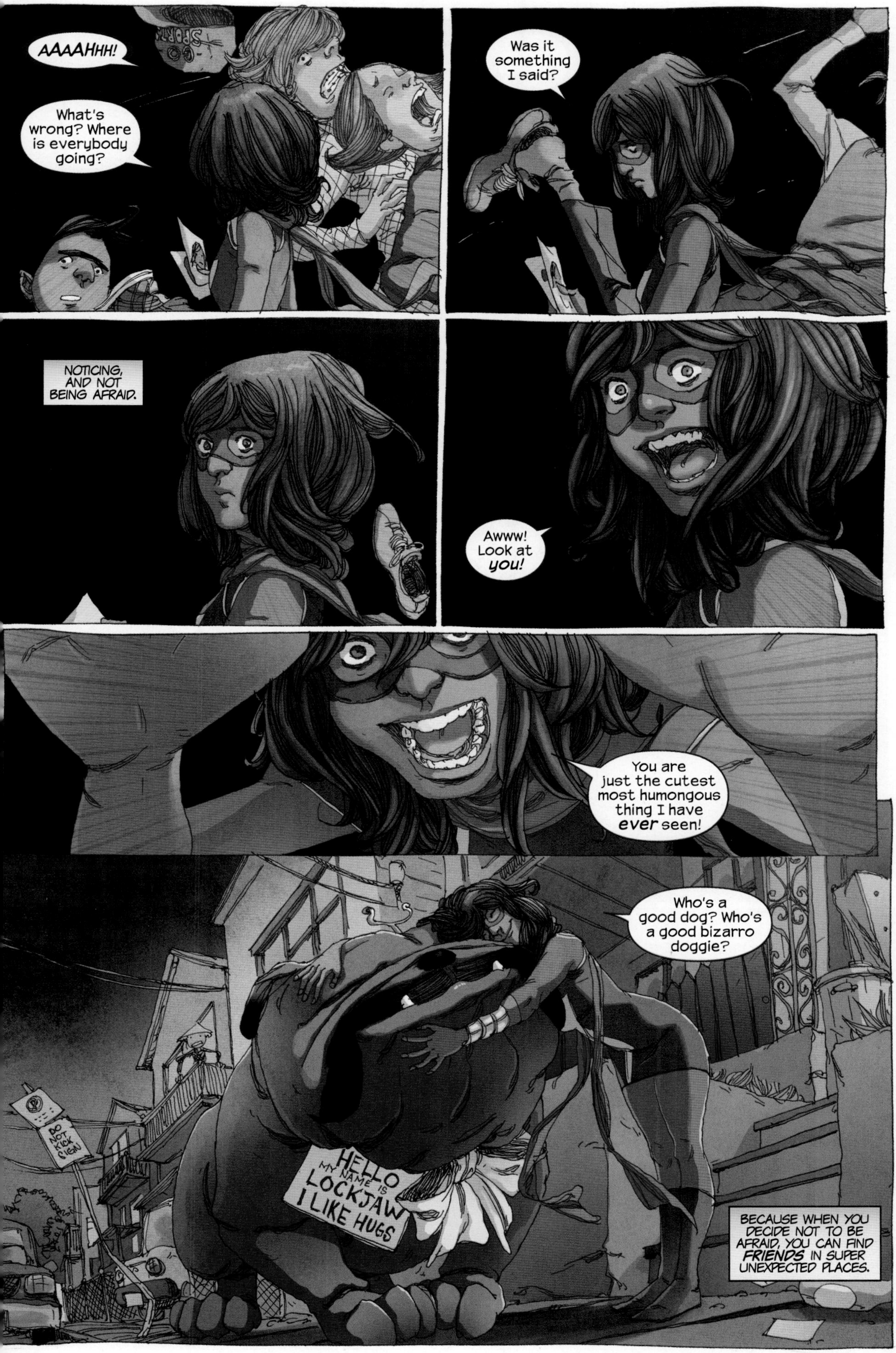
AAAAHHH!
What's wrong? Where is everybody going?
Was it something I said?
NOTICING, AND NOT BEING AFRAID.
Awww! Look at *you!*
You are just the cutest most humongous thing I have *ever* seen!
Who's a good dog? Who's a good bizarro doggie?
DO NOT KICK SIGN
HELLO MY NAME IS LOCKJAW I LIKE HUGS
BECAUSE WHEN YOU DECIDE NOT TO BE AFRAID, YOU CAN FIND *FRIENDS* IN SUPER UNEXPECTED PLACES.

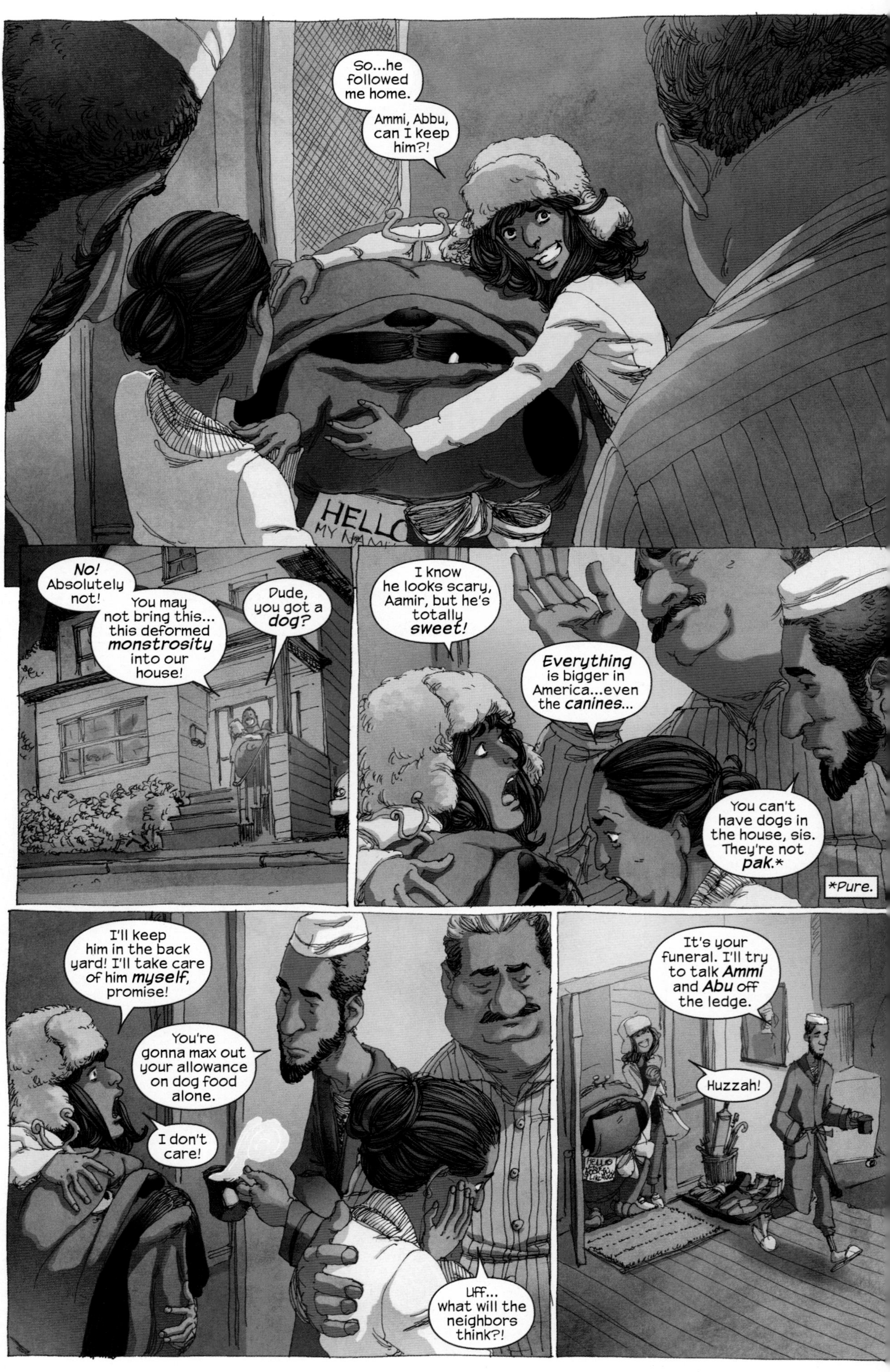

So...he followed me home.
Ammi, Abbu, can I keep him?!
HELLO MY NAME
No! Absolutely not!
You may not bring this... this deformed monstrosity into our house!
Dude, you got a dog?
I know he looks scary, Aamir, but he's totally sweet!
Everything is bigger in America...even the canines...
You can't have dogs in the house, sis. They're not pak.*
*Pure.
I'll keep him in the back yard! I'll take care of him myself, promise!
You're gonna max out your allowance on dog food alone.
I don't care!
Uff... what will the neighbors think?!
It's your funeral. I'll try to talk Ammi and Abu off the ledge.
Huzzah!

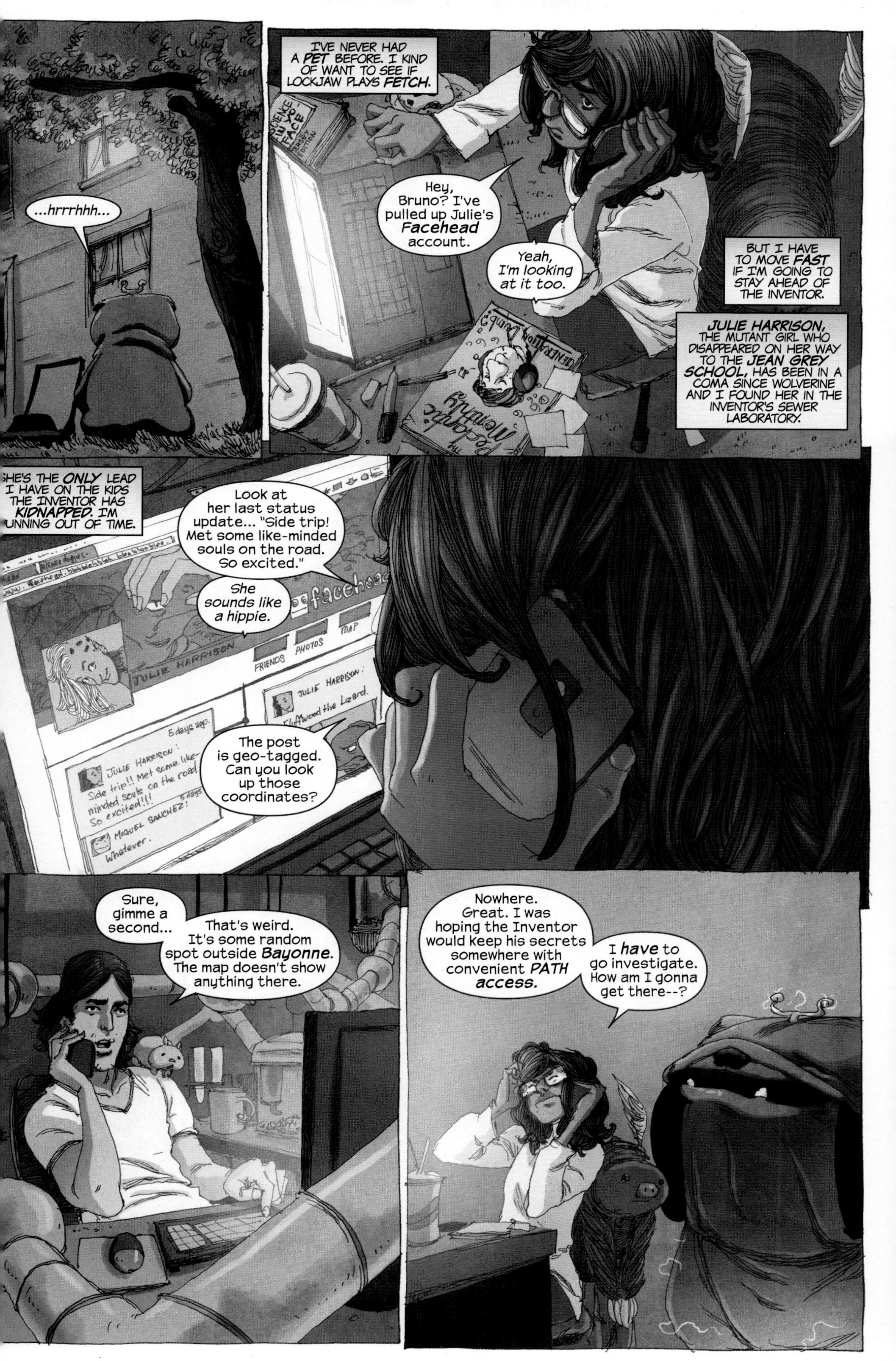
...hrrrhhh...
I'VE NEVER HAD A PET BEFORE. I KIND OF WANT TO SEE IF LOCKJAW PLAYS FETCH.
Hey, Bruno? I've pulled up Julie's Facehead account.
Yeah, I'm looking at it too.
BUT I HAVE TO MOVE FAST IF I'M GOING TO STAY AHEAD OF THE INVENTOR.
JULIE HARRISON, THE MUTANT GIRL WHO DISAPPEARED ON HER WAY TO THE JEAN GREY SCHOOL, HAS BEEN IN A COMA SINCE WOLVERINE AND I FOUND HER IN THE INVENTOR'S SEWER LABORATORY.
SHE'S THE ONLY LEAD I HAVE ON THE KIDS THE INVENTOR HAS KIDNAPPED. I'M RUNNING OUT OF TIME.
Look at her last status update... "Side trip! Met some like-minded souls on the road. So excited."
She sounds like a hippie.
JULIE HARRISON
FRIENDS
PHOTOS
MAP
JULIE HARRISON: Side trip!! Met some like-minded souls on the road So excited!!!
MIGUEL SANCHEZ: Whatever.
The post is geo-tagged. Can you look up those coordinates?
Sure, gimme a second...
That's weird. It's some random spot outside Bayonne. The map doesn't show anything there.
Nowhere. Great. I was hoping the Inventor would keep his secrets somewhere with convenient PATH access.
I have to go investigate. How am I gonna get there--?

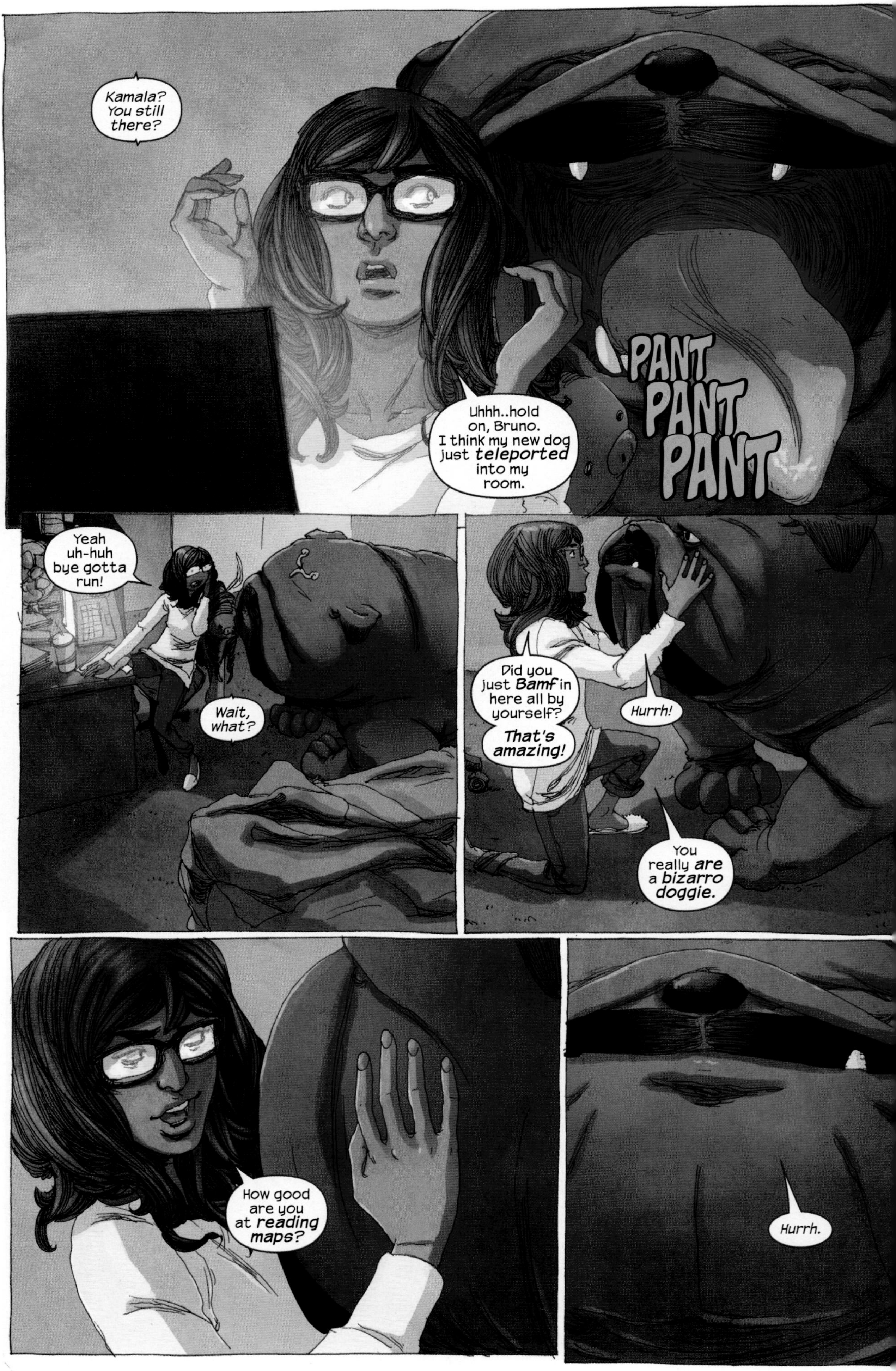
Kamala? You still there?
Uhhh..hold on, Bruno. I think my new dog just teleported into my room.
PANT PANT PANT
Yeah uh-huh bye gotta run!
Wait, what?
Did you just Bamf in here all by yourself?
That's amazing!
Hurrh!
You really are a bizarro doggie.
How good are you at reading maps?
Hurrh.

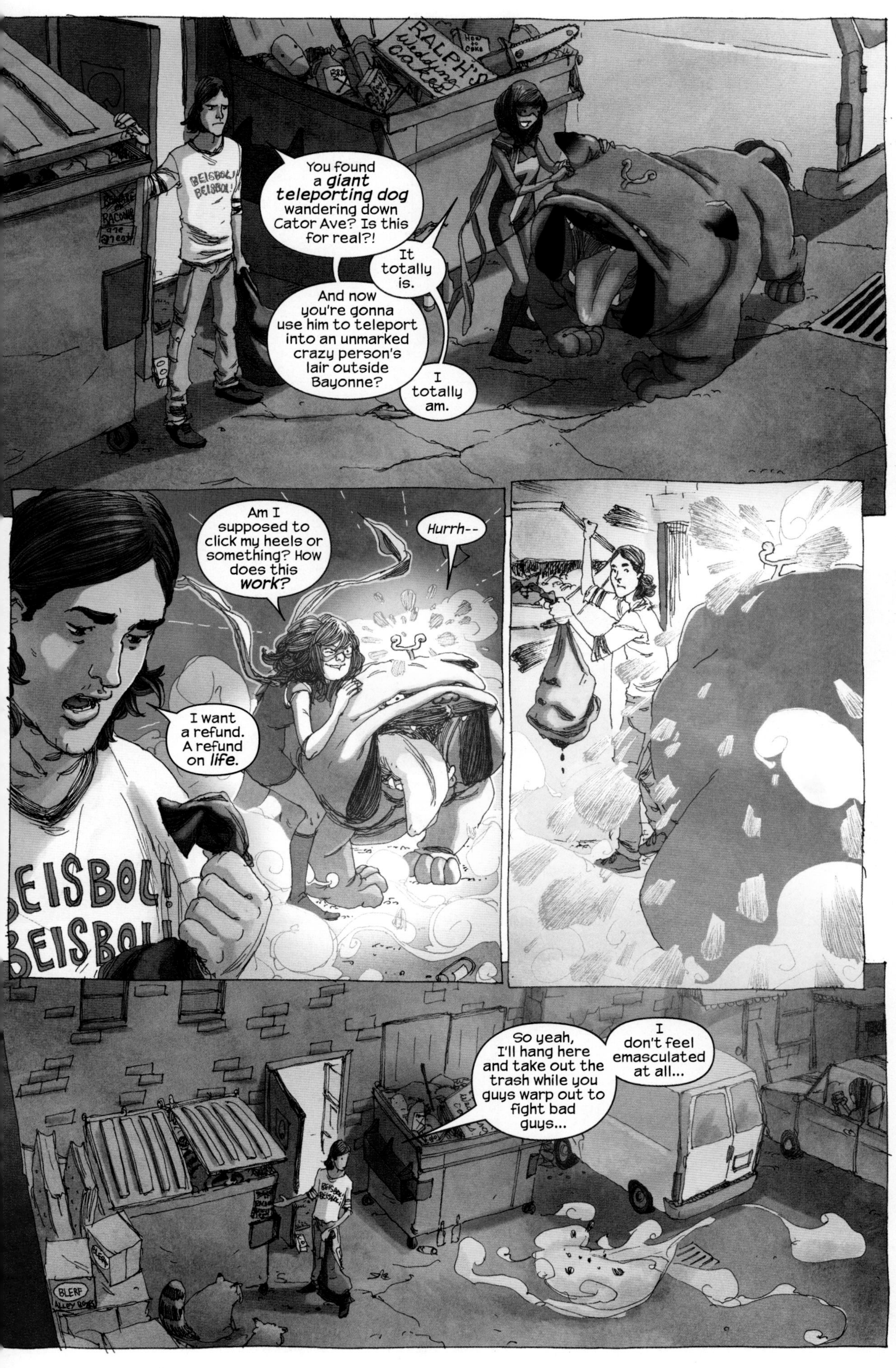
RALPH'S Wedding Cakes
BEISBOL! BEISBOL!
You found a **giant teleporting dog** wandering down Cator Ave? Is this for real?!
It totally is.
And now you're gonna use him to teleport into an unmarked crazy person's lair outside Bayonne?
I totally am.
Am I supposed to click my heels or something? How does this **work?**
Hurrh--
I want a refund. A refund on ***life.***
BEISBOL! BEISBOL!
So yeah, I'll hang here and take out the trash while you guys warp out to fight bad guys...
I don't feel emasculated at all...
BLERF

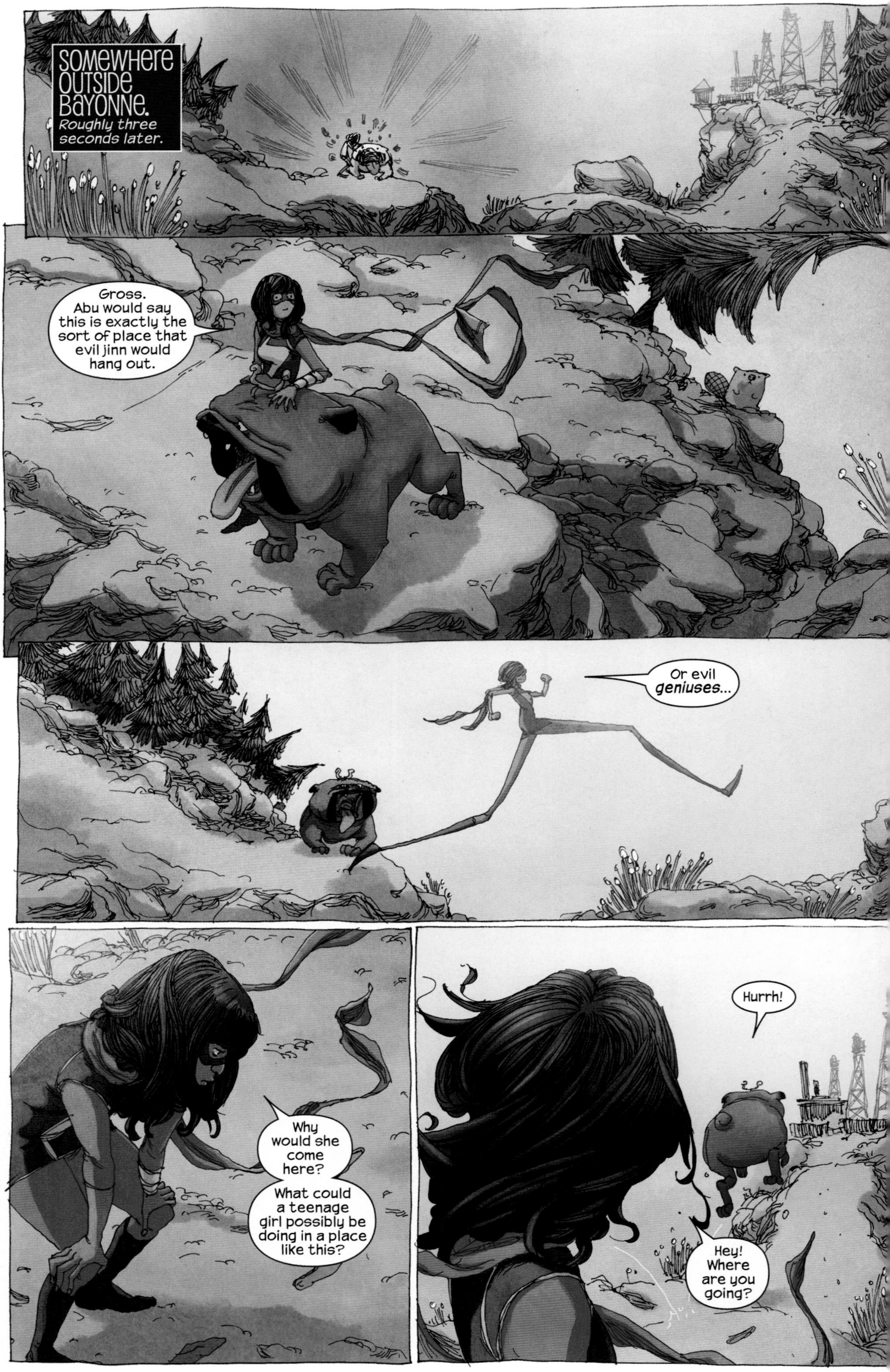
SOMEWHERE OUTSIDE BAYONNE.
Roughly three seconds later.
Gross. Abu would say this is exactly the sort of place that evil jinn would hang out.
Or evil geniuses...
Why would she come here?
What could a teenage girl possibly be doing in a place like this?
Hurrh!
Hey! Where are you going?

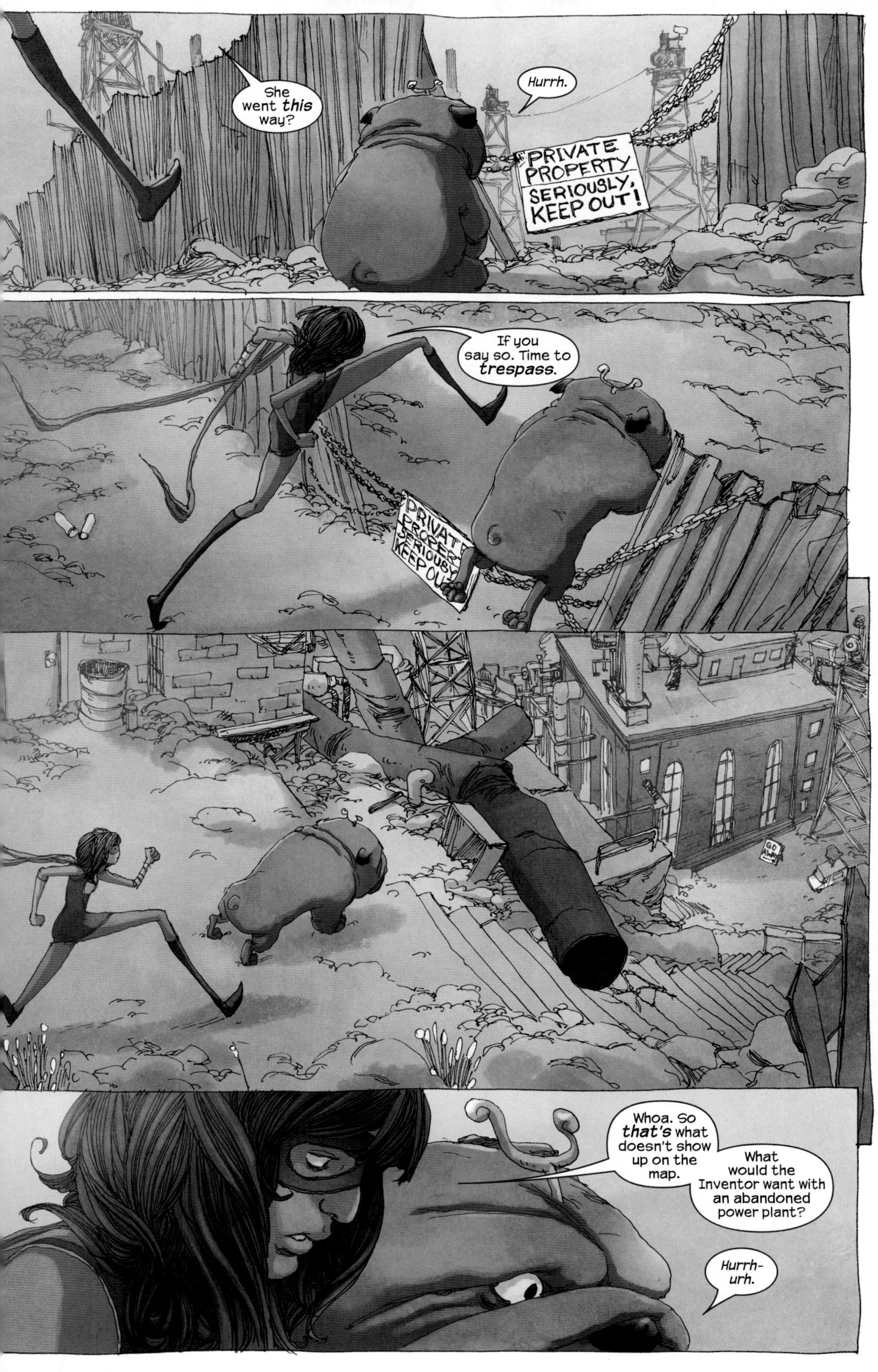

She went this way?
Hurrh.
PRIVATE PROPERTY SERIOUSLY, KEEP OUT!
If you say so. Time to trespass.
GO AWAY
Whoa. So that's what doesn't show up on the map.
What would the Inventor want with an abandoned power plant?
Hurrh-urh.

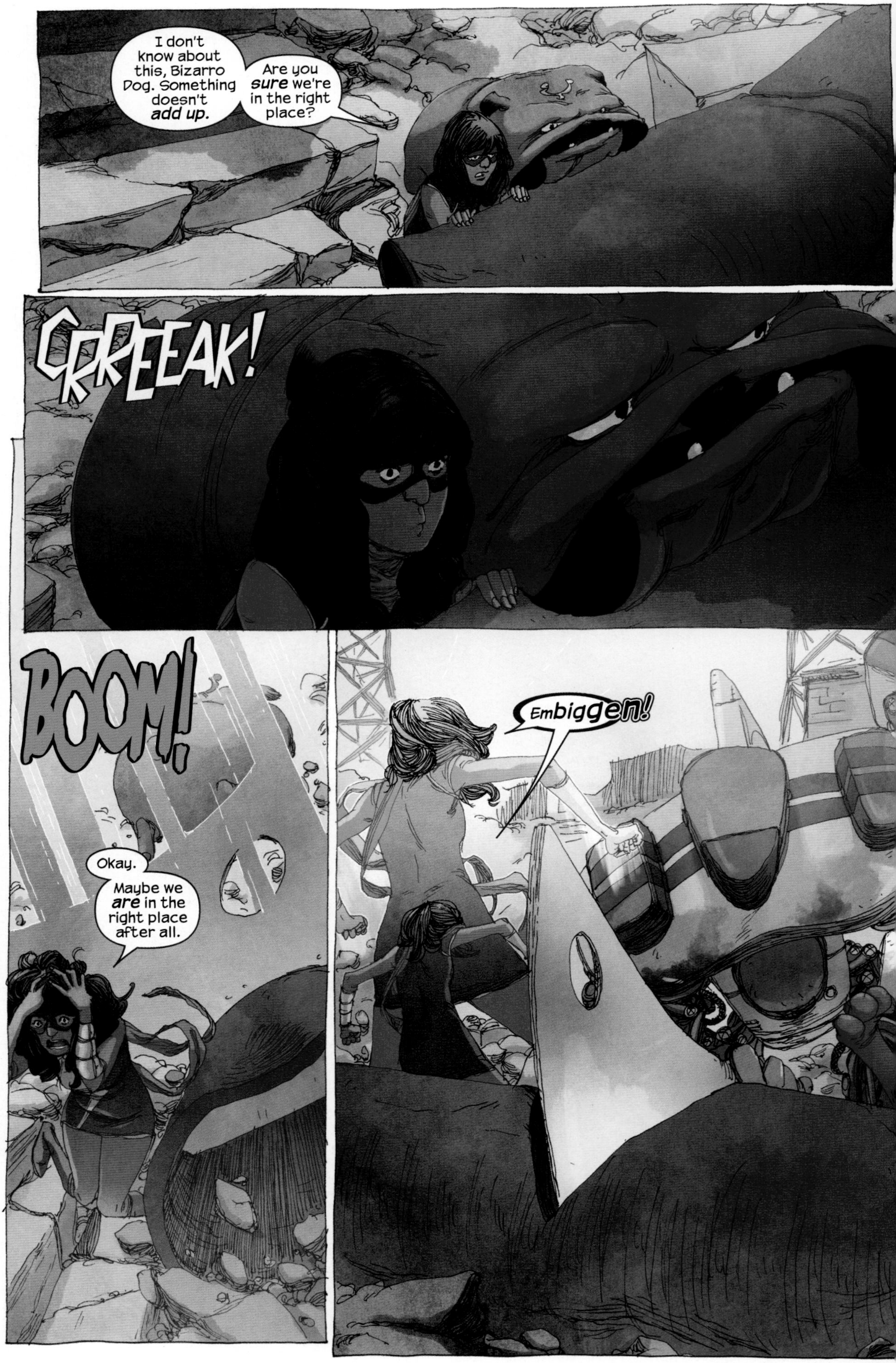
I don't know about this, Bizarro Dog. Something doesn't add up.
Are you sure we're in the right place?
CRREEAK!
BOOM!
Okay.
Maybe we are in the right place after all.
Embiggen!

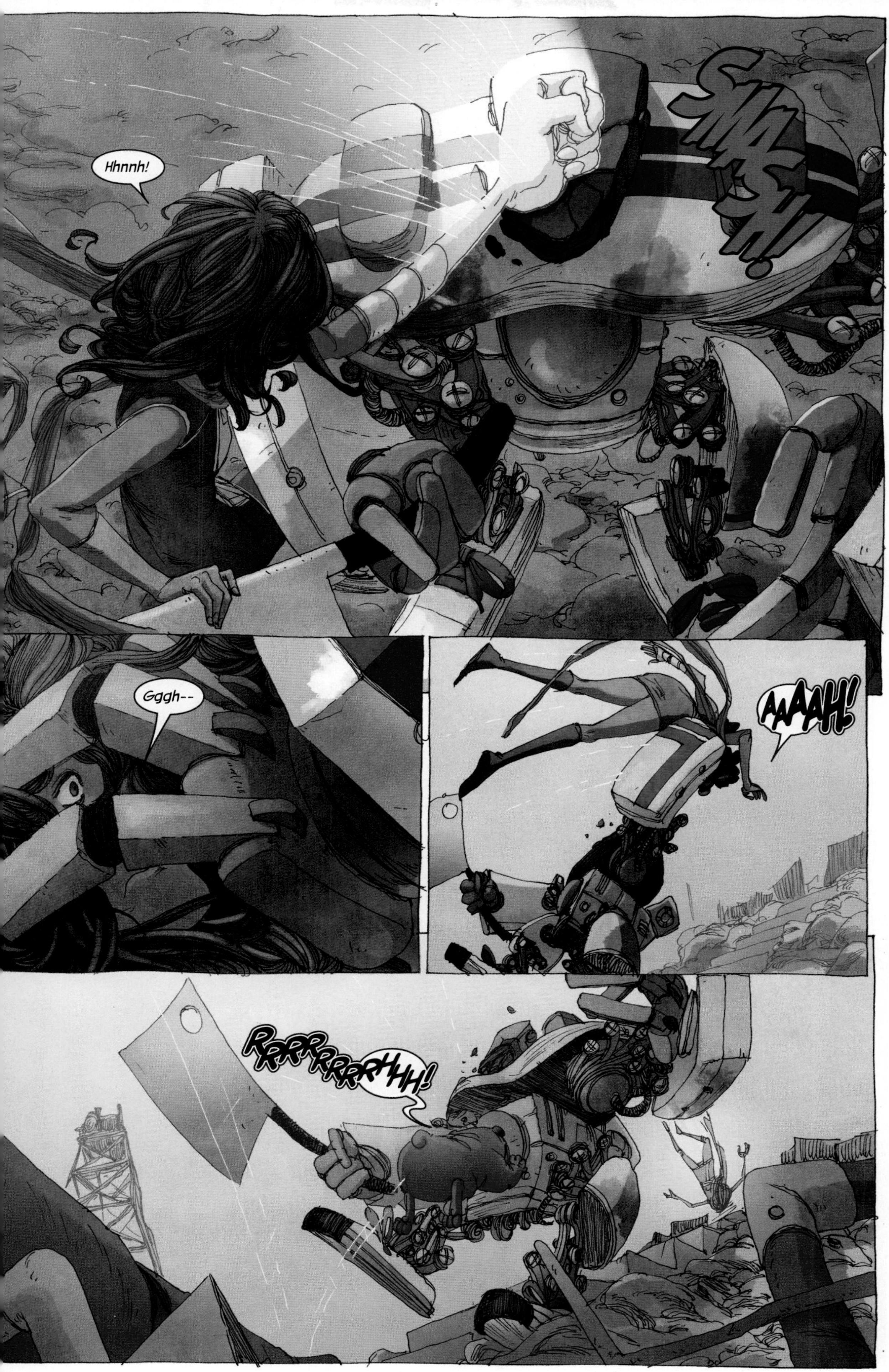
Hhnnh!
SMASH!
Gggh--
AAAAH!
RRRRRRRRRHHH!

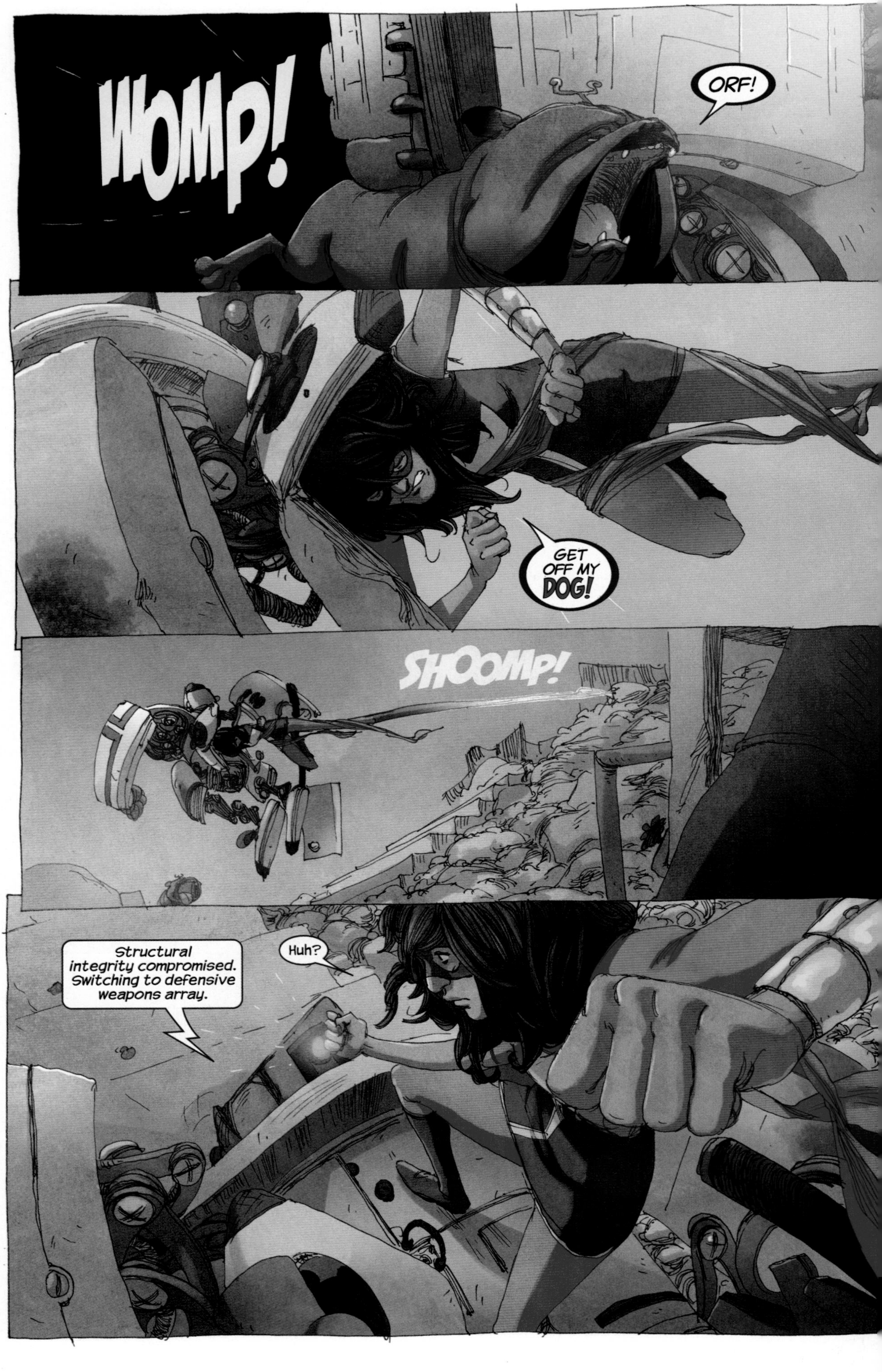
WOMP!
ORF!
GET OFF MY DOG!
SHOOMP!
Structural integrity compromised. Switching to defensive weapons array.
Huh?

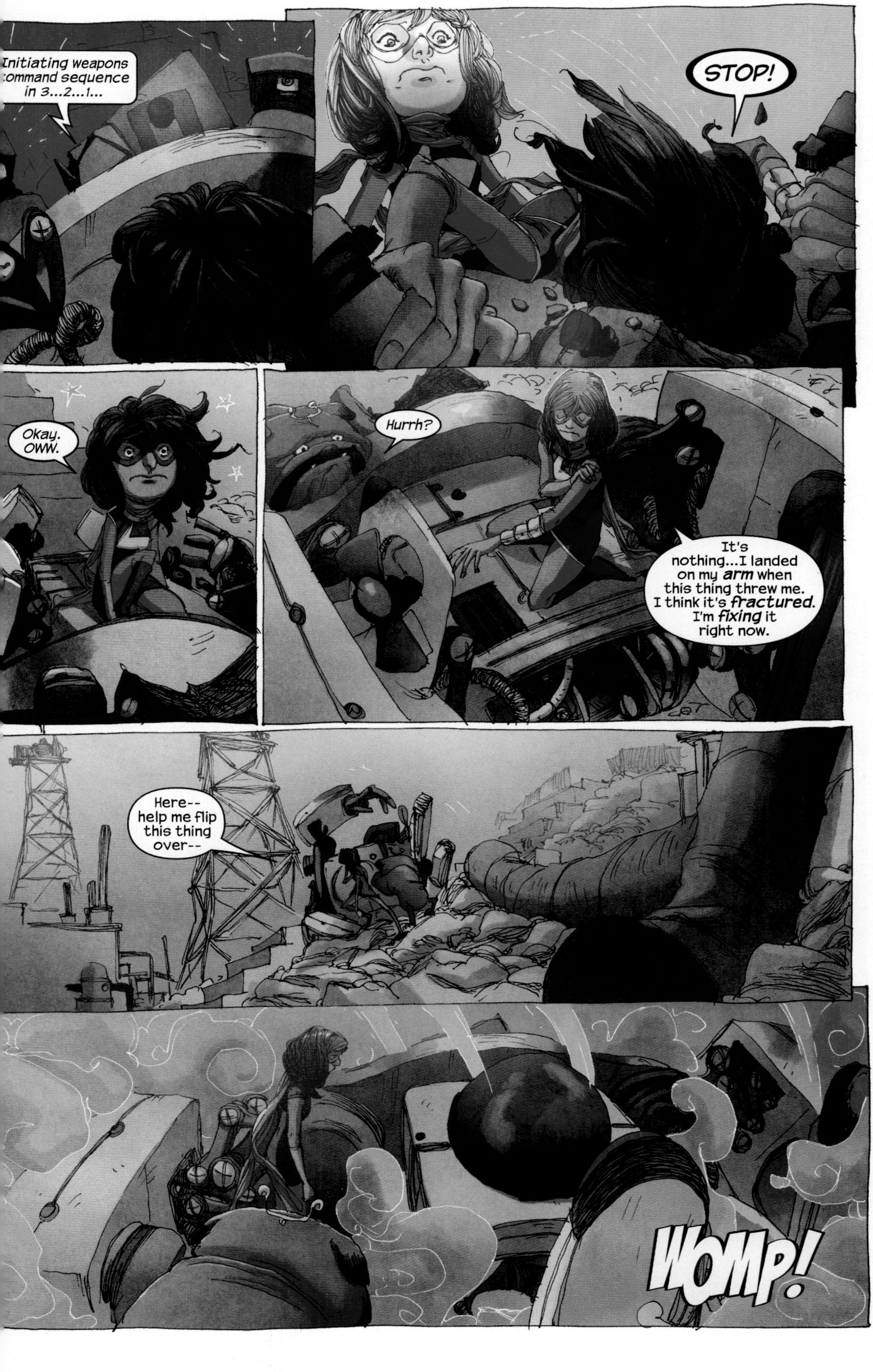

Initiating weapons command sequence in 3...2...1...
STOP!
Okay. OWW.
Hurrh?
It's nothing...I landed on my arm when this thing threw me. I think it's fractured. I'm fixing it right now.
Here-- help me flip this thing over--
WOMP!

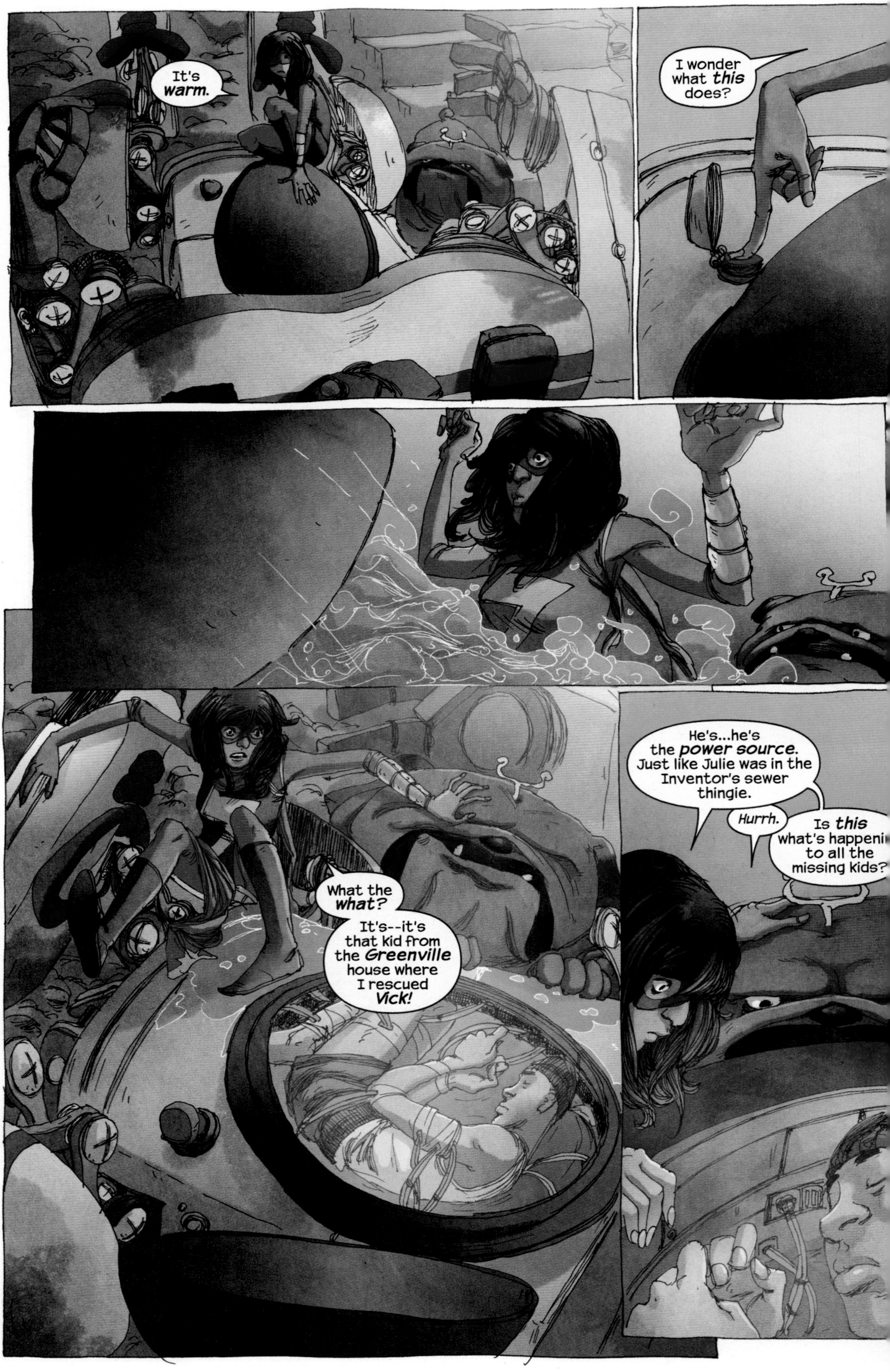
It's *warm.*
I wonder what *this* does?
What the *what?*
It's--it's that kid from the *Greenville* house where I rescued *Vick!*
He's...he's the *power source.* Just like Julie was in the Inventor's sewer thingie.
Hurrh.
Is *this* what's happeni to all the missing kids?

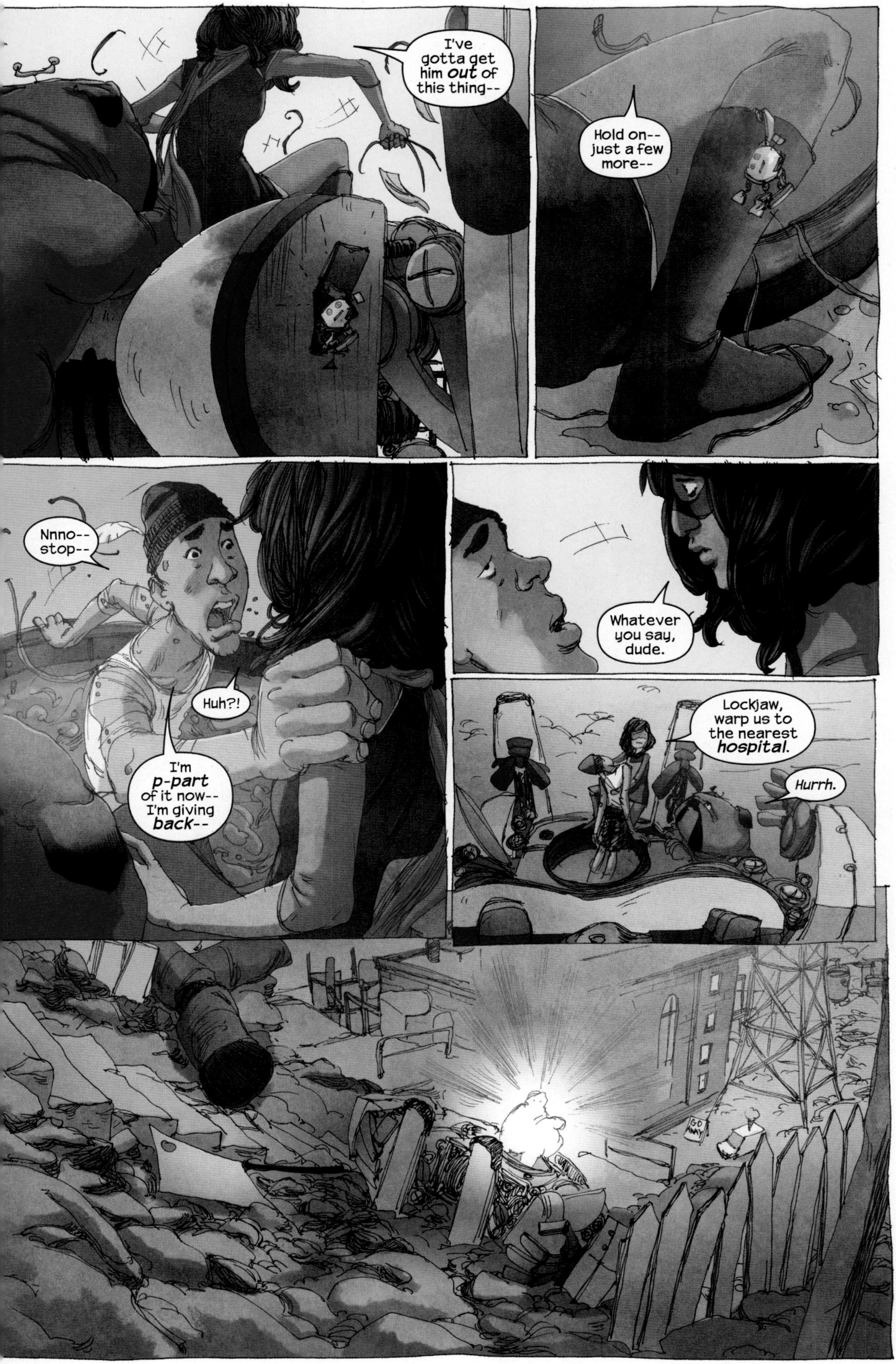
I've gotta get him out of this thing--
Hold on-- just a few more--
Nnno-- stop--
Huh?!
I'm p-part of it now-- I'm giving back--
Whatever you say, dude.
Lockjaw, warp us to the nearest hospital.
Hurrh.
GO AWAY

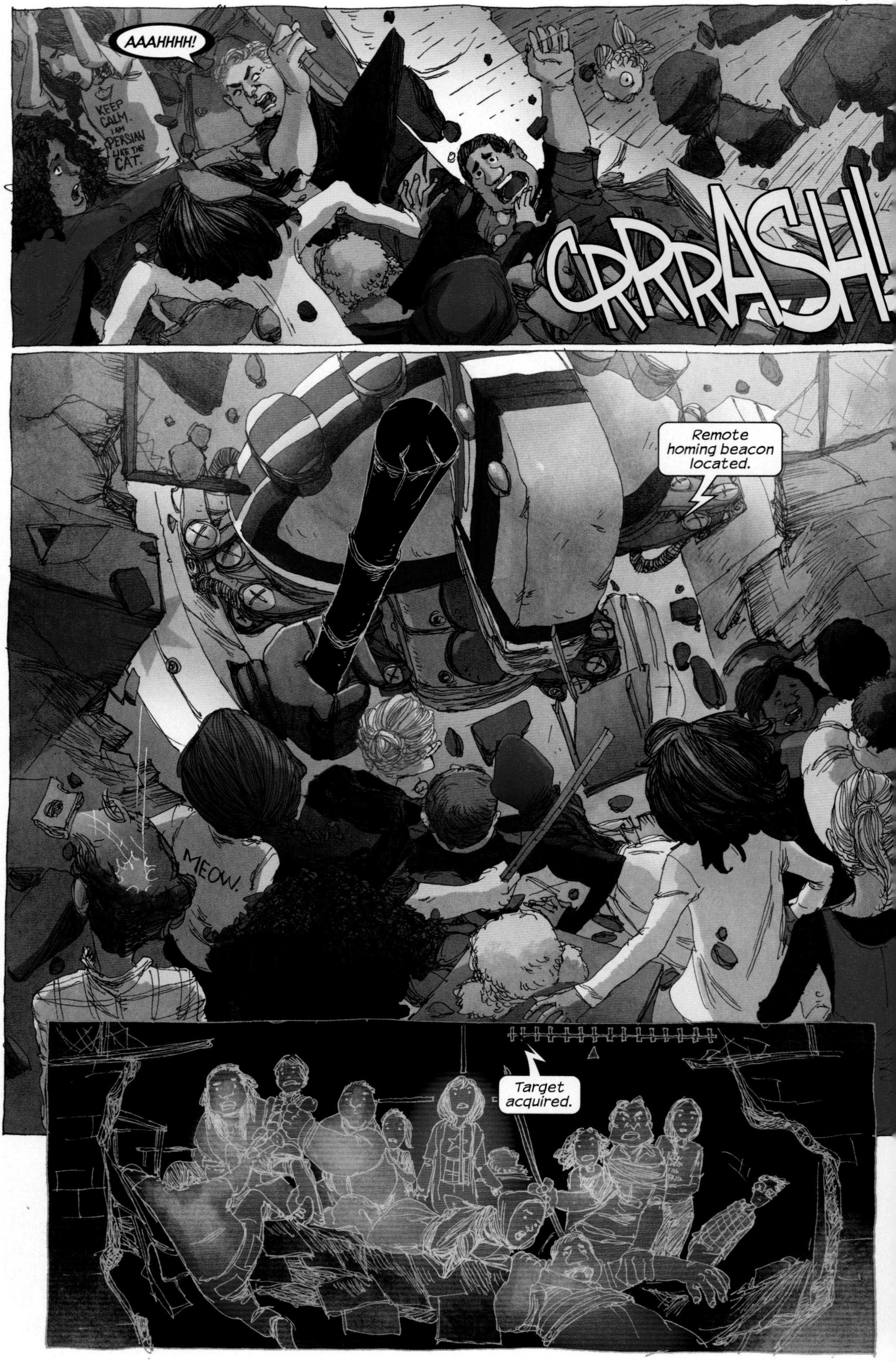
AAAHHHH!
KEEP CALM. I AM PERSIAN LIKE THE CAT.
CRRRASH!
Remote homing beacon located.
MEOW!
Target acquired.

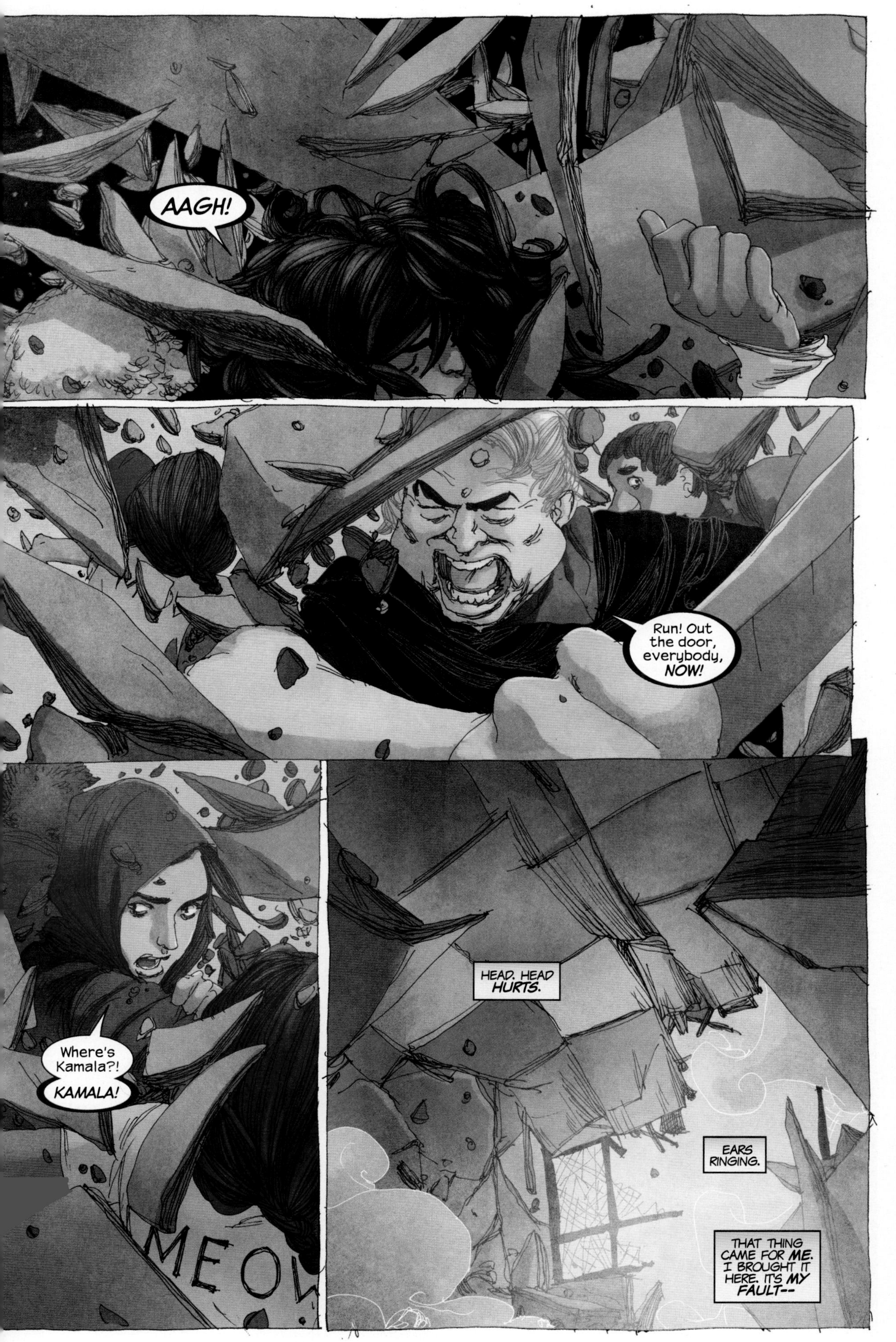
AAGH!
Run! Out the door, everybody, NOW!
Where's Kamala?!
KAMALA!
MEOW
HEAD. HEAD HURTS.
EARS RINGING.
THAT THING CAME FOR ME. I BROUGHT IT HERE. IT'S MY FAULT--

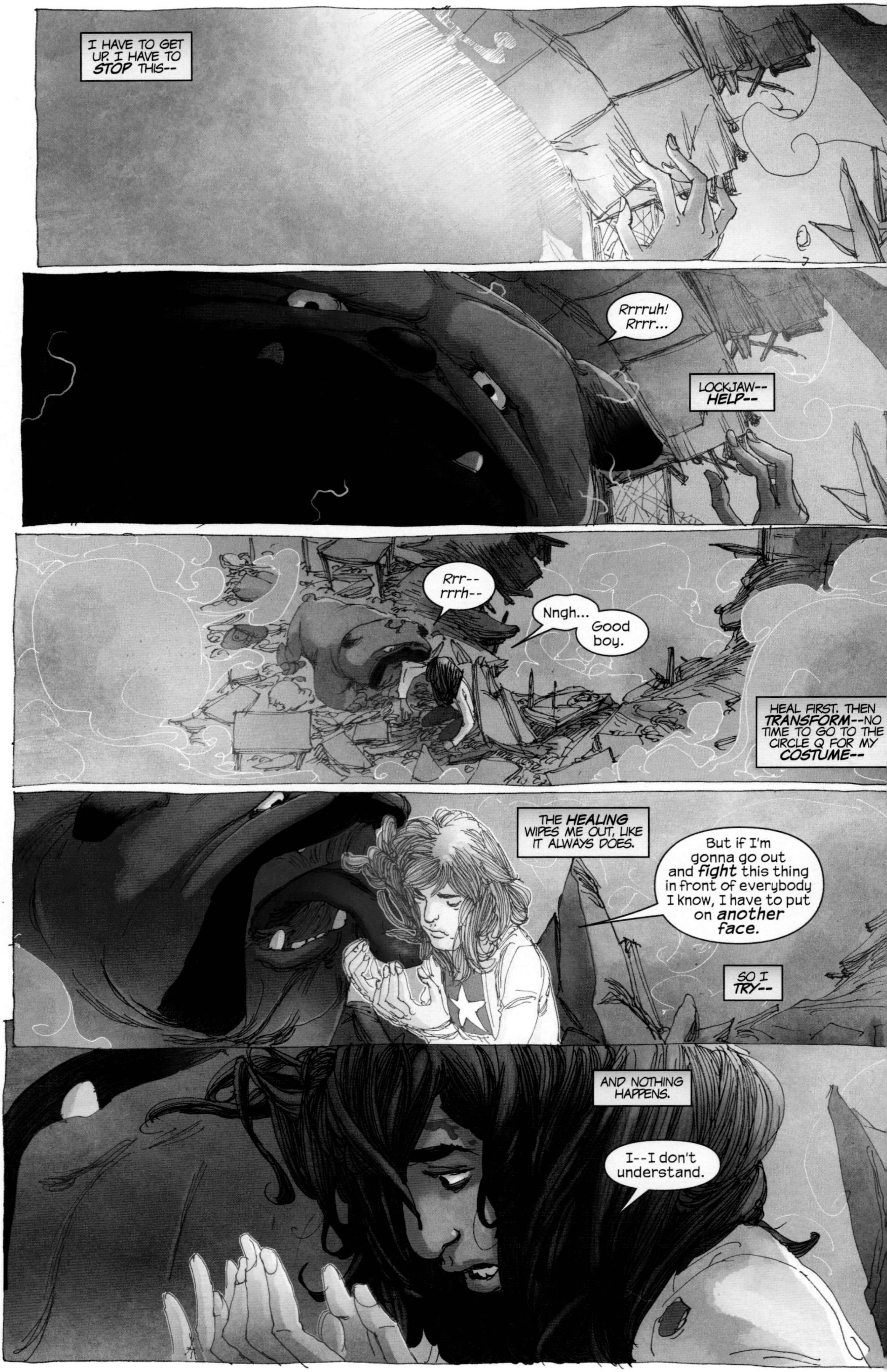

I HAVE TO GET UP. I HAVE TO *STOP* THIS--
Rrrruh! Rrrr...
LOCKJAW-- *HELP*--
Rrr-- rrrh--
Nngh... Good boy.
HEAL FIRST. THEN *TRANSFORM*--NO TIME TO GO TO THE CIRCLE Q FOR MY *COSTUME*--
THE *HEALING* WIPES ME OUT, LIKE IT ALWAYS DOES.
But if I'm gonna go out and *fight* this thing in front of everybody I know, I have to put on *another face.*
SO I *TRY*--
AND NOTHING HAPPENS.
I--I don't understand.

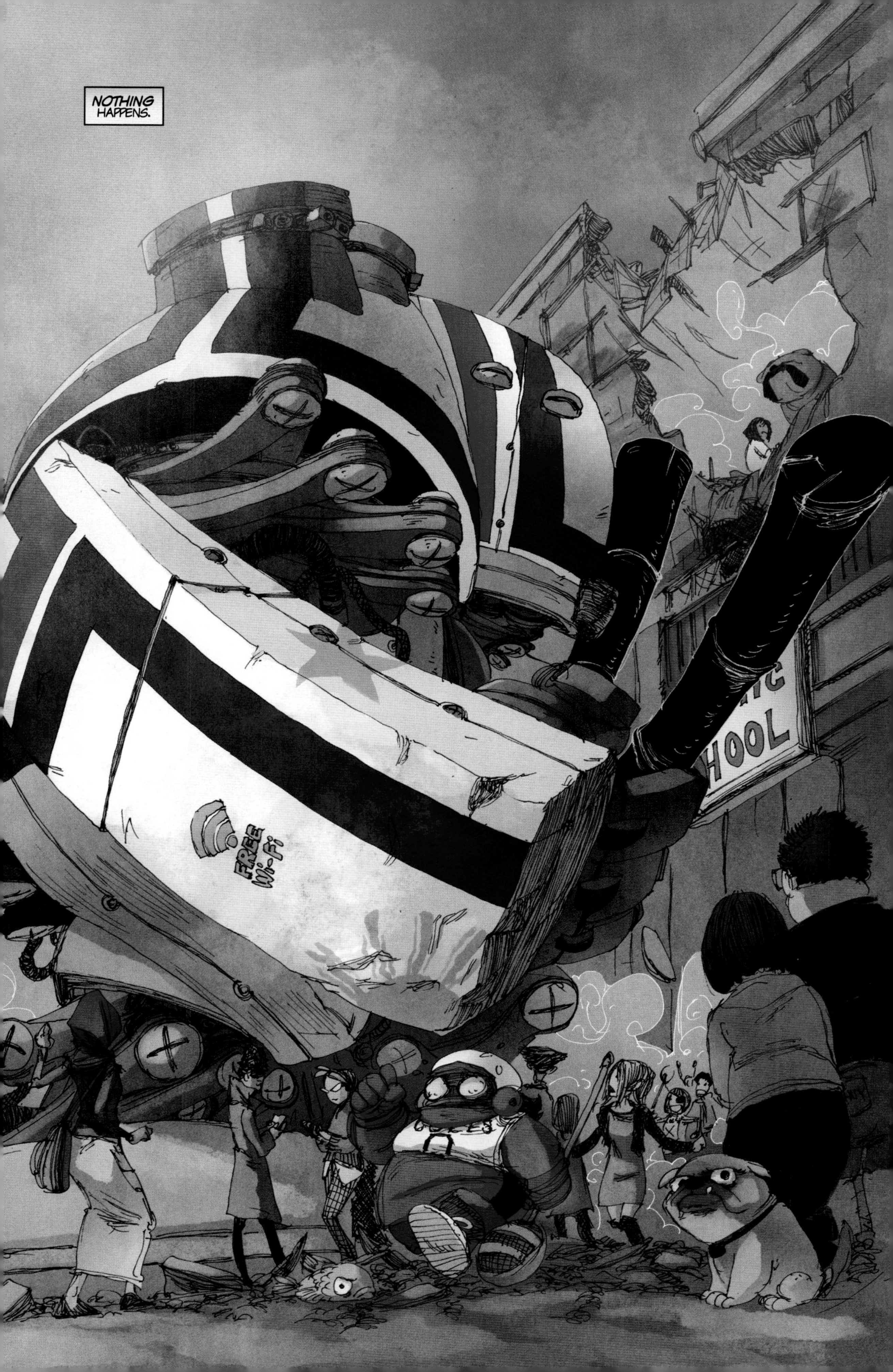
NOTHING HAPPENS.
FREE Wi-Fi
HOOL

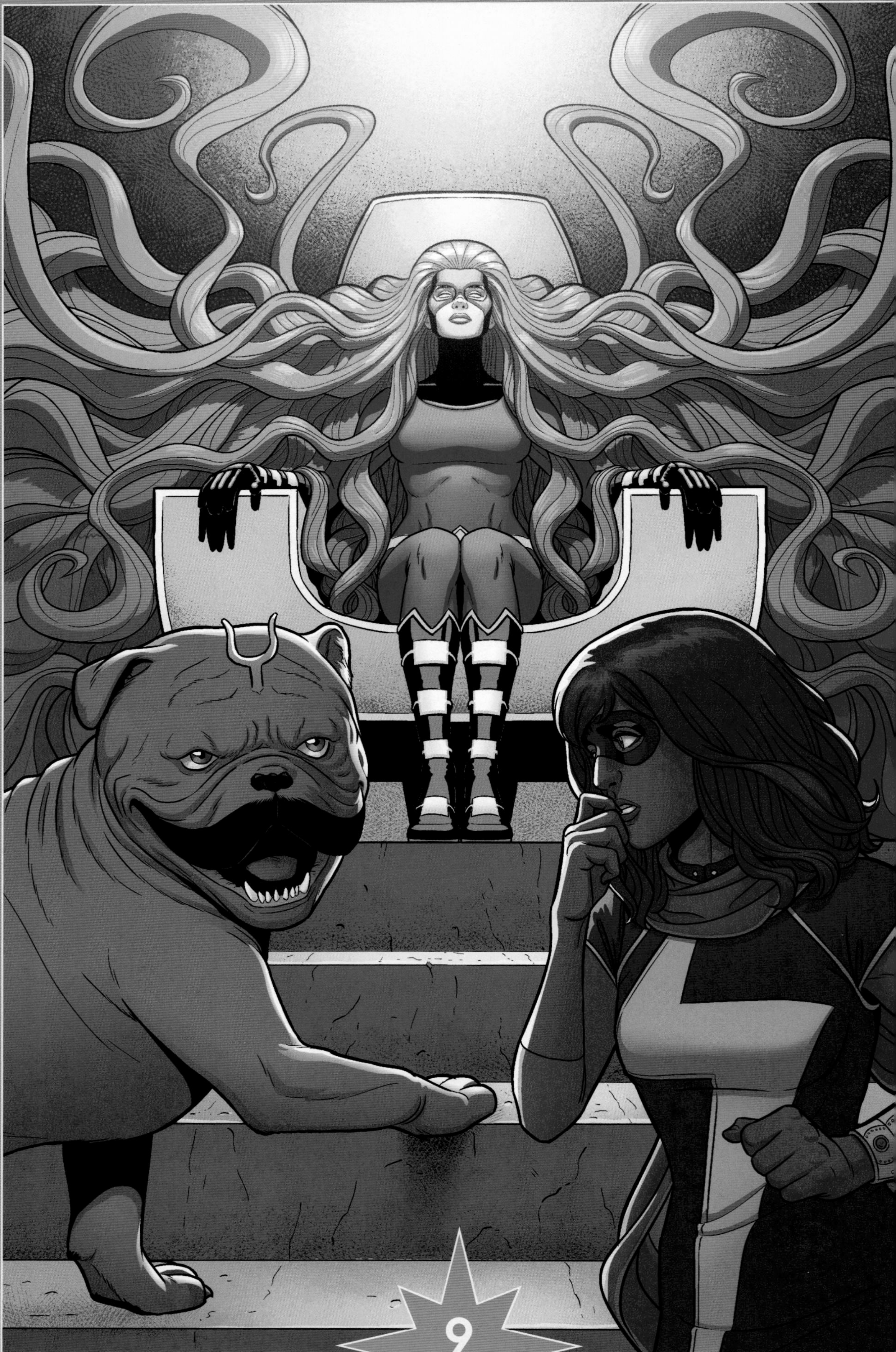
9

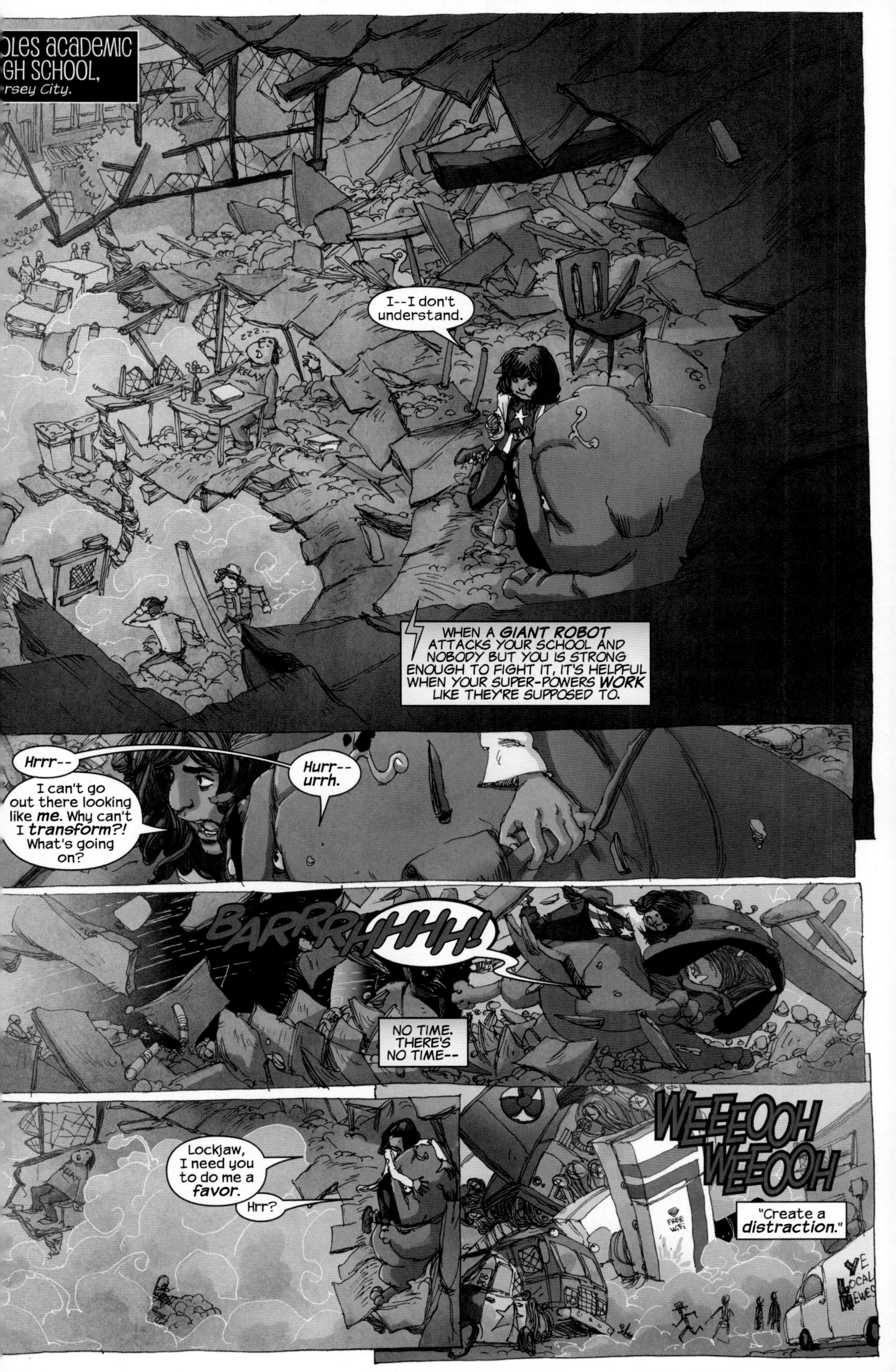

OLES ACADEMIC
GH SCHOOL,
rsey City.
I--I don't understand.
ZZZ...
RELAX
WHEN A GIANT ROBOT ATTACKS YOUR SCHOOL AND NOBODY BUT YOU IS STRONG ENOUGH TO FIGHT IT, IT'S HELPFUL WHEN YOUR SUPER-POWERS WORK LIKE THEY'RE SUPPOSED TO.
Hrrr--
I can't go out there looking like me. Why can't I transform?! What's going on?
Hurr--urrh.
BARRRHHHH!
NO TIME. THERE'S NO TIME--
Lockjaw, I need you to do me a favor.
Hrr?
WEEEOOH WEEEOOH
"Create a distraction."
FREE WiFi
YE LOCAL NEWES

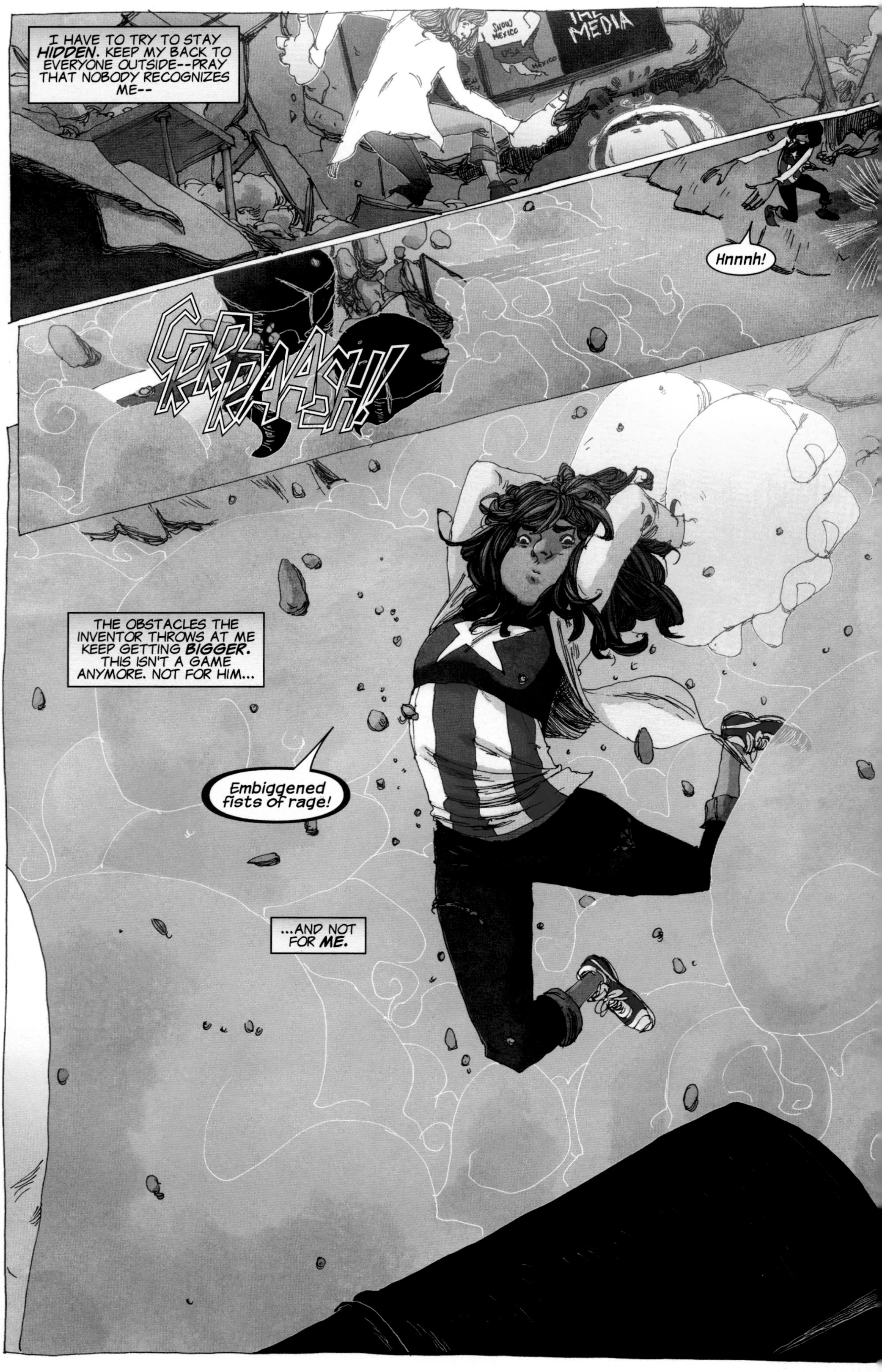
I HAVE TO TRY TO STAY HIDDEN. KEEP MY BACK TO EVERYONE OUTSIDE--PRAY THAT NOBODY RECOGNIZES ME--
THE MEDIA
Hnnnh!
GRRBAKASH!
THE OBSTACLES THE INVENTOR THROWS AT ME KEEP GETTING BIGGER. THIS ISN'T A GAME ANYMORE. NOT FOR HIM...
Embiggened fists of rage!
...AND NOT FOR ME.

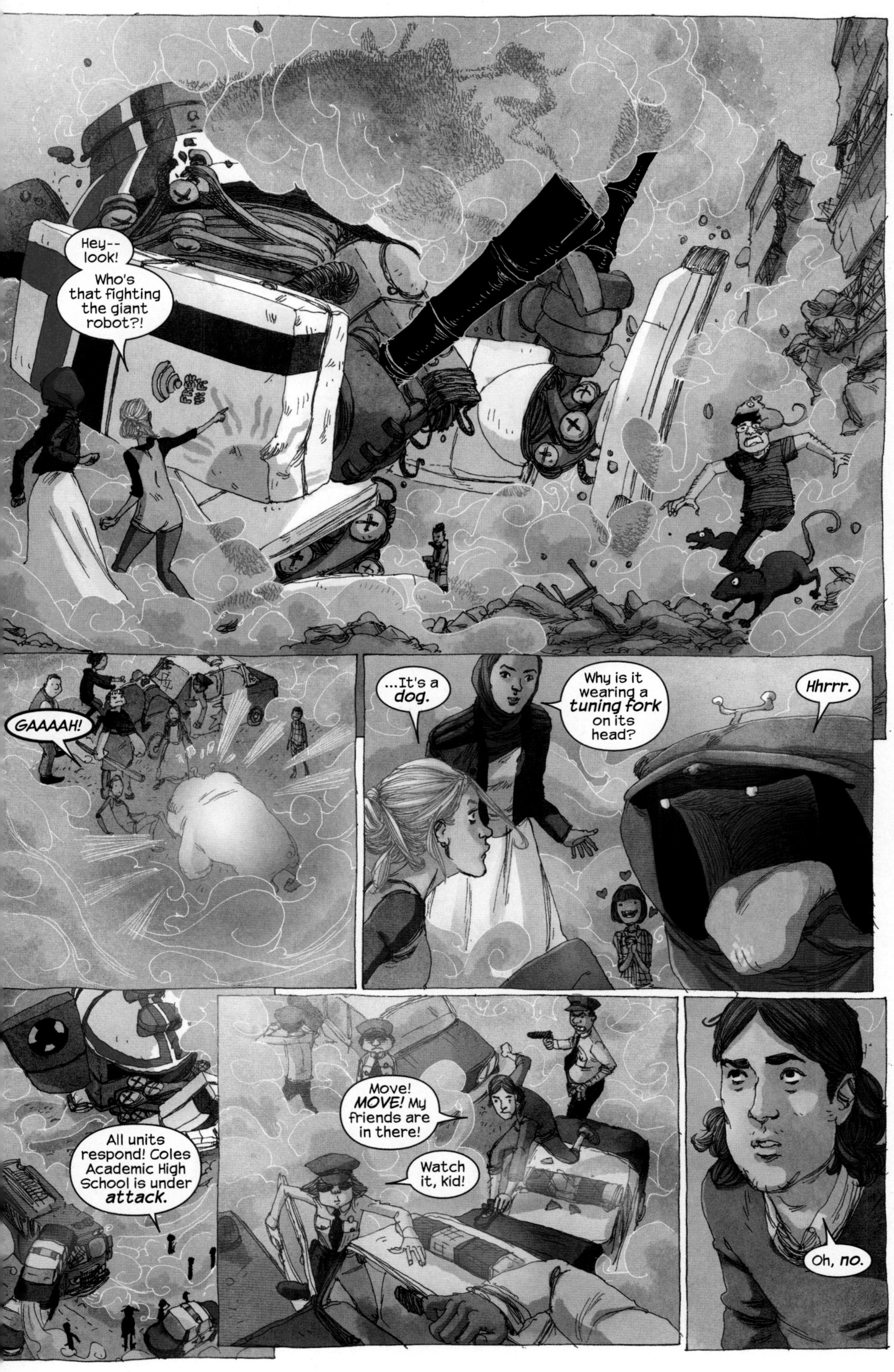
Hey-- look!
Who's that fighting the giant robot?!
GAAAAH!
...It's a dog.
Why is it wearing a tuning fork on its head?
Hhrrr.
All units respond! Coles Academic High School is under attack.
Move! MOVE! My friends are in there!
Watch it, kid!
Oh, no.

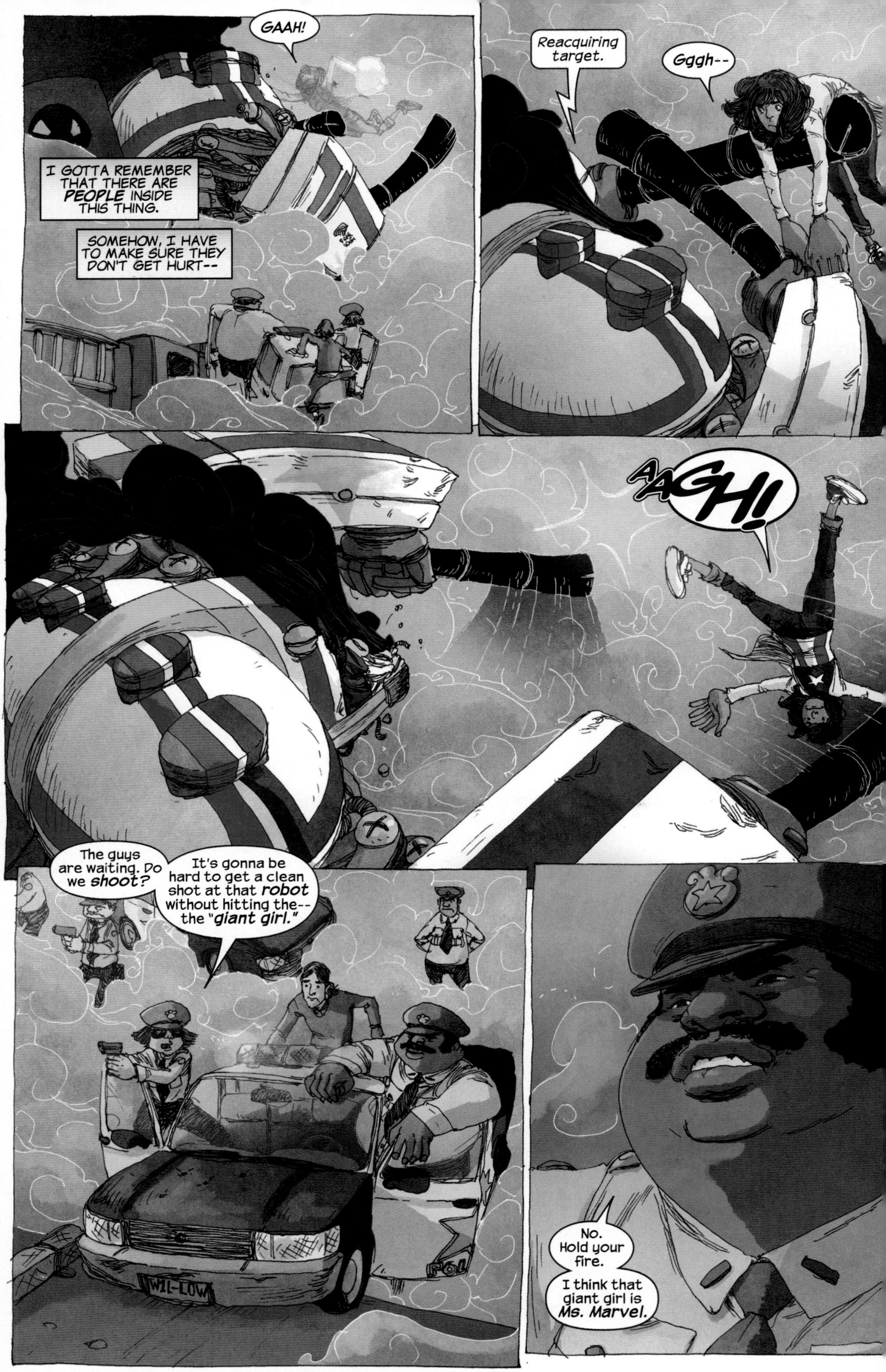

GAAH!
I GOTTA REMEMBER THAT THERE ARE PEOPLE INSIDE THIS THING.
SOMEHOW, I HAVE TO MAKE SURE THEY DON'T GET HURT--
Reacquiring target.
Gggh--
AAGH!
The guys are waiting. Do we shoot?
It's gonna be hard to get a clean shot at that robot without hitting the-- the "giant girl."
WI1-LOW
No. Hold your fire.
I think that giant girl is Ms. Marvel.

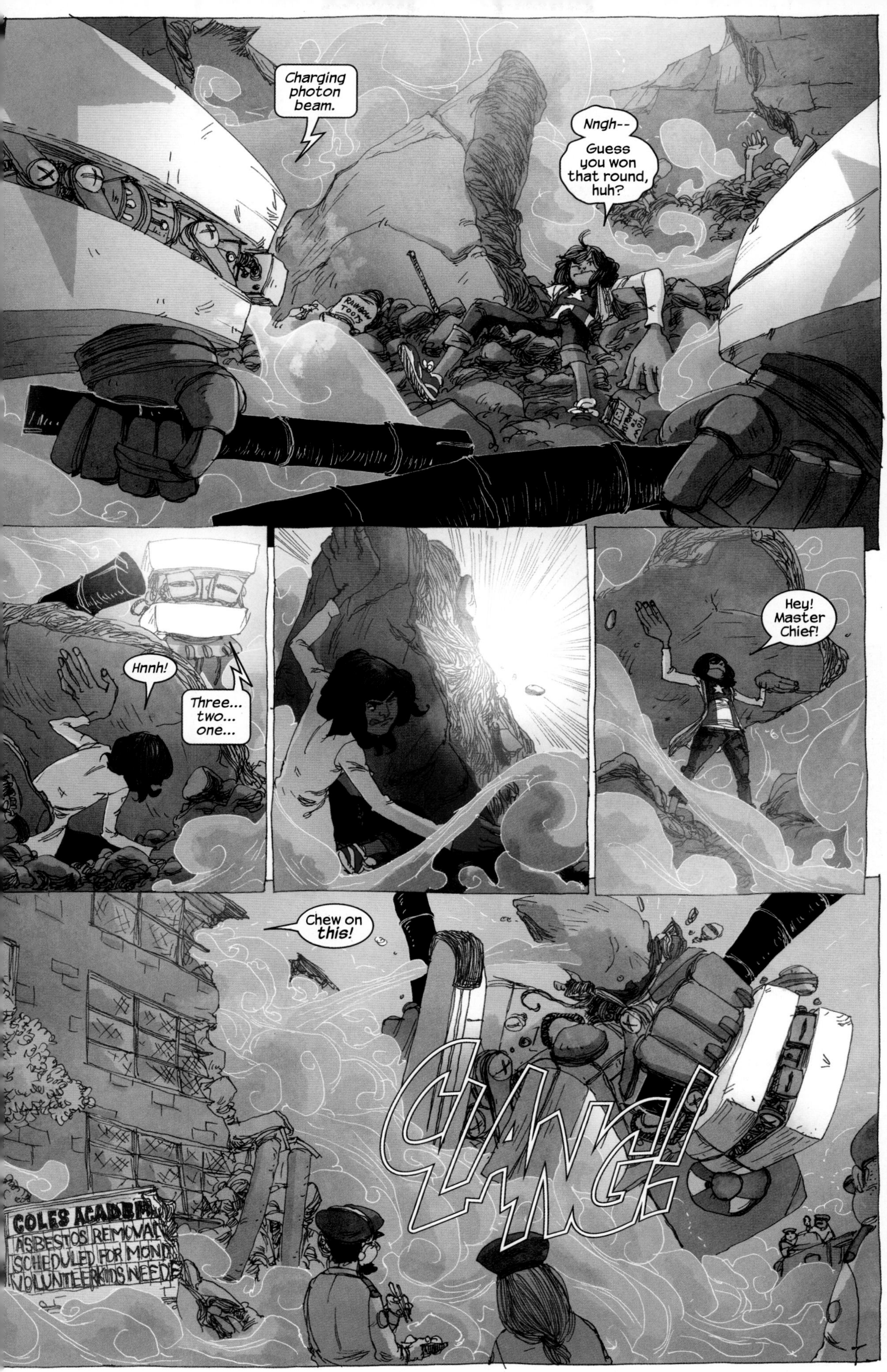
Charging photon beam.
Nngh--
Guess you won that round, huh?
RAINBOW TOOTS
Hnnh!
Three... two... one...
Hey! Master Chief!
Chew on this!
CLANG!
COLES ACADEM
ASBESTOS REMOVAL
SCHEDULED FOR MOND
VOLUNTEER KIDS NEEDE

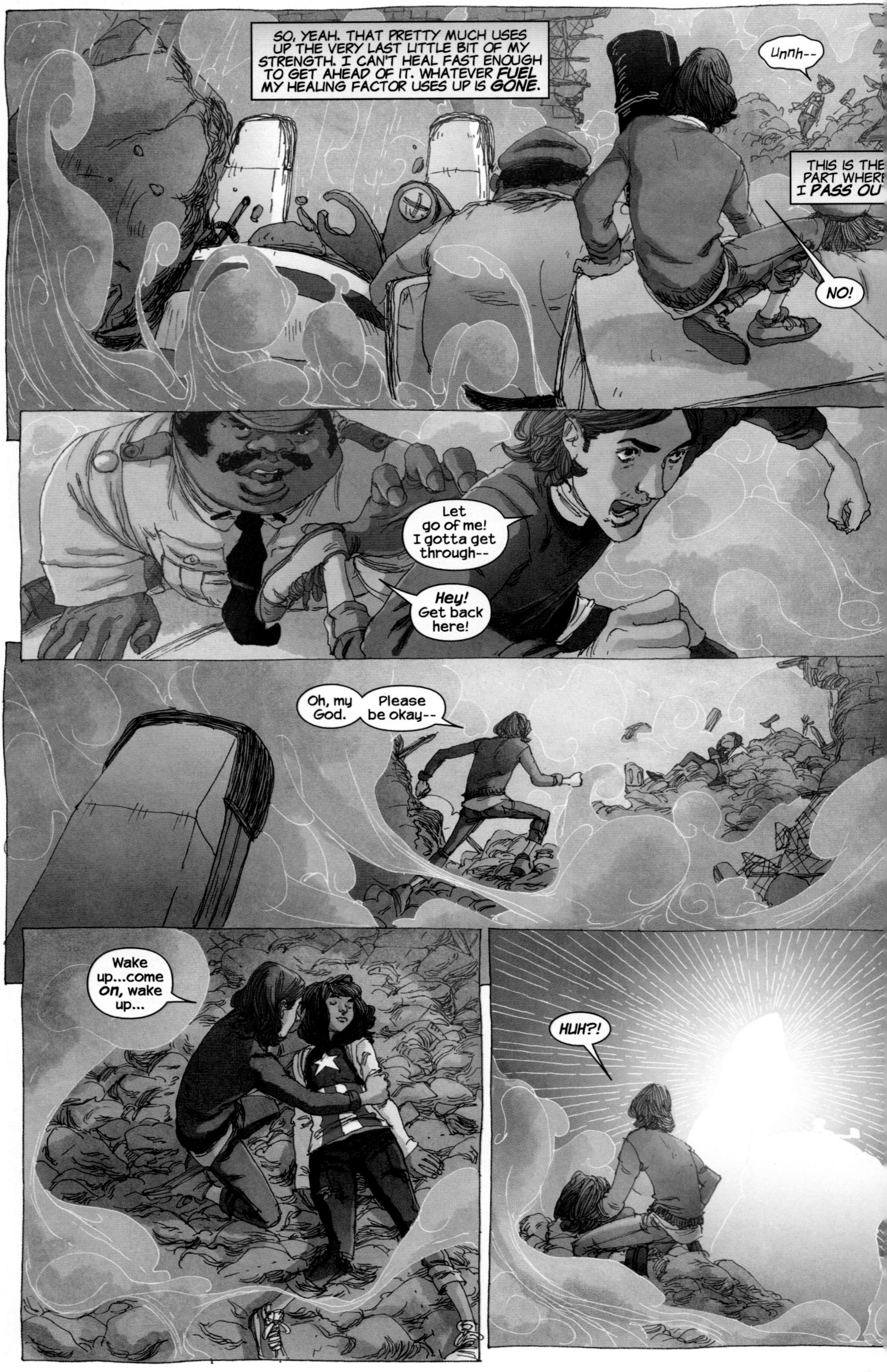
SO, YEAH. THAT PRETTY MUCH USES UP THE VERY LAST LITTLE BIT OF MY STRENGTH. I CAN'T HEAL FAST ENOUGH TO GET AHEAD OF IT. WHATEVER FUEL MY HEALING FACTOR USES UP IS GONE.
Unnh--
THIS IS THE PART WHERE I PASS OU
NO!
Let go of me! I gotta get through--
Hey! Get back here!
Oh, my God.
Please be okay--
Wake up...come on, wake up...
HUH?!

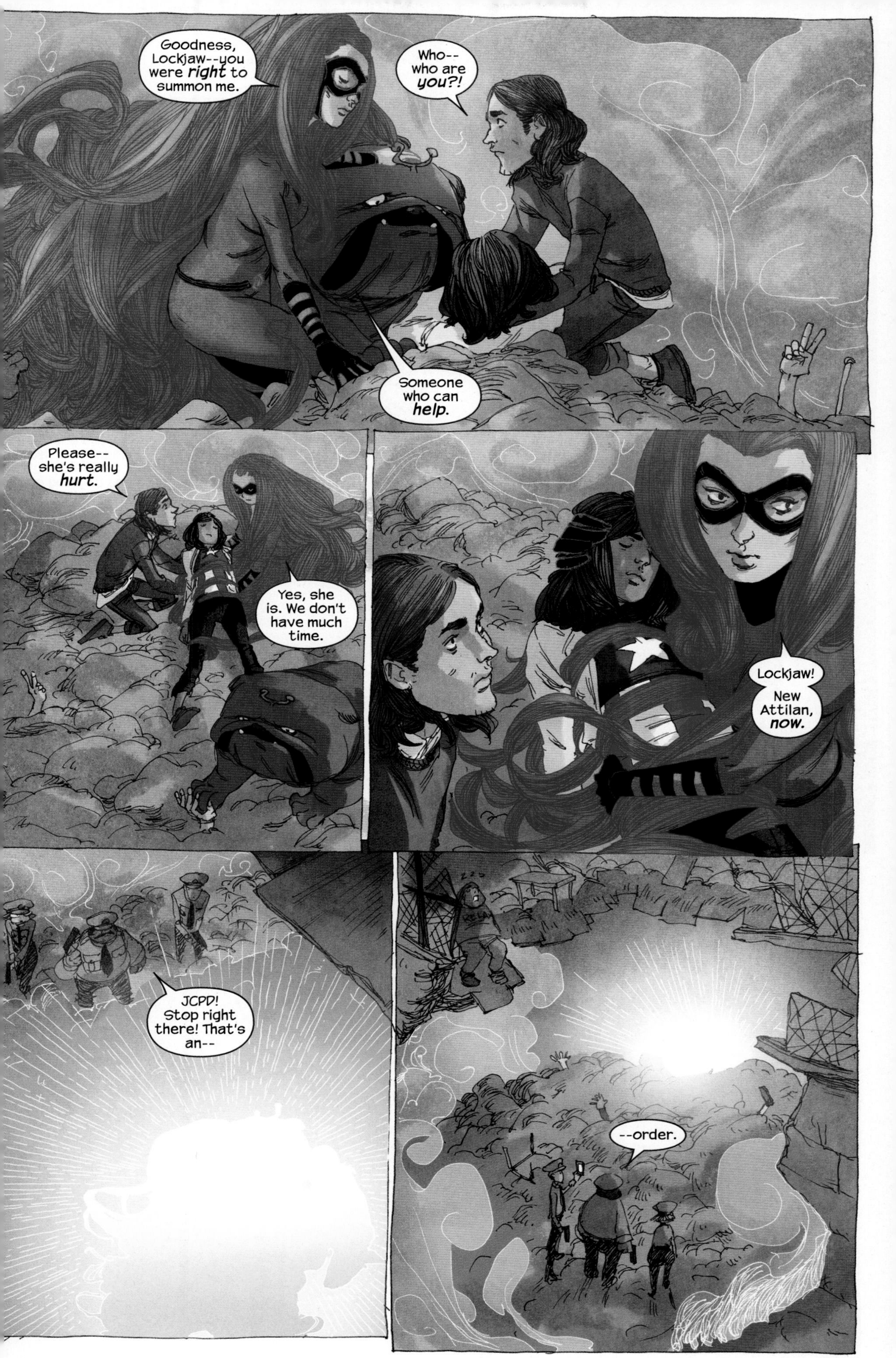

Goodness, Lockjaw--you were *right* to summon me.
Who-- who are *you?!*
Someone who can *help*.
Please-- she's really *hurt*.
Yes, she is. We don't have much time.
Lockjaw! New Attilan, *now*.
JCPD! Stop right there! That's an--
--order.

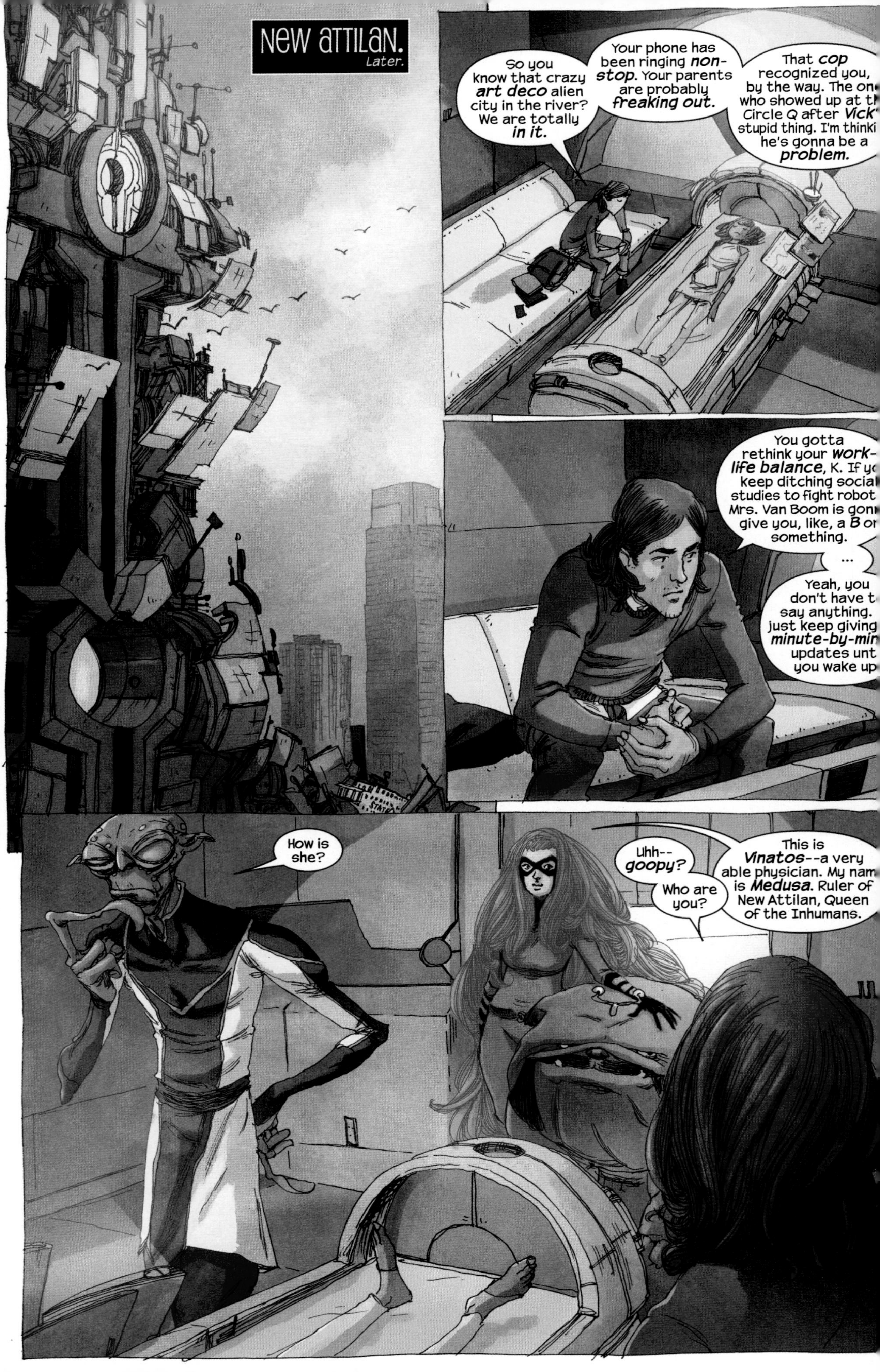

NEW ATTILAN.
Later.
So you know that crazy art deco alien city in the river? We are totally in it.
Your phone has been ringing non-stop. Your parents are probably freaking out.
That cop recognized you, by the way. The one who showed up at the Circle Q after Vick
stupid thing. I'm thinki
he's gonna be a problem.
You gotta rethink your work-life balance, K. If yo
keep ditching social studies to fight robot
Mrs. Van Boom is gon
give you, like, a B or something.
...
Yeah, you don't have t
say anything.
just keep giving
minute-by-mi
updates unt
you wake up
How is she?
Uhh-- goopy?
Who are you?
This is Vinatos--a very able physician. My nam
is Medusa. Ruler of New Attilan, Queen of the Inhumans.

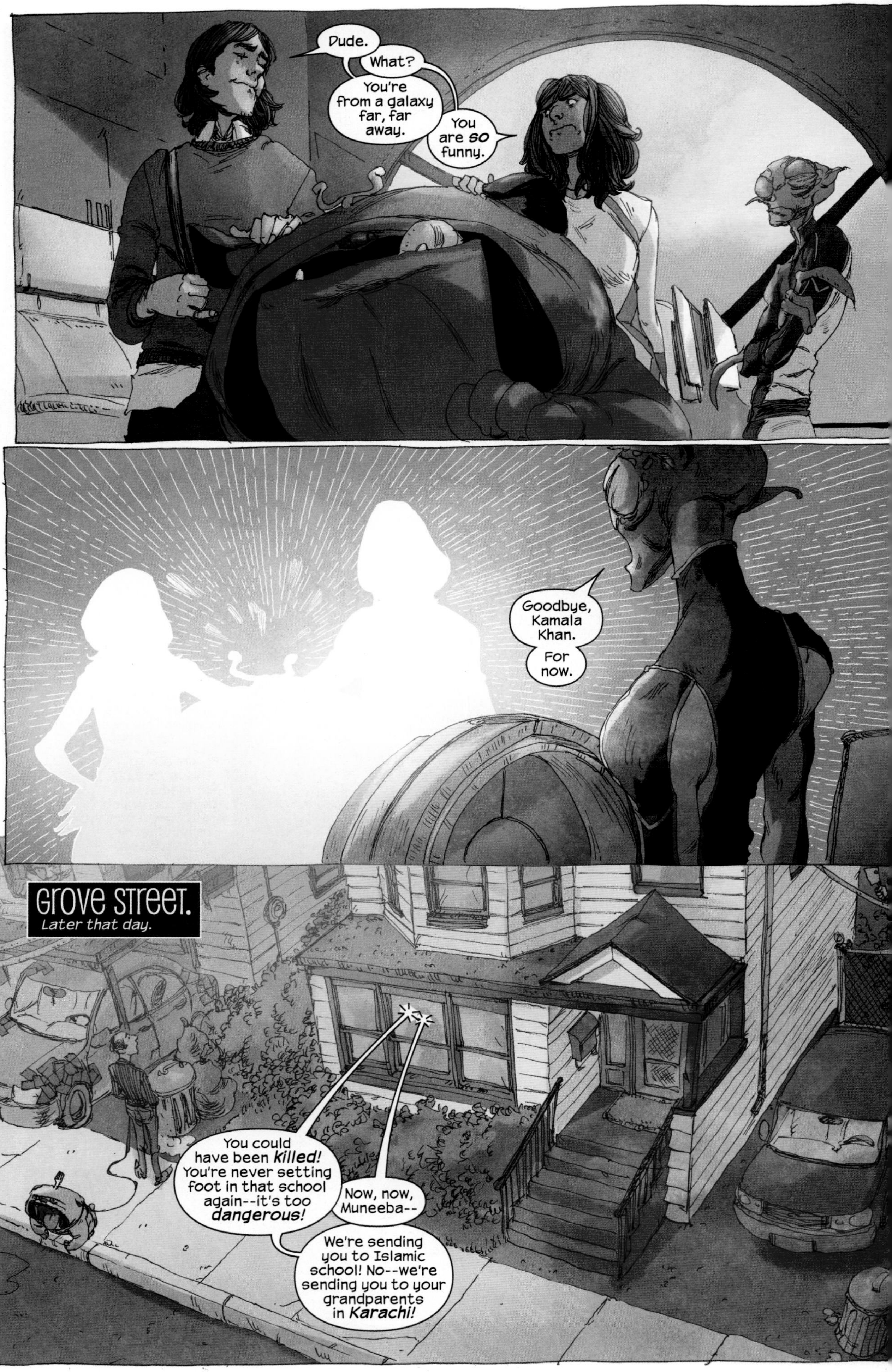
Dude.
What?
You're from a galaxy far, far away.
You are *SO* funny.
Goodbye, Kamala Khan.
For now.
GROVE STREET.
Later that day.
You could have been *killed!* You're never setting foot in that school again--it's too *dangerous!*
Now, now, Muneeba--
We're sending you to Islamic school! No--we're sending you to your grandparents in *Karachi!*

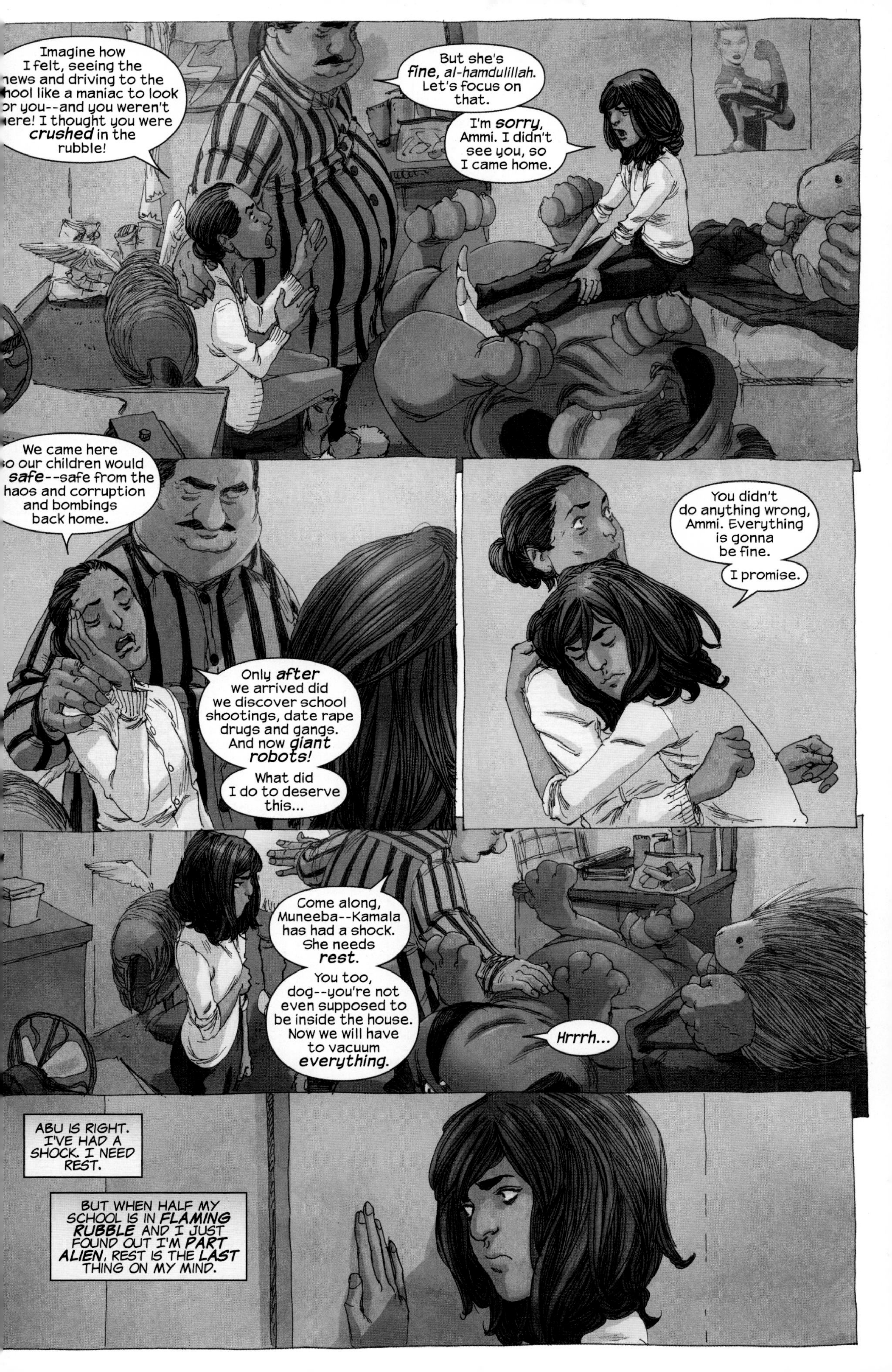
Imagine how I felt, seeing the news and driving to the chool like a maniac to look or you--and you weren't ere! I thought you were *crushed* in the rubble!
But she's *fine*, *al-hamdulillah*. Let's focus on that.
I'm *sorry*, Ammi. I didn't see you, so I came home.
We came here o our children would *safe*--safe from the haos and corruption and bombings back home.
Only *after* we arrived did we discover school shootings, date rape drugs and gangs. And now *giant robots!*
What did I do to deserve this...
You didn't do anything wrong, Ammi. Everything is gonna be fine.
I promise.
Come along, Muneeba--Kamala has had a shock. She needs *rest*.
You too, dog--you're not even supposed to be inside the house. Now we will have to vacuum *everything*.
Hrrrh...
ABU IS RIGHT. I'VE HAD A SHOCK. I NEED REST.
BUT WHEN HALF MY SCHOOL IS IN *FLAMING RUBBLE* AND I JUST FOUND OUT I'M *PART ALIEN*, REST IS THE *LAST* THING ON MY MIND.

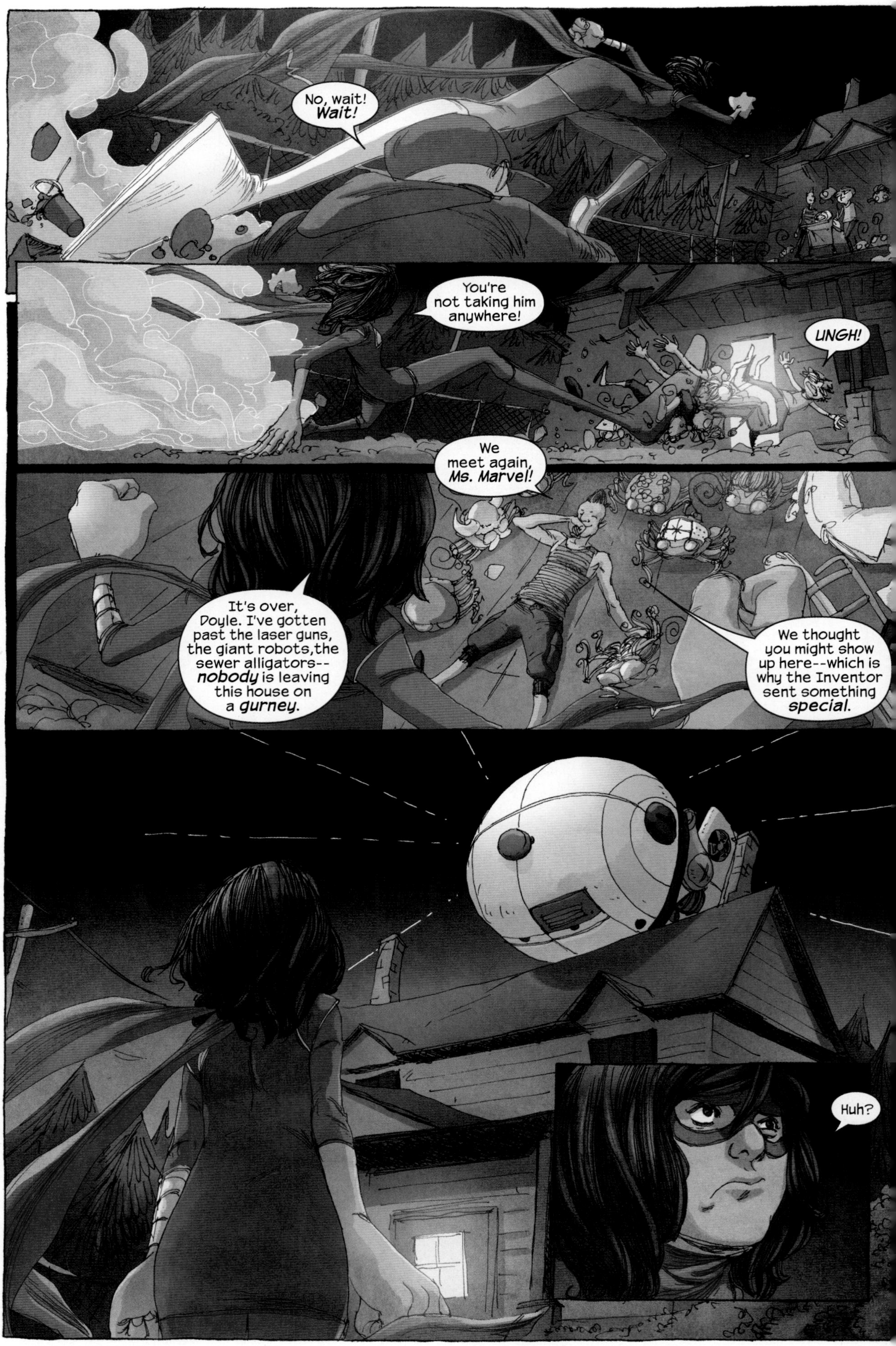
No, wait! Wait!
You're not taking him anywhere!
UNGH!
We meet again, Ms. Marvel!
It's over, Doyle. I've gotten past the laser guns, the giant robots, the sewer alligators-- nobody is leaving this house on a gurney.
We thought you might show up here--which is why the Inventor sent something special.
Huh?

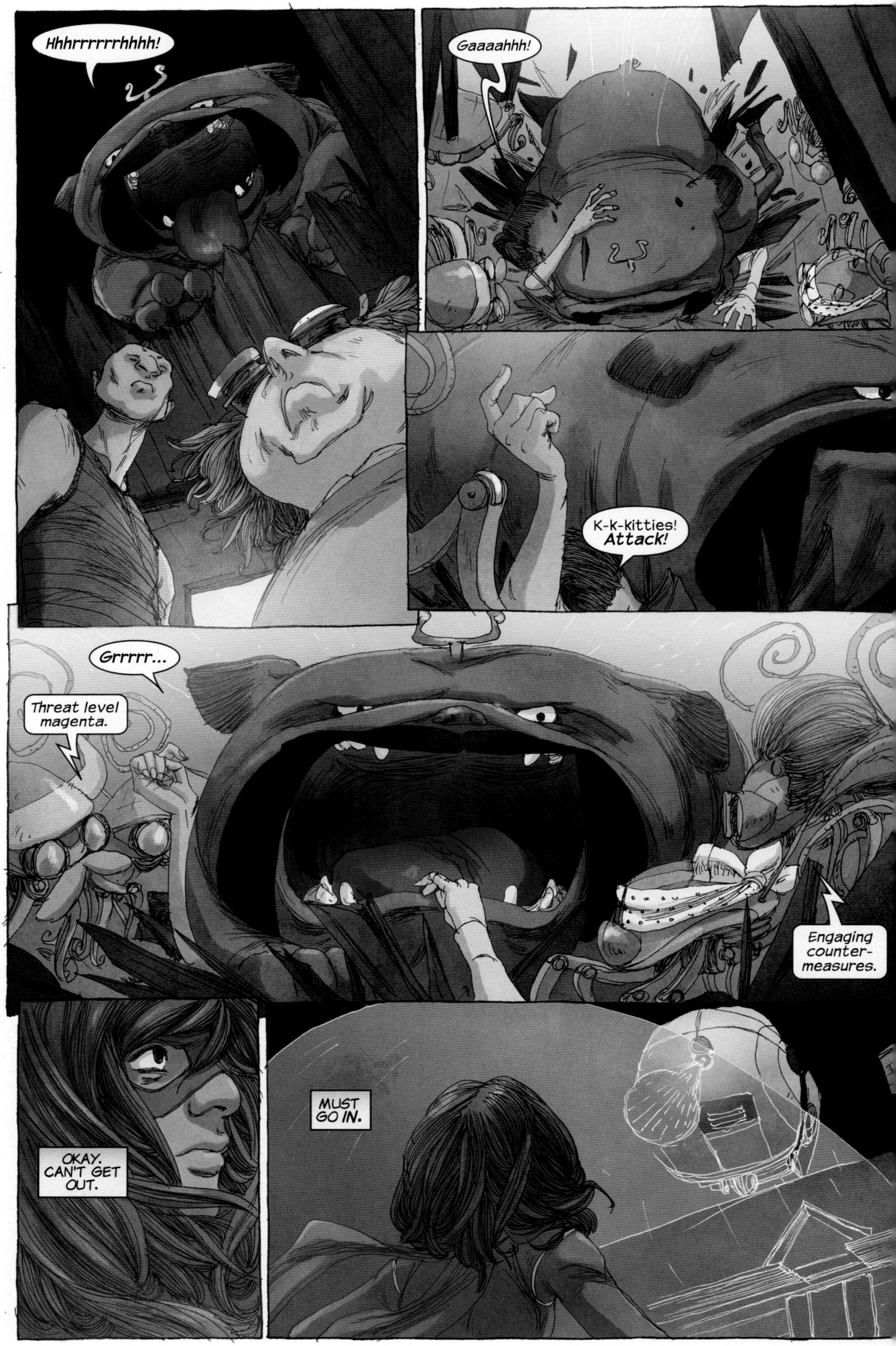
Hhhrrrrrrhhhh!
Gaaaahhh!
K-k-kitties! Attack!
Grrrrr...
Threat level magenta.
Engaging counter-measures.
OKAY. CAN'T GET OUT.
MUST GO IN.

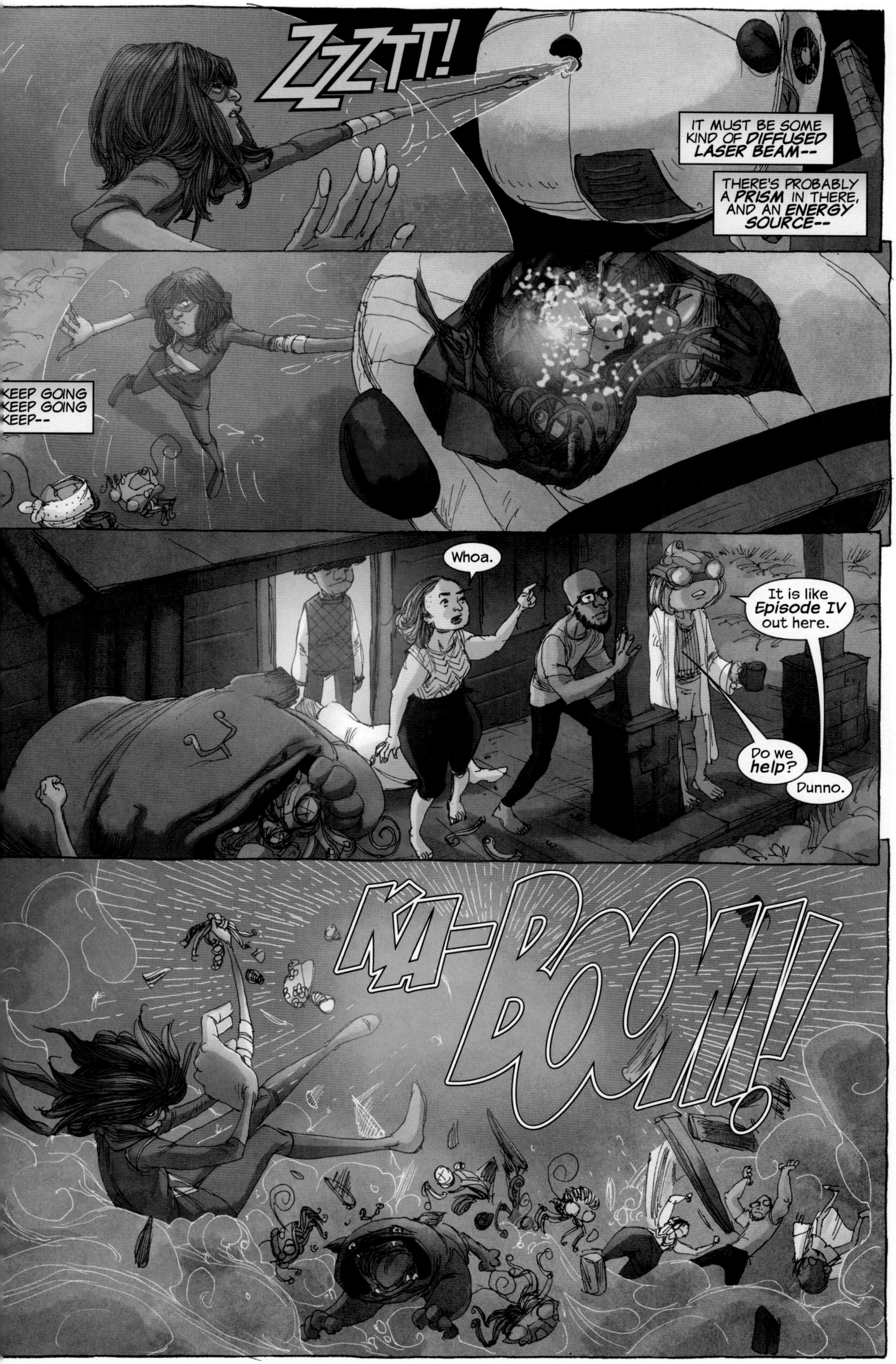
ZZZTT!
IT MUST BE SOME KIND OF DIFFUSED LASER BEAM--
THERE'S PROBABLY A PRISM IN THERE, AND AN ENERGY SOURCE--
KEEP GOING KEEP GOING KEEP--
Whoa.
It is like Episode IV out here.
Do we help?
Dunno.
KA-BOOM!

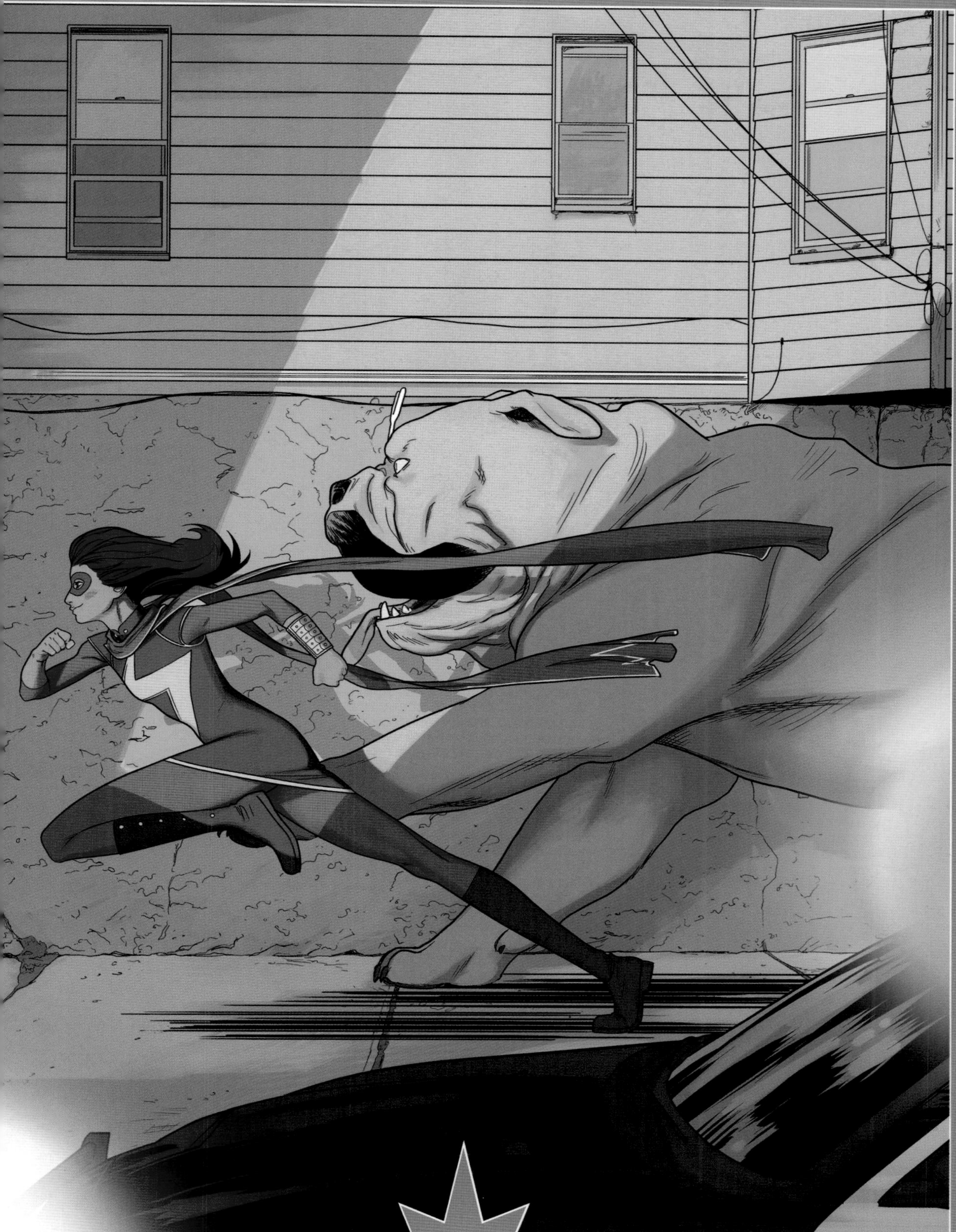
10

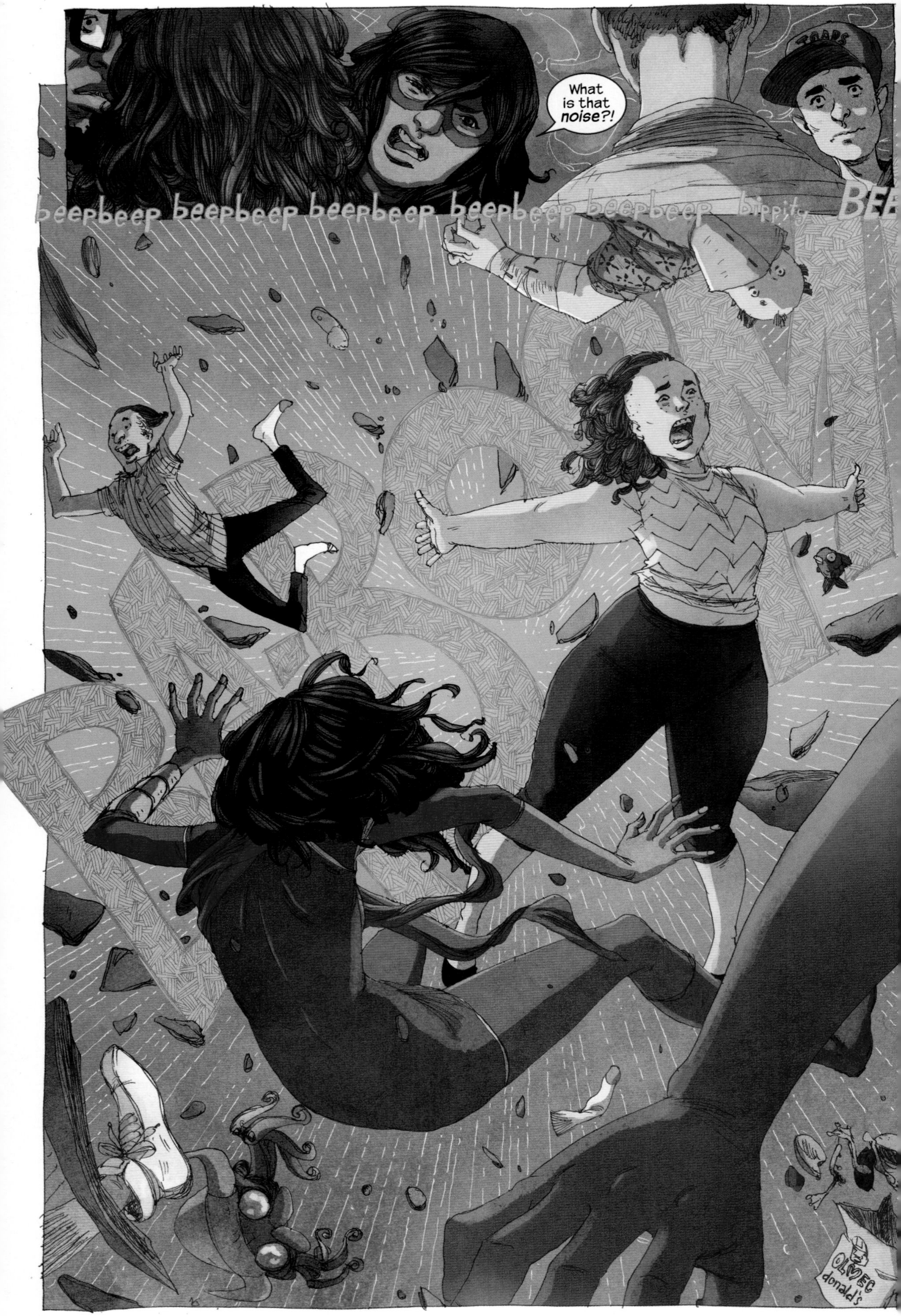
What is that noise?!
beepbeep beepbeep beepbeep beepbeep beepbeep bippity BEE
OLMEC donald's

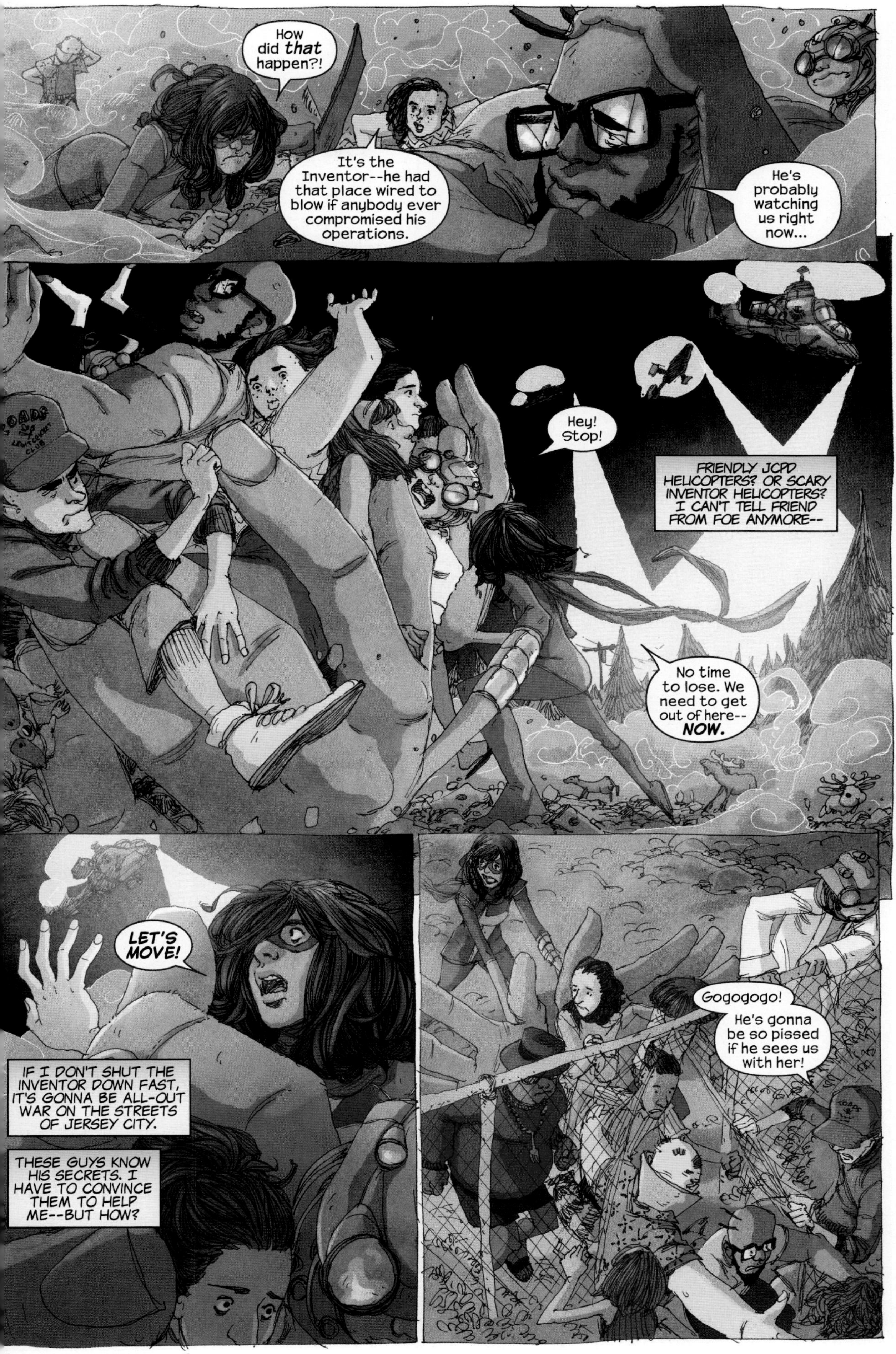
How did *that* happen?!
It's the Inventor--he had that place wired to blow if anybody ever compromised his operations.
He's probably watching us right now...
Hey! Stop!
FRIENDLY JCPD HELICOPTERS? OR SCARY INVENTOR HELICOPTERS? I CAN'T TELL FRIEND FROM FOE ANYMORE--
No time to lose. We need to get out of here-- **NOW.**
LET'S MOVE!
IF I DON'T SHUT THE INVENTOR DOWN FAST, IT'S GONNA BE ALL-OUT WAR ON THE STREETS OF JERSEY CITY.
THESE GUYS KNOW HIS SECRETS. I HAVE TO CONVINCE THEM TO HELP ME--BUT HOW?
Gogogogo!
He's gonna be so pissed if he sees us with her!

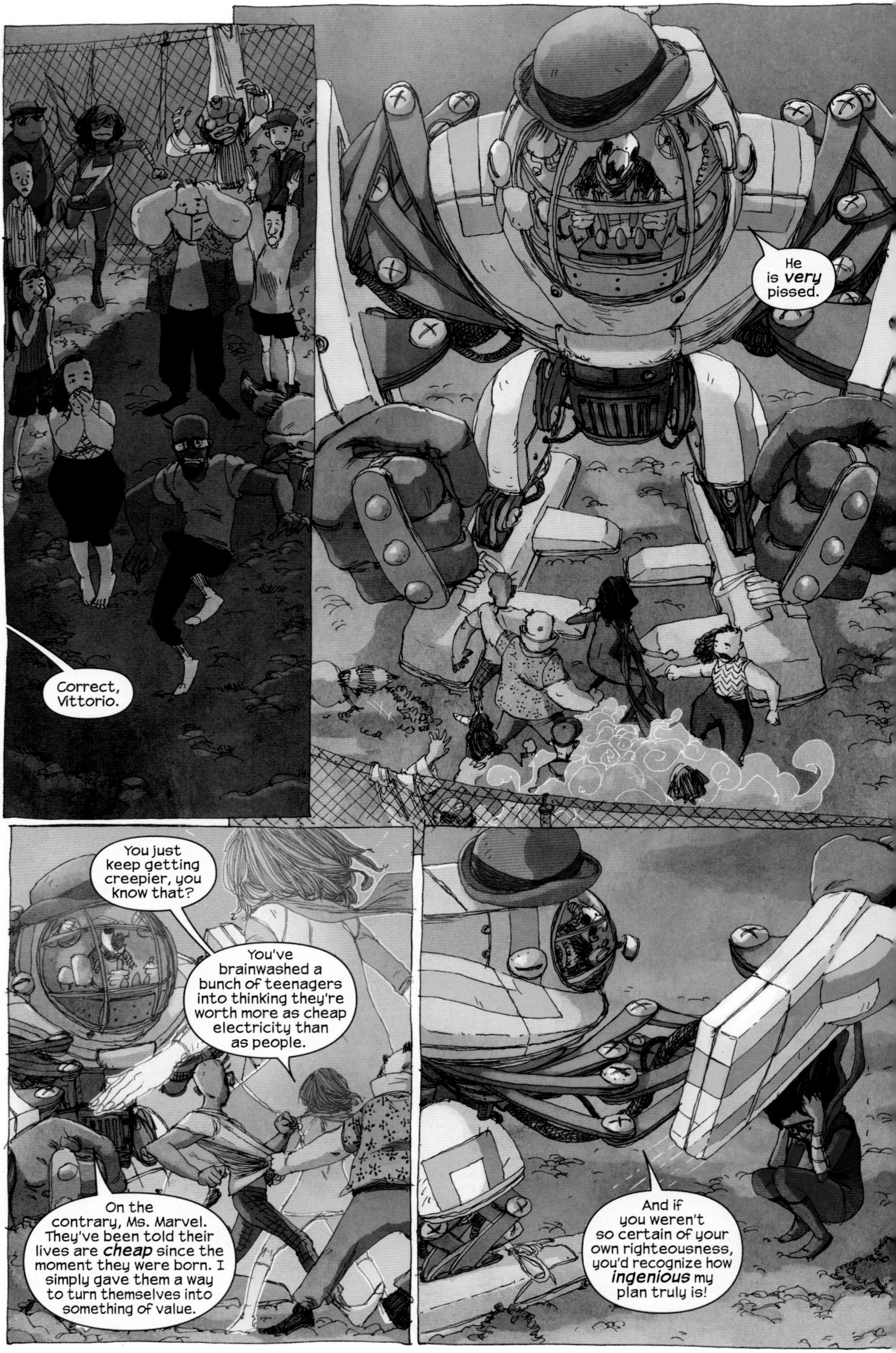
He is *very* pissed.
Correct, Vittorio.
You just keep getting creepier, you know that?
You've brainwashed a bunch of teenagers into thinking they're worth more as cheap electricity than as people.
On the contrary, Ms. Marvel. They've been told their lives are *cheap* since the moment they were born. I simply gave them a way to turn themselves into something of value.
And if you weren't so certain of your own righteousness, you'd recognize how *ingenious* my plan truly is!

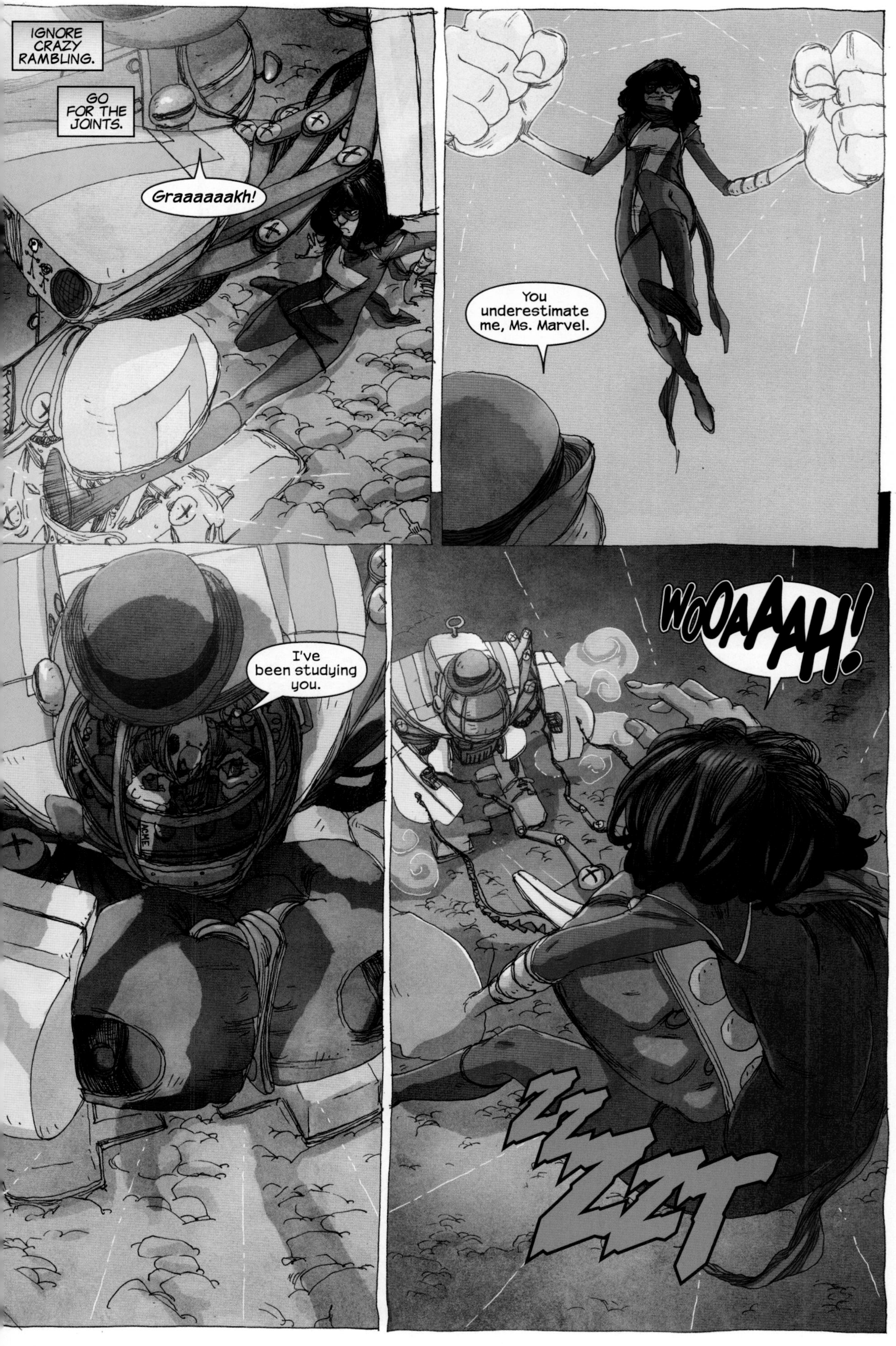

IGNORE CRAZY RAMBLING.
GO FOR THE JOINTS.
Graaaaaakh!
You underestimate me, Ms. Marvel.
I've been studying you.
WOOAAAAH!
ZZZZT

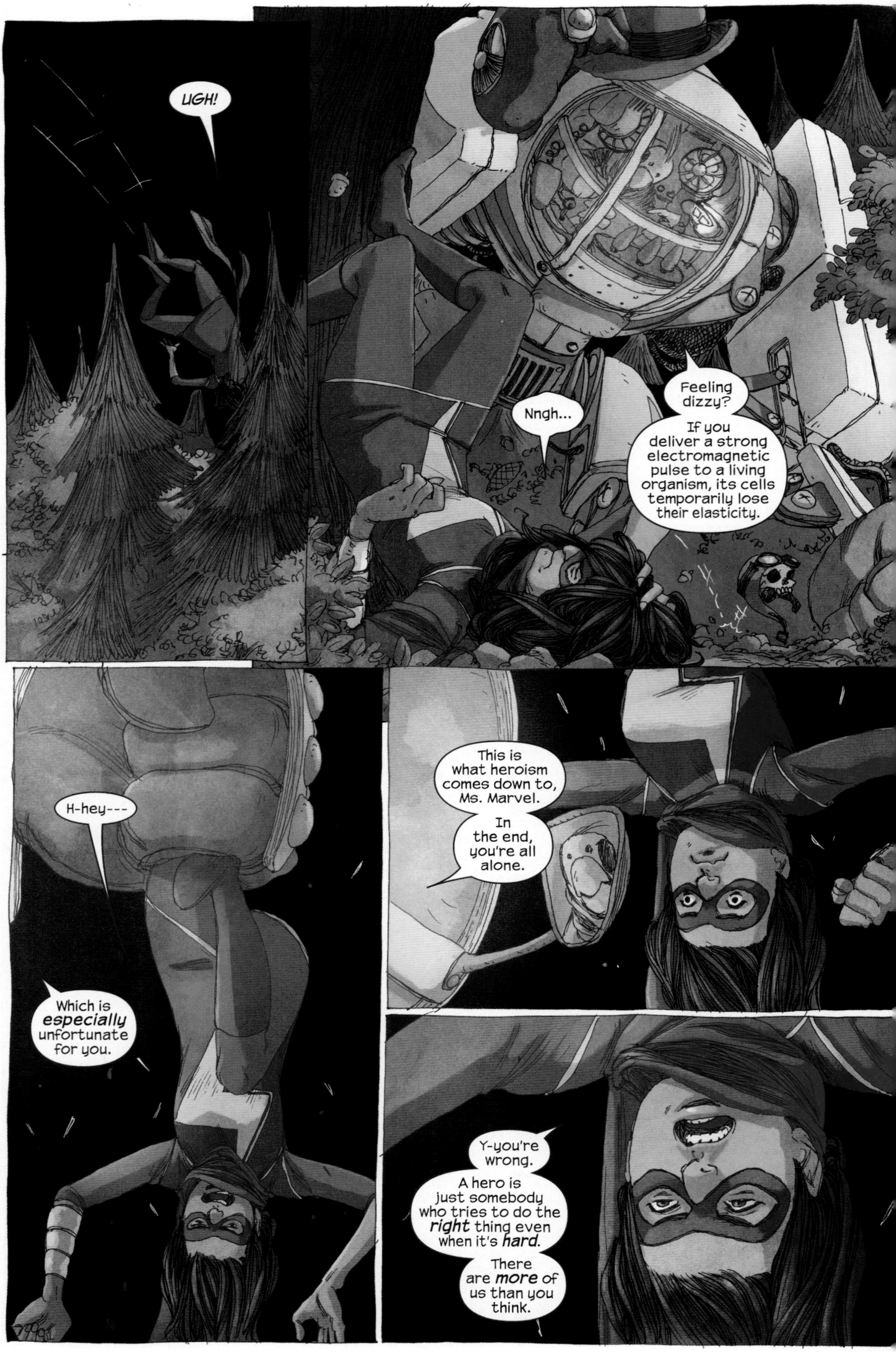
UGH!
Feeling dizzy?
If you deliver a strong electromagnetic pulse to a living organism, its cells temporarily lose their elasticity.
Nngh...
H-hey---
Which is especially unfortunate for you.
This is what heroism comes down to, Ms. Marvel.
In the end, you're all alone.
Y-you're wrong.
A hero is just somebody who tries to do the right thing even when it's hard.
There are more of us than you think.

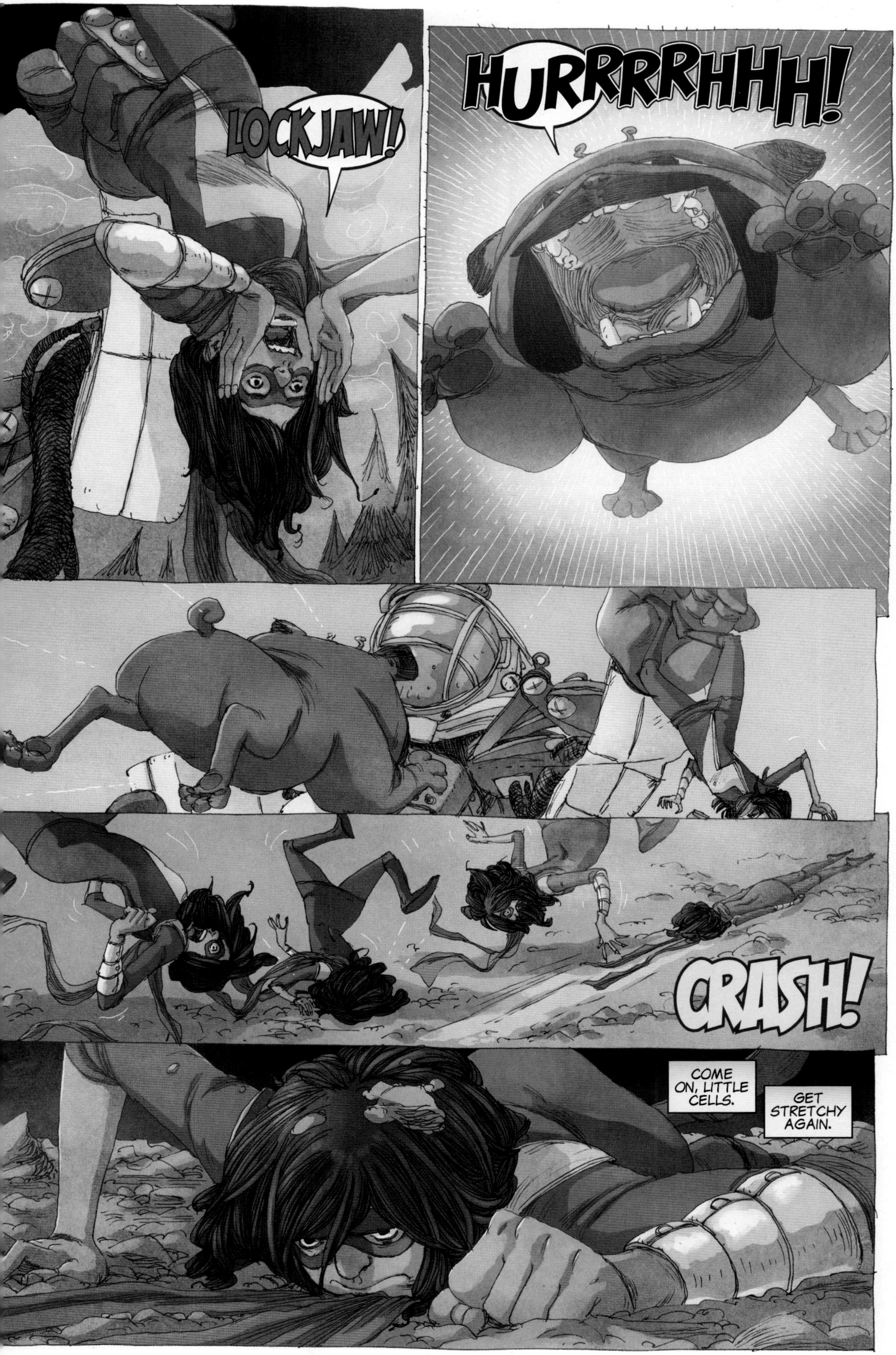
LOCKJAW!
HURRRRRHHH!
CRASH!
COME ON, LITTLE CELLS.
GET STRETCHY AGAIN.

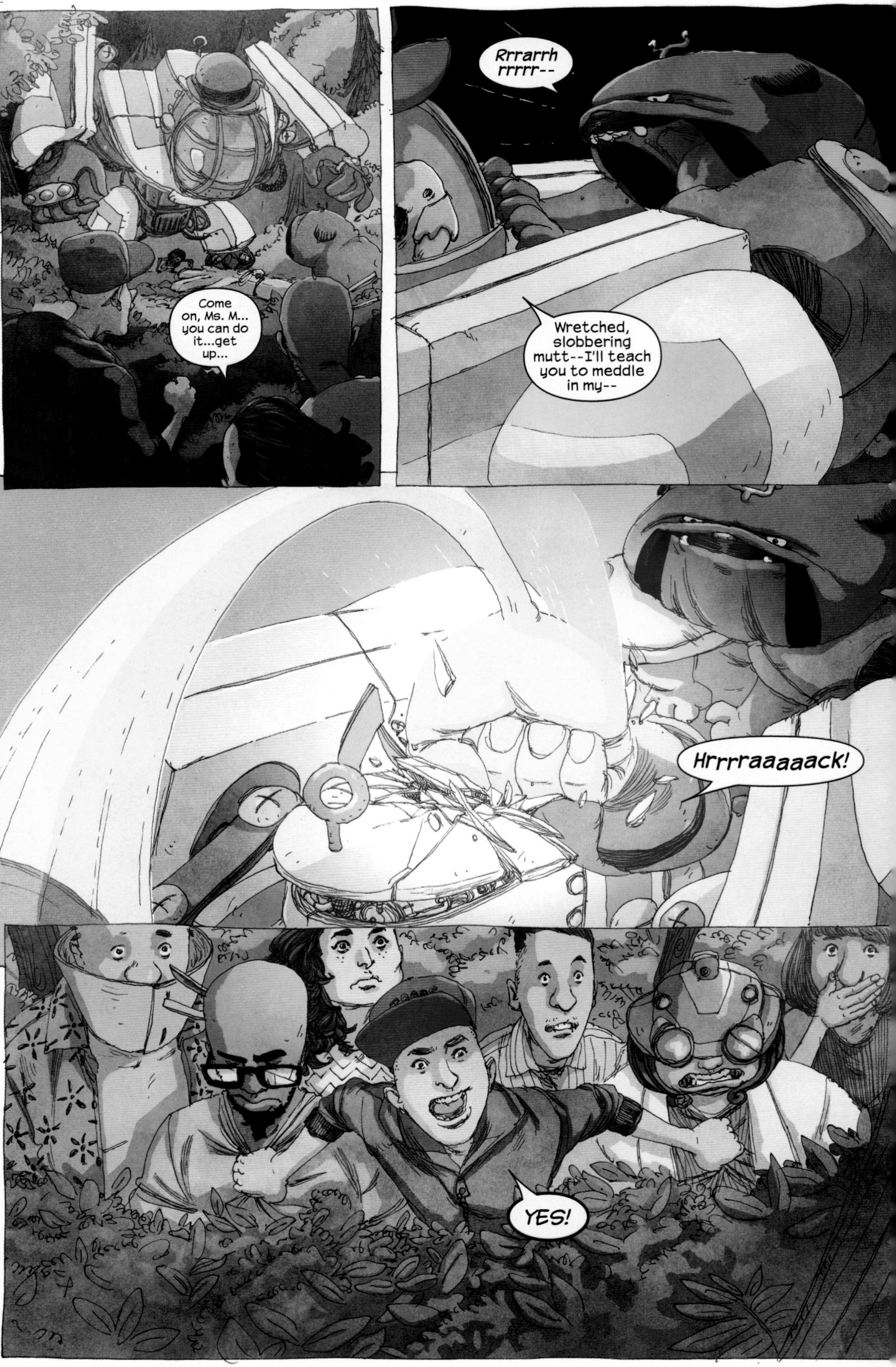
Come on, Ms. M... you can do it...get up...
Rrrarrh rrrrr--
Wretched, slobbering mutt--I'll teach you to meddle in my--
Hrrrraaaaack!
YES!

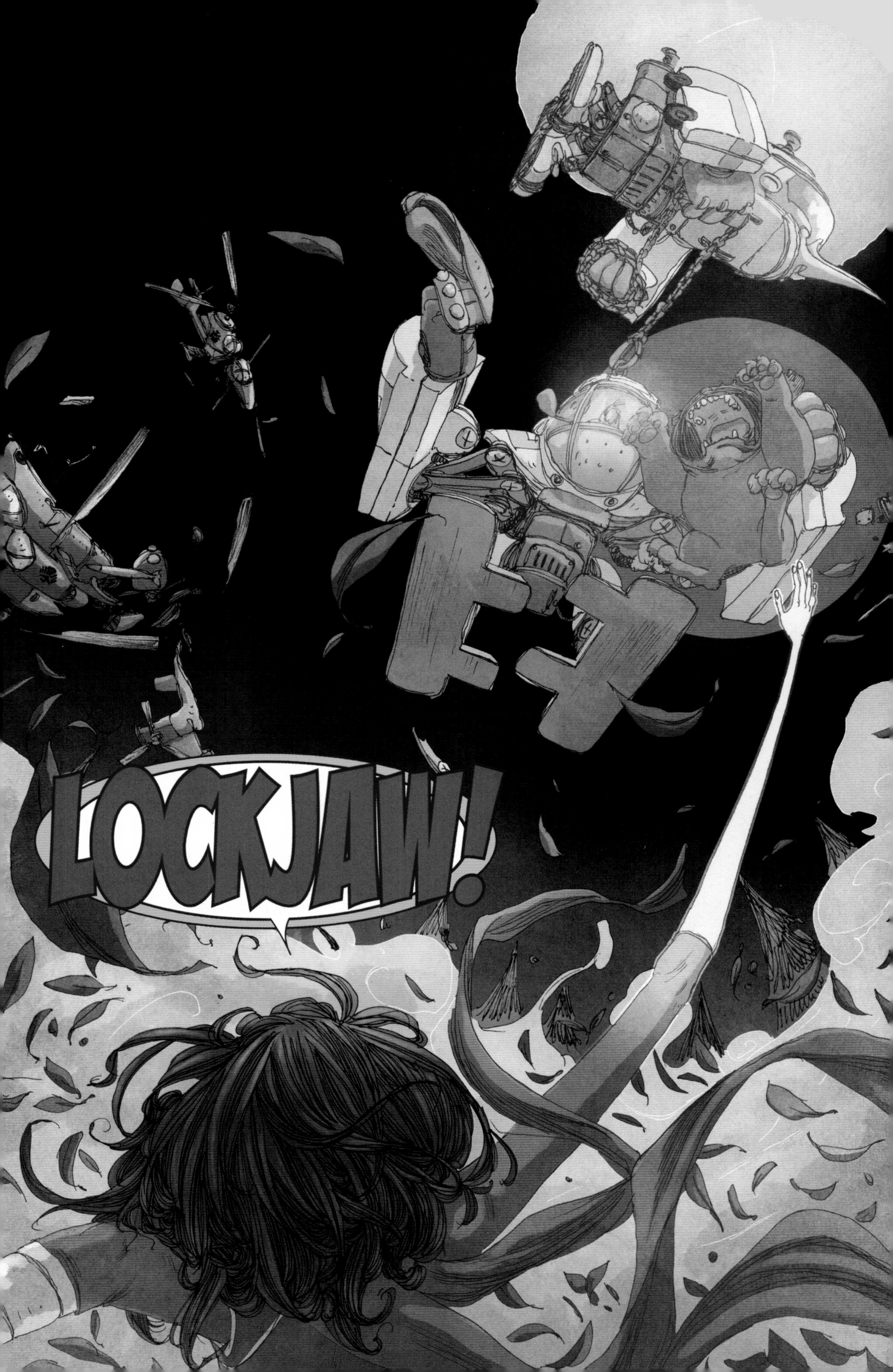
LOCKJAW!

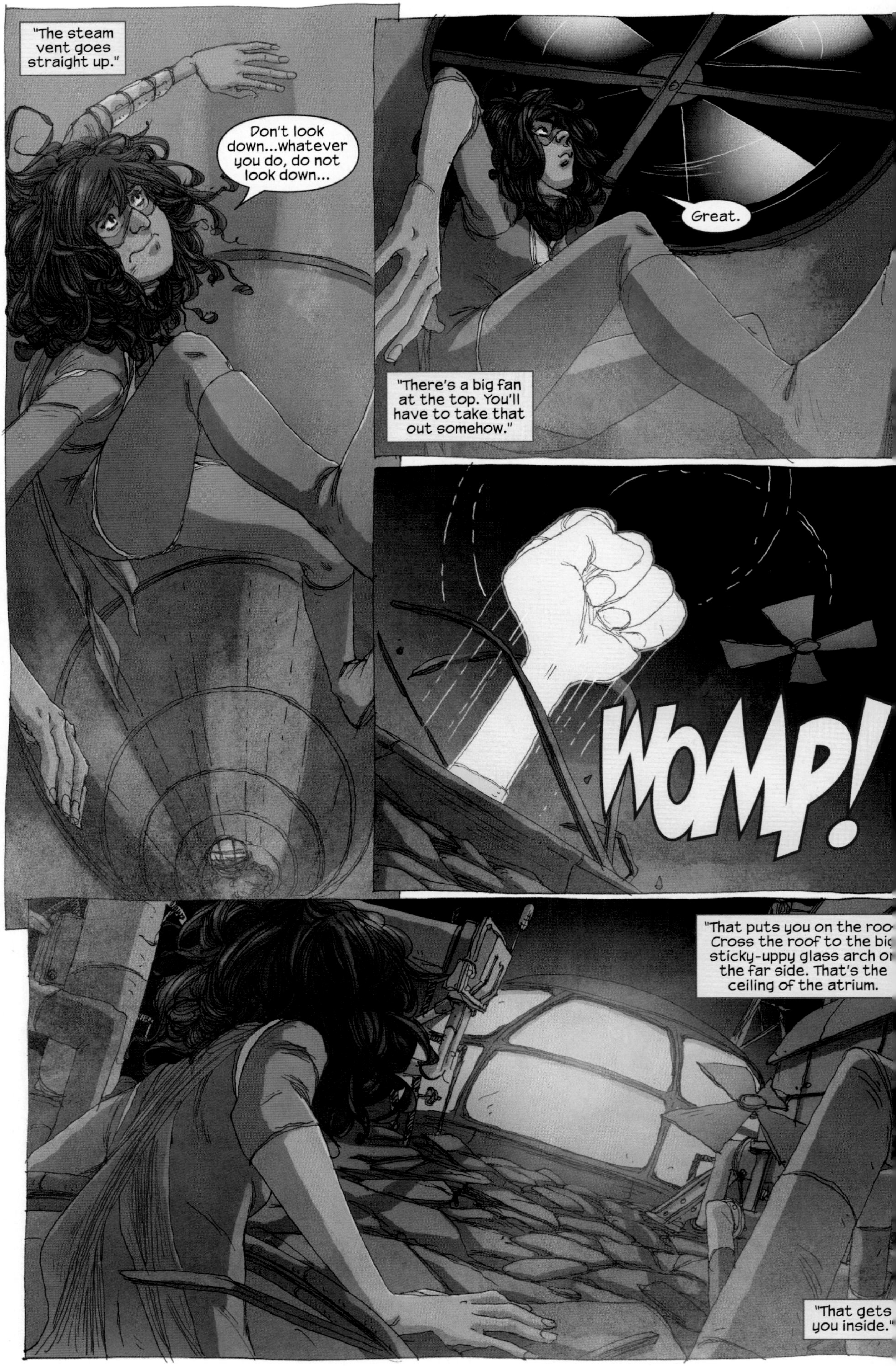
"The steam vent goes straight up."
Don't look down...whatever you do, do not look down...
Great.
"There's a big fan at the top. You'll have to take that out somehow."
WOMP!
"That puts you on the roo Cross the roof to the bi sticky-uppy glass arch o the far side. That's the ceiling of the atrium.
"That gets you inside."

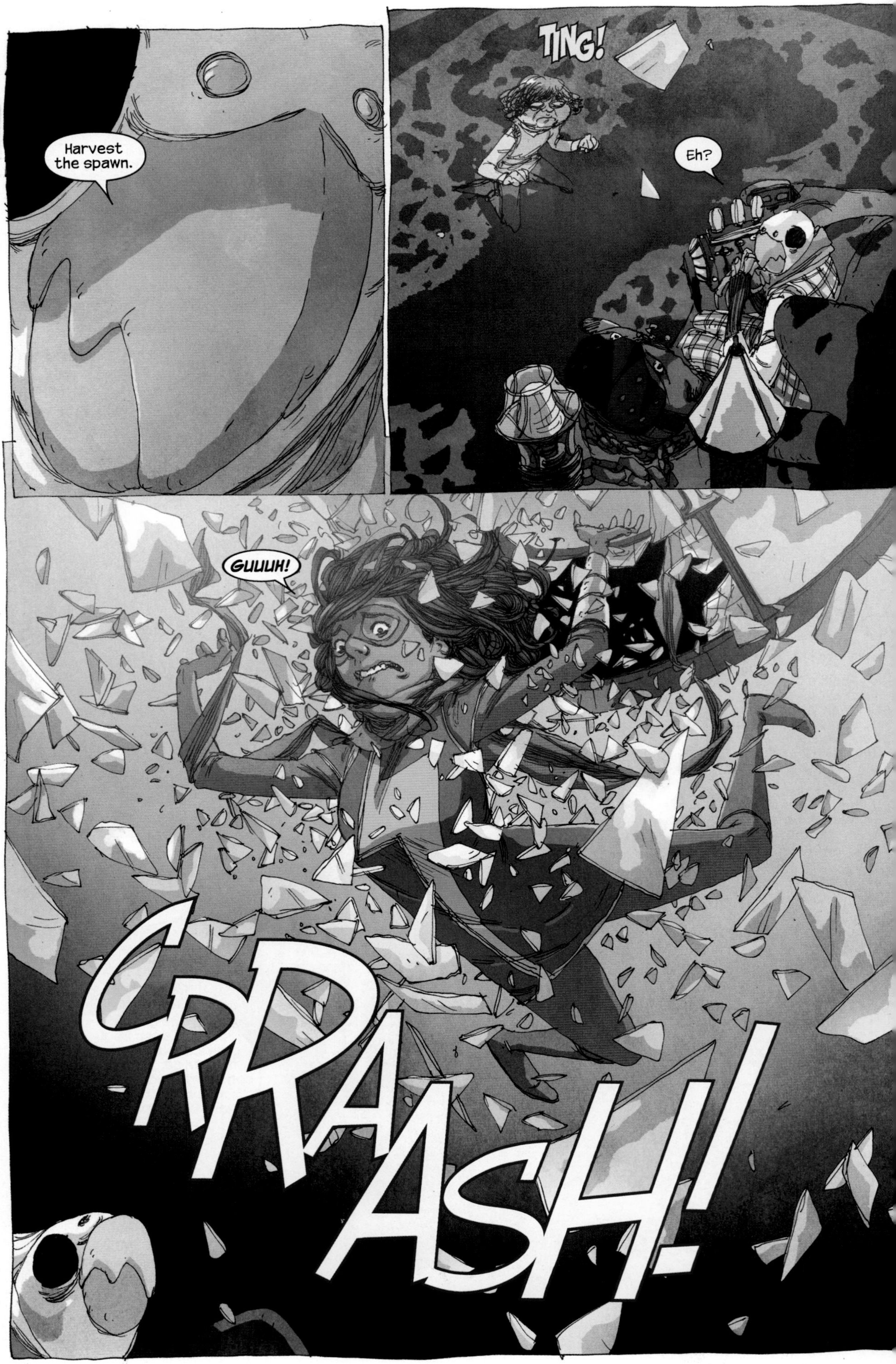
Harvest the spawn.
TING!
Eh?
GUUUH!
CRRAASH!

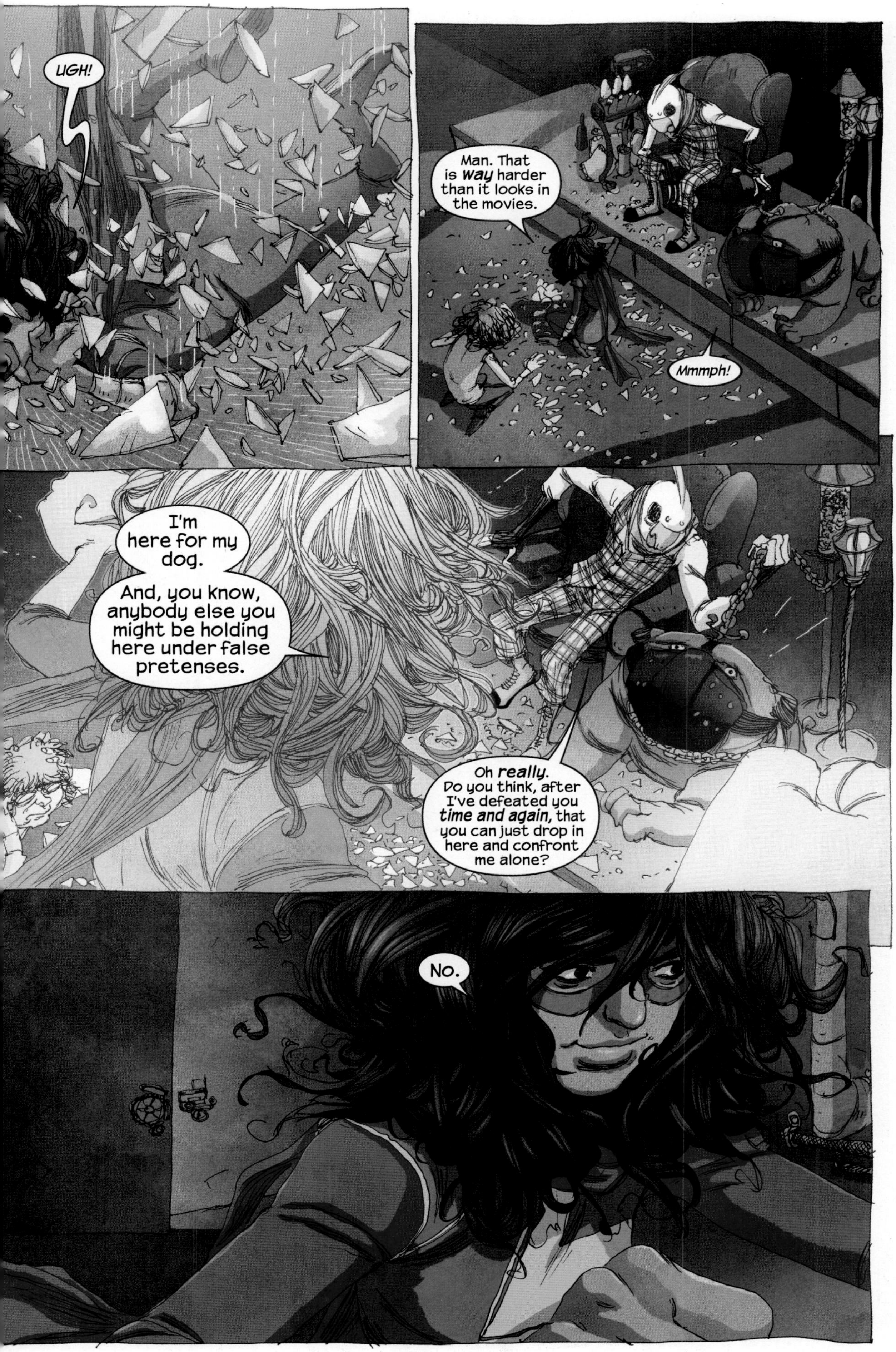
UGH!
Man. That is *way* harder than it looks in the movies.
Mmmph!
I'm here for my dog.
And, you know, anybody else you might be holding here under false pretenses.
Oh **really**. Do you think, after I've defeated you *time and again*, that you can just drop in here and confront me alone?
No.

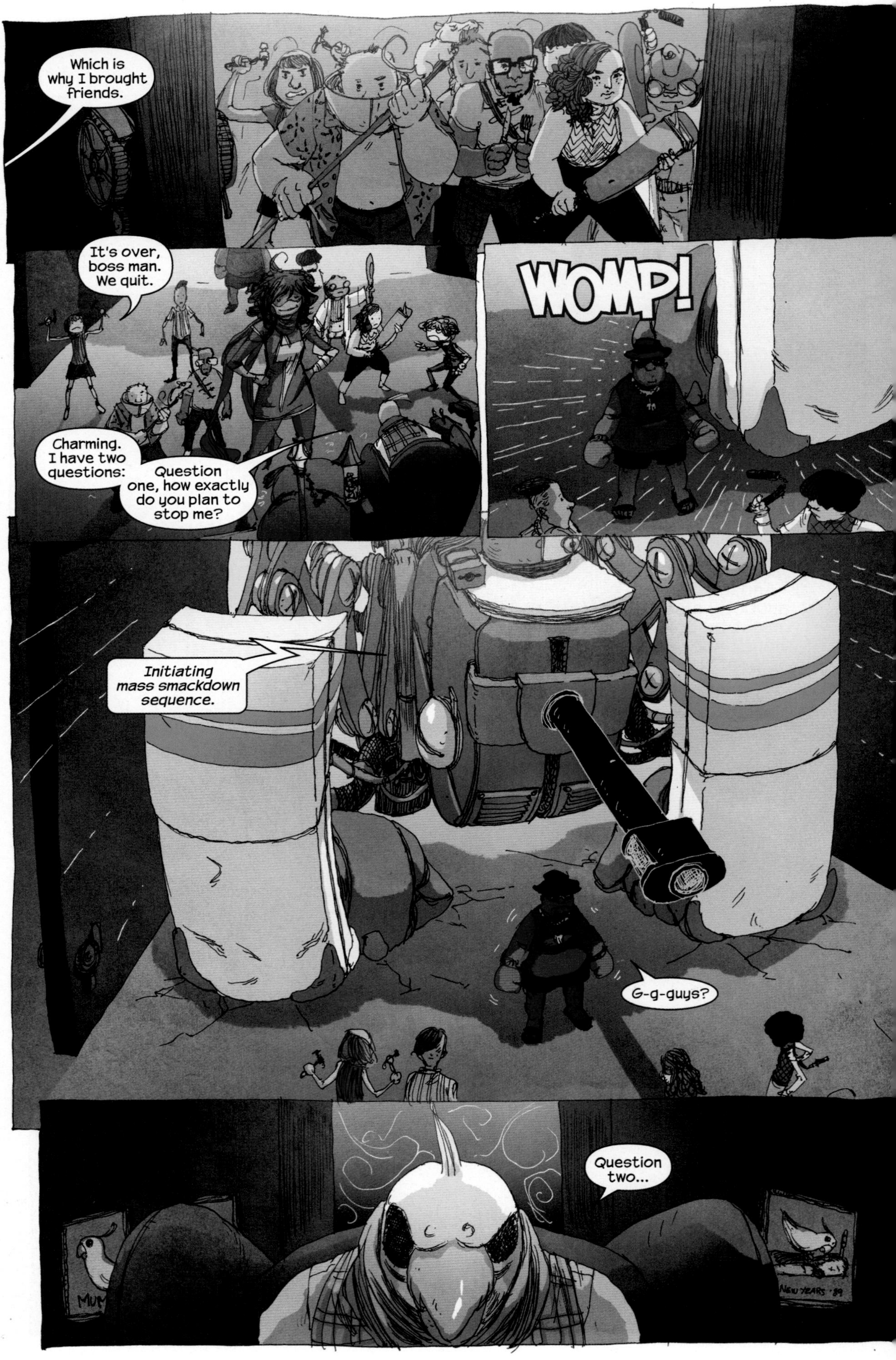

Which is why I brought friends.
It's over, boss man. We quit.
Charming. I have two questions:
Question one, how exactly do you plan to stop me?
WOMP!
Initiating mass smackdown sequence.
G-g-guys?
Question two...
NEW YEARS '89

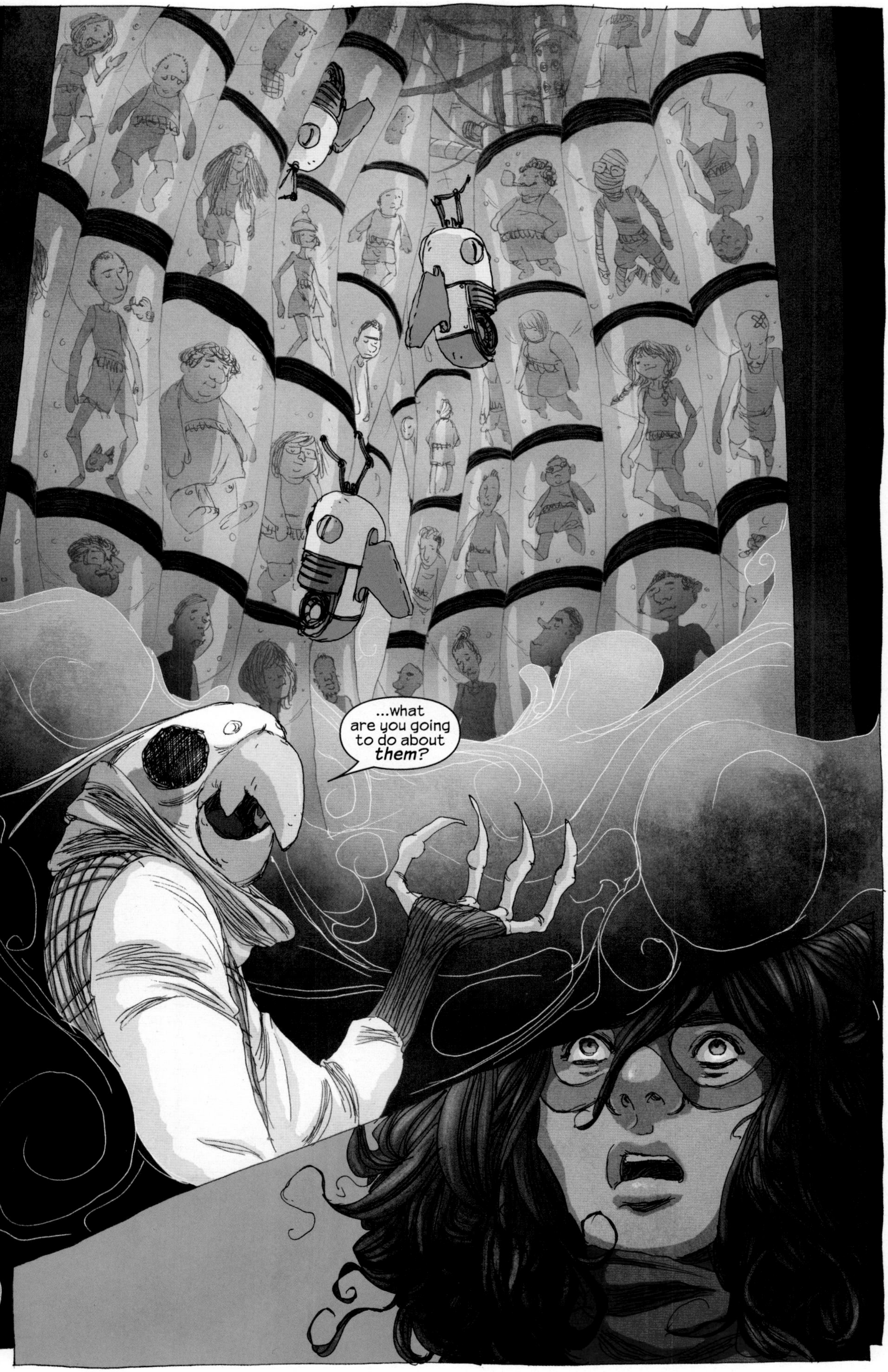
...what are you going to do about *them*?

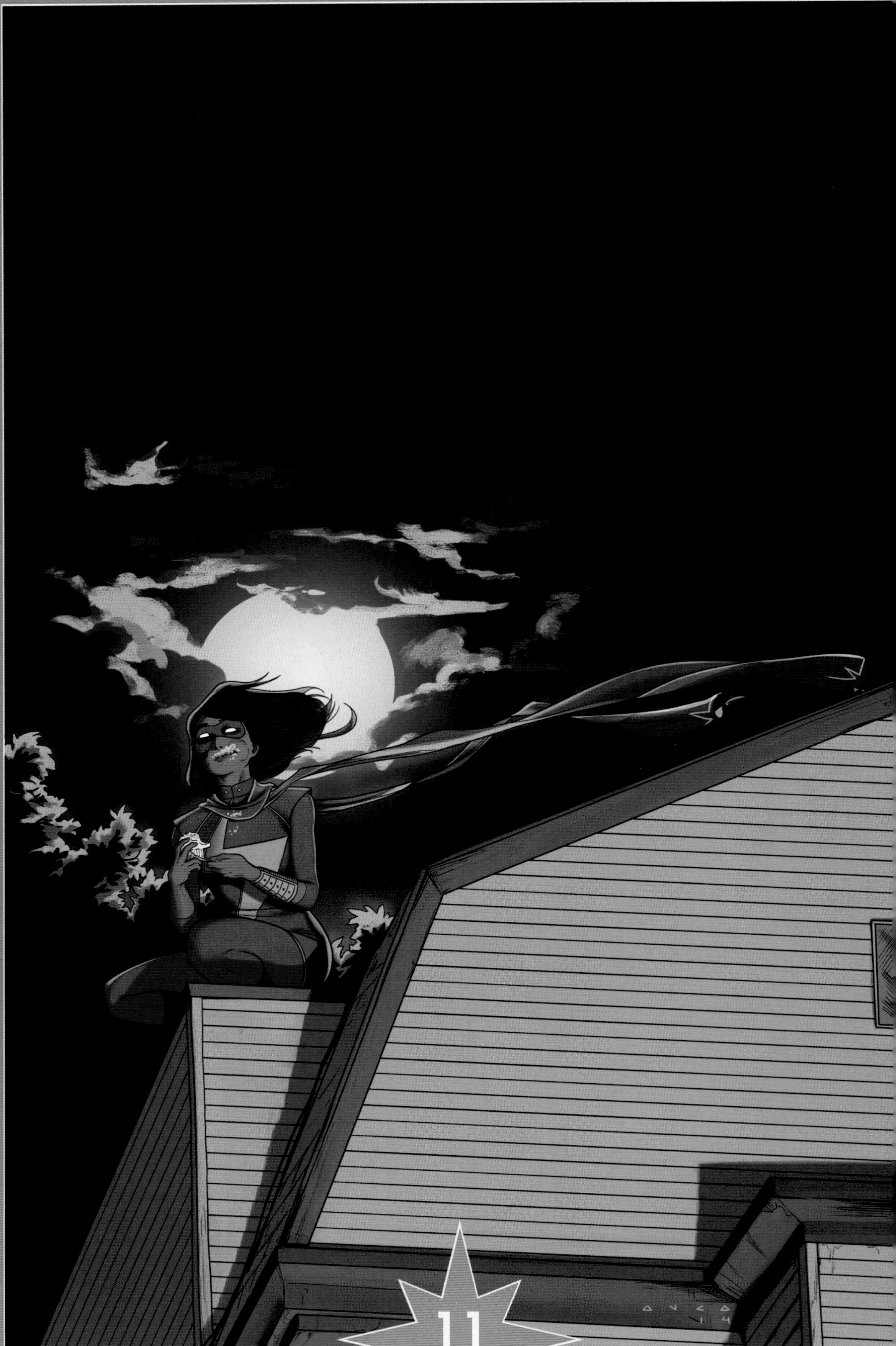
11

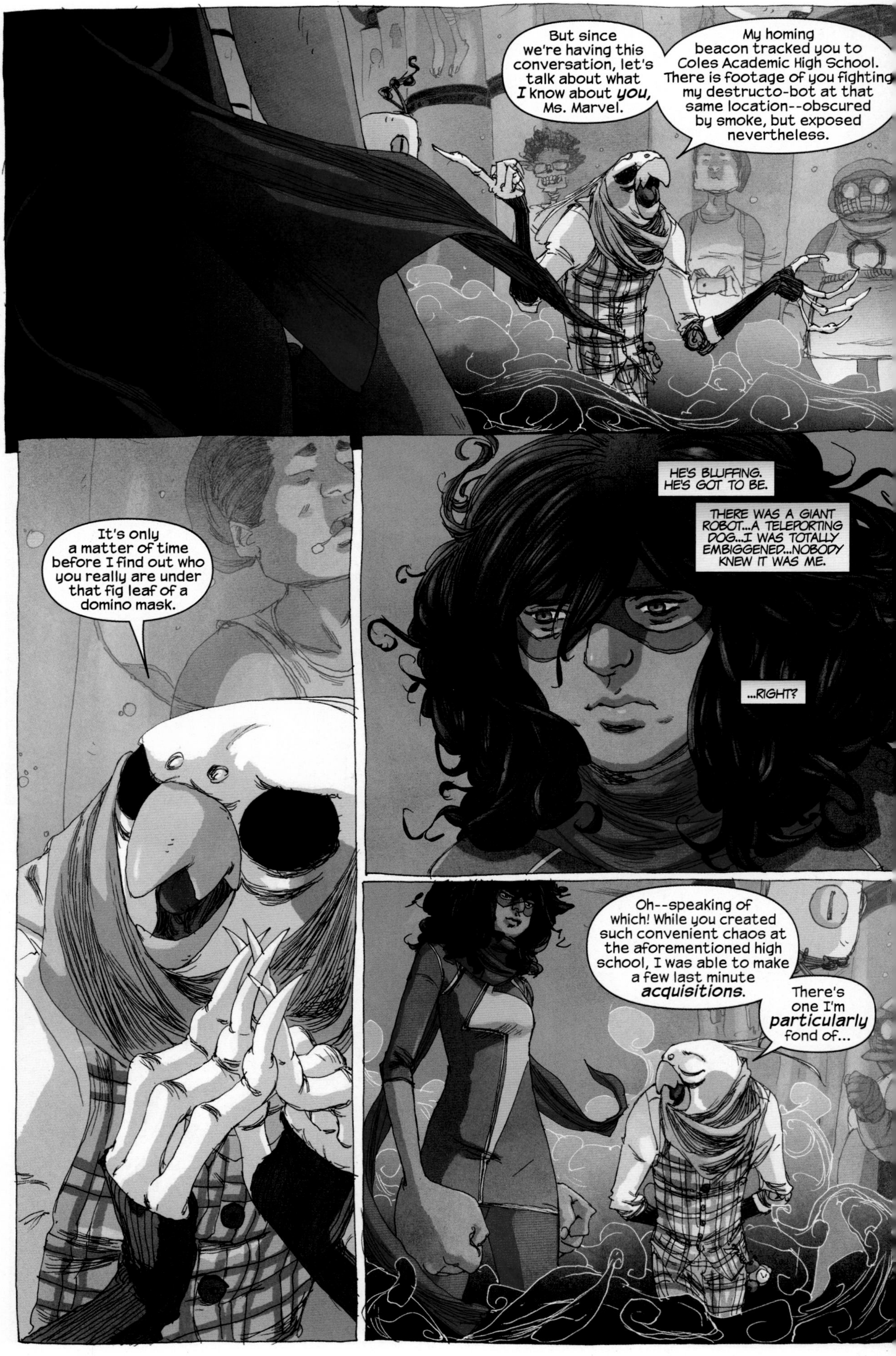
But since we're having this conversation, let's talk about what I know about *you,* Ms. Marvel.
My homing beacon tracked you to Coles Academic High School. There is footage of you fighting my destructo-bot at that same location--obscured by smoke, but exposed nevertheless.
It's only a matter of time before I find out who you really are under that fig leaf of a domino mask.
HE'S BLUFFING. HE'S GOT TO BE.
THERE WAS A GIANT ROBOT...A TELEPORTING DOG...I WAS TOTALLY EMBIGGENED...NOBODY KNEW IT WAS ME.
...RIGHT?
Oh--speaking of which! While you created such convenient chaos at the aforementioned high school, I was able to make a few last minute ***acquisitions***.
There's one I'm ***particularly*** fond of...

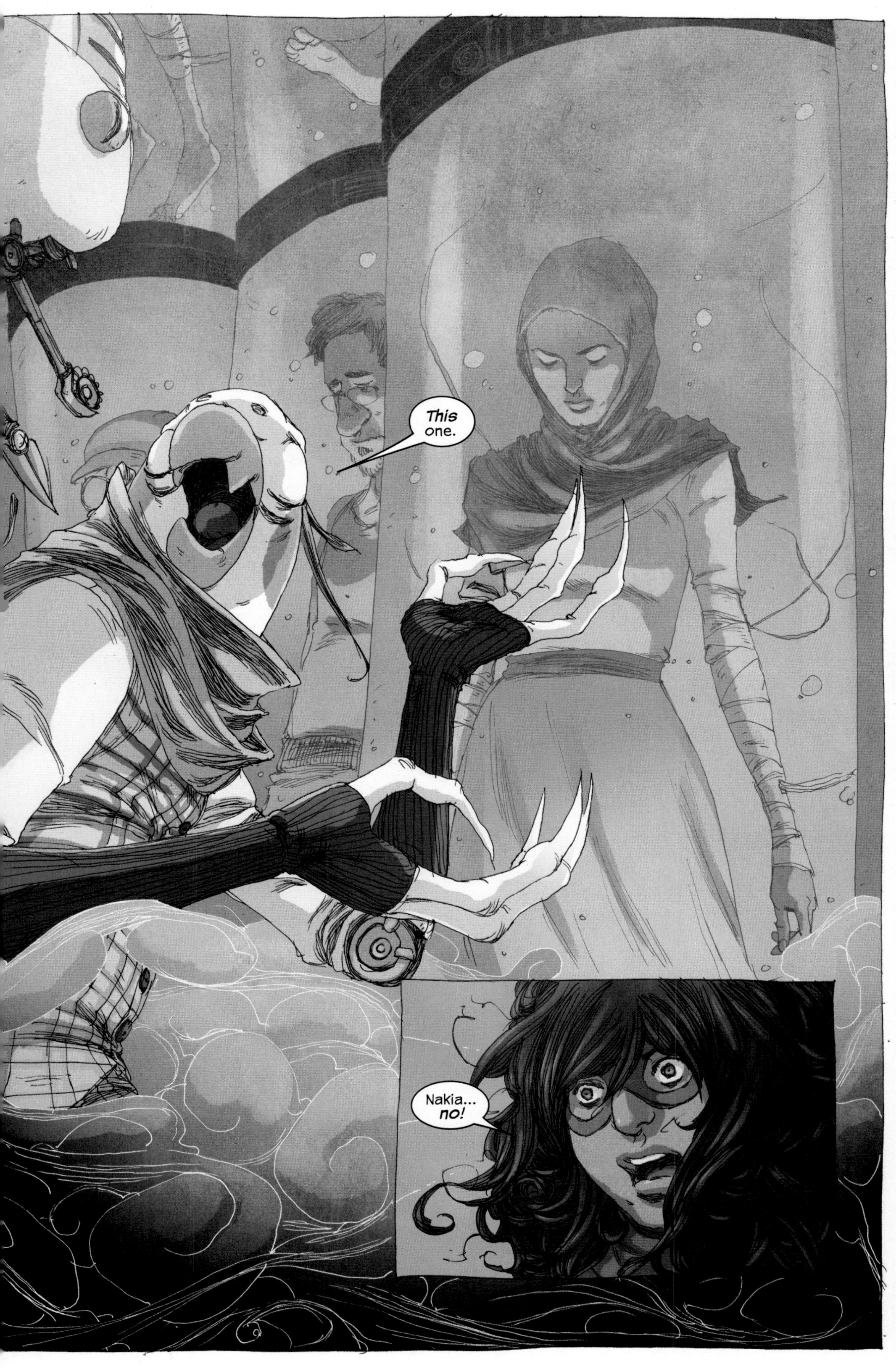
This one.
Nakia... no!

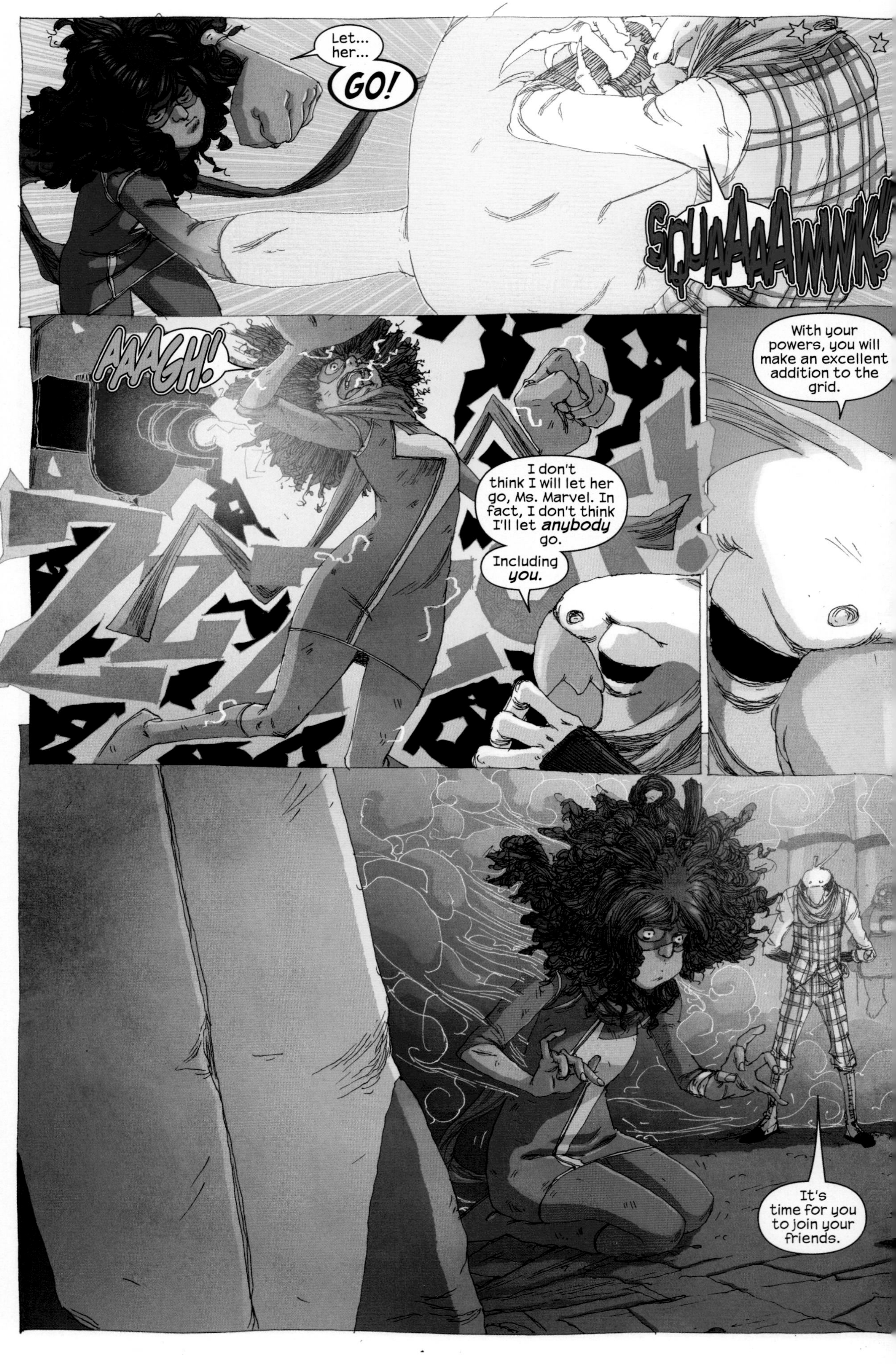
Let... her... GO!
SQUAAAAWWK!
AAAGH!
I don't think I will let her go, Ms. Marvel. In fact, I don't think I'll let anybody go.
Including you.
With your powers, you will make an excellent addition to the grid.
It's time for you to join your friends.

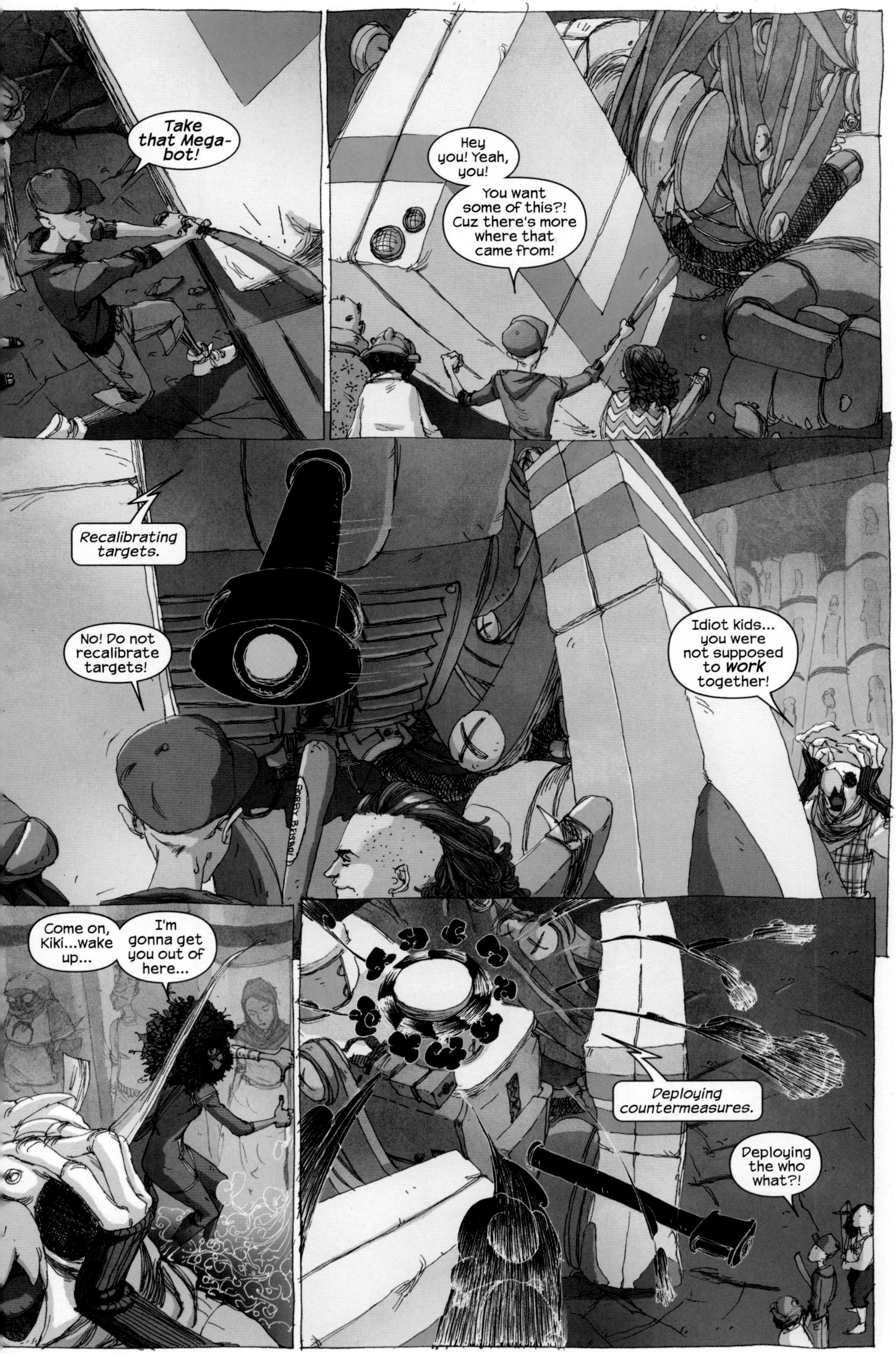

Take that Mega-bot!
Hey you! Yeah, you!
You want some of this?! Cuz there's more where that came from!
Recalibrating targets.
No! Do not recalibrate targets!
Idiot kids... you were not supposed to *work* together!
Come on, Kiki...wake up...
I'm gonna get you out of here...
Deploying countermeasures.
Deploying the who what?!

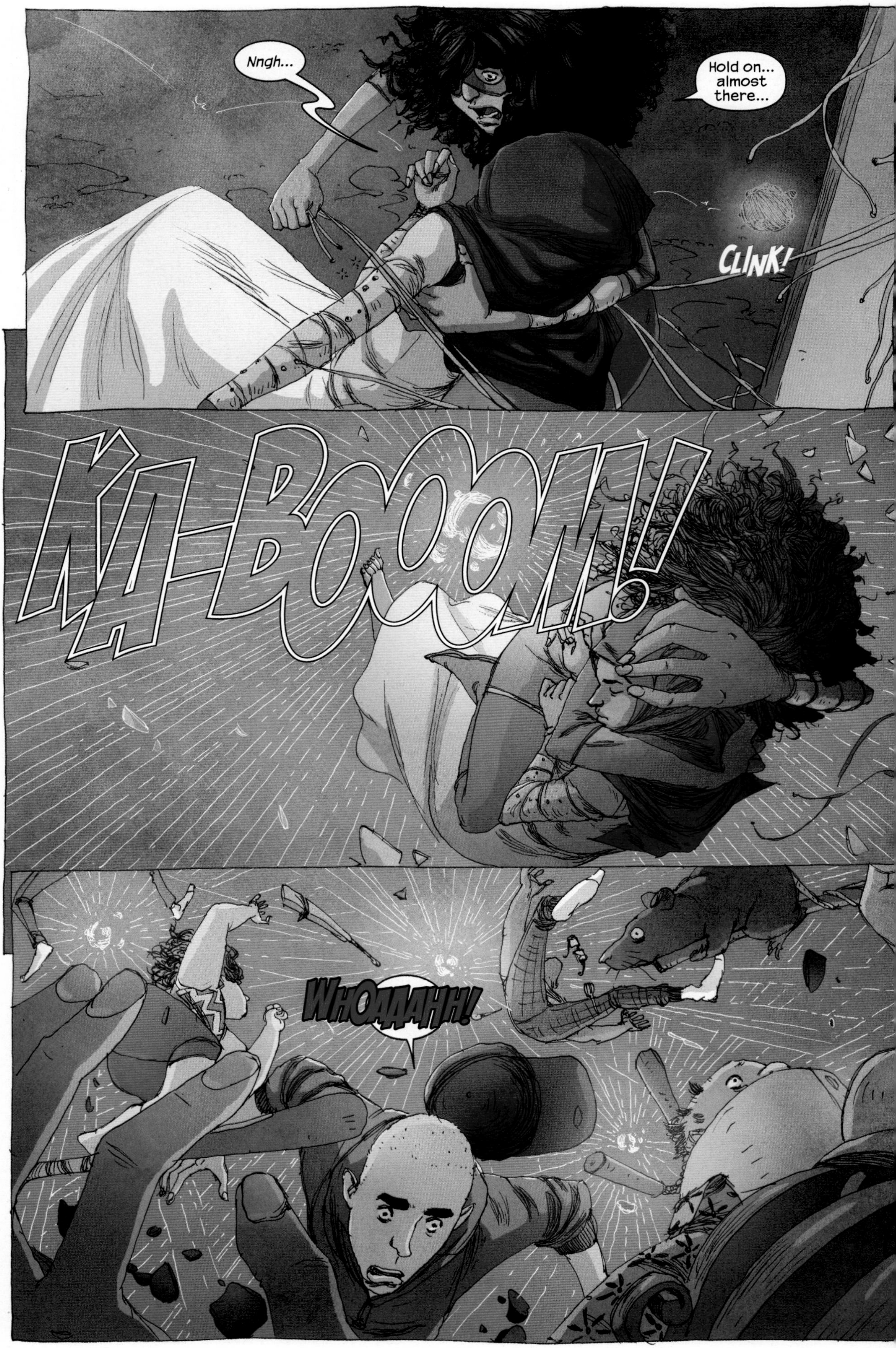
Nngh...
Hold on... almost there...
CLINK!
KA-BOOOM!
WHOAAAHH!

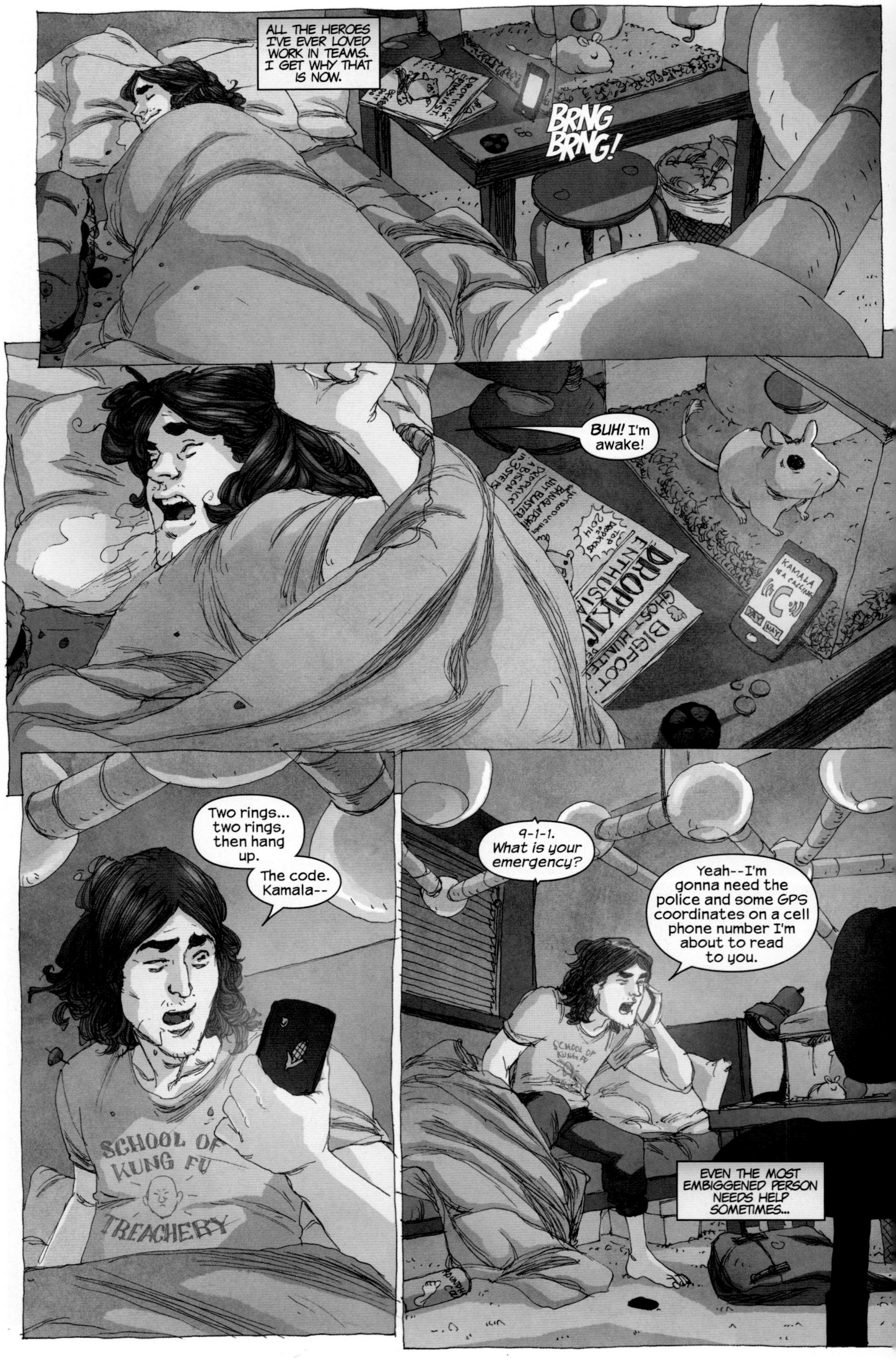

ALL THE HEROES I'VE EVER LOVED WORK IN TEAMS. I GET WHY THAT IS NOW.
BRNG BRNG!
BUH! I'm awake!
KAMALA IS A CALLING
YAY NAY
DROPKICK ENTHUSIAST
BIGFOOT GHOST HUNTER
Two rings... two rings, then hang up.
The code. Kamala--
SCHOOL OF KUNG FU
TREACHERY
9-1-1. What is your emergency?
Yeah--I'm gonna need the police and some GPS coordinates on a cell phone number I'm about to read to you.
EVEN THE MOST EMBIGGENED PERSON NEEDS HELP SOMETIMES...

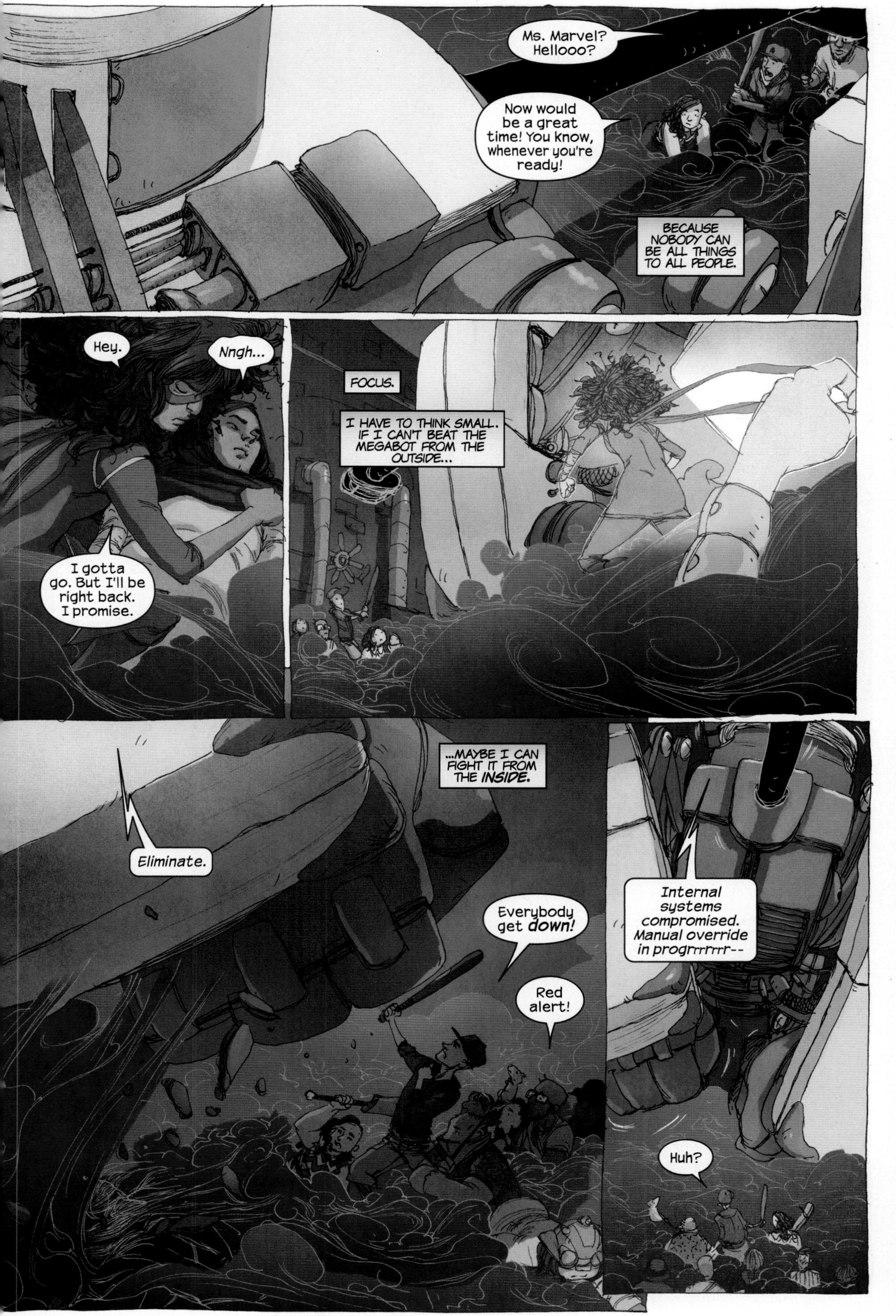
Ms. Marvel? Hellooo?
Now would be a great time! You know, whenever you're ready!
BECAUSE NOBODY CAN BE ALL THINGS TO ALL PEOPLE.
Hey.
Nngh...
I gotta go. But I'll be right back. I promise.
FOCUS.
I HAVE TO THINK SMALL. IF I CAN'T BEAT THE MEGABOT FROM THE OUTSIDE...
...MAYBE I CAN FIGHT IT FROM THE *INSIDE.*
Eliminate.
Everybody get **down!**
Red alert!
Internal systems compromised. Manual override in progrrrrrr--
Huh?

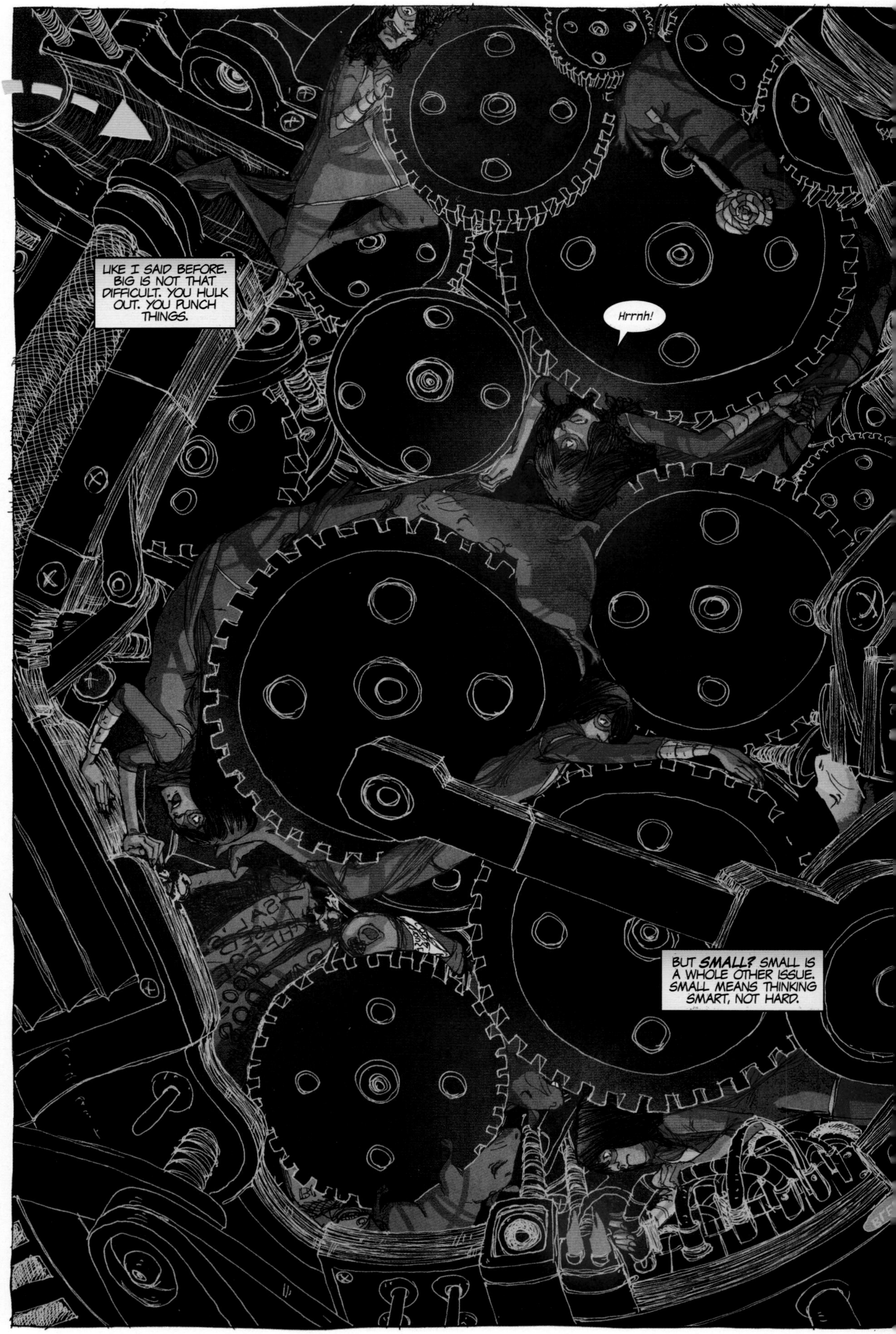
LIKE I SAID BEFORE. BIG IS NOT THAT DIFFICULT. YOU HULK OUT. YOU PUNCH THINGS.
Hrrnh!
BUT SMALL? SMALL IS A WHOLE OTHER ISSUE. SMALL MEANS THINKING SMART, NOT HARD.

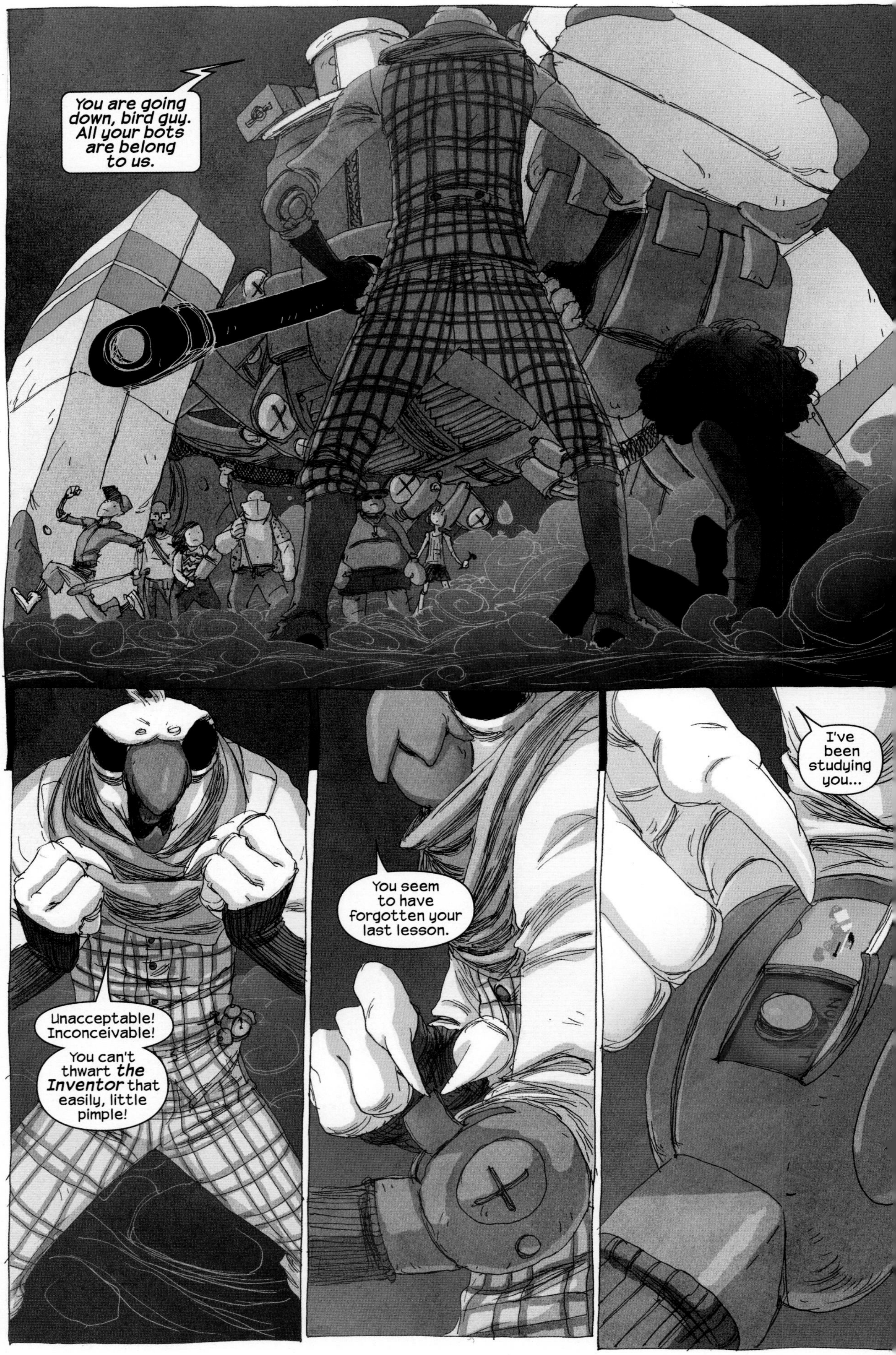
You are going down, bird guy. All your bots are belong to us.
Unacceptable! Inconceivable!
You can't thwart *the Inventor* that easily, little pimple!
You seem to have forgotten your last lesson.
I've been studying you...

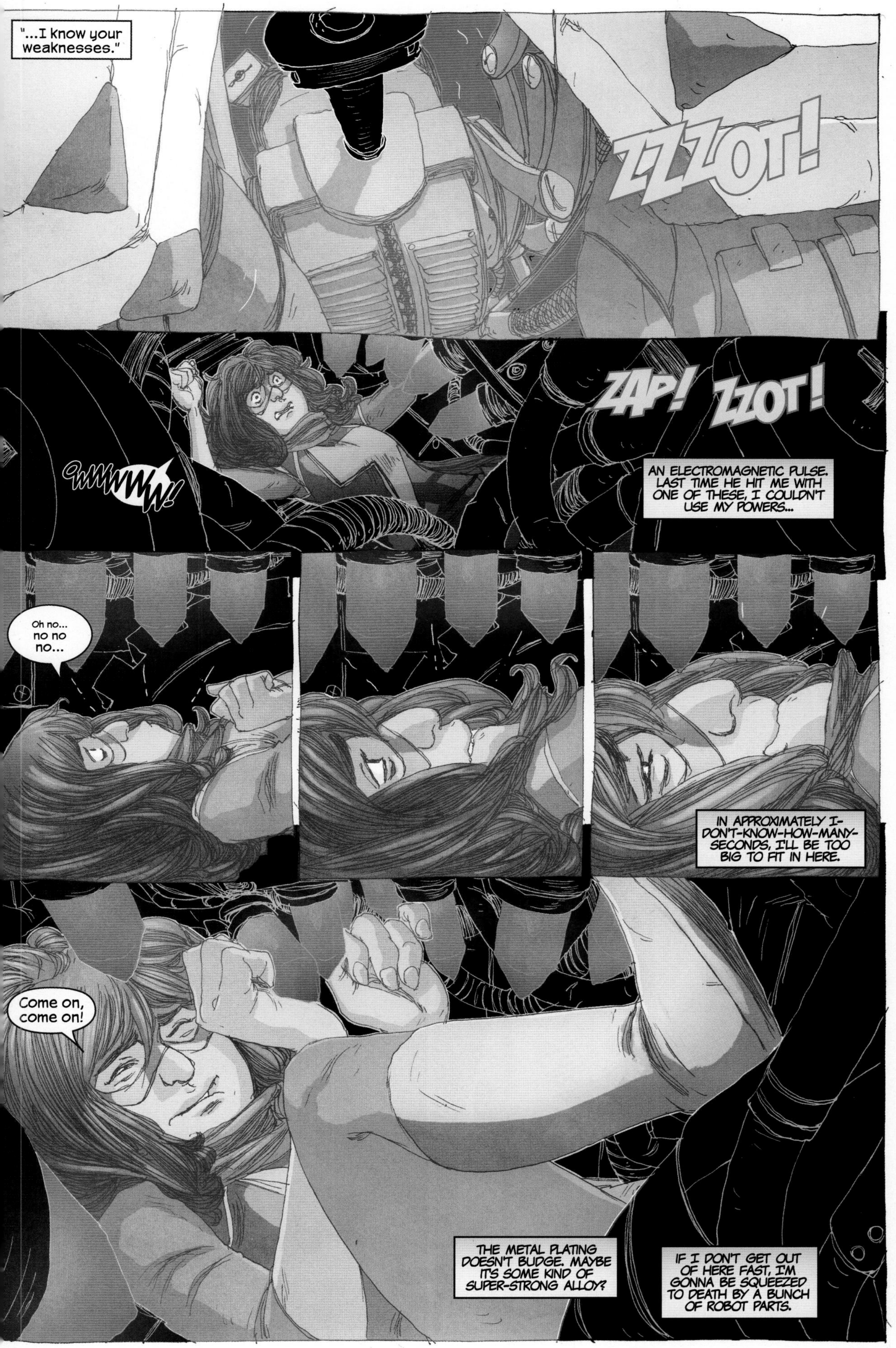
"...I know your weaknesses."
ZZZOT!
ZAP! ZZOT!
QWWWWN!
AN ELECTROMAGNETIC PULSE. LAST TIME HE HIT ME WITH ONE OF THESE, I COULDN'T USE MY POWERS...
Oh no... no no no...
IN APPROXIMATELY I-DON'T-KNOW-HOW-MANY-SECONDS, I'LL BE TOO BIG TO FIT IN HERE.
Come on, come on!
THE METAL PLATING DOESN'T BUDGE. MAYBE IT'S SOME KIND OF SUPER-STRONG ALLOY?
IF I DON'T GET OUT OF HERE FAST, I'M GONNA BE SQUEEZED TO DEATH BY A BUNCH OF ROBOT PARTS.

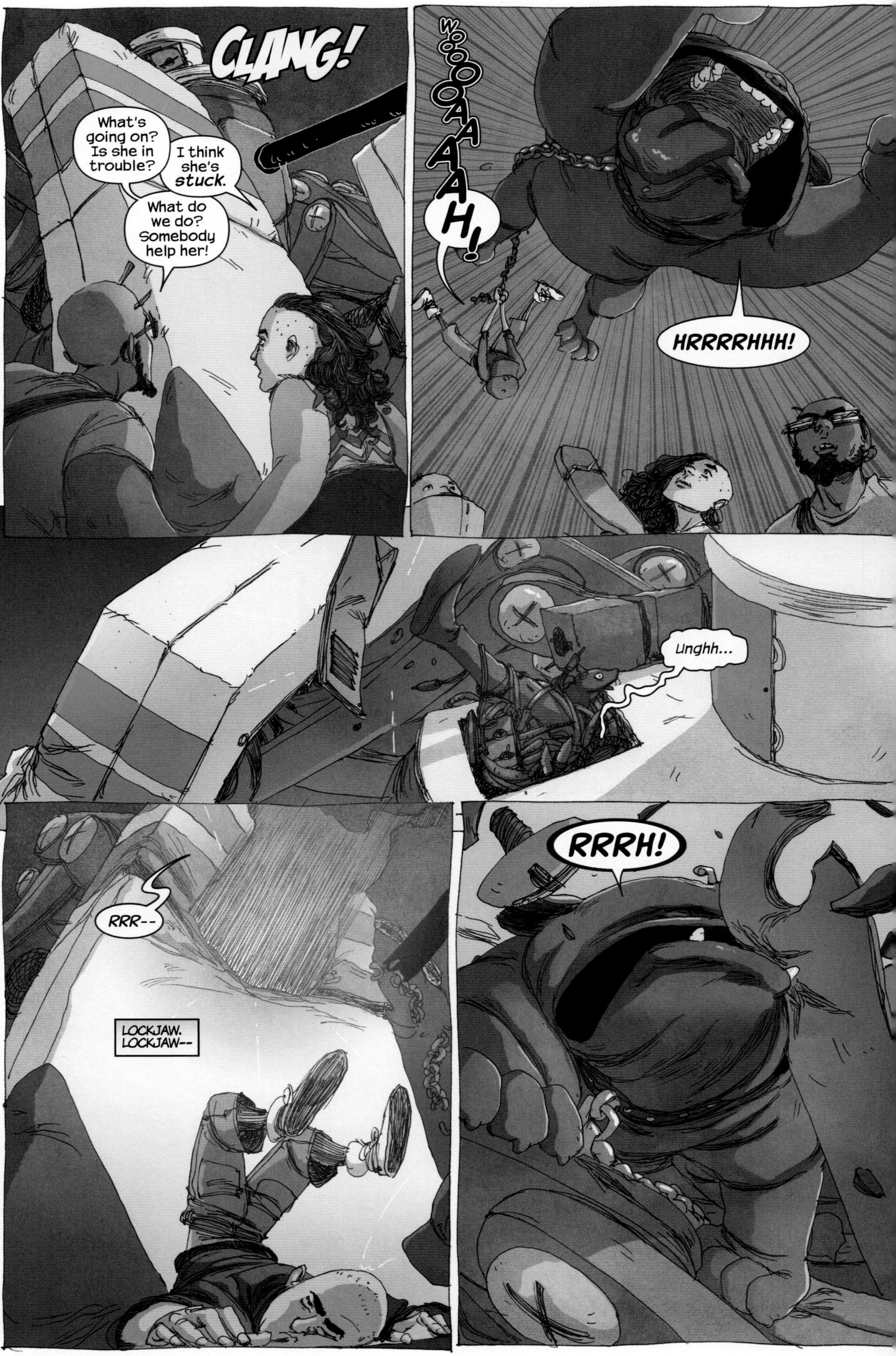

CLANG!
What's going on? Is she in trouble?
I think she's *stuck*.
What do we do? Somebody help her!
WOOOOAAAAAH!
HRRRRHHH!
Unghh...
RRR--
LOCKJAW. LOCKJAW--
RRRH!

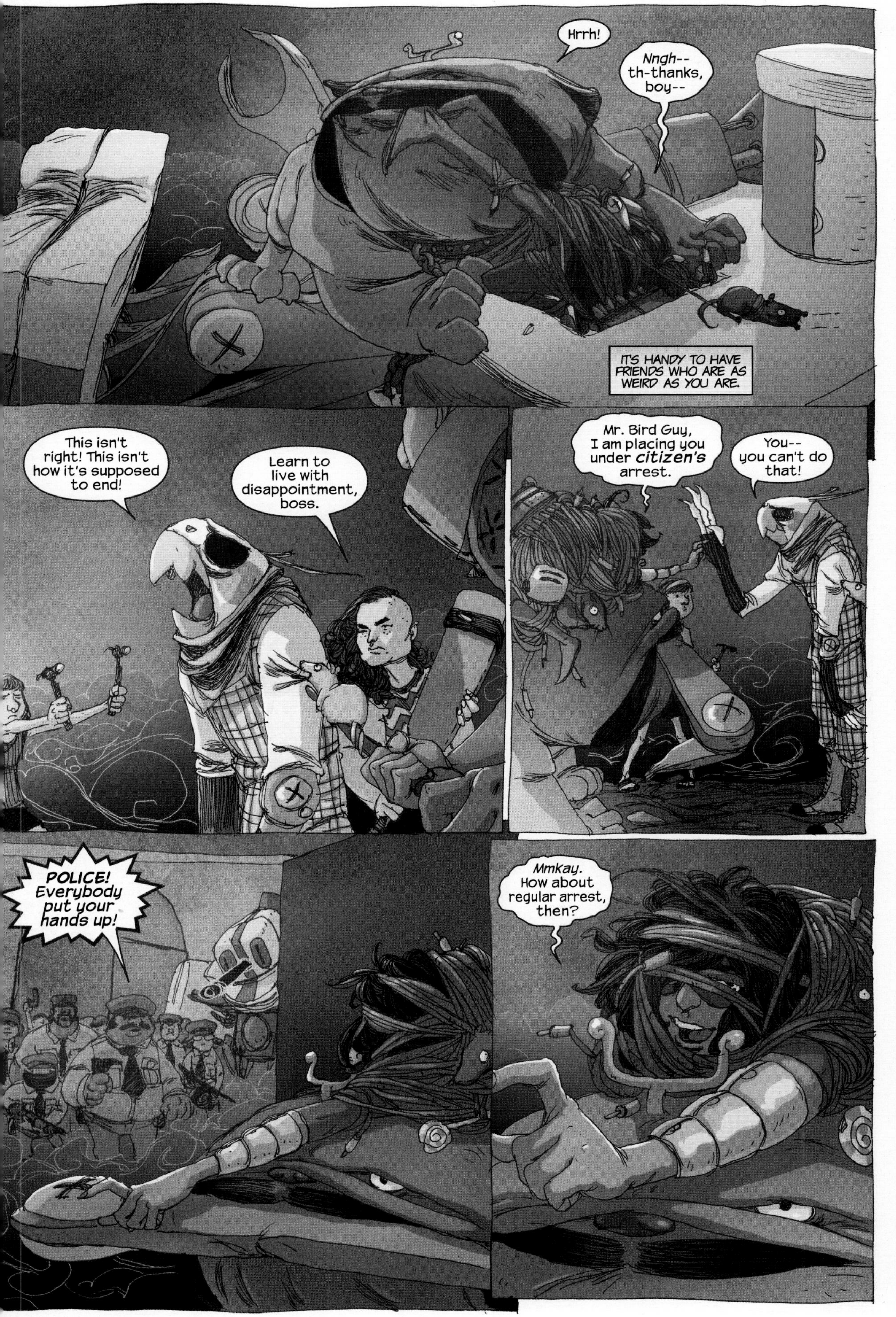
Hrrh!
Nngh-- th-thanks, boy--
IT'S HANDY TO HAVE FRIENDS WHO ARE AS WEIRD AS YOU ARE.
This isn't right! This isn't how it's supposed to end!
Learn to live with disappointment, boss.
Mr. Bird Guy, I am placing you under citizen's arrest.
You-- you can't do that!
POLICE! Everybody put your hands up!
Mmkay. How about regular arrest, then?

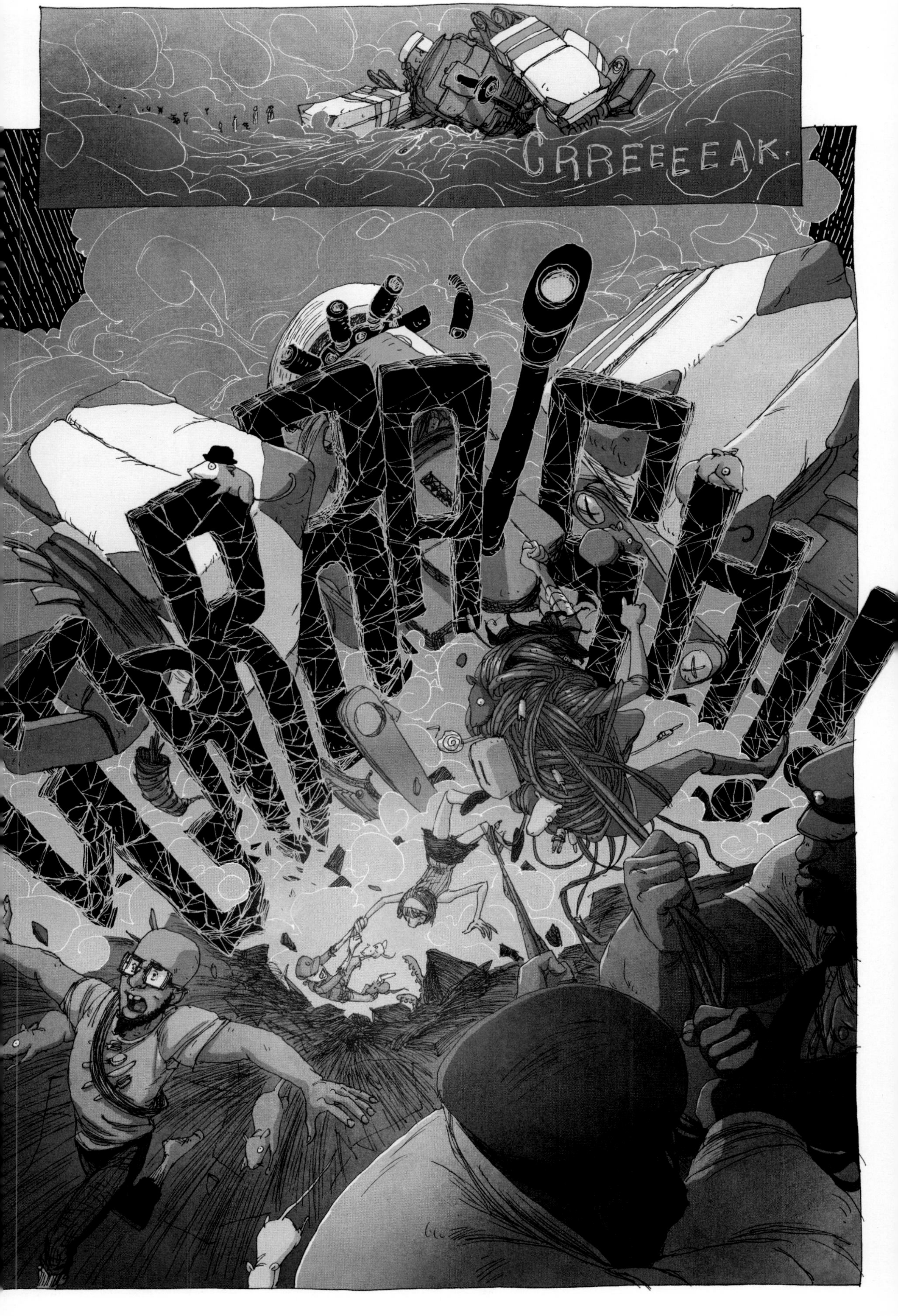
CRREEEEAK.

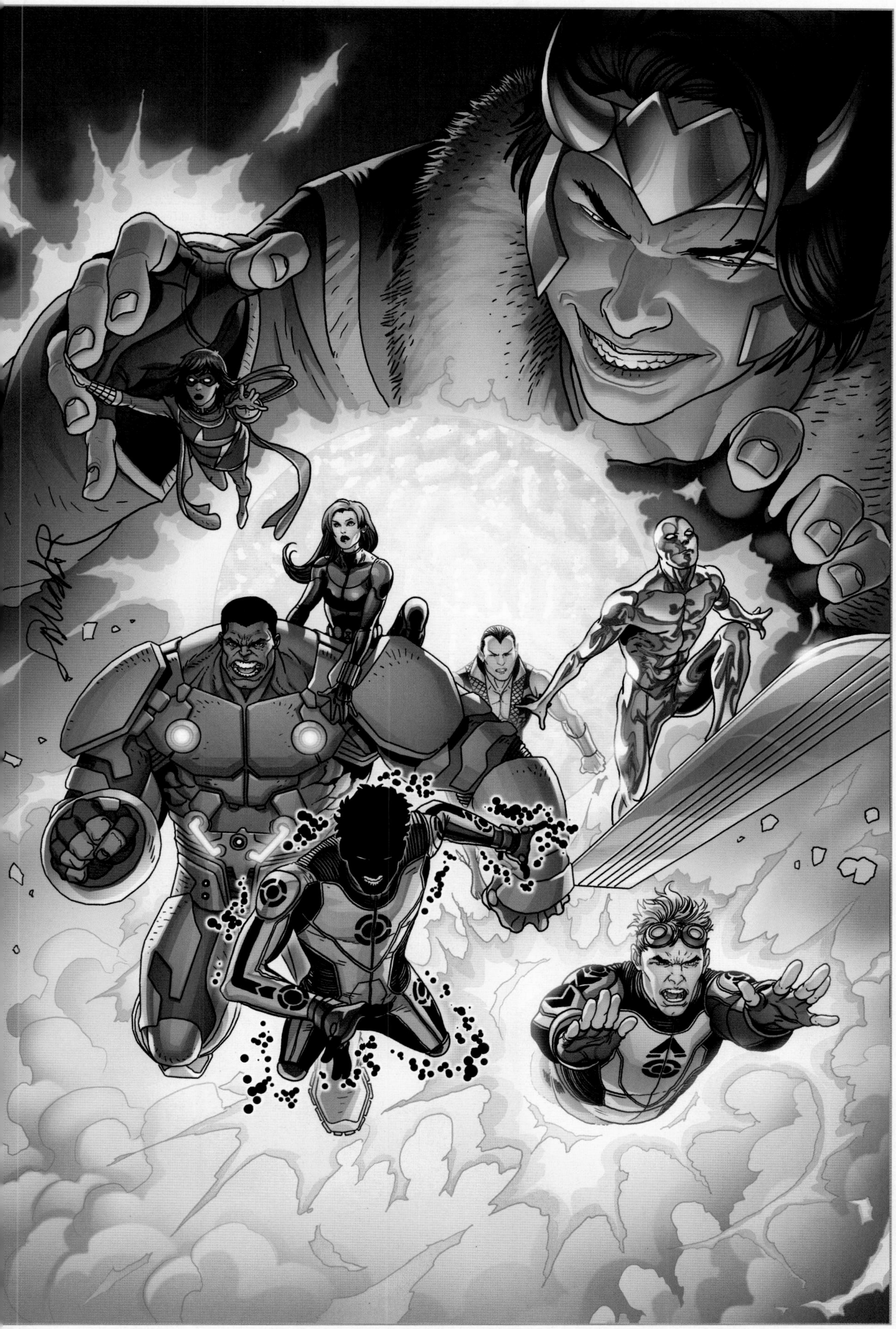

ALL-NEW MARVEL NOW POINT ONE #1
BY SALVADOR LARROCA & LAURA MARTIN

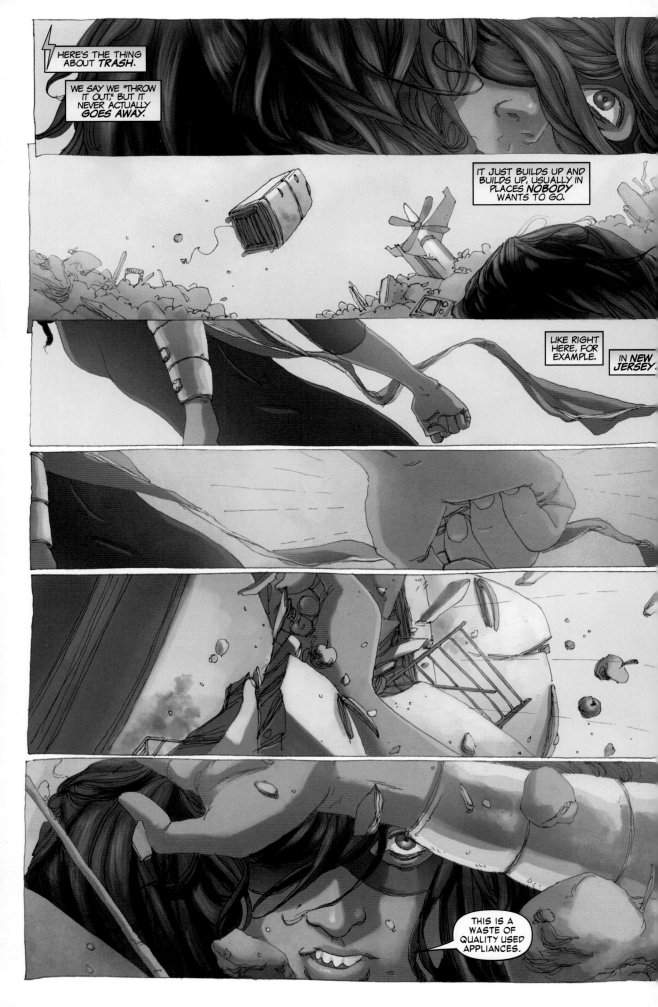

HERE'S THE THING ABOUT **TRASH.**

WE SAY WE "THROW IT OUT," BUT IT NEVER ACTUALLY *GOES AWAY.*

IT JUST BUILDS UP AND BUILDS UP, USUALLY IN PLACES **NOBODY** WANTS TO GO.

LIKE RIGHT HERE, FOR EXAMPLE.

IN *NEW JERSEY.*

THIS IS A WASTE OF QUALITY USED APPLIANCES.

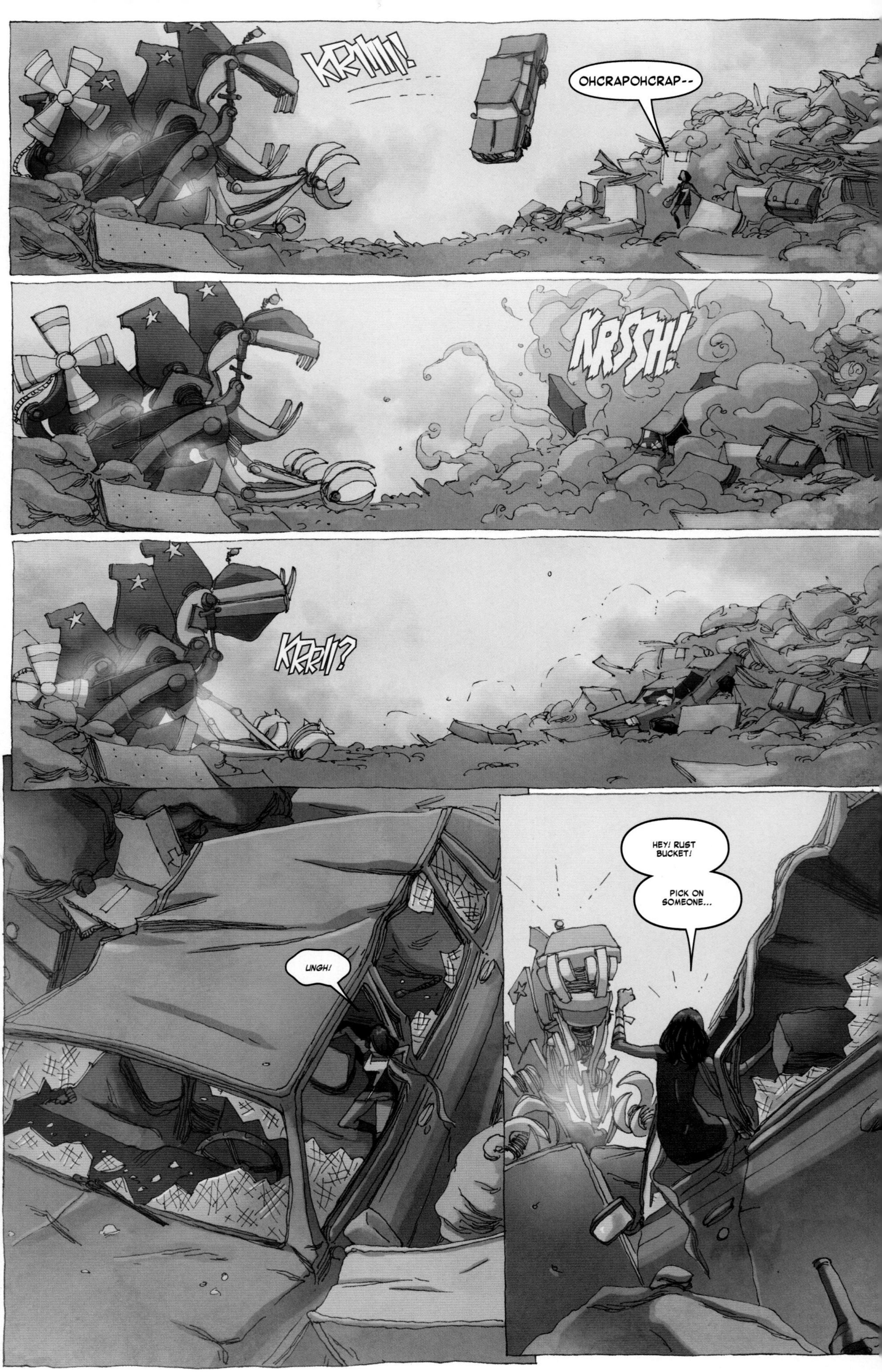
KRIIII!
OHCRAPOHCRAP--
KRSSH!
KRRII?
UNGH!
HEY! RUST BUCKET!
PICK ON SOMEONE...

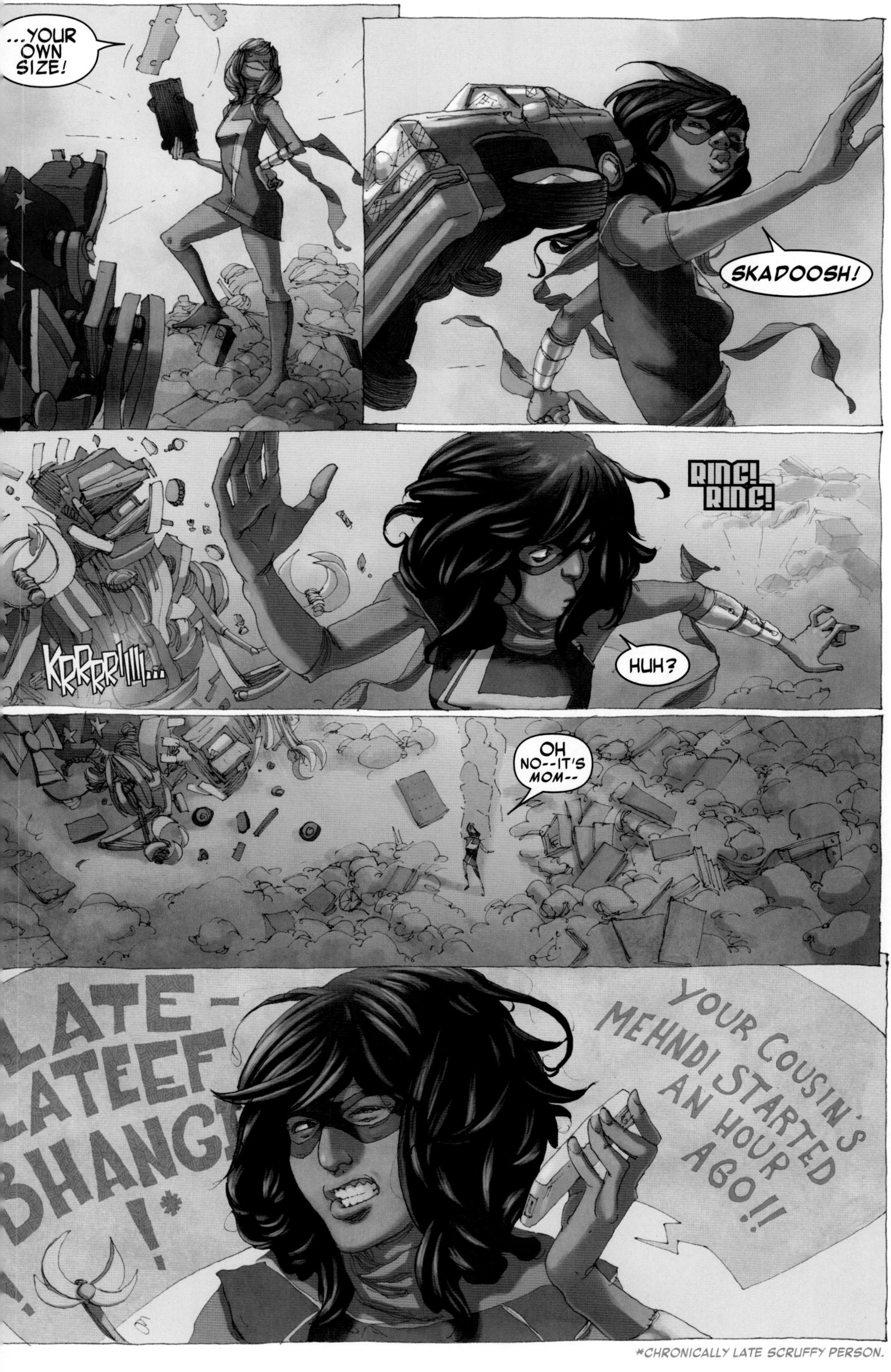
...YOUR OWN SIZE!
SKADOOSH!
RING! RING!
KRRRRR!!!!...
HUH?
OH NO--IT'S MOM--
LATE-LATEEF BHANG!*
YOUR COUSIN'S MEHNDI STARTED AN HOUR AGO!!

*CHRONICALLY LATE SCRUFFY PERSON.

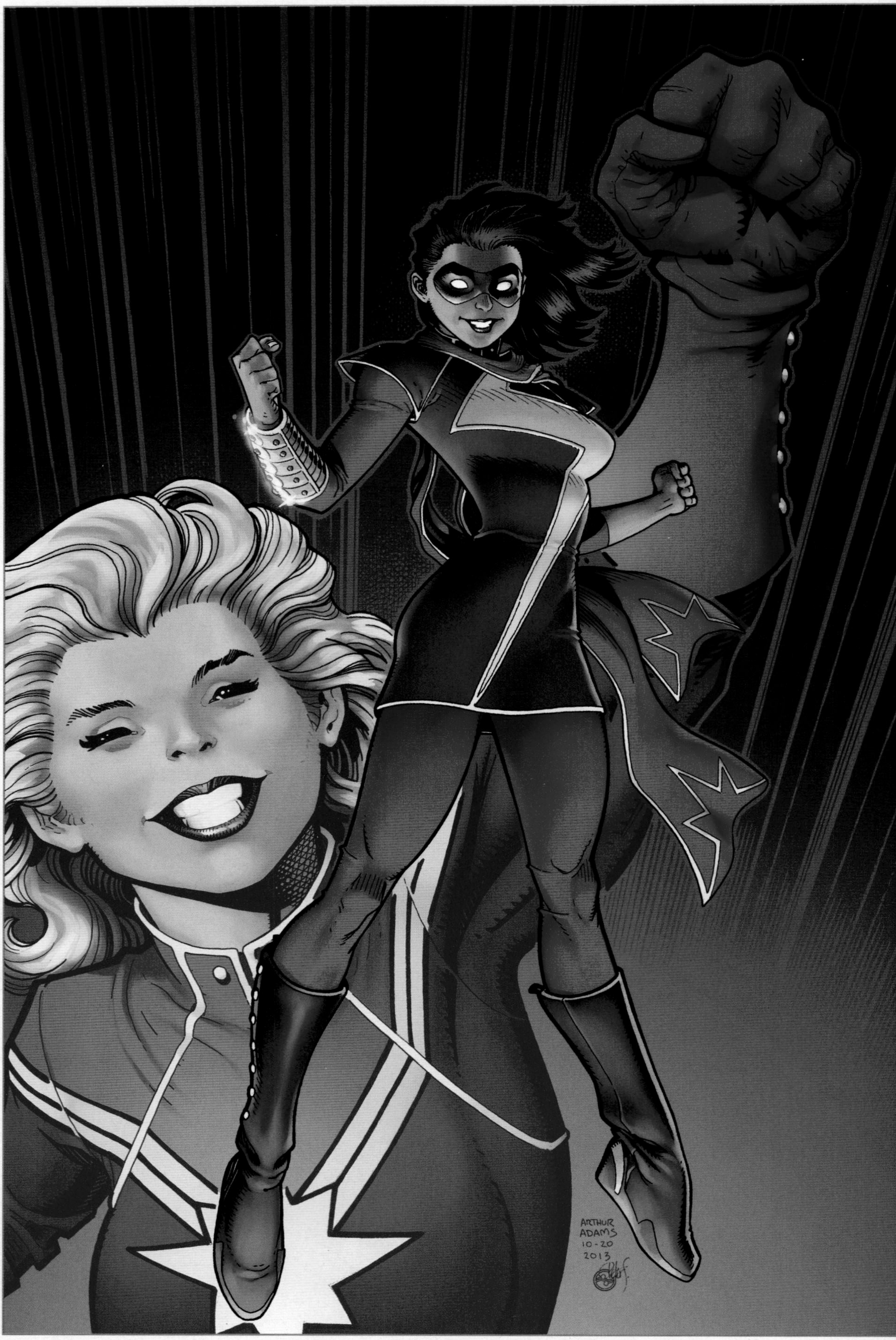
ARTHUR
ADAMS
10-20
2013

MS. MARVEL #1 VARIANT
BY ARTHUR ADAMS & PETER STEIGERWALD

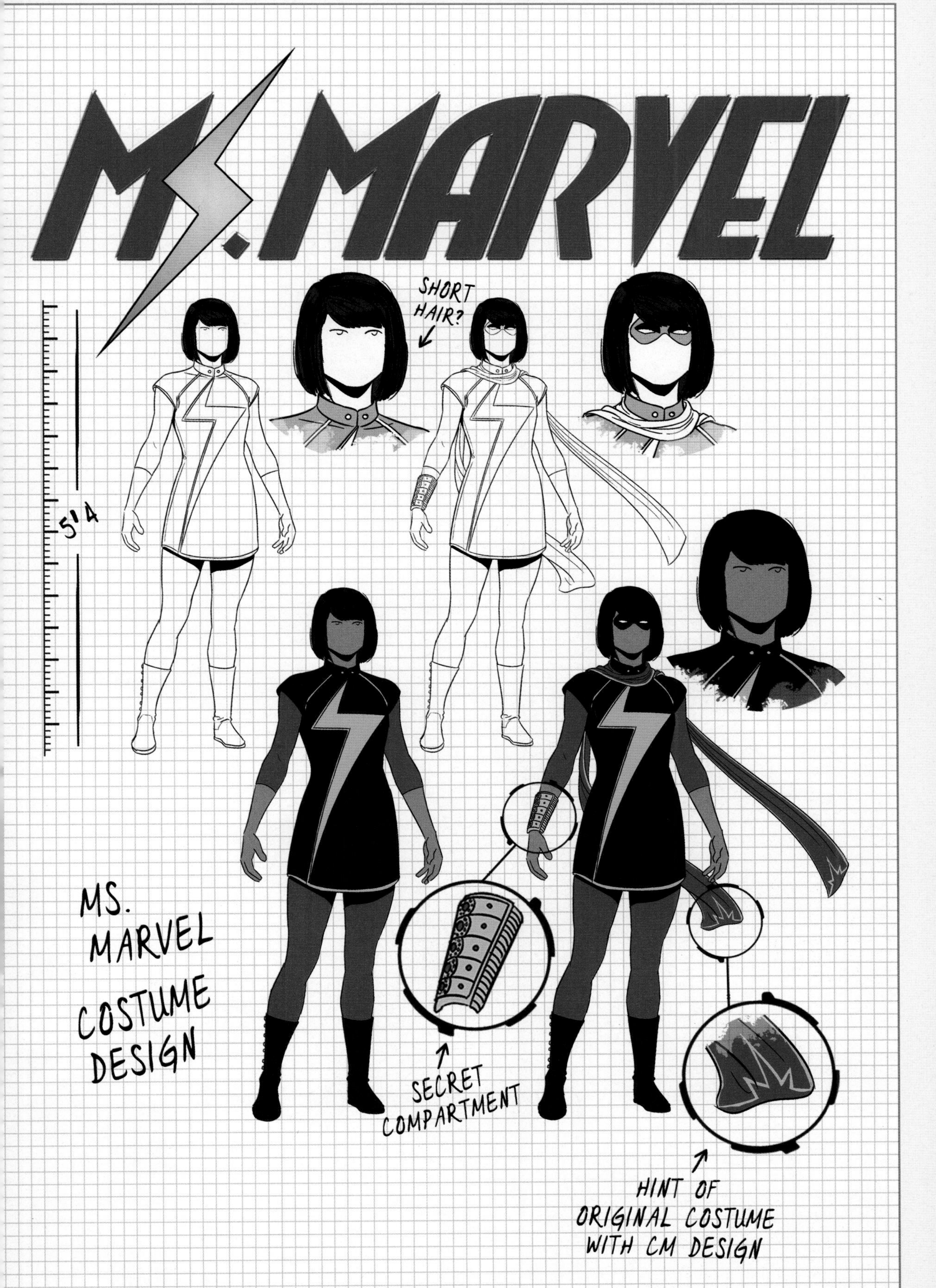
MS. MARVEL
SHORT HAIR?
5'4
MS. MARVEL COSTUME DESIGN
SECRET COMPARTMENT
HINT OF ORIGINAL COSTUME WITH CM DESIGN

MS. MARVEL #1 DESIGN VARIANT
BY JAMIE MCKELVIE

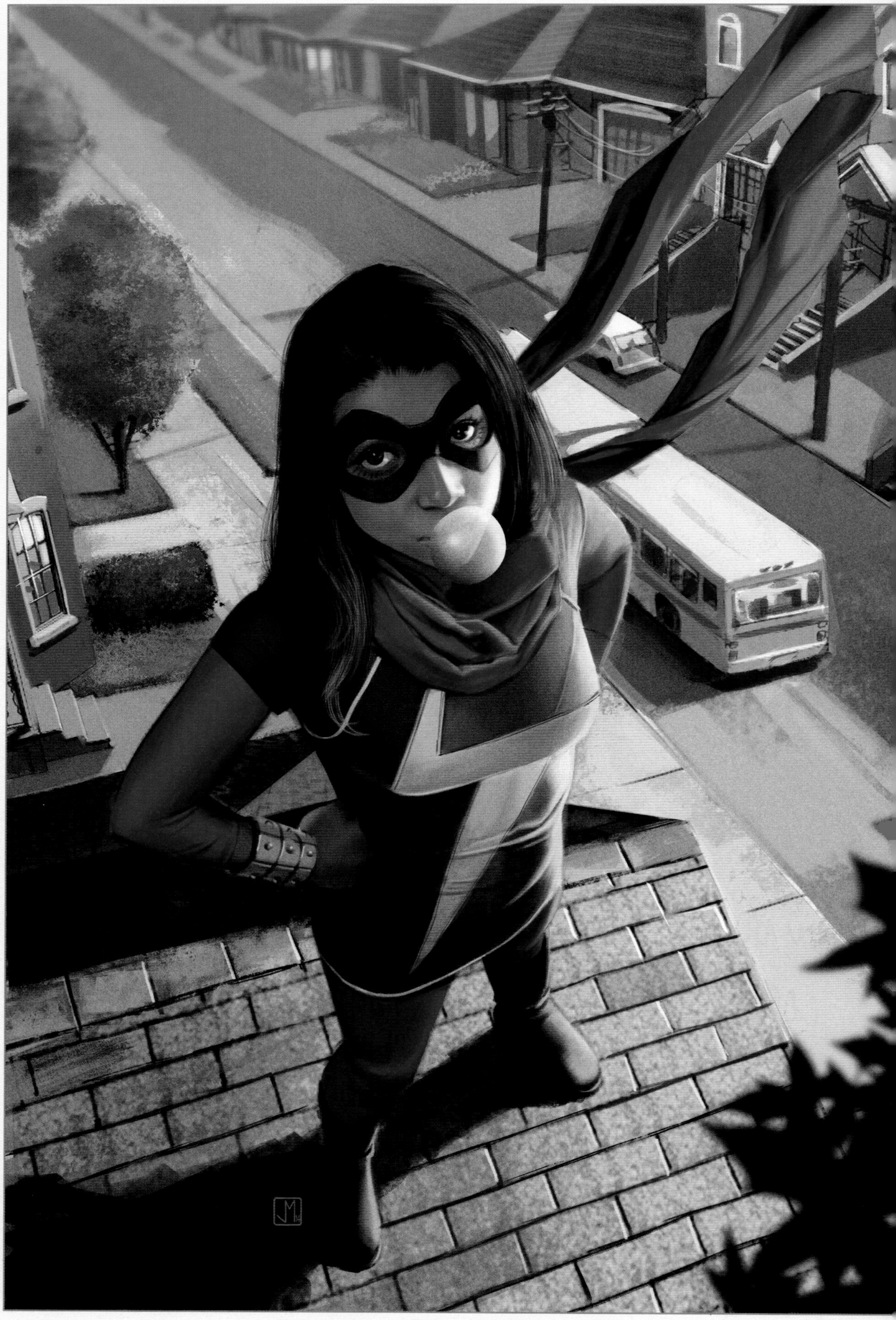

MS. MARVEL #2 VARIANT
BY JORGE MOLINA

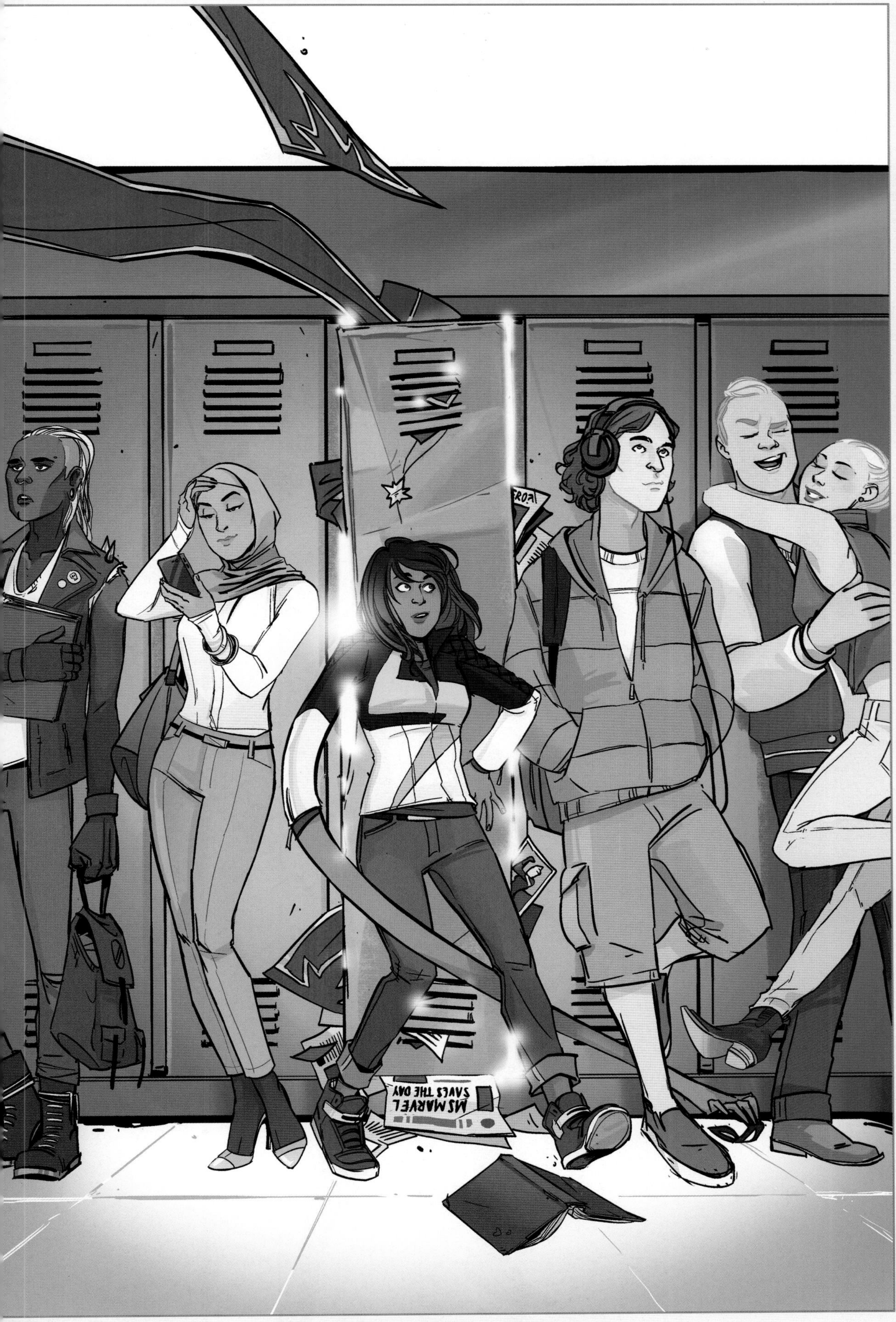
MS MARVEL
SAVES THE DAY

MS. MARVEL #3 VARIANT
BY ANNIE WU

adrian alphona sketchbook

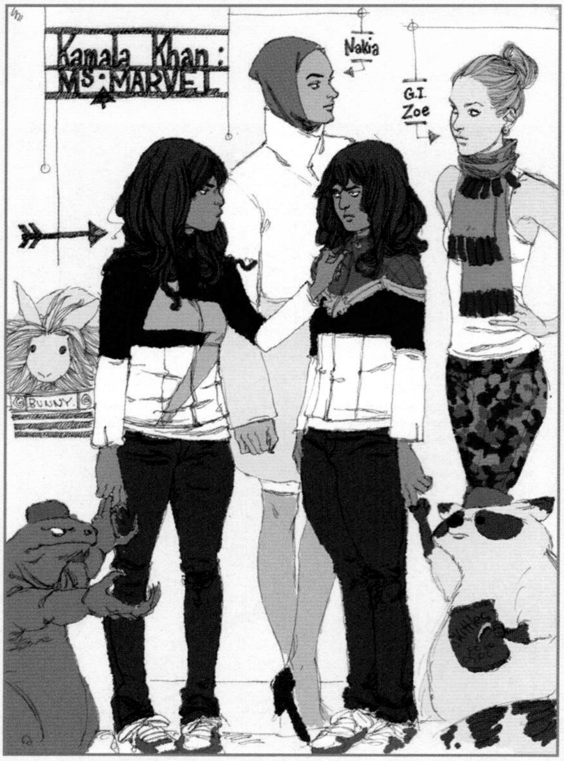
Kamala Khan:
Ms. MARVEL
Nakia
G.I.
Zoe
BUNNY

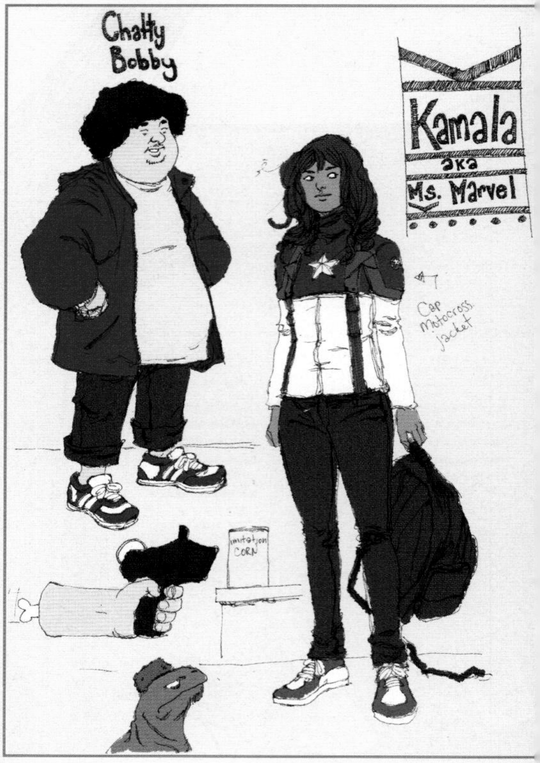
Chatty
Bobby
Kamala
aka
Ms. Marvel
Cap
Motocross
jacket
imitation
CORN

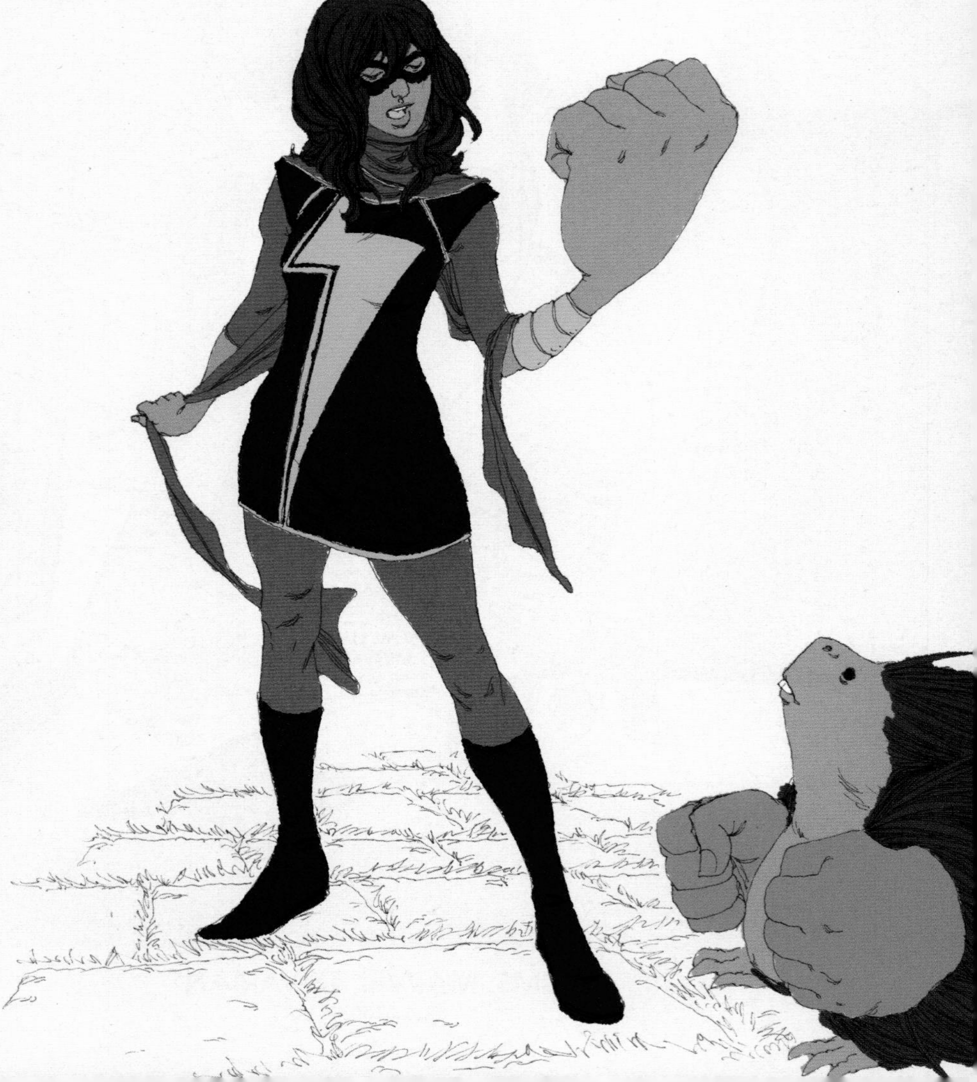

inks to color process

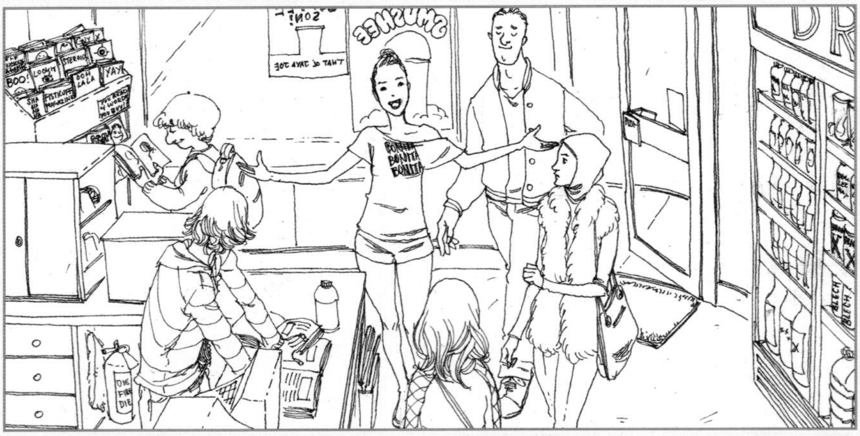

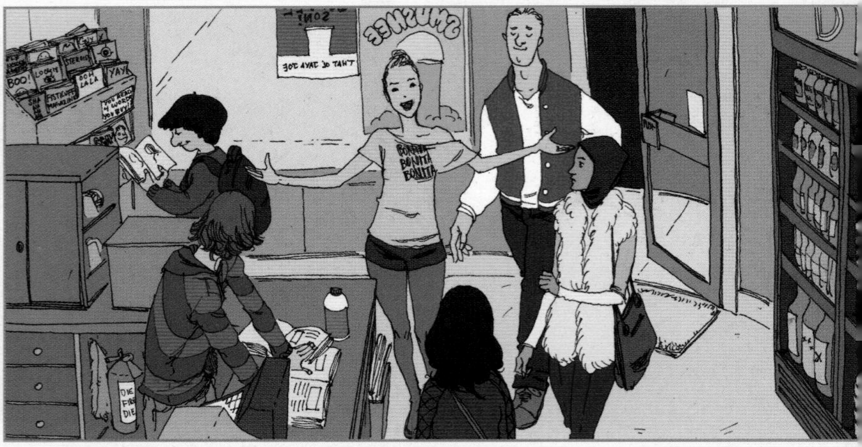

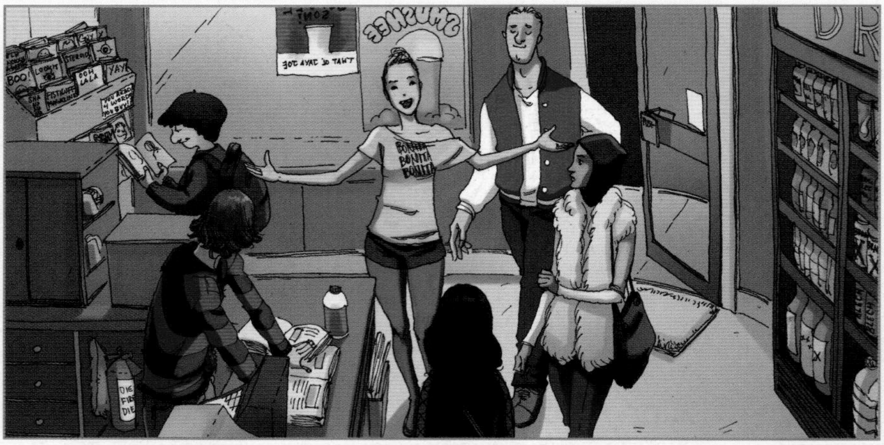

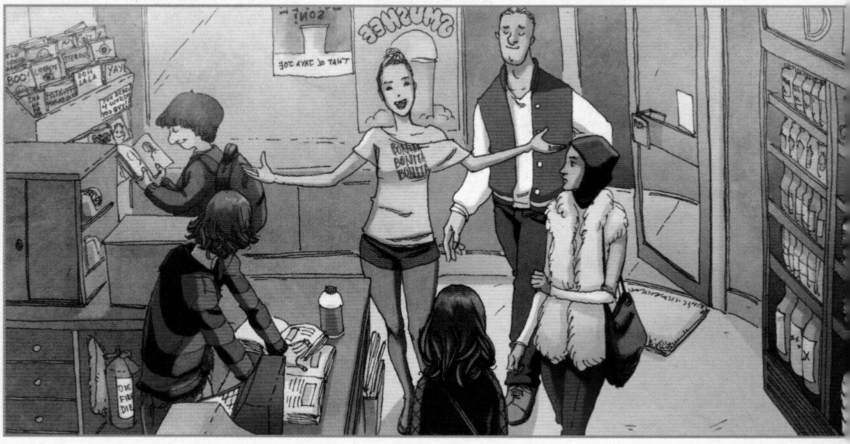

#8, page 2 by adrian alphona

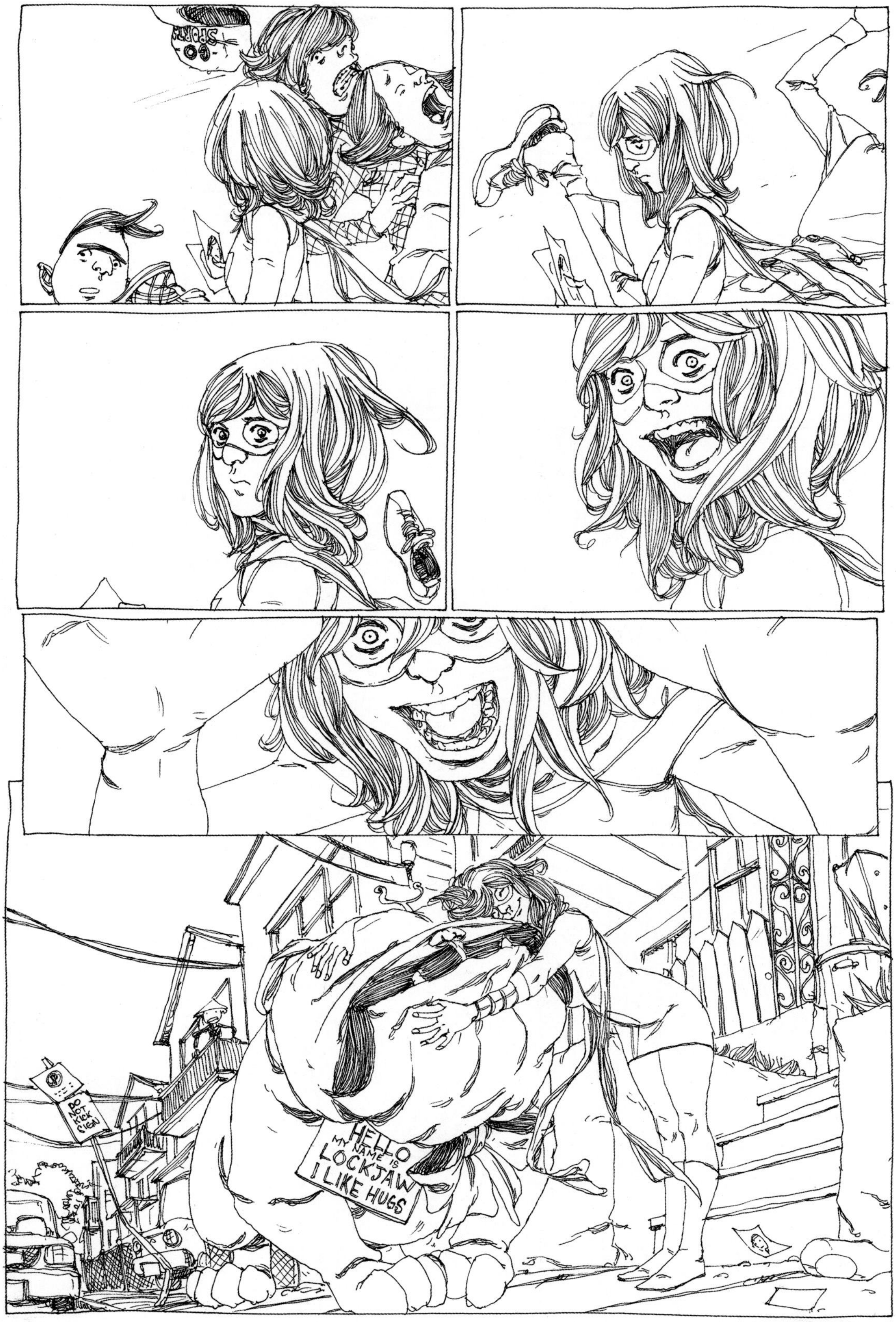
GO SPORTS
DO NOT KICK SIGN
HELLO MY NAME IS LOCKJAW I LIKE HUGS

#8, page 15 by adrian alphona

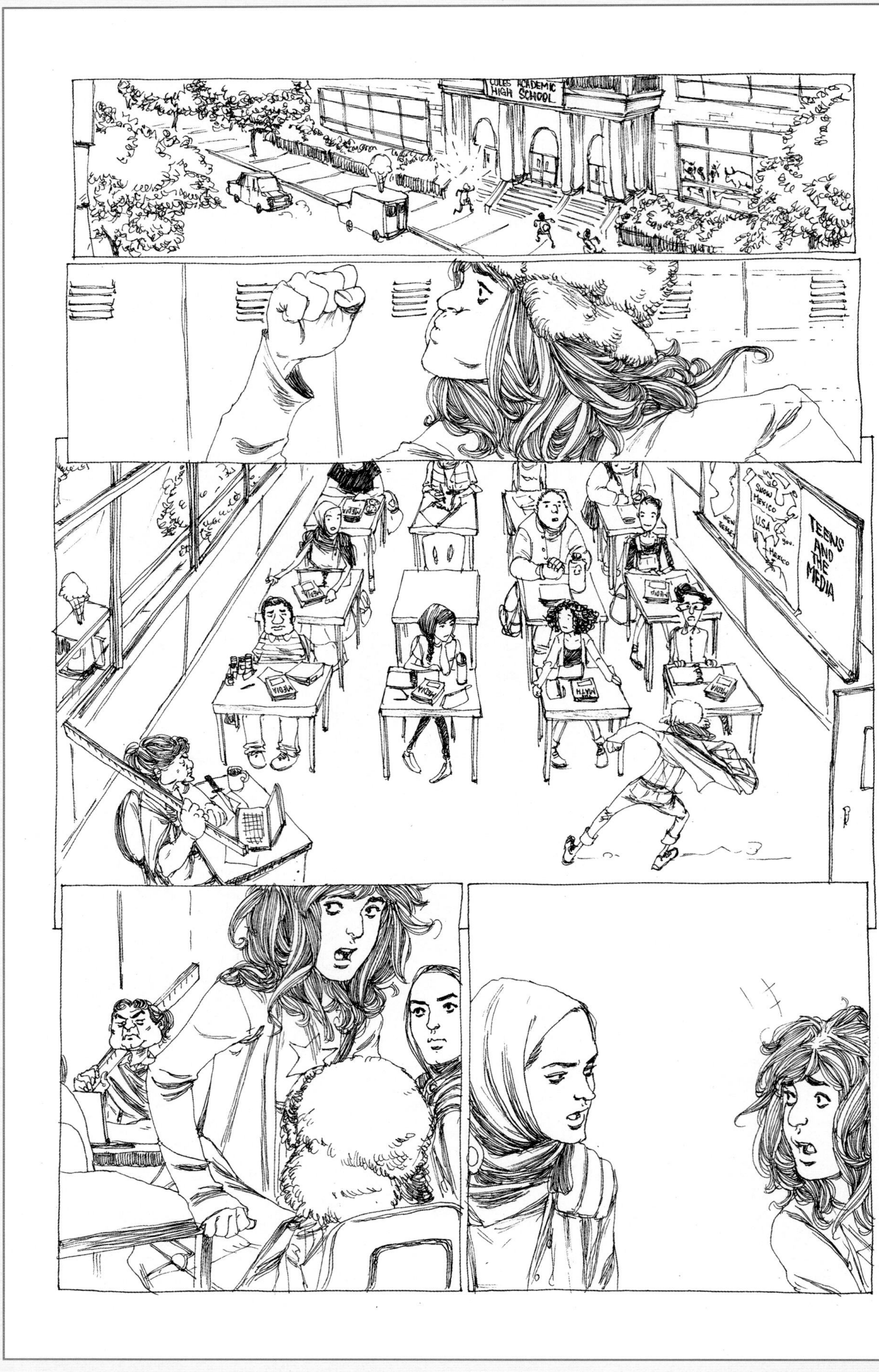
COLES ACADEMIC HIGH SCHOOL
TEENS AND THE MEDIA
MEDIA
MATH

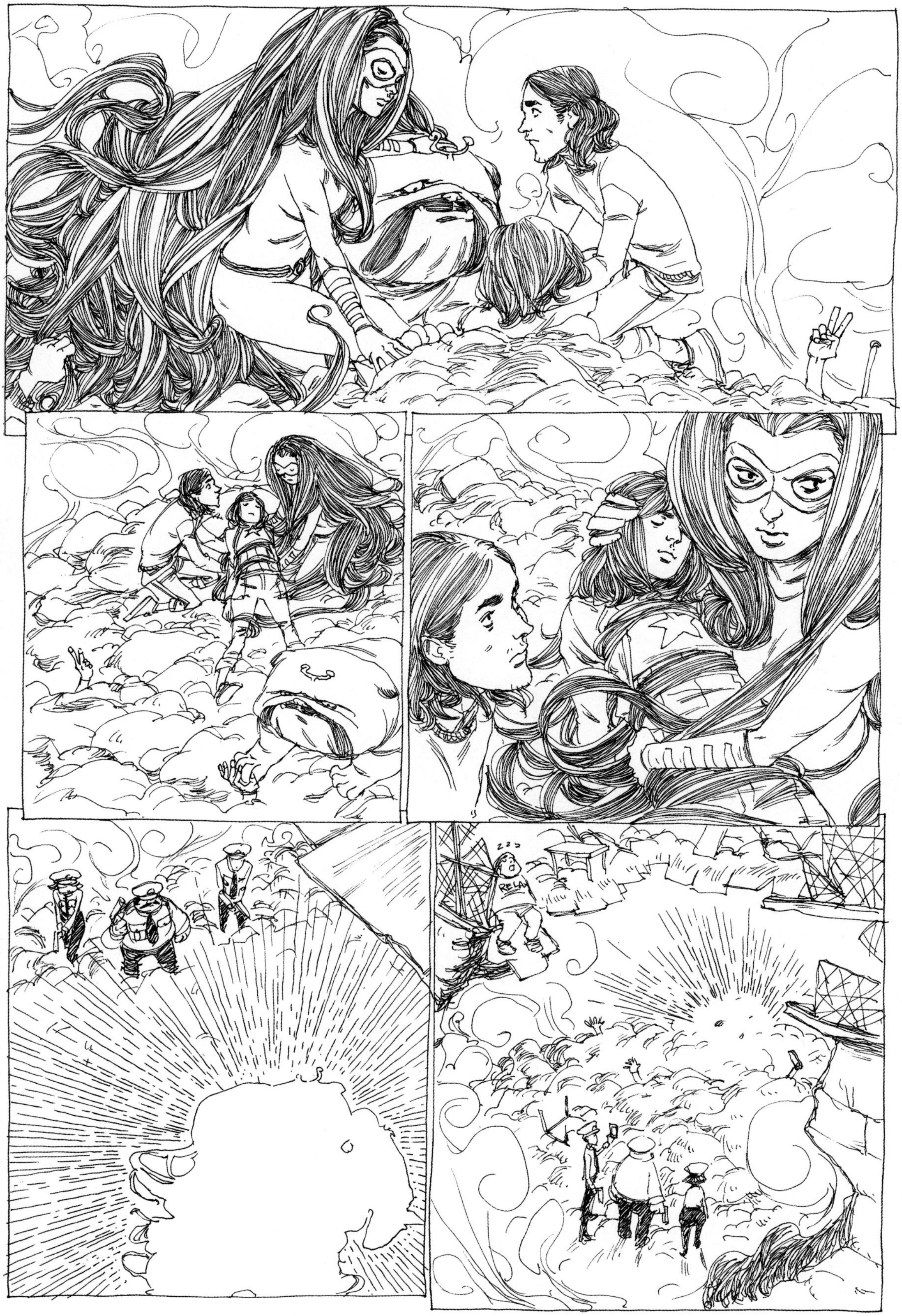

#10, page 3 by adrian alphona

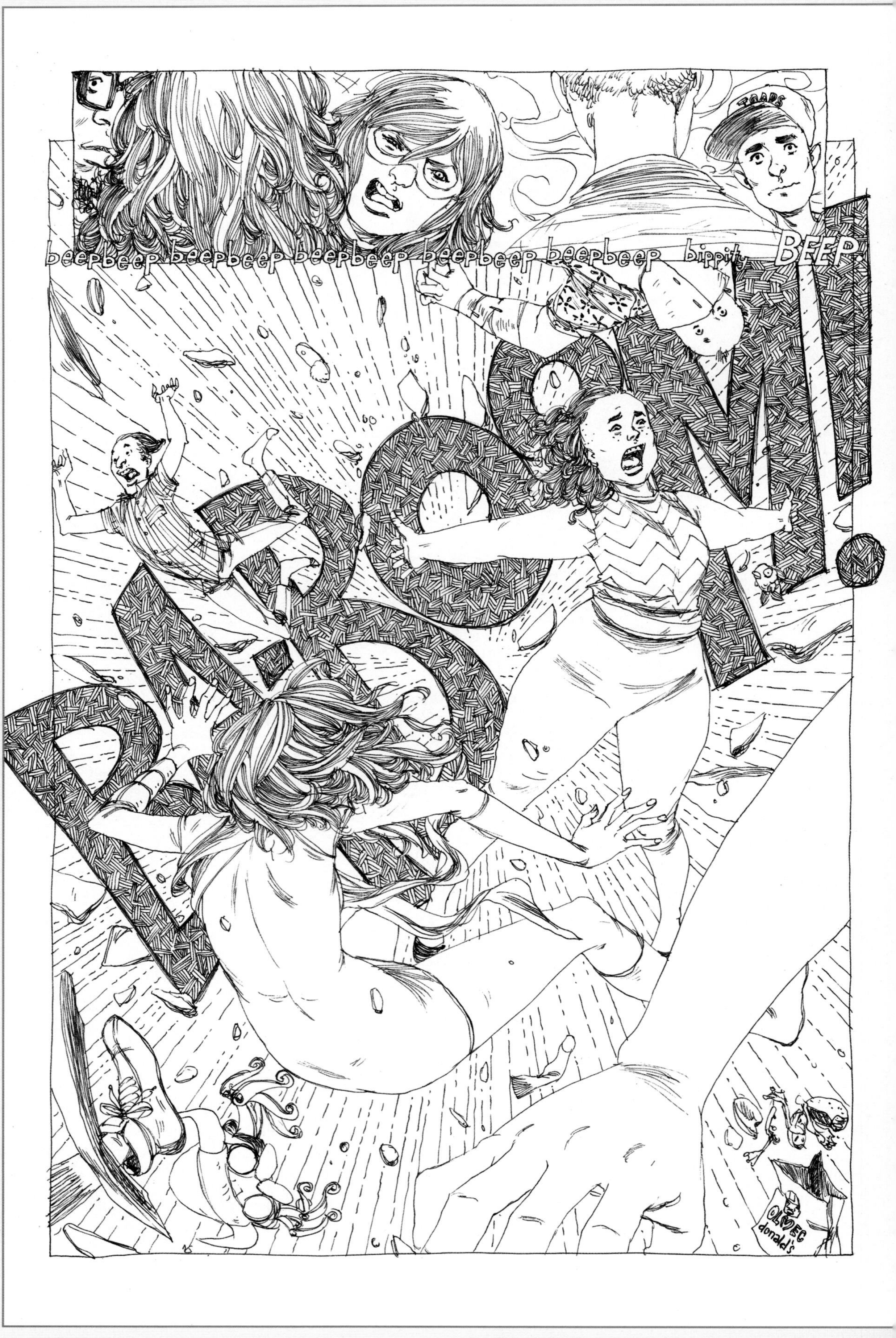
beepbeep beepbeep beepbeep beepbeep beepbeep bippity BEEP.

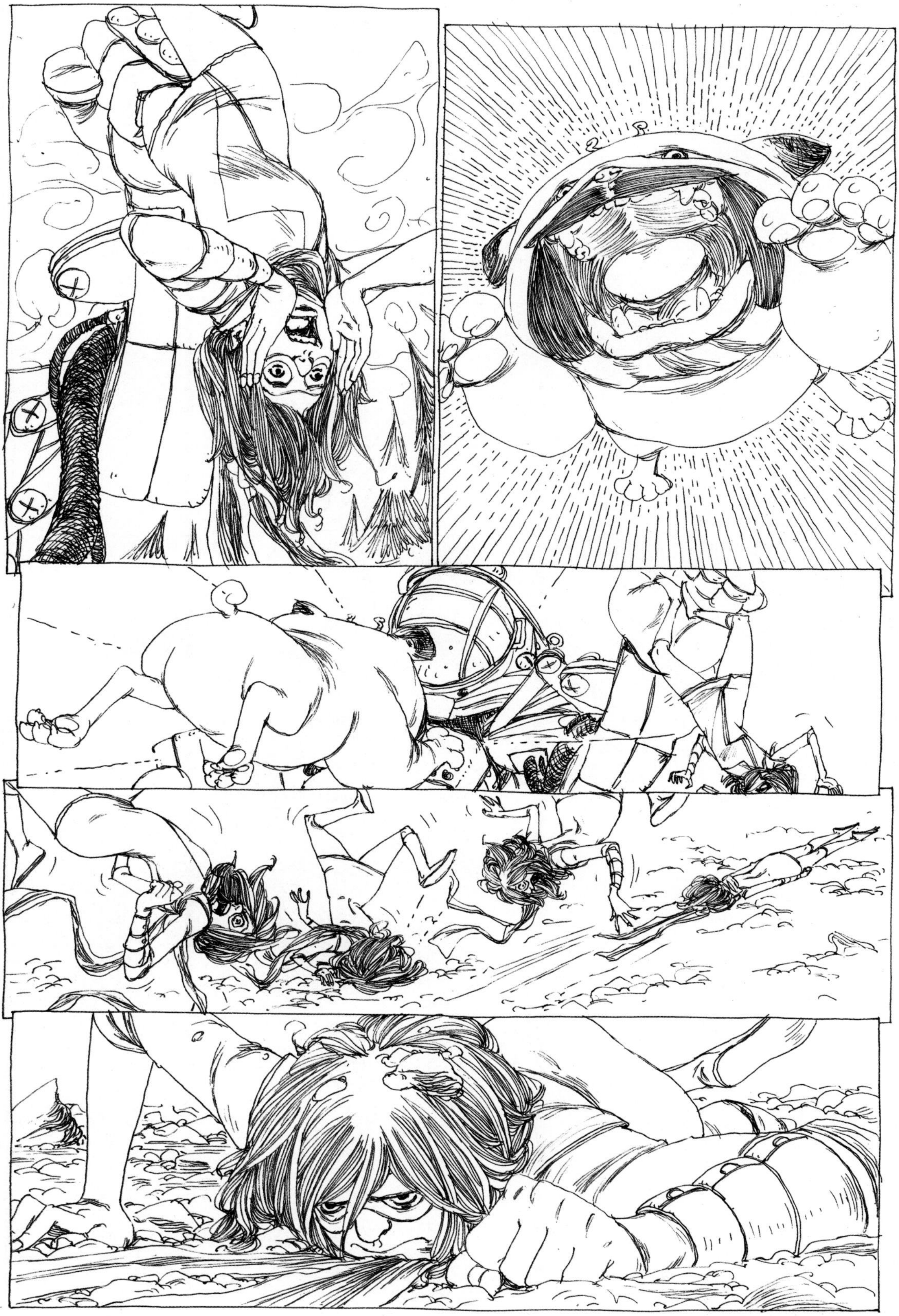

#11, page 4 by adrian alphona

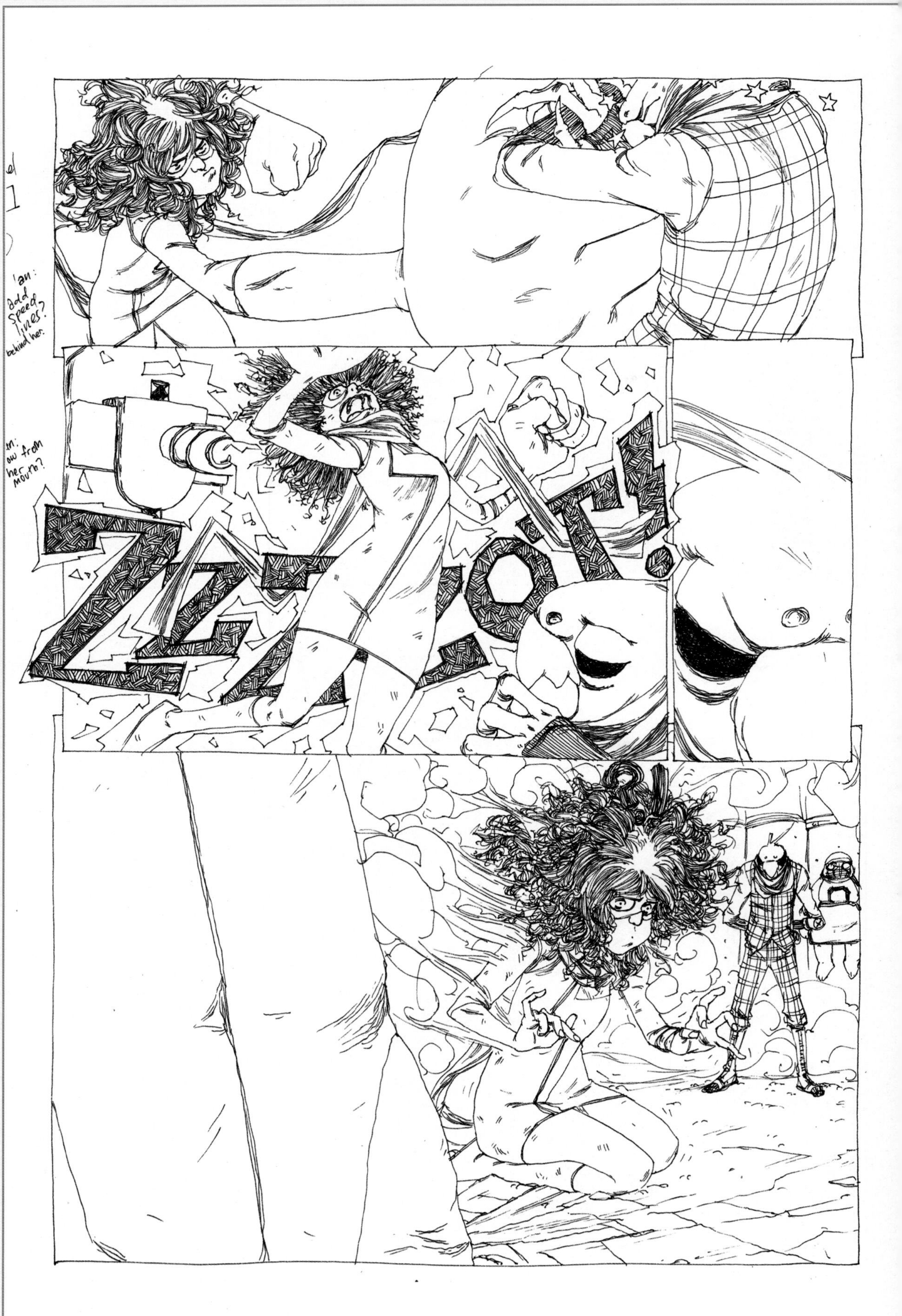

'an: add speed lines? behind her.
an: ow from her mouth?
ZZZOT!